COMPARATIVE HEALTH CA

Federalism Studies

Series Editor: Søren Dosenrode

The end of the Cold War profoundly altered the dynamics between and within the various states in Europe and the rest of the World, resulting in a resurgence of interest in the concept of federalism. This shift in balance has been further fuelled by the increase in the number of conflicts arising from the disaffection of the diverse ethnic or religious minorities residing within these states (e.g. Sudan, Iraq). Globalization is forcing governments not only to work together, but also to reconsider their internal roles as guarantors of economic growth, with regions playing the major part.

Federalism Studies offers academics a complete and in-depth understanding of federalism and intergovernmental relations in historical, theoretical and comparative contexts. Intended to be international and interdisciplinary in scope, the books in the series are designed to build a common framework for the constructive analysis of federalism. Contributions are welcome on topics which explore federalism as a theory; as a political system and as a form of conflict management.

Comparative Health Care Federalism

Edited by

KATHERINE FIERLBECK
Dalhousie University, Canada

HOWARD A. PALLEY
University of Maryland, USA

Routledge
Taylor & Francis Group

LONDON AND NEW YORK

First published 2015 by Ashgate Publishing

2 Park Square, Milton Park, Abingdon, Oxon, OX14 4RN
605 Third Avenue, New York, NY 10017

Routledge is an imprint of the Taylor & Francis Group, an informa business

First issued in paperback 2020

British Library Cataloguing in Publication Data
A catalogue record for this book is available from the British Library.

The Library of Congress has cataloged the printed edition as follows:
Comparative health care federalism / [edited] by Katherine Fierlbeck and Howard A. Palley.
    p. ; cm. -- (Federalism studies)
 Includes bibliographical references and index.
 ISBN 978-1-4724-3231-5 (hardback)
 I. Fierlbeck, Katherine, editor. II. Palley, Howard A., editor. III. Series: Federalism studies.
 [DNLM: 1. Delivery of Health Care. 2. Health Policy. 3. Federal Government. WA 540.1]
 RA363
 362'.0425--dc23

2014045274

ISBN 978-1-4724-3231-5 (hbk)
ISBN 978-0-367-73820-4 (pbk)

I would like to acknowledge both the Canadian Institutes of Health Research and the European Union Centres of Excellence for providing financial support for my ongoing work on health care federalism. A warm hug of thanks goes out to my indefatigable research assistant, Marcella Firmini, as well as to the usual web of family, friends, and colleagues who help me through each book project.

—KF

*To the memory of my mother, Henrietta Palley,
and to Marian, Elizabeth, Amelia and Charlotte.*

—Howard A. Palley

Contents

List of Figures

List of Tables

Notes on Contributors

Gwyn Bevan is Professor of Policy Analysis and Head of the Department of Management at the London School of Economics and Political Science. He has worked as an academic at Warwick Business School, St Thomas' Hospital Medical School, and Bristol Medical School. He has also worked in industry, as a consultant, for the Treasury, and for the Commission for Health Improvement (2001–2003), where he was Director of the Office for Information on Healthcare Performance. His current research includes studies of outcomes of the natural experiment of different policies in UK countries for the NHS and schools following devolution.

James Warner Björkman is Professor Emeritus of Public Policy and Administration at the Institute of Social Studies, The Hague (the Netherlands) and past Chair of the International Political Science Association's Research Committee on Comparative Health Policy. With degrees from the University of Minnesota (BA 1966) and Yale University (MPhil 1969, PhD 1976), he was Professor of Public Administration and Development at Leiden University (1990–2008) and episodically Visiting Professor at the International Centre for the Promotion of Enterprise in Ljubljana (Slovenia), University of Namibia (Windhoek), Ritsumeikan University (Japan), and Stellenbosch University (South Africa). Previously a faculty member at the University of Wisconsin-Madison and Executive Director of the International Institute of Comparative Government in Lausanne (Switzerland), he held appointments in Sweden (Linköping University), England (Essex University), India (Institute of Economic Growth), Pakistan (Institute of Development Economics), and Yale University. During 1987–1990 he directed the American Studies Research Centre, Hyderabad, India; during 1996–1999 he was Deputy Rector of the Institute of Social Studies. He has published 15 books and over 80 journal articles and reviews.

Tatiana Chubarova is Head of the Center for Economic Theory of the Social Sector in the Institute of Economy at the Russian Academy of Sciences in Moscow, Russia. She also teaches at the Moscow School of Economics, Moscow State University, and the Moscow State Institute of International Relations. She was educated at the Moscow State Institute of International Relations (MS 1986). She holds a Candidate of Science Degree in International Economy from the Russian Academy of Sciences and a PhD (Social Policy) from the London School of Economics and Political Science. She is an Executive Secretary of *Upravliniye Zdravookhraneniem* (*Journal of Health Management*) as well as a member of New Economic Association (Russia) and International Political Science Association (IPSA). She is the author (and co-author) of four books and has contributed to numerous journals. Professional interests cover health and social policy in a comparative perspective; organisation and financing of health care; corporate social responsibility; and gender issues.

Sheelah Connolly is Research Fellow within the Academic Unit of Neurology, Trinity College Dublin. She was awarded a PhD in Epidemiology from the Centre for Public Health at Queen's University Belfast. In addition, she holds an MSc in Health Economics from the University of York, England. Her research interests lie in the area of the social and demographic determinants of health and health services usage.

Stephen Duckett is Director of the Health Program at the Melbourne-based think tank, Grattan Institute. He has held top operational and policy leadership positions in health care in Australia and Canada including as Secretary of what is now the Commonwealth Department of Health. He has a reputation for creativity, evidence-based innovation, and reform in areas ranging from the introduction of activity-based funding for hospitals to new systems of accountability for the safety of hospital care. An economist, he is a Fellow of the Academy of Social Sciences in Australia.

Katherine Fierlbeck is McCulloch Professor of Political Science at Dalhousie University. She has cross-appointments in Community Health and Epidemiology, International Development Studies, and European Studies, and is a member of the European Union Centre of Excellence. Her most recent books are *Health Care in Canada* (2011) and *Health Care Federalism in Canada: Critical Junctures and Critical Perspectives* (with William Lahey; 2013). She and William Lahey are currently leading a Canadian Institutes for Health Research team on innovative methodological approaches in health care federalism.

Scott Greer is Associate Professor of Health Management and Policy at the University of Michigan, School of Public Health. Author or editor of eight books, his most recent include *The Politics of European Union Health Policies* (2009), *European Union Public Health Policies* (with Paulette Kurzer; 2013), and *Federalism and Decentralization in European Health and Social Care* (with Joan Costa-i-Font; 2013). He is currently leading a study of health systems governance for the European Observatory on Health Systems and Policies, and finishing a book with Margitta Maetzke on the role of the state in English, German, and United States health care.

Natalia Grigorieva is Professor of Political Science and Head of the Centre of Comparative Social Policy and Social Administration in the School of Public Administration at the Lomonosov Moscow State University (MGU), Moscow, Russia. She is Editor in Chief of the *Journal of Health Management* (Russia) and Adviser to the Deputy of the Committee for Health Care Policy of the State Duma, the Federal Assembly- (Parliament) of the Russian Federation; and consultant for the Gender Theme Group, UN (Russia). She is an active researcher in the field of comparative social policy with a special interest in health care policy. Her latest two monographs (of more than 150) are: V. Sadovnichi, N. Grigorieva, and T. Chubarova, *From Tradition to Innovation: Modern Health Care Reforms* (2012), and N. Grigorieva and T. Chubarova, *Modern Health Care: Policy, Economics, Management* (2013). Publications in English include: 'Health Care in the CIS' in the *Routledge International Encyclopedia of Women* (2001); 'Health Status in Russia' in *The Role of the State in Economic Growth and Socio-economic Reforms: Human Development Report* (2002/2003); 'Public Health Policy and the Gender-based Approaches' (2003); and 'Family Strategies of Modern Russian Students' in *Work Family Conflict Resolution* (ILO Sub-regional Office for Eastern Europe and Central Asia 2009).

Michael K. Gusmano is Associate Professor of Health Policy and Management at the New York Medical College and Research Scholar at The Hastings Center. His research interests include the politics of health care reform, comparative health systems, aging, health and health care inequalities, and normative theories of policy analysis. In addition to his appointments at New York Medical College and The Hastings Center, Dr Gusmano holds adjunct appointments at Columbia University and Yale University. His most recent book, *Health Care in World Cities* (2010), documents the implications of national and local health care policies for access to care in New York, London, and Paris. He holds a PhD in political science from the University of Maryland at College Park and a Master's in Public Policy from the State University of New York at Albany. He was also Post-doctoral Fellow in the Robert Wood Johnson Foundation Scholars in Health Policy Program at Yale University (1995–1997). Dr Gusmano is President-elect of the American Political Science Association's Organized Section on Health Politics and Policy. He serves on the editorial boards for the *Journal of Health Politics, Policy and Law*, *Health Economics Policy and Law*, and *The Hastings Center Report*.

Achim Lang is Senior Lecturer of Political Science and Public Administration at the University of Konstanz (Germany). His research focus includes interest groups, health politics, and innovation policy. He published on different aspects of eHealth in Europe (*Telemedicine and eHealth, das Gesundheitswesen*) and has edited *Innovation Policy and Governance in High-technology Industries* which also featured medical technology.

Lenaura De Vasconcelos Costa Lobato has a PhD in Public Health from the School of Social Work at Fluminense Federal University (Rio de Janeiro, Brazil). Her area of research is in social policy, health and social assistance policies and systems, and health reform in Brazil. She is also a researcher for the National Council for Scientific and Technological Development. Recent publications in

English include *Policy Analysis in Brazil* (co-editor and co-author (in press)) and 'Changes and Challenges in Brazilian Health Care System' (with J. Vaitsman and J.M. Ribeiro), in H.S. Rout (ed.), *Health Care Systems: A Global Survey* (2011).

Margitta Mätzke is Professor at the Institute for Politics and Social Policy at the Johannes Kepler University in Linz, Austria. She completed her PhD in Political Science at Northwestern University, Evanston, Illinois in 2005, and received the venia legendi in Political Science from the University of Gottingen, Germany in 2012. She currently works on comparative health and welfare state policy, and has published several book chapters and journal articles in publications including *Social Politics*, *Journal of Health Politics, Policy and Law*, *Journal of Public Policy*, *German Policy Studies*, *Journal of European Social Policy*, *Journal of Policy History*, and *Social Policy and Administration*.

Theodore R. Marmor is Professor Emeritus of Public Policy, Management, and Political Science at Yale University. His most recent co-authored books are *Politics, Health and Health Care* (with Rudolf Klein; 2012) and *Social Insurance: America's Neglected Heritage* (with Jerry Mashaw and John Pakutka; 2014).

Nicholas Mays is Professor of Health Policy in the Department of Health Services Research and Policy at the London School of Hygiene and Tropical Medicine where he has been since 2003. He also directs the Department of Health-funded Policy Research Unit in Policy Innovation Research. He first became interested in how the health services operate in the different countries of the United Kingdom while working at Queen's University Belfast in the early 1990s.

Kieke G.H. Okma has worked with a variety of government agencies in the Netherlands and international organisations, including the World Bank, for over 25 years. Since 2004, she has been living in New York and works as an international health consultant and academic. Her teaching included posts as Associate Professor at the Catholic University Leuven (2003–) and the Wagner School of Public Services, New York University (2008–2011), Visiting Professor at Cornell University (2009–2011), and Professeur Invitée at the Conservatoire National des Arts et Métiers in Paris (2012). Other activities include editorial board membership of *Health Policy*, *Journal of Health Politics, Policy and Law*, and the *Journal of Health Services Research and Policy*, among others. Kieke Okma has widely lectured and published on a broad range of issues of health policy, health politics, and international comparison. Recent publications include: 'Changing Health Care Systems of the World', *Wiley Encyclopaedia of Health* (2014); 'Swiss and Dutch "Consumer-driven Health Care": Ideal Model or Reality?' (with L. Crivelli), *Health Policy* (2013); 'Will Dutch-style Managed Competition Work with the Irish System?' (opinion), *Irish Journal of Public Policy* (January 2013); 'Managed Competition for Medicare? Sobering Lessons from the Netherlands' (with J. Oberlander and T.R. Marmor), *New English Journal of Medicine* (2011); *Six Countries, Six Reform*

Models? The Health Reform Experiences of Israel, the Netherlands, New Zealand, Singapore, Switzerland and Taiwan, edited by K.G.H. Okma and L. Crivelli (2009); *Comparative Studies and the Politics of Modern Medical Care*, edited by T.R. Marmor, R. Freeman and K.G.H. Okma (2009); and 'Comparative Perspectives on National Values, Institutions and Health Policies' (with T.R. Marmor and S.R. Latham), *Sociology of Health and Illness*, edited by C. Wendt (2006).

Howard A. Palley is Professor Emeritus of Social Policy at the School of Social Work, and Distinguished Fellow at the Institute for Human Services Policy at the School of Social Work of the University of Maryland, Baltimore. He has authored or co-authored a number of studies on health service delivery policies and long-term care policies in the United States, Canada, Sweden, the Republic of Korea, Japan, Ukraine, and Israel. His current research is on the delivery of health care services in Canada. His publications have appeared in the *International Journal of Health Services*, *International Political Science Review*, *Journal of Health Politics*, *Policy and Law*, *Journal of Health and Social Policy*, *Inquiry*, *Health and Social Work*, *Publius*, *Social Service Review*, *Social Policy and Administration*, *Milbank Quarterly*, and the *Journal of Aging and Social Policy*. He has served on the Science Advisory Board of Health Canada and is currently a member of the state of Delaware Health Facilities Authority. He has received Fulbright Awards to the Republic of Korea, Taiwan, and Ukraine. Howard Palley has written widely on the subject of the development of health care programmes and policies and long-term care programmes and policies for the elderly and the disabled in the United States and internationally – inclusive of nursing home care, and in-home and community-based care. He is co-author of *The Chronically-limited Elderly: The Case for a National Policy for In-home and Supportive Community-based Services* and editor of *Community-based Programs and Policies: Contributions to Social Policy Development in Health Care and Health Care-related Services* (2009). Recently, he has co-authored *The Political and Economic Sustainability of Health Care in Canada: Private-sector Involvement in the Federal Provincial Health Care System* (2011).

Ixchel Pérez Durán is a Postdoctoral Researcher at the Institut Barcelona d'Estudis Internacionals (IBEI) and Adjunct Professor in the Department of Political and Social Sciences, Universitat Pompeu Fabra. Her research interests focus on accountability in public policy, accountability in European welfare states, European Parliament oversight, and interest group influence in European Union agencies.

A. Venkat Raman is Associate Professor at the Faculty of Management Studies (FMS), University of Delhi and teaches HRD and Health Policy. His research interest is particularly focused on exploring public–private partnership models to improve access to equitable health services for the poor and the underserved. He received his master's degree from Tata Institute of Social Sciences, Mumbai, and

PhD from FMS, Delhi University. Before entering academics, Dr Raman worked with NGOs in urban slums, and rural and tribal communities. He has more than 20 years of teaching, research, consulting, and advisory experience. He has been associated with many bilateral and multilateral development agencies including the World Bank, USAID, and DFID in several programme interventions in Asia and Africa. He has several research publications including *Public–Private Partnership in Health Care in India: Lessons for Developing Countries* (with Prof. Bjorkman; 2009), based on extensive field research in India. He was a member of the working group on PPP for the 11th Five Year Plan, Government of India and served in many committees. Currently Dr Raman provides technical (advisory) support for some of the states in India. His other areas of interest include demand side financing, service delivery innovations, and human resource in health sector.

Mônica de Castro Maia Senna is Associate Professor of Public Health at the Federal Fluminense University (UFF) in Brazil. Currently the coordinator of the Post-graduate Programme in Social Policy at the UFF, she is also the vice-coordinator of the Centre for Public Policy Analysis and Evaluation. Published papers focus on policy analysis, and especially on the health care reform process and the policy implementation of social assistance in Brazil. Professor Senna completed her doctor of science degree at the National School of Public Health (ENSP – Escola Nacional de Saúde Pública), Oswaldo Cruz Foundation (FIOCRUZ – Fundação Oswaldo Cruz).

Harold Stöger received his PhD from the University of Salzburg, Department of History and Political Sciences. At present, he is Senior Lecturer and Researcher at the Institute of Social Policy at the University of Linz in Austria. He is the author of numerous articles, book chapters, and contributions to international academic conferences. His current research interests focus on the politics of welfare state transformation in Austria and in comparative perspective, on variations of old-age poverty and pension systems in the European Union, and on the impact of federalism on public policy-making.

Federico Toth is Assistant Professor in Political Science at the University of Bologna, where he teaches in the areas of organisation theory and health systems. His research concerns health care policy in comparative perspective. Among his latest publications are 'Healthcare Policies Over the Last 20 Years: Reforms and Counter-reforms', *Health Policy* (2010); 'Is There a Southern European Healthcare Model?', *West European Politics* (2010); 'The Italian Civil Service System' (with R. Lewanski) in F. van der Meer (ed.), *Civil Service Systems in Western Europe* (2011); and 'The Choice of Healthcare Models: How Much Does Politics Matter?', *International Political Science Review* (2013). He is currently writing a book on the Italian health care system, with a special focus on the ongoing process of regionalisation.

Chapter 1

Comparative Policy Analysis, Health Care, and Federal Systems

Katherine Fierlbeck and Howard A. Palley

The field of comparative health policy has grown almost as exponentially as health expenditure itself. Once viewed as a very specific product of a particular cultural and institutional context, health policy has increasingly been placed under the lens of comparative political scientists (e.g., Marmor, Freeman, and Okma 2009; Saltman 2012; Marmor and Klein 2012; Greer and Costa-Font 2013). Much of this has been driven by the realisation that, while many countries increasingly face the same kinds of intransigent problems, some are better able to address these issues than others. The hope is that, by understanding how other states address these problems, we may be able to learn effective ways to solve or mitigate complex issues. The worry is that we may discover that, while the problems are common to us all, the solutions must be unique.

The methodological premise of this book is that the study of health care federalism is underrepresented in the field of comparative political science. Much of the existing work on comparative health policy per se has a national focus. This is because comparative analysis, to make sense, must compare similar things. By breaking down health care data into a more granular presentation, we can learn about variations in health care delivery that may indicate substantial equity and access issues between regions. This may include relative levels of public and private expenditure, the proportion of the population not covered by health insurance, wait times across regions, access to primary care, demographic indicators, and so on. While it is commonly acknowledged that federal structures are in fact quite important variables in explaining why specific health policy outcomes arise in particular states (e.g., Tuohy 1999), there are very few systematic studies which focus on the dynamics between federal and regional governments (and between regional governments) across a number of federal states.

The Changing Face of Health Care Federalism

'Federalism' is a notoriously loose term; 'the kind of political phenomenon that cannily eludes and frustrates grand theoretical system-building' (Ward and Ward 2009: 2). In this book we include entities such as the European Union and China (which cannot usefully be compared to 'true' federal states). To allow for a wide scope of analysis, we employ Elazar's definition of federalism as simply 'the mode of organization that unites separate polities within an overarching political system by distributing power among the general and constituent governments in a manner designed to protect the existence and authority of both' (1972: 2). One rather interesting observation that this volume highlights is that both formal and 'quasi' (or 'hybrid') as well as simply 'functional' federal systems exhibit very similar kinds of dynamics. In the realm of health care federalism, the distinction between formal and de facto federal systems is much less important than other characteristics (such as the disparity in size between units within each system, the particular powers granted to them, or the disposition of political agents to act). Two of the cases presented here are, according to the respective authors, 'hybrids' between federal and unitary systems (such as Spain and the United Kingdom); others, such as China and Italy, are functional though not legal federal systems. Some federal states (such as Germany and Austria) are 'power sharing' systems, in which both national and regional governments oversee health care, but are given quite distinct roles in the process; others (such as Canada) are 'power separating' systems, which attempt – rather unsuccessfully – to delineate clear authority for health care in one jurisdiction or the other. And, in the fascinating case of the European Union, even when clear authority over health care is explicitly given to individual member states, participation in a 'purely economic' federal system can have significant and unintended consequences for the governance of health care by discrete jurisdictions. As Bevan, Connolly, and Mays note, very few federal systems actually exhibit relative equality between regions in terms of size, fiscal capacity, or legal powers, and it is often the particular asymmetry situated within a specific institutional context which is most relevant in explaining the precise nature of the dynamics of federal health systems.

We have attempted to include a generous cross-section of federal, functional federal, and quasi-federal states across geographical regions. Many of the federal states are European, and we have also included the European Union itself as this federal structure plays an increasingly important role in many aspects of European health policy. We include North America and Australia and, in addition, we have made a point of incorporating the major BRIC states (Brazil, Russian, India, and China). Due to limitations of size and time, we have been unable to include other interesting federal states (such as Switzerland and South Africa). But we trust that the case studies which we offer here will provide a representative sample of policy-making across disparate federal states and states with highly devolved governance structures.

Analytically, there are two separate questions which underlie the studies in this volume. The first is the question, addressed in each discrete chapter, of how the institutional structure of each federal system affects the nature of each health care system. The second question which arises (in the comparison between these chapters) is whether the nature of health care federalism itself is changing in a systematically and qualitatively distinct manner.

Federal structures do not evolve in a vacuum; they change in response to the world on which they are imposed. Health care is a particularly vexing policy area for federal systems. This is because federal institutions are designed to be solid, stable, and predictable legal frameworks for political and civil relationships. The problem is that the nature of health care provision today is highly complex, cross-jurisdictional, and quickly evolving. Even within living memory, health technology was once quite rudimentary. Health care often amounted to little more than the warehousing of patients (for example, in tuberculosis sanatoriums or mental asylums). Information often rested in the hands of the medical profession alone. The pace of change was slow, as was the relative cost of health care as a proportion of public spending. Public health care was generally a matter of private or charitable concern. Communication between discrete healthcare jurisdictions was minimal. Today, communication can be instantaneous. Huge data banks and the utilisation of websites permit the analysis of information, ending physicians' monopoly over medical decision-making. At the same time, policy decisions require a level of technical expertise few career civil servants enjoy. Cost containment of ever-burgeoning health services has become politically imperative. Health care, again, is a completely different creature from what it was only a few generations ago. Those born into a highly localised system are living out their days in much denser and interconnected one.

But the management of this complexity has become an issue. We now have a sense of how technologies can be used to make health care more efficient and more effective: anecdotal accounts and pilot studies provide optimistic encouragement that health care can be redesigned into a more effective and sustainable system. Yet there is also increasingly a concern with the misuse of expensive technology and costly pharmaceuticals. But (unless one has complete faith in the ability of the market to distribute health care resources) this kind of reordering cannot be done spontaneously and anarchically; there must be some form of coordination. Communication must be facilitated; best practices must be collected and disseminated. Even collaborative activity cannot be achieved extemporaneously: it must be negotiated and facilitated. Effective and complex (and usually expensive) systems cannot easily be developed by smaller or poorer jurisdictions. The point is that *some* form of policy coordination must exist in order efficiently to utilise the capacity afforded by new technologies. And in federal states, policy coordination is rarely a simple task.

The growth in complexity of health care as a policy issue has made health care governance difficult enough. But the ceaseless increase in health care expenditure has heightened the tension between governments within federal states even more emphatically. The political dynamics of contemporary health care federalism, then, are the legacy of two overlapping narratives: decentralisation and cost containment. These debates, in turn, have had considerable implications for equity (including access to health care), accountability, and the coordination of health care services and governance structures.

Few countries were unaffected by the trend to decentralisation in the provision of public services. In retrospect, of course, the unrestrained enthusiasm for decentralisation in health care was quite remarkable given how fragmented and inchoate its theoretical justifications were. The romance with decentralisation was driven by a number of factors. In some countries, such as Spain, Brazil, and Russia, federalism has been a fairly recent policy solution to a history of authoritarian rule. Similarly, the devolution of one British National Health Service into four separate ones was an explicitly political decision regarding larger issues of governance. In other states, both federal and unitary, the allure of New Public Management led to a greater functional decentralisation. The New Public Management school held that, while overarching goals could and should be articulated in a hierarchical manner, the execution of these aims was best achieved by those who had a clear sense of the granular detail of service provision (the principle of 'steering, not rowing'). Significantly, the first major policy experiment with New Public Management reforms was performed by Mrs Thatcher upon the National Health Service before it radiated into other policy areas. Within the field of economics, as well, one particular stream of literature from Hayek (1937) to Tiebout (1956), Oates (1972), and Weingast (1995) argued that making discrete subnational jurisdictions accountable for cost expenditure was an efficient means of limiting expenditure, while critics responded that this approach led to patterns of inequitable access to health care services (Minow 2003; Rosenau 2007; Vladeck and Rice 2009).

What have been the consequences of three decades of decentralisation? As a number of health policy analysts have already argued, the bloom is off the rose: while decentralised structures still exist for either practical political reasons or because of theoretical assumptions of the utility of decentralisation, a number of clear consequences have arisen. On the positive side, more centrifugal forms of federalism have compelled state actors to develop new mechanisms in order to facilitate coordinated activity or (at worst) to prevent regions from acting at cross-purposes, either deliberately or unconsciously. Two interesting examples here are Canada and Brazil: in the former, the decision of the national government to step away from health policy has meant a need for provinces to find more innovative ways of communicating and working together more effectively. Here there are clear examples of lateral governance between provincial governments, and of a fascia of non-governmental networks supporting common policy development. While many argue that this form of soft governance is not as effective as one in which the central government plays a more engaged role, it does present an interesting approach in cases where the central government *refuses* to play a role. In the case of Brazil (and, to a lesser extent, in China and the new Russian Federation), new structures of multilateral governance have been established to accommodate the fact that public health care provision is a complicated relationship between federal, regional, and municipal governments.

But the trend to decentralisation has, to a large extent, not been an advantageous one for health care. Contributors to this volume were invited to examine constructive consequences of health care decentralisation in their respective jurisdictions: if one of the most common theoretical justifications of decentralisation is the capacity for innovation at the local level, then what have been some of these outcomes? While several contributors acknowledged that their particular federal systems did permit the development of a plethora of pilot programmes, they also noted the inability of federal states efficiently to translate policy successes more widely across jurisdictions. Additionally, they observed that without substantial assistance from the central government for health care, there was an inability to reach the goals of improving health care in poor regions. But, as James Björkman and A. Venkat Raman observe in reference to the Indian state of Kerala, it is not purely a matter of whether regional governments have the authority (or the money) but also whether they are able to use available money and authority. More generally they note that, where a state lacks the capacity to fulfil its basic functions, 'there is a risk that decentralisation will exacerbate problems rather than reduce them. But in countries where a state is committed to the devolution of power to local tiers of government, decentralisation can enhance service delivery'.

To an extent, the literature promoting the greater decentralisation of health care provision, or funding, or regulation did not discount the likelihood that a 'patchwork quilt' effect would result from such a reorganisation. But the discussion of decentralisation occurred at a time when the total expenditure on health care as a percentage of GDP was, on average, a third lower than today. And, while the 1980s did have periods of critical economic fluctuation, the strategy of decentralising authority over health care was seen, in part, as a means of restraining costs by making individual regions more accountable for their spending. For very specific political reasons, as many of the contributions to this book explain, there was little restraint in health care spending following decentralisation and – somewhat more surprisingly – there was often little accountability as well. In sum, what this comparative survey highlights is that the experiment with health care decentralisation in federal states over the past few decades has led to three major issues: greater inequality between regions; poor accountability in health care governance within and between regions; and a critical lack of coordination of health care governance within federal systems.

Equity

The dynamics of decentralised federal structures combined with the severe economic conditions following recessions in the mid-1990s and late 2000s set the conditions for a considerable amount of cost-shifting between jurisdictions in order to stabilise the budgets of those jurisdictions which were not directly responsible for the provision of public health services. This is one very clear area in which the comparative presentation of national-level data tells us very little, for, in those jurisdictions where regional governments were largely responsible for maintaining health care services, national governments were able to reduce budget deficits by downloading costs to regional ones. These regional governments, in turn, often did not possess the legal capacity to raise sufficient revenues to meet the increased costs associated with the delivery of health care services, or simply did not have the population or resource tax base that could provide these additional revenues. The result has been a noticeable increase in disparity between regions. In Canada, for example, while such disparities are not as transparent, some provinces nonetheless spend almost half of their resources on health care, while others utilise closer to 30 per cent. While the provinces have similar levels of health care, the poorer provinces must use a higher proportion of their available resources on health care due to popular political demand, which means much more constrained spending in policy areas that have nothing to do with health care per se. These differences in regional capacity also raise the issue of how to address the mobility of patients (and providers) within federal systems. In Italy, for example, where patients can chose the hospital in which they prefer to receive treatment irrespective of regional boundaries, the mobility of patients is so noticeable that net patient outflow can be used as a marker of the quality of health care in any particular region (if patients are satisfied with the treatment options within their home region, they would have no reason to travel outside of it).

Accountability

The even more remarkable observation this volume highlights is the failure of strategies of decentralisation to secure greater accountability in the governance of health care. Some of the contributors to this volume have provided empirical measurements to evaluate the relative performance of regional jurisdictions within federal states. Given the insistence of earlier theoretical literature on the value of decentralisation in making policy decisions more accountable and more efficient, the results are quite intriguing. Ixchel Pérez Durán, for example, constructs a detailed framework to measure the relative level of accountability in health care jurisdictions across Spain. Using three separate metrics (the extent to which regions' health authorities are governed by a formal framework of rules; the extent to which regional health care regulation provides binding obligations on governments; and the level of openness and transparency in the activities of health authorities), she is able to rank the level of accountability across Spain's regions. She also examines some possible explanations for the variability in accountability across Spain's 'autonomous communities'. In the first place, she notes, those regions which have enjoyed an autonomous status for a much longer period exhibit no more accountability than those which were, until relatively recently, under central control. Her second observation is that those regions which rely more heavily upon the private administration of services show a lower level of accountability than those utilising a greater degree of publicly administered health care services. Thirdly, she notes, the measurement of accountability is generally lower in regions led by political parties which do not have a national presence. Similarly, Chubarova and Grigorieva compare the economic and health indicators for each region of the Russian Federation with the actual execution of state guarantees for free-of-charge health services across regional jurisdictions. They find that Moscow, with some of the most robust health *and* economic indicators (and best-developed health infrastructure) placed poorly in living up to the guarantee of free access to health services compared to some less well-off jurisdictions. (However, while 'free', often many health services are unavailable in these poorer areas).

But if some devolved federal structures present problems for the accountability of regions' health authorities to their own citizens, others illustrate distortions arising in the mode of accountability (or lack thereof) *between* regions within federal systems. Both the United Kingdom and Italy are examples of this kind of a relationship. In the former, the process of devolution in 1999 led to a particular federal relationship in which three of four regions are governed by two legislative levels, while the fourth – England – has only one. This, as Bevan, Connolly, and Mays point out, means that the political representatives of non-English constituencies have a legislative voice in English health policy, while English MPs have no input in the health policy-making in Scotland, Wales, or Northern Ireland. One result of this has been that funding increases to the English health system were subject to significant sanctions for failure to meet specific indicators (such as wait times), while other regional parliaments did not make this funding conditional upon performance. Data gathered by the authors shows that England was more effective in improving the performance of its NHS; but because health authorities in the devolved regions were only responsible to their respective national parliaments rather than the national Treasury, there was political capital to be gained in these regions by *not* ceding to the English model.

In Italy, there is a clear division between northern and southern regions' success at controlling health care expenditure. As in the United Kingdom, health care funding is distributed at the national level to regional governments. Those in northern regions have been able to impose fairly strict constraints on health care spending, while those in the south, where health care resources are more frequently used for political purposes (such as patronage appointments, especially in areas of high unemployment), tend to experience consistent health care deficits. As Federico Toth writes, this is partly due to the lack of financial discipline, but also partly due to the high level of interregional mobility of patients, which puts further strain on the southern regions as they must reimburse northern jurisdictions for the large number of southerners who travel north for treatment. Ultimately, the poor performance of the southern regions has effectively led to growing recentralisation in health care governance, as the national government has been obliged to appoint health care administrators in delinquent states, significantly curtailing regional autonomy. This, in turn, has led to greater tensions with the northern regions, which have been strongly in favour of greater fiscal autonomy.

One of the most damning flaws of theories of decentralisation was their propensity to assume, without a clear comprehension of the power dynamics underlying the political relationships within each state, that greater decentralisation of health care provision would necessarily mean better accountability. In Italy, for example, decentralised health care decision-making in several southern regions was simply captured by the established system of local patronage. In China, however, the opposite was true: health care decentralisation did not lead to greater accountability at a local level because of the stranglehold that the national NCP party has upon local officials. As Michael Gusmano points out, local decision-makers clearly understand that they are answerable to national party officials, and not local health care consumers, regardless of the formal institutionalisation of decentralised health care structures.

Coordination

All federal systems have issues with the coordination of health policy, but the specific problems they encounter depend very much on the particular manifestation of federalism of each country. Canada has perhaps the most decentralised system of health care of all the federal states examined here. Provinces have full authority over almost all key aspects of health care provision, and they are responsible for funding over 80 per cent of all health care costs, and this may rise even higher. Less well-off provinces and territories are more dependent on the availability of federal expenditures in the determination of such spending. Consequently, there is little formal coordination between jurisdictions which, unsurprisingly, has meant a great deal of difficulty in communicating best practices, establishing clear channels of communication (especially during public health crises), coordinating health human resources, establishing effective purchasing strategies for pharmaceuticals, and so on. But if this 'watertight compartments' model of federalism is problematic, more integrated forms of federalism present their own drawbacks.

As Stephen Duckett argues, Australia's 'marble cake' model of interwoven jurisdictional responsibilities is characterised by attempts by jurisdictions to offload costs to each other or to avoid responsibility for unpopular outcomes. Blame shifting, he notes, is endemic. Overlapping responsibilities and multiple veto points in health policy-making severely inhibit important policy reform. Recognising this, the Commonwealth government has made some recent attempts at assuming greater responsibility for the costs of public hospitals but, as this measure requires a transfer of tax revenue from the states to the federal government, it was met with a less than enthusiastic response from the states themselves.

Even in federal states in which the functional division of responsibility in health care is clearly set out, policy distortions nonetheless remain. As Duckett argues, one of the problems with federal systems embracing shared funding responsibilities is that each government 'may see the health system simply as those parts of the health system that it funds'. This dynamic is quite clear in both Austria and Germany, 'power-sharing' federal states which delineate the functional responsibility of each level of government in health policy-making. Both countries are characterised by a similar form of social insurance, the governance of which is highly centralised. But, as Margitta Mätzke and Harald Stöger (on Austria) and Achim Lang (on Germany) explain, the hospital sector in both countries is much more decentralised. Thus outpatient care (governed by social insurance regulations) is largely under the purview of the national government, while inpatient care (within the hospital sector) is more firmly under regional control. Cost shifting occurs not simply between governments per se, but between inpatient and outpatient sectors. The Länder are responsible for the operation of hospitals, but not for raising the revenue for them; thus overcapacity in the hospital sectors remains 'politically and electorally attractive'. Austria, in consequence, continues to spend the largest share of its health budget on hospital care, a figure that is higher than any other European state. In Germany, the schism between social insurance (outpatient care) and the hospital sector (inpatient care) exists in a similar manner but, as Lang explains, German Länder are subject to strong balanced-budget regulations. They have attempted to meet these requirements by cutting expenditure and by selling state properties and companies to private investors; these, pointedly, include a large proportion of hospitals. This, in turn, has led to marked discrepancies between private hospitals, which can use their superior access to capital markets to provide additional funding resources, and public hospitals, which cannot.

The evocative optimism of decentralisation was the hope that pushing decision-making on local services down to the local level would make decision-makers more accountable and, in this way, improve the quality of services and the effectiveness of public spending. But, as most authors in this volume observe, the decentralisation of responsibility over health care often was not accompanied by a distribution in funding or expertise to allow local political authorities to engage in constructive policy-making and improved delivery of health care services at the local or regional levels. Without adequate funding, substate governments cannot provide services at a level expected by their constituents (and, in some cases, required by federal legislation). Without the technical expertise to implement and regulate health services, and without the administrative expertise needed to negotiate with powerful service providers, smaller substate governments can become even less effective in providing public health care. At the same time, there are very clear political reasons for central governments refusing to cede such powers: these may involve the lack of confidence that regions will use their authority effectively and constructively (as in Italy), or it may be that centralised health policies sometimes serve as efficient 'vote-buying machines' for whatever national parties happen to be in power (as Björkman and Venkat Raman observe in India). The capacity for decentralisation in health policy to lead as easily to *less* political accountability as it is to result in more has, in many cases, led to a discernible attempt by many states to recentralise the control over health care; although, as some states have discovered, once formal jurisdiction has been ceded to the regions, it is not always as easy to recover it.

Theorising Health Care Federalism

To reiterate an earlier point, what this volume attempts to do is to provide a series of nuanced discussions of the dynamics of health policy in a number of federal states. The policy discussion has shown remarkable coherence across federal states: the last two decades have been powerfully informed by the idea of decentralisation as a means of securing greater accountability in how funds are spent, and how services are provided. More recently, the consequences of this policy direction have been uniformly criticised and, while these criticisms vary, they highlight the rise of regional inequalities, the distortion in relations of accountability, and the serious lack of coordination of health policy within federal states.

But what do these discussions tell us about how we should study health care federalism? While there has been an explosion of cross-national dialogue in comparative health policy, notes Marmor (2012: 2), the field of comparative health policy remains somewhat under-theorised. To a large extent this is because the analytical tools which we use are quite derivative: they have been appropriated from other policy fields, and the 'fit' with the new subject matter is often not as close as it could (or ought) to be. This is especially relevant for the field of comparative health policy federalism, where analytical instruments have been crafted for very different fields than health care. For example, a comparative analysis of immigration or tax policy may have little to say about the comparative nature of health policy, especially when the former are undertaken at a national level, and an instance is where the latter is largely determined at a substate level.

A useful starting-point for political scientists is the usual broad basket of significant variables consisting of 'institutions, interests, and ideas' (Hall 1997; Hall and Taylor 2001). Some combination of these three variables will generally go far to explain the unique political relationships between political actors in various federal systems (as well as in non-federal systems). But this may not be enough to explain the dynamic quality of these relationships: not only do we need to understand why things are the way they *are*, but we must also attempt to comprehend the reasons that they are *changing*. The starting point for most policy analysis is usually an examination of the institutional factors which provide the armature for what state and substate governments can legitimately do. Constitutions, legislation, political structures, and health care financing systems are also useful to examine because they are relatively stable over time and can be analysed in relation to more transitory variables such as political administrations or economic cycles. Policy-making, and especially health policy-making, in federal states is usually influenced by the level of institutional fragmentation within each state. The relative level of centralisation or decentralisation established by the particular institutional framework of federalism does, to a large degree, explain the capacity (if not necessarily the direction) for substantial policy change. Despite the fact that federal design is one of the most significant institutional variables explaining why health policy outcomes differ substantially from country to country (e.g., Immergut 1992; Tuohy 1999), it is much less helpful in explaining why (and how) these systems do in fact change, however infrequently or hesitantly, as such change involves a multitude of variables (Palley, Pomey, and Owens 2012). This is, of course, the dominant critique of institutionalist theory. A strict institutionalist approach is very good at demonstrating why systems are able to resist change, but less helpful in understanding why, at times, significant change does in fact occur as such change also, of course, involves a multitude of variables. To address this explanatory deficit, a structural institutionalist approach adopted the narratives of 'path dependency' and 'critical junctures'. This approach was originally articulated in economic theory (the paradigm being the dominance of the inefficient QWERTY keyboard) and was quickly adopted by some political scientists to explain a range of political outcomes (including labour movement politics in Latin America: e.g., Collier and Collier 1991). It was then picked up by health policy analysts (Wilsford 1993) and quickly became the dominant explanatory focus for comparative health policy (e.g., Tuohy 1999), usually incorporating the concept of a transitory 'window of opportunity'. Within two decades, however, dissatisfaction with the analytical utility of this approach began to accumulate (Brown 2010). In response, Wilsford (2010) indicated a more 'flexible' and modest view of the claims of the term 'path dependency'.

As constructivists might say, the perception of what is theoretically possible is inherently limited by the dominant way in which we interpret the world. In other words, the overemphasis upon institutionalism to explain health policy reinforces the danger of crystallising our theoretical understanding which limits our capacity to understand the way in which the world in unfolding in front of us. This concern has led to the development of a more nuanced view which considers the role of institutions, both state and nonstate, in the development of public policy, but only as one relevant variable in the determination of public policies such as health care policy (March and Olsen 1984; Olson 1965; Jacobs 2007).

It would be a mistake to downplay the role of institutions too much. As Marmor and Okma succinctly write in this volume, 'institutions matter'. This is particularly true in the United States, where a highly decentralised federal structure has made major coherent reforms exceptionally difficult. But, as this volume also illustrates, it is the particular historical development of every individual state's institutional structures which set the parameters for governments' policy-making. As Bevan, Connolly, and Mays describe, for example, the political and institutional character of Scotland, Northern Ireland, and Wales (going back as far as the sixteenth century) can be discerned in these regions' contemporary policy responses to health policy following devolution in 1999. As important as institutions are in determining health policy outcomes, however, they are often variables which *constrain* choice, rather than ones which mobilise activity.

Another important variable is the discursive environment within which health policy develops and operates. Political scientists will often identify the specific political culture or set of values which define a community to explain policy-making decisions. Ideological positions, however, are not the only kind of discursive variables that are relevant, for it is important to examine the conceptual fads and fashions in health policy development, and to identify the epistemic communities which influence the way in which we think about what kinds of health policies are viable, relevant, and desirable. As noted above, the recent experimentation with decentralisation in many jurisdictions was not the result of sustained empirical investigation but, rather, an intellectual flirtation with an idea the principles of which, in retrospect, seem remarkably overstated. And, as numerous studies in this volume describe, the fixation upon decentralisation has led to considerable inequities (and political tensions) between regions, has diminished the accountability of regional decision-making bodies, and has exacerbated the problems of coordination within federal states.

One of the most critical, but underdeveloped, variables in understanding the formation of health policy is the relationship between national and substate governments. An examination of the way in which national, regional (and sometimes municipal) governments' interests interact is imperative in comprehending policy outcomes. As most authors in this volume note, the volume of cost-offloading and blame-shifting in federal states is quite substantial. Depending on the country, other major stakeholders' interests (physicians' associations, private insurance, hospital, or pharmaceutical corporations, unions, and so on) may also be decisive in a given situation. It is also important to be able to parse the political landscape above and beyond the health care sector, as health policy outcomes can also simply be externalities driven by wider political decisions. But the discernment of relevant interests as key variables in policy outcomes is a far more difficult exercise than the identification of pertinent institutions. Key players often do not wish to advertise their influence. And interests shift fluidly and continually in response to the larger political and economic environment.

For this reason, it is also crucial to understand the fiscal and economic bases of health policy. This is probably self-evident in jurisdictions where spending on health services consumes half of the regional budget. But it is also important in comprehending why and how the regulatory environment affects jurisdictions' capacity to provide the kind of health care they deem appropriate. As Scott Greer explains, for example, it is the European Union's attempt to achieve a disciplined control of member states' economies which has resulted in an unexpected (and arguably illegitimate) centralisation of control over health policy-making. 'Federalism' and 'economic variables' are often seen as two quite distinct elements in the determination of health policy, but there have been far fewer attempts to understand how the two variables interact. The school of market-preserving federalism, for example, has attempted to redesign federal institutions so that they impose an inexorable logic of cost-containment upon regional governments (e.g., Qian, Yingyi, and Weingast 1997; McKinnon 1997); a strategy that, some argue, has particularly adverse consequences.

A final, and even more overlooked, explanatory variable in understanding health policy-making in federal states is the nature of health care itself. Health care systems are often viewed as static and passive arenas in which political and intellectual battles are played. But health care can be not only the *subject* of investigation but, at times, the *key force* for change itself. Once a relatively simple and localised matter, health care is now a complex and rapidly evolving phenomenon which involves policy-making beyond substate or even state boundaries. The surveillance and control of pathogens, the joint procurement of pharmaceuticals, the monitoring of post-market performance of pharmaceuticals, the coordination of training and staffing of health care professionals, and the cross-jurisdictional development of standards, benchmarks, and performance indicators are vibrant examples of the ways in which health care has expanded beyond jurisdictional boundaries. Interjurisdictional policy formulation is essential when individual subnational units have little capacity to develop highly complex measure on their own, but it is also important when individual regions must address larger events and outcomes over which they have little direct control. Such interjurisdictional policy formulation, as several contributors note, often requires the national government to play a coordinating role, as well as a significant role in funding.

It is probable that many relevant developments in health care were not pronounced until the digital revolution became undeniable by the twenty-first century. Healthcare advances through the 1980s and 1990s were already palpable, but they centred more squarely upon pharmaceutical development than upon information technology. This, of course, in itself had significant implications for the way in which health care was provided, as the potential for outpatient care increased exponentially. It also had a considerable effect on overarching health care expenditure (spending on drugs, unsurprisingly, skyrocketed); on the distribution of health care across the population (whether pharmaceuticals were insured publicly or privately became far more important); and on the influence of pharmaceutical corporations on health policy formulation (as in the United States, eclipsing the influence of doctors' organisations themselves). By the second decade of the twenty-first century, however, the technology underlying health care had transformed into a truly digital revolution. The reason for this revolution is what Topol (2012: vii) calls an 'unprecedented super-convergence'. Such a revolution, he notes 'would not be possible were it not for the maturation of the digital world technologies – ubiquity of smart phones, bandwidth, pervasive connectivity, and social networking. Beyond this, the perfect digital storm includes immense, seemingly unlimited computing power via cloud server farms, remarkable biosensors, genomic sequencing, imaging capabilities, and formidable health information systems'.

Yet another potentially revolutionary application of digital technology is the phenomenal advances made in data processing. The use of cloud storage technology to store digital information enables the pooling of data and can now permit clinical trials to incorporate even larger populations. This, in turn, allows researchers 'to extrapolate regularity patterns from the data algorithmically [...] Emphasis will thus move away from the traditional knowledge base towards understanding of quantitative data clouds at a global level, consequently homogenizing both results and performance' (*International Innovation* 12 May 2013). Computer simulation modelling is also being used to evaluate health policy (e.g., Sobolev and Kuramoto 2010; Hashemian et al. 2012). In sum, then, the technological tools we have with which to create health care provide an explosive array of possibility in the way in which care systems can be reconfigured, but health policy analysts are slow to think about the ways in which this will shape not only health care but also health care *policy* and, inevitably, the politics of health care policy.

Conclusion: Health Care Federalism in a Globalised World

Why focus on federal states in comparative health policy? One reason is that federal states are relatively ill-served by comparative studies which, at best, view federalism as a relevant but static institution. By focusing on the dynamic relationships between substate actors themselves, between substate and national governments, and even between substate units and non-governmental actors, one develops a much more nuanced account of the policy formulation and the politics behind it. By comparing patterns of substate activity across countries, one becomes better able to evaluate claims about how federal systems do (or ought to) operate. And, to the extent that governments often evince a propensity to embrace theoretical models without due consideration of how (and even whether) these ideas have performed in practice, a comparative evaluation of federal systems can offer what Marmor et al. call 'a defense against explanatory provincialism' (2009: 13).

Another reason to think hard about federal dynamics is that, in a sense, we all live in federal systems now. Even small, compact states exist within a larger concatenation of political and economic systems. While debates over health policy may remain, as some have argued, stubbornly parochial (Marmor, Freeman, and Okma 2009: 4), the increasing globalisation of markets, regulatory frameworks, and surveillance systems have resulted in the 'greater internationalisation of public policy' (Adolino and Blake 2011: 4; see also Blank and Burau 2010). This paradox is deeper than might appear at first glance: for as the world becomes increasingly integrated through the establishment of such global connexions, policy systems are at the same time becoming more fragmented. Also, in spite of international trends, the actual implementation of health care policy in federal, quasi-federal, and functional federal systems is refracted through the cultural, ideological, political, organisational and financial arrangements of diverse national health care systems (Gagnon and Iacovino 2007; Riggs 1964).

If federal systems ever did exist as either 'watertight compartments' or concentric circles of authority, they certainly do not do so now. A better hermeneutic with which to think about modern federal systems may be the notion of 'neo-medievalism', or systems focused on overlapping and cross-cutting spheres of authority (also termed 'overlapping independent bargaining systems': see Bull 1977; Wright 2000). For a number of reasons rigid command and control methods of implementation are difficult to apply to complex federal health delivery systems. By thinking about ways in which such systems can best be implemented, even political systems which are not formally considered to be federal states can benefit from a clear understanding of best (and worst) practices of federal health care systems.

Chapter 2

Austria

Margitta Mätzke and Harald Stöger

Introduction

Federalism in Austria presents a shifting image. On the one hand, Austria is one of
Europe's established federal polities. Its subnational provinces, the Bundesländer,
'can be traced back to the Habsburg Empire, with the former Crown lands
(Carinthia, Styria, Tyrol, and so on) maintaining their names' (Karlhofer and
Pallaver 2013: 43) and upholding strong regional identities after the demise of the
Austro-Hungarian Empire (Erk 2004: 4). On the other hand analysts are quick to
point out the country's formidable bureaucratic legacy and the powerful unitary
tendencies in the Austrian Constitution (Obinger 2002: 223), party system and
society, the famous corporatism and last but not least the welfare state (Obinger
2005). The image of 'A Federation without Federalism' (Erk 2004) and the notion
of 'Strong Parties in a Weak Federal Polity' (Obinger 2005) appear inaccurate,
however, when examining policy making in specific policy fields. Here we find
substantial regional autonomy, insofar as the activities of regional governments
are quite salient in citizens' perceptions (Engelmann and Schwartz 1981: 88) and
there is considerable regional influence on decision making and implementation.

The health policy field is one such area in which both the oscillating image
of Austria's federal–unitary state and the salience of the subnational level in
determining the political feasibility of reform can be observed. Internationally,
Austria's health system is classified among the social insurance systems (Wendt
and Kohl 2010) and, as such, is governed centrally. Social insurance organisation
is uniform across the country: regulations for governance structures, decision
making prerogatives, contribution rates and the minimum range of health services
reimbursable under social health insurance are the same in all regions.[1] There is
administrative decentralisation in the system, but this is not meant to translate into
significant political power on the part of regional social insurance organisations.
There is, however, a notable difference between the formal constitutional statutes
and the reality of political structures and dynamics in the Austrian political system
(Karlhofer and Pallaver 2013: 42). Administrative decentralisation does in fact
translate into considerable amounts of regional and local influence. Medical
service provision in the outpatient care sector is the domain of independent medical

---

1 Variation exists across different *occupational groups*' social insurance organisations,
but not across territorial jurisdictions.

professionals; they shape actual patterns of medical care and enjoy the amounts of medical autonomy that doctors have in most health systems. Where Austria stands out, however, is in the regionalism of its hospital sector. Here regional governments are the central players in the planning, investment, and delivery of care. More than 60 per cent of beds are in hospitals under regional or municipal ownership (Hofmarcher and Quentin 2013: 190)[2] so that in the hospital sector social health insurance is not the financial and regulatory hub. Rather, the Bundesländer are, and this is consequential in several respects.

In the first place, fiscal pressures and governments' economic strategies directly impact the hospital sector and health policy making at large in Austria. Secondly, the central government's capacity to curb the growth of hospital expenses and implement strategies of fiscal restraint is dependent on the cooperation of the Bundesländer. Legislating major health reforms requires Bundesländer consent, so that political constellations on the subnational level are crucially important for national health policy making. Thirdly, because this is the case, it is the hospital sector that dominates much of health policy making in Austria. The Austrian history of health care cost containment is a history of attempts at controlling hospital expenses. Federalism is the crucial institutional framework in which this history has played itself out.

This chapter will give an account of that history and its underlying logic. The following two sections will briefly describe the main characteristics of federalism and the health system's institutions in Austria. Then the fiscal challenges that the country has faced and the Austrian political system's readiness to address these challenges will be analysed. The last section outlines the central government's attempts to install some measure of control over the hospital sector and the role of federalism in this endeavour. The conclusion highlights a few central points and places them in a broader context.

'A Federation without Federalism'[3] in Austria?

Austria is a paradigmatic case of consensus democracy and social partnership, but strikingly little is known internationally about its federal political system. Despite the relatively small size of its population (roughly 8 million), Austria has nine subnational Bundesländer which significantly vary in their size and character. In terms of historical lineages it would seem intuitively plausible that the successor of the multinational Habsburg Monarchy would have a federal state structure; yet at the same time it is equally obvious that the empire's formidable bureaucratic legacy makes for a powerful political centre, along with its grand capital city (Obinger 2005: 182). As in neighbouring Germany, the formation of the federation took place during times of political strife, in search of national

---

2   Data for 2010.
3   This is the title of an article by Jan Erk (2004).

identity (Hadley et al. 1989: 83), and the institution of social insurance, with its uniform rules across all territories and its universalistic appeals, was a vehicle for bringing about further centralisation and tighter loyalties of blue- and white-collar employees to the institutions of the new polity (Obinger 2005: 185).

After World War II the Austrian political system was restored on the basis of the federal constitution of 1920 but, since then, has been subject to several constitutional amendments, which all tended to be 'centrist', rather than strengthening regional governments' prerogatives (Engelmann and Schwartz 1981: 86). The unitary characteristics of the Austrian political system are most pronounced with regard to formal legislative institutions. Austria's upper house of parliament (the Bundesrat) is not an effective means of defending territorial interests (Obinger 2002: 248): it can call for a suspension of legislation, but not veto it.

The distribution of authority across territorial jurisdictions is uneven across policy fields, which makes it difficult to classify Austria along mainstream typologies of comparative federalism research (Fallend 2013). There are 'policy areas clearly under central jurisdiction (Article 10), those covered by central legislation but under provincial administration (Article 11), and those where there is central framework legislation, but detailed provincial regulations (Article 12). Residual powers remain with the provinces (Article 15)' (Engelmann and Schwartz 1981: 85). Most social policy fields, including (in principle) health, are defined as being under the legislative competency of the central government (Article 10, 12 B-VG). Centralisation also characterises the country's fiscal system (Obinger 2002: 250), in which the federal government collects most of the taxes and allocates them to the Bundesländer in a procedure of vertical financial equalisation (Obinger 2005: 208). Constitutional and administrative structures find their match in political parties, interest associations (which are all geared toward the political centre (Karlhofer 2002: 235)) and an 'ethno-linguistically homogeneous societal structure, where divisions are nationwide, rather than territorial' (Erk 2004: 2).

Given all those unitary tendencies, the strong position of the Bundesländer in much of social policy legislation comes as a surprise. They are, however, heavily involved in administering federal programmes or implementing federal framework legislation, and because of this central role, they can wield strong influence over enactment and implementation of social policies (Karlhofer and Pallaver 2013: 42). That influence is mirrored in a party system that, although hierarchical and geared toward the political centre in Vienna, is asymmetric in the distribution of power across regions. There are partisan strongholds in some of the Bundesländer, and the governors of those strongholds have extremely strong positions in the central government parties (Karlhofer and Pallaver 2013: 46f). In that sense, Austrian federalism has been described as 'party federalism' (Hadley et al. 1989: 97). Regional power through the party system plays itself out informally, in the pre-parliamentary review of legislation and in conferences of the Bundesländer governors (Obinger 2005: 197). The principal constitutional mechanism for securing regional political influence is in Article 15a of the Austrian Constitution, which allows Bundesländer and the federal government to negotiate treaties (Staatsverträge) about issues on which the national parliament can only establish framework legislation, because the Länder are in charge of implementation. Much of social policy legislation, and all legislative decisions about hospital planning, takes the form of such '15a' agreements (Lehner 2008: 20ff).

Article 15a treaties, Austria's principal form of cooperative federalism, restore some of the constitutional prerogatives of the Bundesländer in the face of their potent de facto power positions in many social policy fields. This accounts for the asymmetric effect of federalism on the Austrian welfare state, which has never been a constraint on governments' ability to expand welfare benefits, as many welfare state scholars conjectured (Castles et al. 2005). When it came to enacting new social policies, concentration of formal decision making authority in the political centre allowed the federal government much leeway and smoothed the path of welfare state expansion. This also holds in the health sector. From the perspective of Länder governments, hospital investment has long been politically expedient and welcome: as an upgrade of local social service infrastructures, especially as long as the resources needed for investment and operating costs consisted of reimbursements from social insurance and the central government. Cost containment in the hospital sector is another matter, though, and Bundesländer employ their considerable political influence to prevent overly harsh spending cuts. In the health policy field there has been relatively little interest in activities that accentuate regional diversity, policy experimentation or even competitive downgrading, so that there is no restraint on a dynamic that is essentially expansionary. This expansionary thrust is built into the organisational and financing structures of the Austrian health system: regional authority over the spending-intensive task of hospital financing with no responsibility for raising the revenue is what characterises fiscal and regulatory arrangements and the political institutions in the policy field. To these we will turn in the following section of the chapter.

The Allocation of Authority in Health Policy

The image of Austria's health system reflects that of the country's state structures: the first impression is one of considerable centralisation, much of which dissolves, however, when taking a closer look at precise policies and political dynamics. The image of centralisation is conveyed by the country's social health insurance system, financing 52.4 per cent of the country's health care costs in 2010; this is 65.2 per cent of *public* health expenditure and amounts to 4.6 per cent of gross domestic product (GDP) (Hofmarcher and Quentin 2013: 85 and 97). Social insurance is extremely visible especially in the primary care sector. It is also extremely politicised, with the social partners, the government, and doctors' association in regular negotiations regarding the parameters of the system. Based on compulsory membership, social health insurance covers virtually the entire population, and in the outpatient care sector it forms the organisational core, regulating health care funding, residents' entitlement to health services, and health care providers' incomes. The federal constitution puts the federal government in charge of social insurance legislation. The legislative basis is the General Social Insurance Act (ASVG) of 1956 and a number of narrower laws establishing rules for the insurance systems of particular occupational groups, such as farmers, civil servants, and the self-employed.[4] Despite attempts at unifying the system, it has remained fragmented, with benefits, contribution rates, and copayments varying among the different occupational sickness funds (Heitzmann and Österle 2008).

The governance structure of Austrian social health insurance is strongly influenced by self-government, a dominant administrative principle for organising the internal structure of the 19 health insurance funds, with social health insurance organisations enjoying autonomy from government intervention and their supervisory boards staffed by representatives of the social partners, rather than appointees of the government. Self-governance also applies to the peak organisation of social insurance agencies, the Federation of Austrian Social Insurance Bodies (Hauptverband der Sozialversicherungsträger HVB), which represents the joint interests of social insurance organisations in the political arena. While theoretically in charge of regulating the social insurance sector, the HVB depends on the cooperation of its member organisations, and this rules out an effective leadership role (Tálos 2006; Trukeschitz et al. 2012: 160ff). Self-government applies, finally, to the medical profession, in which the college of physicians represents the interests of doctors in health policy making and in negotiations with health insurance funds over physicians' remuneration in the outpatient care sector.

Health insurance institutions are responsible for ensuring the service guarantee in outpatient care. They perform this function primarily by contracting with physicians and to a significantly lesser extent through the provision of their own services (Theurl 1999: 336). While the federal framework legislation assigns the responsibility to contract with the Austrian college of physicians to the social insurance peak association, the HVB, in practice negotiations are taking place on the regional level, with the result that 'final contract and fee agreements are very diverse across different social security institutions and Länder' (Hofmarcher and Quentin 2013: 53). To obtain a higher degree of coordination, the peak organisation HVB acts as a co-negotiator and signs the agreements together with the individual insurance funds (Trukeschitz et al. 2012: 175f), but so far health insurance funds and the regional colleges of physicians have successfully resisted these attempts at

---

4   There are nine regional sickness funds (Gebietskrankenkassen), covering the vast majority of employees (white- and blue-collar) based on residence. Six large companies have company-based social health insurance funds (Betriebskrankenkassen). The self-employed, civil servants, railway and mining workers, and farmers are insured by their own health insurance bodies, which have fewer members and are not organised alongside territorial principles.

centralisation. While health insurance funds' revenue is raised by levying income-related contributions from the employees and employers, subsidies from general revenue have resulted in closer financial interrelations between the state and the social insurance system, albeit not necessarily in a greater amount of direct state control (Obinger 2005: 213f). Autonomy from ministerial instruction, social self-government, and regional and occupational fragmentation combine to form a governance structure that renders social health insurance extremely unwieldy and hard to penetrate by reform-minded political entrepreneurs.

Social health insurance tells only half the story of the Austrian health system. There is a second 'regulatory circuit' (Theurl 2001: 160) of Austria's health system, in which the subnational level of government is much more important, and this is the hospital sector. In this area legislative competencies are shared among the different levels of government, building on Article 12 of the federal constitution and complementary federal laws, especially the Federal Hospitals Act (Kranken- und Kuranstaltengesetz) of 1951 (Gottweis and Baumandl 2006: 759f). The role of the federal government is confined to setting up the framework legislation, while the Länder are responsible for the more detailed legislation and implementation. The service guarantee for hospital care is the responsibility of the Bundesländer. They provide hospital capacities within their territories either by running their own hospitals or by contracting out to other hospital providers, such as church-affiliated charities, municipalities or private providers. At present, the majority of the hospital beds (55.5 per cent) are in hospitals owned by the Länder (Hofmarcher and Quentin 2013: 190).

Hospital financing is divided among the central government, social health insurance, the Bundesländer, and the municipalities. In 2010 social insurance covered (on average, across the nine Länder) 43 per cent of hospital expenses, the federal government 14 per cent, the Länder 33 per cent, and local authorities 10 per cent (Hofmarcher and Quentin 2013: 124). Because of this dual structure of hospital financing, with social insurance and the Länder bearing the lion's share of the financing burden, and social health insurance itself dominated by regional social insurance organisations, the regional level is the administrative and organisational hub of Austrian inpatient care. Bundesländer hold crucial veto positions with regard to regional planning and decision making and in federal health reform processes. The division of tasks in the hospital sector has necessitated close cooperation, especially between the federal and the Länder governments. This has been taking the form of Article 15a agreements, in which rather comprehensive package deals were negotiated, resulting in a range of federal and provincial laws. These agreements are usually valid for a fixed term of four years, and they regulate planning and financing in the hospital sector, including investment in large medical equipment (Hofmarcher et al. 2006: 135ff).

The emphasis placed on Article 15a treaties between the Länder and the federal government in the governance of the health system has engendered a 'negotiation-oriented' health policy style, which fits well with the norms of Austrian consensus democracy. That at least is one possible reading of the situation in the Austrian health sector. Here it has become widespread to argue that federalism and corporatism are two alternative, but complementary power sharing arrangements (Lijphart 1985; Pelinka 1999; Karlhofer 2002). But there is also the opposite view: that federalism and corporatism sometimes work *against* each other, because corporatism, in order to be an effective governance tool, needs the high degree of centralisation (for which Austria, in many policy fields, is a model case) and this structure is being undermined by devolving power to subnational jurisdictions (Encarnación 1999). The frequent use of Article 15a treaties, in which the central government and the Länder seek to install some measure of central coordination in a policy field where this is lacking lends some support to this latter reading. It is in fact the prevalent assessment of hospital governance in Austria (Gottweis and Baumandl 2006: 761).

The allocation of responsibility and decision making prerogatives is the central issue in this assessment. Dividing responsibility for the service guarantee between the Bundesländer and social health insurance (Theurl 1999: 136) prevents the development of a coherent health policy strategy. Nationwide regulation must then resort to Article 15a agreements, and there is always the possibility that the Länder will veto those treaties and thus prevent innovation in health system governance. The difference in financing and governance structures of inpatient and outpatient care accentuates the coordination problems between in- and outpatient care. Problems at the interface between ambulatory care and the hospital exist in all health systems, but incentive structures in the Austrian system give rise to all kinds of cost-shifting attempts on the part of the actors in each of the sectors, resulting in an overextended hospital sector (Hofmarcher and Quentin 2013: 191; Riedel and Röhrling 2009: 101) and inefficiencies in the provision of care. Of all European countries, Austria spends the largest proportion of its health budget – 36 per cent of public health spending – on hospital care (Bachner et al. 2012: 44), and this is widely perceived as a deeply problematic situation. Health policy-making – especially under conditions of austerity – has been dominated by attempts at reforming governance structures in the hospital sector and, more specifically, installing more federal government control in that sector (Gottweis and Baumandl 2006: 760). These attempts will be the focus of attention in the following sections of the chapter.

Economic Challenges and Austria's Readiness to Respond

Economic challenges to the health system take the form of two overlapping processes. One derives from general budgetary pressures, which many health systems began to encounter as early as in the 1970s, when first calls for curbing public spending reached the political agenda and became manifest in social policy debates. With Austrian hospital finances to a large part borne by public budgets, hospital financing has been one of the first targets in calls for budget consolidation, even though austerity measures in response to the oil price shocks of the 1970s have generally been mild in Austria. Since the mid-1990s, when Austria became a full member of the European Union, the macro-economic stability criteria of the Maastricht Treaty, later the 1997 Stability and Growth Pact and the recent European Fiscal Compact of 2012 have increased the pressure to consolidate public budgets. Irrespective of their partisan affiliation all federal governments of Austria endorsed the agenda of moderation in public spending, and Bundesländer and municipalities all affirmed their support for this agenda as well. Austria is currently violating the European budget criteria, so that fiscal pressures on all levels of government increasingly overshadow domestic policy making. The large share of social insurance funding in the Austrian health system has a twofold effect. On the one hand it shields social insurance finances from the pressure of budget consolidation to some extent, because social insurance organisations have their own budgets and some degree of organisational autonomy. On the other hand health insurance contributions become a political issue, making the sector susceptible to efforts at lowering payroll taxes.

The other economic challenge for the health system is the long-term shift from an overall context of welfare state expansion to retrenchment. Even though Austria was a late-comer as far as the transition toward a regime of welfare state retrenchment is concerned (Obinger 2005: 210), fiscal pressures became manifest in the health system strikingly early. It was as early as in the 1970s that first calls for health care cost containment reached the political agenda in many advanced industrial countries, as 'the financing of personal medical care everywhere became a major financial component of the budgets of mature welfare states' (Marmor et al. 2005: 333). This holds for Austria in particular, because of its peculiar combination of governance and financing structures. In terms of governance, the health sector is relatively far removed from the purview the national health ministry's intervention; yet, at the same time, the large share of tax financing in its hospital sector causes fiscal strain on the general budget to directly impact health finances. As a result, reform efforts in that sector, seeking to control the development of spending, started as early as 1978. Attempts at cost containment, of course, are not the same as cost control, as we will see when tracing the recent reform trajectory of Austria's health policy in the next section.

In view of rising international demands for fiscal discipline a broad consensus evolved among Austrian policy makers to strengthen efforts at budget consolidation (Bundeskanzleramt 2013). Given the heavy involvement of the state and the ballooning hospital expenditures, it is not surprising that this sector has come under heightened scrutiny, even though the declared goal is not to cut back on health spending, but merely to align its growth trajectory with that of GDP (Bundesministerium für Gesundheit 2013). Especially with regard to the hospital sector, there is broad agreement on the principal shortcomings (Theurl 1999: 335–40). All diagnoses, in one way or another, point to the fragmentation of responsibilities, and here especially to the dual structure of hospital financing, as bifurcated between social health insurance and public budgets. This not only creates incentives for spending expansion, it also amounts to a lack of coordination in hospital investment, causing overcapacities in the inpatient care sector and duplication of investment in large scale technical equipment. It moreover deepens the dualism of in- and outpatient care, with starkly differing financing and regulatory schemes, and no coherent nationwide health policy strategy, resulting in the inefficient allocation of resources.

Austria's ability to address these problems is institutionally and normatively circumscribed. It is institutionally constrained by the governance structures of social insurance and federalism, as described above. Normatively the fate of health reform is shaped by the principal notions of fairness and good governance that prevail in Austria's health sector. Guiding norms of health governance, although not uncontested, have been surprisingly stable and consistent across time and across the various areas of health policy. The predominant policy frame (Surel 2000) in health policy builds on the idea that in order to address the complex challenges in this field, state intervention must play a leading role (Theurl 1999: 152). This view corresponds with the tradition of welfare state development in Austria and enjoys the support of the vast majority of policy makers and the public. State intervention is acceptable as long as it does not violate the principles of self-government and social partnership. There is a competing market-oriented policy approach, held mainly by part of the health economists' profession and by the Austrian Chamber of Commerce (WKO), who call for managed competition as a means of raising cost-efficiency and improving transparency for the patients (Trukeschitz et al. 2012), and for better conditions for private health care providers, especially in the hospital sector. However, this competing policy frame has not exerted a strong influence over the Austrian health reform debate; the state-oriented outlook has remained dominant.

The Health Policy Response

Health policy responses to economic challenges are not only hemmed in by norms and institutions; they also depend on a range of influential actors of the health system, such as the social partners, the Austrian College of Physicians, the Federation of Austrian Social Insurance Bodies (HVB), and by the governors of the Bundesländer. The latter are particularly powerful actors in both policy making and the implementation of health reforms. This is especially pronounced in the inpatient care sector. Here specification of federal skeleton legislation is delegated to regional agencies ('Health Platforms', as they are called), in which Länder representatives are in the dominant position. In this environment the success of national hospital reform initiatives depends on the authority of federal authorities to act as a 'ringmaster', establishing the main parameters of the system and monitoring implementation. This includes the ability and the willingness to impose sanctions on the Länder, if evaluation reveals serious implementation deficits. In negotiating agreements about those main parameters, however, federal governments often find themselves constrained by the threat of Bundesländer vetoing legislation that violates their interests.

The Bundesländer often rely on more informal ways of shaping reform results. In particular, they hold informal governors' conferences (Landeshauptleutekonferenzen) to stake out joint governors' positions. Given this unanimity and, and by implication, broad legitimacy, it is practically impossible for federal governments to enforce measures that go against these joint Länder demands (Karlhofer and Pallaver 2013). A second source of governors' influence rests on their strong affiliations with the two major political parties. Within these parties and as a result, within the governing coalition, the regional governors carry a lot of weight (Hadley et al. 1989). One can thus conceive of the governors as informal veto-players, with the capacity to block or at least to water down federal initiatives. Fiscal equalisation (Finanzausgleich) and the hospital sector are policy areas where the informal veto power of the governors is particularly strong. This does not mean that the status quo cannot be altered, but it certainly slows down the pace of policy innovation in the hospital sector.

The reform trajectory in the field of hospital care can be traced back to the late 1970s, when the federal government and the Länder agreed on the first Article 15a treaty on hospital matters in 1978. Its main objective was to reform the complicated system of hospital finance by establishing a central fund, the Hospital Cooperation Fund (Krankenanstalten-Zusammenarbeitsfonds), and thus establish some measure of federal control over the fragmented hospital sector. Attempting to exercise federal control by means of Article 15a agreements has been the defining trait of Austrian hospital policy ever since. The next major reform, in 1997, sought to install a nationwide scheme of planning hospital capacities and investment in large-scale medical technology. A 'structural commission' at the federal level was established to develop the (legally binding) plan, control its implementation at the regional level, and impose sanctions in cases of non-compliance by the Länder (Theurl 1999: 339). Along with this centralisation of regulatory capacity, however, the reform *decentralised* hospital finance by replacing the federal hospital cooperation fund with nine separate regional funds, which receive their funding from grants by the federal government, the Bundesländer, the municipalities, and the social health insurance system. While the regional hospital funds could potentially become an effective tool for imposing a global budget on regional hospital expenses, the most significant aspect of the hospital plan is that its sanction mechanism was never applied. Political pressure from the Länder governor ensured that the federal government never imposed sanctions on the Länder, regardless of their compliance with the provisions of the hospital plan. The reform did little by way of altering the incentive structures at the Länder-level, which make overcapacities in the hospital sector politically and electorally attractive (Obinger 2005: 216). Even under a system of fixed hospital budgets, the Austrian Bundesländer are still not responsible for raising their revenue; they receive almost all of their resources through the financial equalisation scheme from the federal government (Obinger 2005: 208; Obinger 2002: 250), and therefore global hospital budgets also remained a blunt edge.

The 2005 health reform, a comprehensive and complicated reform package, sought to remedy the weaknesses of the hospital plan by introducing an even more comprehensive planning tool, the Austrian Structural Plan for Health (Österreichischer Strukturplan Gesundheit). This plan was not confined to the hospital sector, but covered the entire health sector including the interface between health care and long-term care and rehabilitation. The key idea was to improve health service integration by bridging the gaps between the different sectors of the system, especially between hospital care and the outpatient sector. Evaluations found the reform to be ambitious, but rather poorly implemented (Bundesrechnungshof 2010), suffering from the same flaw as its predecessors: the lack of effective sanctions. The last comprehensive reform package under review here is based on negotiated agreement between the federal government and the Länder, as usual, and it was finalised in 2013. The reform intensifies the established reform trajectory by integrating hospital planning into a single nationwide system of targets, to be developed jointly among the major stakeholders of the health system, and elaborating a monitoring- and sanctioning mechanism (Bundesministerium für Gesundheit 2013). Implementation is based on a combination of binding targets with cooperative monitoring, involving all relevant stakeholders in the health system.

At the time of writing it is not foreseeable whether the reform measures will live up to the high expectations. Implementation and negotiation of targets for the health system are still not fully completed. In particular, at this point it remains unclear to what extent the involvement of all relevant stakeholders guarantees better implementation; it remains to be seen whether monitoring will generate useful information, and whether sanctioning mechanisms will ever be utilised. It remains to be seen, in other words, whether 'constitutionally determined divisions of responsibility between regional bodies and sectors, which are at the root of the problem of fragmentation in Austrian health care' (Hofmarcher and Quentin 2013: 234) will again remain untouched.

Conclusion

Austria has a well-developed, nearly universally accessible health system, and citizens and most experts agree that it offers high-quality health services (Bundesministerium für Gesundheit 2013). It is a rather expensive health system, however, with Austria ranking sixth[5] among the European countries in terms of health expenditures, and spending 11 per cent of GDP on health in 2010 (Bachner et al. 2012: 32). In this logic of 'debt brakes', high costs and strong cost increases in the health system are especially perilous in areas that are directly financed from tax revenue, rather than 'hidden' in the budgets of social insurance. In Austria this is the area of hospital financing. It is here that politicians, rather than corporatist

---

5   After the Netherlands, France, Germany, Denmark, and Switzerland.

bodies, make decisions about health finances, it is here that tolerance for cost increases might reach its limits. It is also here, interestingly, that Austria stands out as a system with exceptionally high costs. No European country spends as large a share of its health budget (36 per cent) on hospital care, and nowhere in Europe are there more patients admitted to a hospital (Bachner et al. 2012: 54).[6] All major health reforms of the past decades have sought to address this problem, but a sustainable solution has yet to be found.

The reasons for the resilience of the cost-driving elements in Austria's health system are in part an outgrowth of that system's institutions themselves. Two aspects stand out as particularly important. First, in Austria the service guarantee is split up between the social health insurance system (for outpatient care) and the Bundesländer (for hospitals). That aspect alone does not explain the particular economic and political dynamics on the Austrian hospital sector, though. We find the same allocation of responsibilities in Germany (Mätzke 2012), and we also find similar complaints about inefficiencies at the threshold between in- and outpatient care in many health systems. Coordination problems between ambulatory care and hospitals are greatly accentuated by the second institutional trait of the Austrian health system: the financing and governance structures of the two sectors. Because they are in different hands, they function according to different rules, and their politics is also very different. Outpatient care is dominated by the social insurance principle. This is more than a mere financing scheme, but instead encompasses corporatism and social partnership, professional self-government in a field of providers most of whom are independent professionals working in small-scale practice environments (Mätzke 2010: 135f). In the hospital sector, by contrast, medical and nursing staff are salaried employees, mostly working in large organisations, and regulatory and financing institutions are organised along the lines of territorial jurisdictions. These are headed by politicians, who have strong electoral motives besides their substantive interest in having well-organised regional health systems. Financing decisions are in a framework of budgetary politics, not social insurance. And financing decisions take place in a context of federalism.

Federalism, an institution barely discernible as a relevant force in the politics of Austrian welfare state development, perennially in the shadow of Austria's centralised social insurance model, has been the single most important factor of influence in the politics of health care in Austria. Before we argue why this is so, two comments on what Austrian federalism does *not* do – what it has *not* caused, and what *cannot* be observed – are in order.

Horizontal Relationships

In Austria they take the form of 'collusion' (Costa-Font and Greer 2012: 25), meaning that Bundesländer enter their dealings with the central government

---

6   26.5 per 100 residents. The European average is at 15.7. The European average share of the health budget spent on inpatient care is 28.1 per cent (ibid.: 37).

with a joint position, negotiated beforehand in meetings that are not open to the public (Karlhofer and Pallaver 2013: 49). There is not much of a tradition of endorsing distinctions, policy experimentation, or even competition in Austria's federal polity. The motif of subnational jurisdictions as 'laboratories of democracy' has been significant in the historical development of Austrian federalism only once, and even then it was not federalism and regional diversity per se, but the political antagonism that existed in the interwar years between a very Catholic and Conservative country(side) and the Socialist governed capital city of Vienna. This rivalry may have allowed for the growth of innovative social policies and an alternative model of public policy (Obinger 2002: 243; Hadley et al. 1989: 84; Karlhofer and Pallaver 2013: 43) but interregional competition has been no significant dynamic during the Second Republic, and it has played no role in health. Likewise, a 'race to the bottom' dynamic, a danger of 'competitive underbidding', in social standards and welfare state generosity cannot be discerned in Austria.

A Brake on Welfare State Expansion?

Scholars observing welfare state development in federal polities have often observed that federalism inhibits the development of generous social protection systems. Federalism, it is said, empowers opponents of welfare state expansion; it gives them veto possibilities; there may also be competition over low taxes and employer–friendly social policies at work (Castles et al. 2005: 220). Such a thing cannot be observed in Austria. The country was a pioneer in welfare state development; in its beginnings enacted under the monarchy, but subsequently continued in the federal polity. This expansive dynamic can be explained with reference to the centralist traits of Austria's political institutions (Obinger 2002: 245–8): there is the extremely centralised social insurance system, acting as a vehicle of furthering political centralisation; there is the host of constitutional provisions, assigning responsibility for important social policy fields to the centre. There are legislative institutions that grant regional interests no veto powers, thus further enhancing the unitary character of Austria's political system in that respect. The Austrian hospital sector is one of the exceptions, rather than the rule.

One would not, therefore, consider federalism to be important when observing social insurance or welfare state expansion in general. One does find federal state structures to be extremely important when observing the health system's (recent) development, and in particular the hospital sector. Here subnational governments exercise a powerful informal veto, which can effectively prevent reforms from becoming a reality. This veto is not based on constitutional guarantees; in fact, Karlhofer and Pallaver call it 'a natural response to the weakness of federal institutions' (Karlhofer and Pallaver 2013: 197), but it might even be more potent precisely because of its informal quality. It is more unpredictable and much more difficult to circumvent. Two consequences of this informal regional veto stand out as powerful effects of federalism on health care in Austria.

Incentive Structures of Subnational Governments

From the perspective of subnational governments, hospital investment is a very attractive kind of activity: hospitals create high-skilled jobs, local hospitals are popular among the citizens, and they are also significant with regard to the service guarantee for which the Bundesländer bear responsibility. At the same time the Austrian Länder are not in charge of raising their own revenue; instead, their resources are allocated to them in a financial equalisation procedure (Obinger 2002: 250). Thus, spending and raising revenue are not in the same hands, and this is likely to drive up costs. Federal initiatives toward measures of cost control have all tried to install mechanisms of macro-political consultation in the development of guidelines, targets, or health plans, but these did little to alter the local and regional incentive structures with their strong tendency to block austerity policies (Obinger 2005: 208). The National Growth and Stability Pact of 2012 might turn out to become more influential in that regard than all reforms of hospital financing, because this legislation intends to limit overspending on each territorial level and may therefore install a hard budget constraint for the Länder for the first time.

Cost Containment in Public Budgets (It Is Not About the Money!)

In the comparative welfare state literature social insurance systems are sometimes portrayed as 'frozen landscapes' (Palier and Martin 2007). The idea is that social insurance, organisationally partially removed from short-term political intrusions, and removed, also, from electoral dynamics and governed in an environment of self-government and social partnership, should be more resilient to change. Yet, delegating authority to corporatist organisations surrenders part of the government's power (Mayntz 1991) and constrains the scope for reform. Austria's health system, with its large share of public funding, is occasionally portrayed as one in which cost containment is easier, because Austria's governments, with an overall 'higher level of state intervention can also implement effective cost control mechanisms' (Wendt and Kohl 2010: 27). Our account of health reform in Austria cautions against this view. One can neither take the public (as opposed to social insurance-based) portion of the health budget, nor the amount of state intervention as a straightforward indicator for the ease or difficulty of reform. The decisive aspect for the political feasibility of reform is not where finances come from, but how decision making about these finances is structured. In the Austrian hospital sector policy innovation is exacerbated by a governance structure that pretends to be a part of a unitary state when it comes to raising revenue and turns out it has federalist norms and institutions when it comes to spending the money. This structure works well when the overarching dynamic is welfare state expansion; it creates very difficult situations when cost containment is on the political agenda.

Chapter 3
Germany

Achim Lang

Introduction

The German health care system is characterised by federal structures and the corporatist self-regulation of statutory health insurance funds and health care providers.

Like Austria (as the previous chapter describes), federalism enters the German health care system from three directions. First, federal laws concerning health care have to be approved by the upper chamber of parliament, the Bundesrat, which contains representatives from state-level governments (Länder). Second, negotiations over reimbursement and budgeting of outpatient care typically involve representatives from physician and statutory health insurance funds and take place at both the federal and Länder level. Third, political responsibility for inpatient health care lies mainly with Länder governments, which are responsible for hospital planning as well as for the financing of investments. Since the first makes up the history of German health care reforms (and has been widely discussed) and the second is an example of corporatist negotiations (also the subject of much political analysis), I will focus on the last aspect of German health policy: hospital planning and regulation, and the financing of hospital investments. This facet of German health policy is of particular importance as inpatient care makes up roughly half of the total health expenditures (which makes it the cost item with the highest annual growth rate).

The German hospital sector has experienced major ownership changes in the last decade. The privatisation and marketisation of public as well as non-profit hospitals has increased sharply over the past years (Gerlinger and Mosebach 2009). At the same time, Länder governments, which are responsible for hospital financing and regulation, have constantly cut investments in hospitals since German unification. Lacking financial resources, the German hospital sector has become attractive for private hospital companies and investors. This is all the more true since the ageing society promises constant growth projections (Klenk 2011). However, there is considerable variation in hospital financing and hospital privatisation at the Länder level. These developments have attracted much attention by policy makers and the media but have hardly been investigated by the health policy community. This chapter seeks to analyse the determinants of hospital financing and privatisation at the federal state level.

The main argument of this chapter is that the amount of investment funding and the ownership structure of hospitals are affected by government deficits, partisan politics and hospital efficiency. Ownership of hospitals can be distinguished along three dimensions:

- public hospitals operated and owned by central or federal state governments as well as municipalities;
- for-profit hospitals that are run individually or as part of larger partnerships, corporations, or consortia;
- private non-profit hospitals owned by religious or secular organisations such as Catholic or Protestant welfare organisations.

The amount of privatisation is measured as the number of for-profit hospitals in 2010 in each German federal state, relative to the number of hospitals in 1994. Hospital financing comes from two different sources. Global funding includes replacement and maintenance investments in buildings as well as medical equipment. Individual funding includes investments in new buildings and new medical technologies.

The chapter proceeds as follows: the next section provides a short sketch on the type of federalism in Germany. Next, federalist arrangements in the German health care system are summarised. The fourth section details economic challenges for the Länder governments and focuses in particular on low growth rates and high budget deficits. The following two sections depict the evolution of hospital financing and hospital ownership structure in the German Länder from 1994–2010. The effects of party competition, federal state deficits and investment funding are analysed. The final section summarises the findings and discusses the implications.

Federalism in Germany

The main characteristic of German federalism is the cooperative relationship between federal government and federal state governments. The German constitution, or Basic Law, assigns legislative power primarily to the federal government, whereas the Länder governments are responsible for implementing laws adopted by the lower chamber of parliament, the German Bundestag (Benz 1999). Territorial heterogeneity and competition between Länder governments are by and large absent. Article 2 of the Basic Law demands equivalent living conditions in all German Länder. As a result, a complex system of federal government and inter-Länder grants guarantees almost equivalent public services in all German Länder.

Regarding legislative power, the Basic Law distinguishes between exclusive legislative power of the Bundestag and concurrent legislation between Bundestag and federal state parliaments. However, the term 'concurrent' is somewhat misleading since federal legislation has precedence over Länder legislation. Article 72 in the German Basic Law states that the Länder parliaments have the power to act in the area of concurrent legislation (Gunlicks 2013) but, within these areas, the Bundestag may pass a law if Länder governments have not been active on the issue, or if it is designed to promote equivalent living conditions. Länder parliaments have the right to enact divergent laws in areas such as hunting, environmental protection, land-use planning, hydrologic balance and higher education.

Within the exclusive legislative power of the Bundestag there are extensive rights of co-decision with the upper chamber of parliament, the Bundesrat, which consists of representatives of Länder governments. The Basic Law lists all legal areas in which laws passed by the Bundestag require the approval of the Bundesrat. These 'laws requiring approval' are laws that affect Länder government taxes and income, but also laws that assign Länder governments and Länder administrations duties and obligations. Additionally, laws that change the legal or administrative structure of Länder public authority have to be approved by the Bundesrat. Furthermore, there are laws which are subject to a possible objection by the Bundesrat. These objections only have a suspensory effect.

The institutional structure of German parliamentarism and federalism creates tensions and interlocking politics. Benz (1999) summarises the logic of German federalism:

> The division of power, decentralisation, and the participation of *Land* governments in national policymaking are basic features of German federalism. The sharing of legislative, administrative, and financial functions between governments and the widespread orientation toward unity and equality have contributed to the emergence of a system of interlocking politics (*Politikverflechtung*), which is typical of cooperative federalism. (55–6)

The Bundesrat was established during the consultations of the Basic Law in 1949. It was designed to strengthen Länder governments, since many laws started to require the consent of the Bundesrat. However, the cooperation of federal and Länder governments has since then been accompanied by party competition in the parliamentary system that was initially designed after the Westminster model (Benz 1999). The joining of party competition with patterns of cooperation between governments created tensions along two dimensions (Auel 2010; Benz 1999; Burkhart 2009): the decision-making rules and the limited autonomy of Länder governments.

The numerous laws that require the approval of the Bundesrat 'can be abused to block necessary reforms for strategic party-political reasons' (Auel 2010: 232). It is often argued that the German Basic Law built two incompatible features into the German federal structure (Lehmbruch 2000). The cooperative nature of federalism makes compromise between federal and Länder governments necessary. However, party competition makes compromise difficult, because in times of a divided government, when there are differing majorities in the Bundestag and Bundesrat, party competition dominates the need to find compromise. These incompatible features are held responsible for political deadlock. However, as Auel, König, and Bräuniger point out, deadlock situations are generally the exception, even in times of a divided government (Auel 2010; Bräuninger and König 1999).

Another tension arises due to the centralisation of budgetary and legislative powers at the federal level (Auel 2010; Benz 1999). Länder governments face strict limits on their autonomy since they are unable to raise significant revenues. This also restricts competition between the Länder governments. Auel (2010) states that

> the main legislative competencies lie with the federal level, while most executive competencies are assigned to the Länder. The Länder's own exclusive legislative competencies cover only a small number of policy areas, such as local government, policing, education and cultural affairs including the media, to which the 2006 federalism reform added only a few further narrow competencies. (239)

The fiscal equalisation scheme also limits competitive pressure on Länder governments to make structural adjustments (Auel 2010; Benz 1999).

Regarding health care, the Bundestag has precedence in legislative matters but there are extensive rights of co-decision with regard to the Bundesrat. All major policy reforms and programmes in the last decades had to be approved by the Bundesrat. The last two major health care reforms saw intense negotiations between the federal and the Länder governments as well as between governing and opposition parties. In 2004, the Statutory Health Insurance Modernization Act was passed by the governing party coalition of the Social Democratic Party (SPD) and the Green Party (Gründe) and involved negotiations with representatives from the opposition parties, since those parties had a majority in the Bundesrat. As a result, the Statutory Health Insurance Modernization Act contained demands from all political parties for such things as health technology assessments for drug and medical device reimbursement and liberalized contracting between statutory health insurance and health care providers. Even in times of a grand coalition government run by the conservative Christian Democratic Union (CDU) and the SPD (which inevitably has a majority in both houses of parliament), negotiations include representatives from federal as well as Länder parliaments and governments (Pressel 2012). In 2007, the newly established grand coalition government of the CDU and SPD decided to establish a health care fund (Gesundheitsfond) that formed a compromise between election programmes of both governing parties: the All Citizens' Health Insurance Scheme favoured by the SPD and the Capitation Fee Scheme favoured by the CDU. The resulting compromise then included elements from both schemes such as equal contributions by the insured and by employers to this funds and receives morbidity adjusted payments to the statutory health insurance.

Federalism in the German Health Care System: Legal Provisions

Any health care system can be differentiated according to three pillars: financing, service provision, and regulation (Wendt, Frisina, and Rothgang 2009). Länder competencies can be found in all three pillars of the German health care system. However, these competencies are most pronounced in the case of inpatient care. At its base, the German health care system has a statutory health insurance system that covers about 90 per cent of the German population (Simon 2005). Statutory health insurance is mandatory for employees with incomes below a certain threshold (Versicherungspflichtgrenze, or yearly income above €53,550 in 2014). Civil servants are free to choose private health insurance schemes. The additional 10 per cent are covered by private health insurance which is, in the case of civil servants, supplemented by government allowances (Simon 2005; Verband der Ersatzkassen (vdek) 2013). Financing of the German health care system rests primarily on health insurance premiums (statutory insurance is 57.6 per cent of total health expenditure; private insurance is 9.4 per cent). Government expenditures cover 8.6 per cent of total health expenditures while private out-of-pocket expenditures add another 13.2 per cent (Verband der Ersatzkassen (vdek) 2013). The remaining expenditures are covered by nursing care insurance, accident insurance, and the old-age pension scheme, as well as by employers.

Table 3.1   **Health expenditure in the German health care system (in millions of euros, data from 2011)**

	Total	% THE
General government	25.268	8.6
Social security funds*	199.350	67.9
Private insurance	27.723	9.4
Private households out-of-pocket exp.	38.787	13.2
Non-profit institutions serving households	1.337	0.5
Corporations (other than health insurance)	1.335	0.5
Hospitals	85.209	29.0
Nursing and residential care facilities	22.196	7.6
Providers of ambulatory health care	88.072	30.0
Pharmacies	39.795	13.5
Retail sale and other providers of medical goods	19.553	6.7
Other	38.976	13.3
Total Health Expenditure (THE)	*293.801*	*100.0*

Note: * Social security funds include health insurance, pension insurance, and nursing care insurance.
Source: Gesundheitsberichterstattung des Bundes (http://www.gbe-bund.de).

Regarding health care provision, the German health care system is separated between inpatient and outpatient care. More collaborative forms of health provision are still underdeveloped compared to other Organisation for Economic Cooperation and Development (OECD) countries. Outpatient care providers are predominantly freelance physicians operating out of their own office. In contrast, inpatient care rests on private, public, and non-profit hospitals, each category making up about one-third of German hospitals. Physicians are employed by their respective hospitals.

Regulations on health care financing and service provision are provided by the federal and Länder governments as well as by the national peak associations representing health insurance funds and service providers (see also the chapter on Austria in this volume). National peak associations are business associations that organise either regional affiliate associations or sectoral branch associations, and sometimes both. Peak associations in the German health domain are the National Association of Statutory Health Insurance Funds [GKV-Spitzenverband], the German Hospital Federation [Deutsche Krankenhausgesellschaft], the National Association of Statutory Health Insurance Physicians [Kassenärztliche Bundesvereinigung], and the National Association of Statutory Health Insurance Dentists [Kassenzahnärztliche Bundesvereinigung]. Together, these associations form the Federal Joint Committee (G-BA) which decides on services to be included in the statutory health insurance catalogue and its reimbursement (Rosenbrock and Gerlinger 2006).

Federalism enters the German health care system from two directions. First, negotiations about the services to be reimbursed in outpatient care typically take place between national peak associations. Regional affiliates of the national peak associations then negotiate the cost reimbursement contract for the physicians operating within their jurisdiction. This contract covers the total amount of reimbursement that can be distributed to the physicians. In the next step, the regional peak associations negotiate the distribution of the total reimbursement to physicians of different medical disciplines. The same applies to reimbursement for inpatient care that is negotiated between regional affiliates of the National Association of Statutory Health Insurance Funds and the German Hospital Federation.

The second aspect of federalism involves political responsibility for inpatient health care that lies mainly with each Länder government (Böhm and Henkel 2009; Simon 2000). They are responsible for hospital planning as well as the financing of investments. The institutional context of hospital financing and regulation is set by the Hospital Financing Act (KHG) that came into force in 1972. This federal law provides the framework for hospital planning, financing and regulation, although detailed instructions have to be established by the federal state governments. The KHG aims at securing the financial basis for hospitals in order to ensure the supply of inpatient services according to the need of the population (KHG §1). Additionally, the KHG urges Länder governments to consider the needs of hospitals that arise from their ownership structure.

Federal states are responsible for hospital planning in order to meet citizens' health care needs as well as to guarantee economically independent and responsible hospitals. Federal state governments develop hospital plans that cover all hospitals eligible for health insurance reimbursement as well as investment funding. There is no legal entitlement specifying inclusion into the hospital plan (KHG §6). Eligibility does not rest on public ownership of hospitals but covers all sorts of ownership. Hospital plans are developed by public health authorities, usually federal state health ministries, after consultations with major stakeholders and hospital directors (KHG §8). In most Länder the number of stakeholders is limited to the regional affiliates of the national peak associations in German health care (Regional Associations of Statutory Health Insurance Funds, Regional Hospital Association, Regional Association of Statutory Health Insurance Physicians, the regional affiliate of the Association of Private Health Insurers) as well as the three regional affiliates of the German peak associations of communities, municipalities, and counties (Deutsche Krankenhausgesellschaft 2012). However, some Länder such as Northrine–Westphalia have diversified the number of stakeholders that take part in the hospital planning. They additionally include associations of the medical profession, representatives from the Catholic and Protestant church, and trade unions (MGEPA 2013). Hospital plans cover health policy goals and their effects on hospital capacities and staff. Länder governments use hospital plans to implant cost reduction strategies on the hospital sector by constantly redefining the capacity necessary to meet health care demand. Hospital beds per capita are the prime indicator for hospital capacity. As a result, Länder governments try to lower the number of hospital beds in their respective states to reduce costs and lower government expenditure (Böhm and Henkel 2009; Simon 2000).

The KHG established the dual structure of hospital financing as the basic means to secure its goals. Health insurance funds, private as well as compulsory, cover the expenses for health care provision. In the KHG of 1972, hospitals could rely on the principle of cost coverage based on per-diem allowances (Böhm and Henkel 2009). In 1992, the health structure act (GSG) elaborated by the federal government abandoned the principle of cost coverage and introduced hospital budgets and flat fees for health care provision (Tuschen and Quaas 2001). Hospital budgets and reimbursement of treatment expenses were subject to a cap in order to limit the supposed 'cost explosion in health care' (Gerlinger and Mosebach 2009). The total amount of hospital expenditure was pegged to the national wage bill (Simon 2008). Payments were divided into flat fees, a base nursing charge and a departmental per diem. Hospitals had to calculate the expected demand of health care provision and cost (prospective planning) and had to bargain for the reimbursement of these costs with statutory health insurances. However, the difference between actual and expected costs – gains and losses – remain with the hospital owner, thus creating a strong rationale for privatisation. The health care reform of 2000 then introduced diagnosis-related groups which were fully implemented as of 2010 (Böhm and Henkel 2009).

Despite attempts to change the dual financing system and to dismantle the authority of the Länder governments in hospital planning, both remained largely unchanged. Since both issues require the agreement of the Länder health ministries, hospital financing and planning remain in the hands of the states (Böhm 2009). The Health Care Reform Act of 2000 established a performance-based hospital reimbursement system which was supplemented by the Case Fees Act (FPG) in 2002 which created a German version of diagnosis-related groups (G-DRGs). The implementation of G-DRGs started in 2003 and become obligatory by 2004. However, during a so-called convergence phase, hospital budgets still had to be negotiated with statutory health insurance funds on the basis of the hospital's actual costs. The six-year convergence was intended to gradually adjust the individual hospital rate to the average Länder hospital base rate (Böhm 2009).

Regarding investment costs, Länder governments and the federal government agreed to share the investment costs of hospitals. This dual investment financing structure was implemented with the KHG in 1972. Hospitals that are included in the Länder hospital plan are eligible for funding. Investment costs, according to the KHG, include construction costs (new buildings, remodelling or extensions of buildings), equipment acquisition and replacement of capital assets. Investment financing rests on two pillars: global or lump-sum investment costs that contains replacement costs of medical equipment and remodelling of hospital buildings and individual or itemised investment cost that includes construction and extension cost for hospital building and acquisition cost of new medical technologies (KHG §9). The agreement between Länder governments and the federal government lasted only a few years. After the first oil crisis, the federal government unilaterally reduced its payment. In 1984, the dual structure in investment financing was abandoned altogether. Since then, the responsibility to finance investments in hospitals rests exclusively with the Länder governments.

Economic Challenges: Low Growth Rates and High Budget Deficits

The ability to finance hospitals ultimately depends on the revenues generated by Länder governments and is thus subject to economic growth as well as other financial obligations and welfare entitlements. Since German reunification in 1990, the German economy can be characterised by comparatively low rates of economic growth and high unemployment rates (see Figure 3.1). As revenues of Länder governments (and of municipalities) predominantly rest on shares of corporate income tax, taxes on wages and earnings, and the value-added tax, the economic downturn, in combination with high social expenditures and redistributions toward East Germany, has left its mark on the Länder budgets. From 1994 to 2010, Länder government deficits rose by about 250 per cent while the deficits of municipalities almost doubled (see Figure 3.2). However, the German fiscal equalisation system, in which 'richer' Länder governments are obliged to confer intergovernmental grants to 'poorer' Länder governments, has considerably reduced the variance of annual income of the Länder governments (Büttner 2002). As a result, the effects of fiscal deficits are ameliorated among the poorer Länder governments.

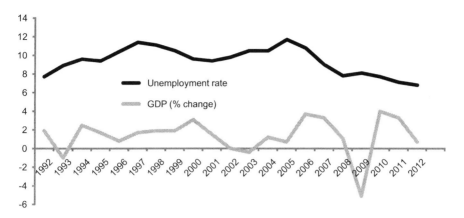

Figure 3.1   Economic growth rates and unemployment in Germany
Source: Destatis, https://www.destatis.de/DE/ZahlenFakten/GesamtwirtschaftUmwelt/Arbeits
markt/Arbeitsmarkt.html.

In particular, East German Länder governments' deficits have grown by about
300–350 per cent (with the exception of Saxony). Against this backdrop, the federal
and Länder governments changed the Basic Law and introduced a balanced-
budget provision that requires a balance between receipts and expenditures of the
federal government by 2016 and for the Länder governments by 2020. As a result,
Länder governments (and municipalities) are eager to cut expenditures in all areas
of Länder responsibility and try to obtain additional revenues by selling Länder
properties and companies to private investors. This strategy has become dominant
across Länder governments.

During the financial crisis, Germany was reluctant to enact fiscal stimulus
programmes in order to stabilise demand; instead, it opted for austerity measures
(Streeck 2010). However, this is only part of the story. In Germany, automatic
stabilisers played an important role in alleviating the macro-economic effects of
the current crisis. 'Automatic stabilizers are usually defined as those elements of
fiscal policy which mitigate output fluctuations without discretionary government
action' (Dolls, Fuest, and Peichl 2012: 279). Automatic stabilisers induce changes
in taxes and government expenditures in order to stabilise aggregate output
(Tödter and Scharnagl 2004). Dolls et al. (2012) point out that social transfers,
such as generous systems of unemployment insurance, played a key role in the
stabilisation of disposable incomes and household demand.

The financial crisis had only a small effect on deficit spending. After the
Lehman default, financial markets penalised fiscal imbalances. High deficit
countries have to accept a higher spread on government bonds compared to
benchmark bonds. Since German government bonds assumed a safe-haven status
(Von Hagen, Schuknecht, and Wolswijk 2011), it became comparatively easy to
finance Länder government debts.

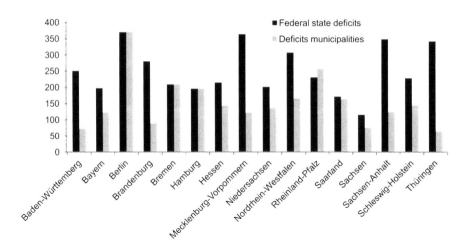

Figure 3.2   Increasing deficits of federal states and municipalities (in per cent from 1994–2010)

Source: Destatis, https://www.destatis.de/DE/ZahlenFakten/GesellschaftStaat/Oeffentliche FinanzenSteuern/OeffentlicheFinanzenSteuern.htm.

Evolution of Hospital Financing in German Federal States: 1994–2010

As mentioned, hospital financing comes from two different sources: investment funding by Länder governments and health service reimbursement by statutory and private health insurance funds. Within investment funding by Länder governments, two different types can be distinguished. Global funding includes replacement and maintenance investments in building as well as in medical equipment. Individual funding includes investments in new buildings and new medical technologies. Both types of investment funding are provided by Länder governments.

Between 1994 and 2010, Länder governments invested about 72,000 euros on global funding and 125,000 euros on individual funding yearly per hospital. Global funding of hospitals changed moderately from 1994 to 2010 (see Figure 3.3). However, there is almost no variation in spending between Länder. In contrast, individual funding varies considerably between federal states. Individual funding remains at low levels in most West German federal states. Exceptions include the federal city states Berlin, Bremen, and Hamburg, where individual funding changed considerably over the course of time. East German Länder had very high volumes of individual funding during the 1990s that have been reduced since the new millennium.

The slow but steady reduction of investment funds provided by Länder governments is not a new phenomenon. Since the introduction of 'income-oriented budgeting' in 1984, Länder governments have opted for the reduction of hospital investment budgets. Income orientation focused almost exclusively on the revenues of Länder governments which adapted hospital investment budgets accordingly.

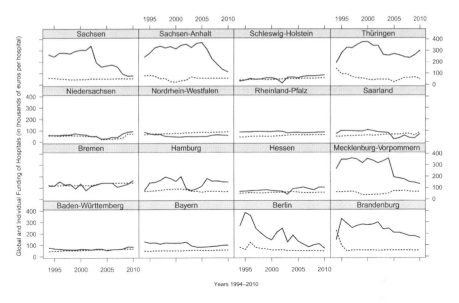

**Figure 3.3   Global and individual funding of hospitals
(in thousands of euros per hospital)**

Note: Solid line: individual funding; dotted line: global funding.
Source: Gesundheitsberichterstattung des Bundes (http://www.gbe-bund.de).

Financial constraints explain part of the decline and stagnation of hospital funding in German federal states (see Figure 3.4). Public deficits constrain the ability of governments to fund hospitals. While global funding is only marginally affected by the financial situation of Länder governments, individual funding has declined rapidly with higher levels of public deficit.

The only exception is the city state of Bremen that kept comparatively high funding levels despite increasing and continuing budget deficits. This exceptional status might be explained by the fact that the Social Democratic Party (SPD) has ruled Bremen since World War II. In the introductory section, I argued that government and party ideology affects funding patterns. This is particularly true for Bremen but also holds true for other German federal states. As Figure 3.3 depicts, the higher the share of seats won by the SPD, the higher the investment spending. The opposite holds for the Liberal Democratic Party (FDP) that promotes spending cuts and less government intervention.

The existence of private hospitals also influences the amount of investment financing. Government funding significantly decreases with the number of private hospitals. Private hospitals have better access to financial markets than not-for-profit or public hospitals. Thus, they are in a position to compensate for the lack of government funding. Federal state governments are fully aware that private hospital companies are able to finance investments through credit and loans.

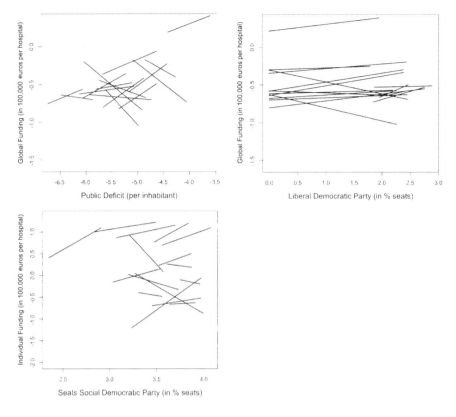

**Figure 3.4   The effect of public deficits and political parties on
            hospital funding**
Source: Gesundheitsberichterstattung des Bundes (http://www.gbe-bund.de).

As a result, Länder governments are able to cut hospital spending in order to reduce the public deficit or to invest in other policy areas.

In sum, hospital financing by Länder governments is dependent on the party composition of federal state parliaments, the extent of Länder public deficits, and the number of private hospitals. Länder public debt reduces the ability of governments to finance hospital investments, while public ownership of hospitals provides an excuse not to do so because private hospital companies have better access to the financial market. A strong Social Democratic Party in Länder parliaments increases government spending as it is predicted by partisan approaches to public policy.

As a result of the decreasing hospital investment funding as well as competitive pressures established by the introduction of disease-related groups, a triple funding system has emerged. The dual funding provided by health insurance funds and Länder governments is 'increasingly complemented by resources acquired on the capital market through debts or equity from selling stocks' (Klenk 2011: 269).

This is not only true for private for-profit hospitals but also public hospitals trying to compensate for decreased funding by using new financial management tools such as asset-backed securities, preferred equity instruments, and cross-border leasing (Klenk 2011). In particular, cross-border leasing became the instrument of choice in the late 1990s when US investors bought German community infrastructure such as public water supply, the sewage water system, or community hospitals and leased it back to the community. Klenk (2011) illustrates these new financial vehicles in the case of two East German municipalities, Chemnitz and Leipzig:

> The CBL transactions of the governorate Chemnitz amount to US$189.4 billion; the Chemnitz Klinikum gGmbH is involved with a sum of US$130.7 billion. In the governorate Leipzig, the total amount of CBL transactions accounts for US$2832.3 billion; the contract with the Städtische Klinikum Leipzig St Georg is for US$344.4 billion (Sächsischer Landtag 2003). The periods of agreement of CBL transactions are extremely long. In the case of the Städtische Klinikum Leipzig St Georg, the contract covers a period of more than 100 years. (269)

While cross-border leasing deals provided an initial relief to strained communal budgets, long-term prospects have been negative. Since already highly-indebted municipalities were the most active in using new financing tools, the negative consequences have worsened the financial situation even further. Most such deals prohibit communities to shut down inefficient communal enterprises and contracts involved several hidden costs, often unknown to the community representative. Furthermore, management decisions in many instances needed consent by the investor.

The Changing Ownership Structure of German Hospitals

The establishment of the G-DRGs with the aim of increasing cost pressure on hospital health services and the decrease in investment funding have put adaptive pressure on hospitals (Heß 2005; Klenk 2011). As a result, the ownership structure of German hospitals has dramatically changed in the last two decades. Ownership changes of public hospitals can be distinguished according to the legal status of the hospital. Formal privatisation involves changes in the legal status of the hospital without affecting the ownership structure. Full privatisation means the hospital was sold to a private provider or financial agent. Municipalities increasingly changed the organisational form of municipal hospitals. Hospitals that have been run under public law are now subject to a formal privatisation process in which the municipality remains the owner or largest shareholder of the hospital, but the health care provision now follows the logic of private management (Klenk 2011). In 2012, almost 60 per cent of public hospitals have changed their legal status from public to private (e.g. limited company). The remaining public hospitals can be divided into two classes: legally autonomous (e.g., foundation) and legally dependent (e.g., government-operated corporation). In 2012, 56 per cent of the remaining public hospitals adopted a legally autonomous status (Statistisches Bundesamt 2013).

The trend to fully privatise public hospitals has been prevalent since the German unification. In 1994, 42 per cent of German hospitals were publicly-owned while private for-profit hospitals accounted for only 17 per cent of all hospitals. In 2010, however, ownership is almost equally distributed across all ownership categories (33 per cent public, 36 per cent not-for-profit, and 31 per cent private). The share of private non-profit hospitals has remained stable over the years (*Statistisches Bundesamt* 2013). In contrast, public hospitals have been continuously sold to private for-profit hospital companies or have been abandoned altogether.

The development of the hospital landscape varies between Länder governments (see Figure 3.5). While in Nordrhein–Westfalen and Rheinland–Pfalz, private for-profit hospitals have had a dominant position since at least the 1990s, all East German Länder (Brandenburg, Mecklenburg–Vorpommern, Sachsen, Sachsen–Anhalt and Thüringen) have experienced a complete transformation of their hospital landscapes. After the German unification, public hospitals clearly dominated in all East German Länder. Since then, private hospitals expanded at the expense of public hospitals. As a result, ownership is almost equally distributed across all ownership categories. However, as Figure 3.5 indicates, developments are far from being simultaneous and hospital landscapes have become ever more diverse.

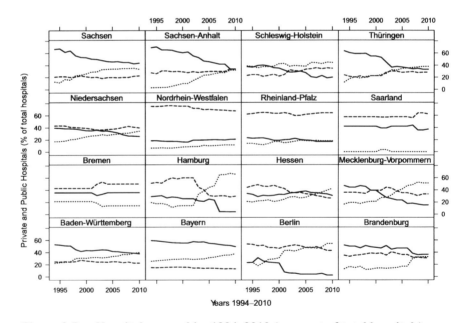

Figure 3.5   Hospital ownership, 1994–2010 (per cent of total hospitals)
Note: Solid line: private hospitals; dashed line: private not-for-profit hospitals; dotted line: public hospitals.
Source: Gesundheitsberichterstattung des Bundes (http://www.gbe-bund.de).

The question remains, what drives the privatisation of German hospitals? And why are there Länder differences? How do the reductions of funding affect hospital ownership?

Funding by federal state governments seems to influence the speed and scope of privatisation. However, most federal states lowered the amount of funding for new medical technologies. As a result, many public hospitals cannot compete anymore with their private counterparts. Böhm states that insufficient investment funding is the main reason for the privatisation process. Due to low funding, municipalities sell their hospitals to for-profit hospital chains:

> Budget constraints leave local authorities unable to make up the investment deficit caused by the states, practically forcing them to sell their hospitals to private operators. An obligation to make necessary investments is often part of the deal. Private operators are not dependent on the states' investment financing because they can raise funds on the capital markets. Private investment funding also has the advantage, compared to public investment support, that it can be deployed flexibly, independently and without excessive red tape. (Böhm 2009)

Economic variables also play a major role in the privatisation of hospitals. The proportion of account days to treatment days measures the efficiency of public hospitals within a Land. Higher values indicate that medical treatment in hospitals comes close to the medical guidelines implemented in the diagnosis-related groups. Higher efficiency of public hospitals reduces the number of private hospitals significantly. These results are in line with previous research on the evolution of German hospitals that hypothesised that public hospitals operate less efficiently than private hospitals and are eventually abandoned by their public owners, in particular municipalities (Augurzky, Engel, and Schwierz 2007; Augurzky, Beivers, and Gülker 2012). Additionally, public hospitals are more affected by changes in treatment reimbursement, due to the introduction of diagnosis-related groups. In 2007, 30 per cent of public hospitals have seen reductions in their budgets. At the same time, high investment needs and insufficient investment fund allocation have deteriorated the competitive position of many public hospitals leading to inefficient health care procedures in comparison with their private competitors (Buscher 2008). Furthermore, private hospitals find it easier to adapt to these cost pressures. According to Klenk, private hospitals have more options to do internal restructuring, such as concentration of health services in DRGs that are more profitable. Additionally, private hospitals may look for new fields of business (e.g., hotel and spa) or choose to cooperate more closely with other private companies or health care providers (Klenk 2013).

Closely related to the efficiency argument is the amount of medical equipment (CRTs, MRTs, etc.) in public hospitals. The amount of high-tech medical equipment also has an impact on the number of private hospitals in a federal state. A number of economic accounts of production systems explain increases in productivity by the implementation of innovative technologies and the rationalisation of production.

The same applies to the German hospital sector. Private hospitals employ more modern equipment and also try to specialise in treatments that receive above average reimbursements. This tendency to concentrate on treatments that guarantee high revenues is frequently been criticised as 'cream skimming' (Simon 1996; Ernst and Szczesny 2006). Furthermore, private hospital companies increasingly outsource staff and try to lower wage costs by circumventing (mandatory) wage agreements with trade unions (Böhm and Henkel 2009; Gerlinger and Mosebach 2009). These cost reduction strategies have made private hospitals more efficient than their public counterparts and give them a significant competitive advantage (Augurzky, Engel, and Schwierz 2007). Public hospitals increasingly imitate business practices and incorporate management concepts with the aim of raising efficiency (Bruckenberger, Klaue, and Schwintowski 2005). The technologisation of health care and the rationalisation of procedures are logical consequences of this process (Elias 1995).

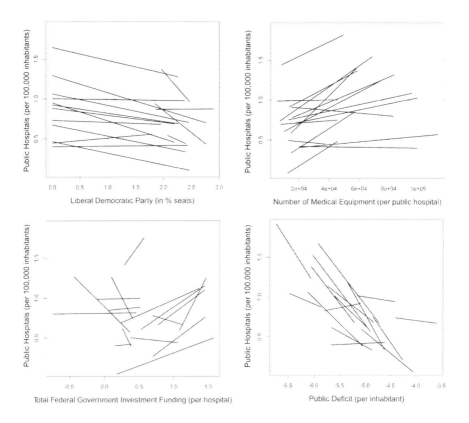

**Figure 3.6   The effect of public deficits, investment funding, technical
equipment, and political parties on ownership of public hospitals**
Source: Gesundheitsberichterstattung des Bundes (http://www.gbe-bund.de).

Political factors intensify the technologisation and rationalisation of health care in the hospital sector. The pro-market Liberal Democratic Party (FDP) not only endorses the reduction of hospital beds and a competitive hospital market but also deliberately worsens the situation of public hospitals by reducing itemised expenditures in new medical technologies. Private for-profit hospitals with their superior access to the capital market can compensate for the lack of government funding. In contrast, many municipalities, in particular those municipalities in federal states that have to shoulder high public debts cannot afford to enhance their hospitals on an equal scale. Party ideology makes little difference for the privatisation process. The number of seats has no effect on the share of private hospitals. The effect of party ideology is mediated by the financing of itemised investments with the SPD more in favour of public funding than the FDP. The conservative Christian Democratic Union (CDU) covers a middle ground between the two other parties.

Conclusion

German federalism has its greatest impact on health care provision with respect to investments in new technology and infrastructure in inpatient care. Länder governments not only assign investment funds to public as well as private hospitals in their jurisdiction but also regulate the number of hospital beds per inhabitant and the quality of inpatient care. Länder governments have constantly cut investments in hospitals since German unification. Lacking financial resources, the German hospital sector has become attractive for private hospital companies and investors. As a result, inpatient care has experienced major ownership changes in the last decade. The privatisation and marketisation of public as well as non-profit hospitals has increased sharply. The main driver of investment cuts and hospital privatisation are the increasing deficits of Länder government budgets. However, there is some variation in hospital financing and hospital privatisation at the Länder level. Länder governments, including the pro-market liberal party FDP, have been devoted to cut investments in hospitals and to pave the way for private hospitals to acquire and merge with public ones. More left-wing Länder governments have been more reluctant to reduce investments and to ease the privatisation of formerly public hospitals. Private for-profit hospital companies have superior access to the capital market and therefore are able to compensate for the lack of government funding. As a result, they have the capacity to acquire the latest medical technology in order to specialise in highly cost-effective DRGs. This gives them a cost advantage compared to their public competitors. At the same time, Länder (and municipal) government budgets are relieved from balancing hospital and municipal deficits as well as increasing hospital investment funding.

This flexibility in investment funding and hospital privatisation seems to suggest that German federalism has improved the responsiveness of the inpatient sector. However, cooperative German federalism leaves Länder governments little room for political manoeuvres. Since Länder governments are unable to significantly raise revenues or reduce expenditures, privatisation is one of the few remaining options available for Länder governments. As a result, political parties may accelerate or slow down the privatisation process, but there seems to be no way to halt it. This supports the thesis which holds that a more decentralised form of federalism can be disadvantageous to health care systems as it impedes the ability of federal states to respond effectively to changing circumstances. German Länder have not enough capacity to respond incisively and consistently to challenges of globalisation, ageing society populations, or growing fiscal debts. However, it is not the fragmentation of Länder health care systems that matters here but overall political and budgetary constraints set by cooperative federalism.

Chapter 4

Spain

Ixchel Pérez Durán

Introduction

The aim of this chapter is to analyse the accountability for health policy in the quasi-federal system of Spain. Since health policy in Spain has a decentralised design, whereby autonomous communities (ACs) are responsible for its implementation, this analysis focuses on this level of government.

In particular, this study assesses formal accountability for health policy in Spain's 17 ACs, by examining the mechanisms to inform and justify three key elements of the implementation phase of the policy: the responsible actors, the resources, and the policy results (Pérez Durán, forthcoming). In order to measure the level of formalisation, this study identifies whether ACs have a specific legal framework for accountability, if this set of rules establishes the obligation to account, and if it stipulates the public character of the information produced in the process of accountability.

The structure of the chapter proceeds as follows. First, I present an institutional and economic description of the quasi-federal system of Spain. Second, I describe some basic elements of Spanish health policy. Third, I develop the measurement of the level of accountability for health policy across Spain's 17 regional governments. Finally, this study identifies relevant variables that could provide possible explanations for the variation in the levels of accountability across Spanish regions. These include the presence of governments led by non-state-wide parties, public versus private management, and the length of time that any given region's health care system has enjoyed greater autonomy from central control.

Institutional and Economic Description of the Quasi-federal System of Spain

After 40 years of dictatorship, the Spanish Constitution of 1978 'established a delicate balance between centralisation and regional autonomy' (Vandamme 2012: 520). According to Bonafont-Chaqués and Palau-Roqué (2011), the debate between those who defended the political unity of Spain and 'the political demands of those territories that historically had had a strong political autonomy was a central debate that ended with the adoption of a hybrid system of territorial distribution of political power that shares most of the features of a federal state' (1093). Article 2 of the 1978 Spanish Constitution 'recognises and guarantees the right to autonomy of the nationalities and regions of which it is composed, and the solidarity amongst them all', and although the word 'federal' does not appear in the 1978 Constitution, some scholars have emphasised that it is inspired by a 'quasi-federal' or 'federalising' philosophy (Moreno 1997: 65).

The Spanish State of Autonomies [*Estado de las Autonomías*] meets some essential characteristics of federal systems: the presence of two orders of government, distribution of legislative and executive authority, and allocation of revenue resources and expenditure (Maiz et al. 2010).

The Presence of Two Orders of Government

On the one hand, 'there are two parliamentary bodies (the *Cortes Generales* and the *Parlamentos Autonómicos*)', and, on the other, 'a two-fold level of government (president and central government, president and AC government)' (Aja 2003: 103). Just like Spain's central parliament, each AC has a Legislative Assembly 'elected by universal suffrage in accordance with a system of proportional representation which shall ensure, moreover, the representation of the various areas of the territory; a Governing Council with executive and administrative powers and a President elected by the Assembly' (Article 152, Spanish Constitution). Also, institutions of the ACs are regulated by their respective Statutes of Autonomy [*Estatutos de Autonomía*] and by their regional laws. The process of political decentralisation created 17 ACs from 1979 to 1985, of which seven of them achieved the maximum degree of political autonomy in the early 1980s. In addition, some of the so-called historical autonomous communities (e.g., the Basque Country, Navarra, Catalonia, Galicia, and Andalusia) followed a special route to become ACs, having additional political jurisdiction over issues such as language (Galician, Basque, and Catalan), a civil code (Catalonia and the Basque Country), and/or a special fiscal status (the Basque Country and Navarra). These differences are recognised by the Constitution and each of the Statutes of Autonomy and are explained mainly by cultural and historical factors (Bonafont-Chaqués and Palau-Roqué 2011: 1093).

Distribution of Legislative and Executive Authority

According to Article 149 of the Spanish Constitution, the central government has exclusive competence (or monopoly) over regulation of citizenship, immigration, defence, foreign policy, foreign trade, criminal and commercial law, currency, infrastructure, transport, customs, economic stability, and basic social security legislation. Other competences – such as education, health, or environment – involve the concurrent intervention of the national government and the ACs, whereby the former establishes the basic laws and the later carry out the implementation of such policies. ACs have thereby the responsibility to provide a wide range of regional public goods and services, which specifically impact the wellbeing of people living within their territory. These include town and country planning, housing, regional public works, infrastructure and transport, farming, environment, culture, tourism, and sports, as well as health and education, two basic public services provided by the welfare state (Gil-Serrate et al. 2011: 2632).

Allocation of Revenue Resources and Expenditure

The process of decentralisation in Spain 'has been asymmetrical on both its revenue and its expenditure sides' (León 2011: 84). In general, it can be said that there are two financing systems: the Foral regime, applicable to the Basque Country and Navarre; and the Common regime, which is applicable to the rest of the ACs. The main difference between them lies in their taxing authority. Under the Foral regime, major taxes are fully administered by regional governments (León 2011: 85), and their revenue partially transferred to the state to compensate for general services provided. In the Common system of financing, the central government traditionally established the majority of taxes and transferred a portion to the ACs (Aja 2003: 135). Within the last 20 years a number of reforms (e.g., 1992, 1996, 2001, 2009) have modified and replaced the Common system 'with a mix of grants and transferred taxes' (Gil-Serrate et al. 2011: 2632), which grants more responsibilities to regional governments (e.g., 50 per cent of VAT in 2009; income tax ceded to ACs) (León 2012). Finally, as regards the expenditure responsibilities, two paths have been followed: the first, called 'fast-track process' provided executive and legislative powers in matters of health, education and environmental policy to the so-called 'historical communities' (Basque Country, Navarre, Catalonia, Canary Islands, Galicia, Andalusia, and Comunidad Valenciana) during the 1980s; while the second mechanism, referred as the 'slow-track process', consisted of a much slower transfer of those spending responsibilities to the remaining ACs, during the second half of the 1990s (León 2011). In the following section, this study analyses such transfers in the case of health policy.

Health Policy in Spain

In Spain, two paths were followed in the decentralisation of health policy to the ACs. As mentioned, the 'historical communities' were pioneers in the process of decentralisation (including the decentralisation of health policy), which was carried out at different speeds, resulting in different years of transfer of this policy to the Spain's regional governments. Several scholars have emphasised that the decentralised nature of this policy stems from the demand for greater self-government made by the historical nationalities (Moreno 2009; Gallego 2003; Navarro 2004). This demand led to the decentralisation of health policy in Catalonia in 1981, Andalusia in 1984, Basque Country and Valencia in 1987, Galicia and Navarre in 1990, and the Canary Islands in 1995. The process culminated in 2002 with the transfer of health competencies to the other 10 ACs that were still managed by the National Health Institute (Cantarero-Prieto and Lago-Peñas 2012; Moreno 2009).

Health policy in Spain is a multilevel policy that involves three levels of government: the central government, autonomous communities and local governments. Implementation lies directly with the governments of the ACs and, therefore, is a decentralised policy. The multilevel design of this policy means that the central government is responsible for overall coordination of the National Health System (NHS), basic health legislation, the establishment of health information systems, drug and medication policy, regulation of the provision of basic services, human resources, and regulation of the quality of services provided, among others. ACs are responsible for implementing this policy in their respective health systems, having the competence to legislate in this area. Local governments are also involved since they participate in health boards, assuming basic responsibilities for health control.

Although 'the public funding of health policy through taxes was established in 1989', its public character 'would materialise after the 1999 budget, which was the first budget that provided for a health system fully funded through taxes' (Pérez-Giménez 2000: 254). To be incorporated into the general state budget, the funding of the NHS stopped being dependent on the social security contributions. ACs then began to negotiate with the central government for the resources they would need to carry out their health competences. Coinciding with the last round of NHS decentralisation in 2002, the central government and the ACs substantially changed the way financial resources were allocated. The governments of the autonomous communities increased their involvement in the collection of certain taxes, and in return, took on responsibility for the full cost of health care. This process has resulted in health care being financed primarily by public funds that are directly managed by the ACs, to the point that the central government has no direct influence on health spending decisions taken by the autonomous governments.

Finally, universal health care coverage was developed in an incremental manner. The implementation of the Constitution of 1978 established the right of citizens to health protection and, subsequently, the General Health Care Act of 1986 extended that right to those who fulfilled the requirements of residence. However, access to health care remained linked to the social security contributions. NHS coverage was expanded in 1989 with the Decree on Universalisation and took a step forward in 2000 – with the approval of the Organic Law 4/2000 on the rights, freedoms, and social integration of foreign nationals in Spain, which established the mere fact of residence on the national territory (not nationality or legal residence) as the criterion for access to the public health system (Moreno 2009). According to the National Health Survey in 1993, 98.1 per cent of the population had public health coverage, and in 2003 this reached 99.6 per cent. Finally, in 2012 a reversal took place in the universal right to health care that resulted in the exclusion of irregular immigrants (allowing access only to emergency care, the treatment of serious illnesses, children, and pregnant women).

Accountability for Health Policy in Spain

The analysis of the level of accountability of health policy implementation is based on a framework for analysing and measuring accountability for public policies developed in previous research (Pérez Durán, forthcoming). The measurement of public accountability is focused on the degree of formalisation of the legal framework that regulates two accountability dimensions and three elements of policy implementation. In particular, the assessment of formalisation takes into account the verification of four characteristics: specific, binding, public, and autonomous. The first relates to the existence of a legal framework for accountability, the second refers to the formal obligation to be accountable, the third to the formal establishment of the public nature of the process of accountability, and the last to the formal independence of agencies that monitor the process of information/justification, and those in charge of evaluation/ sanction along the policy process. It is true that the formal aspect does not always coincide with the accountability that is actually carried out in practice. However, the formal development is a necessary condition for accountability to occur since, without formal rules, the information/justification and evaluation/ sanction of policies would be more difficult to be carried out. Above all, without formalisation, accountability would lack consistency and predictability, since it would become something that could occur randomly or even arbitrarily.

The following sections present the assessment of accountability for the responsible actors, the resources and the results of the health policy in Spanish regions. In particular, the analysis focuses on one of the two dimensions of accountability – the informative/justifying dimension – since it is the fundamental principle of accountability (as it is only through the availability of information that governments' actions can be evaluated and sanctioned). Furthermore, from the content analysis of the regulatory framework of the ACs, it was determined that there are no autonomous bodies to monitor the information/justification of health policy. Hence, this study also focuses on the remaining three characteristics of the formalisation: specific, binding, and public.

The degree of formal accountability for health policy will be placed in one of three levels, which indicate different degrees of compliance with the specific, binding, and public character: high levels of formalisation, medium levels of formalisation, and low or no formalisation. Given the decentralised nature of health policy in Spain, the degree of development is considered high when the Autonomous Community has developed a specific regulatory framework for accountability for the responsible actors, the resources and the policy results; when the AC legislation makes it compulsory to inform and justify the implementation elements noted above and when it establishes the contents to be included in the information; and when the formal rules set by the AC make it compulsory to make public all information related to the implementation elements and when they include the processes to be followed for the publication of this information.

To examine formal accountability, this study analyses the existing regulatory framework – legislation in force in 2011 – related to health policies, rights of access to health information, the functioning and organisation of governments, the regulation of public officials and high-ranking personnel, public finance legislation and auditing bodies, at central state and AC levels.

Accountability of the Responsible Actors for Health Policy

Within the basic structures of the state and regional governments there are at least two groups whose decisions and actions have a direct impact on the implementation of this policy: high-ranking officials and health professionals. The first group is responsible for taking overall management decisions related to coordination, regulation, control, and evaluation of policy, and it includes the minister for health, the health secretaries for each AC, members of the governing bodies relating to ACs' health policies – such as secretaries and general directors – and may also include the heads of public health foundations or health consortia. The second group is basically comprised of health personnel from each of the regions, such as doctors and nurses. The central government and the ACs have developed a regulatory framework for the selection, training, management, registration, mobility, evaluation, and disciplinary procedures for health professionals across the NHS. For instance, the central state legislation establishes that public records on health professionals should be accessible to the general population and that they must, at the very least, contain information for each professional such as the name, qualifications, and area of expertise. As the accountability of health personnel is regulated at the central level and is similar in all ACs, this analysis focuses on the level of formal accountability for high-ranking posts in the ACs since, this being a competence of this level of government, there are differences in their respective legal frameworks. In addition, the analysis of accountability of these actors is relevant since they bear the highest level of responsibility in the policy implementation.

Specific Character

ACs do not have specific formal rules to inform/justify the activities carried out by health authorities. However, 11 ACs (Andalusia, Balearic Islands, Basque Country, Canary Islands, Cantabria, Castile-La Mancha, Castile-Leon, Catalonia, Extremadura, Galicia, and Navarre) have been assigned a medium level of formalisation since they have laws on incompatibilities and/or records of activities of high-ranking posts. These ACs do not reach a high level since these laws on record of activities do not regulate the information/justification of high-ranking posts with respect to the exercise of health policy. That is, this type of regulation is limited to information on the activities external to the health policy, in order to avoid conflict of interest.

Although the six remaining ACs (Aragon, Asturias, La Rioja, Madrid, Murcia, and Valencia) also have regulations regarding high-ranking posts, these are deficient in the development of their own legislation on records of activities, or they do not include those responsible in the various forms of management that are included in their health services (autonomous agencies, foundations, or public consortia). This is the reason why a low level of formalisation was assigned to them. For example, the legislation of the community of Madrid states that the heads of autonomous bodies and public institutions are considered high-ranking posts, but excludes those who belong to the hospitals created in the form of entities under public law.

Binding Character

The legislation on records of activities of high-ranking posts of eight ACs (Andalusia, Basque Country, Castile-La Mancha, Castile-Leon, Extremadura, Galicia, La Rioja, and Navarra) makes explicit the 'obligation' of these responsible actors, in the various levels of management, to deliver such records of activities, as well as the 'content' that these records should have, which is why a high level of formalisation has been assigned to them. For example, the legislation of Navarra states that records of activities should include those public or private activities that generate – or could generate – an economic income, or any other remuneration that comes directly or indirectly from a private activity, among others. For their part, the legislation on records of activities of four ACs (Cantabria, Balearic Islands, Catalonia, and Canary Islands) also point out the obligation they have to deliver their statements of activities, but do not establish the content that those records should have, which is why a medium level of formalisation has been assigned. All the other ACs (Murcia, Madrid, Asturias, Aragon, and Valencia) reach a low level of formalisation, because the obligation or the content mentioned above is not made explicit.

Public Character

All the regions covered require appointments of senior health officials to be advertised and made public in their respective official gazettes. However, there are differences with respect to the publicity of such records of activities. Only Andalusia, Cantabria, Castile-La Mancha, Galicia, and Extremadura have a high level of formalisation, since they have concrete procedures that set out how the register of activities of high-ranking officials is to be made public. All five establish that these must be printed in their respective official gazettes and, for Andalusia, Cantabria, and Galicia, it must also be online. For their part, nine ACs (Balearic Islands, Basque Country, Catalonia, Castile-Leon, Navarre, La Rioja, Asturias, Murcia, and Valencia) have a medium level of formalisation, for although they have established that those registers are public, they have not developed the formal rules for them to be advertised, and are solely subject to the legislation on access to public files and records, in which the information is only accessible by means of a formal petition. Finally, Canary Islands, Madrid, and Aragon have a low level of formalisation. The first two because they do not specify whether this information is public; and with regards to the case of Aragon, the register of activities for high-ranking personnel is not made public.

Accountability for Health Policy Results

Once the decentralisation of health policy was completed in 2002, the central government developed some formal rules including provisions for accountability of health policy results, such as the Cohesion and Quality Act (2003), and the Act on Patient Autonomy and Rights and Obligations of Information and Clinical Documentation (2002). The first one was designed to coordinate the different health systems across Spain's 17 regional governments, while the second one was designed to ensure that the same health information was accessible for all users regardless of their place of residence. These formal rules provide for a central Health Information System (HIS) that must be able to provide information on protected population, human and material resources, pharmacy and health products, financing, expectations and citizens' opinion, and 'results' of health policy in all ACs. Although HIS information is considered to be public information, the explicit rules on how this should be made public have not been developed yet. The following section examines the formal development in ACs.

Specific Character

Six ACs (Extremadura, Castile-Leon, Castile-La Mancha, Galicia, Murcia, and Navarre) have laws on health information rights, which establish the right of access to information on the health system, which is why a high level of formalisation has been assigned to them. The ACs of Andalusia, Aragon, Cantabria, and La Rioja have not developed laws on health information; however, their provisions include some rights of access to health information in their general health laws. This is the reason why a medium level of formalisation has been assigned to them. The health legislation of the seven remaining communities (Asturias, Basque Country, Canary Islands, Madrid, Catalonia, Balearic Islands, and Valencia) have a low level of formalisation, since these only incorporate the regulation of patient information – as a health services user – but not the information related to health system outcomes of these ACs.

Binding Character

Provisions in 10 ACs (Galicia, Navarre, Aragon, Extremadura, Castile-La Mancha, La Rioja, Cantabria, Murcia, Castile-Leon, and Basque Country) regulate access to health information as a 'right' and also indicate the content that the information related to the results of this policy should include (i.e., waiting list indicators or the health coverage indicators), which is why a high level of formalisation has been assigned to them. This 'right' is also incorporated in the health legislation of the six medium-level ACs (Asturias, Andalusia, Madrid, Balearic Islands, Canary Islands, and Valencia). However, these do not develop the content that the information on the results of the policy should have – they are limited to information on health services and welfare benefits available and requirements of access – which is why these ACs reach a medium level of formalisation. Catalan health legislation does not make this right explicit, and therefore only reaches a low level of formalisation. Finally, it is worth noting that there are differences in the amount of information each AC reveals. For example, Galicia and Aragon have formally established that citizens have the right to know the information on indicators of efficiency of the NHS, the coverage of their health programmes and information relating to waiting lists.

Table 4.1 **Information about the health policy results that citizens have the right to know**

ACs	HPI	SWBA	QMI	EQCHS	EINHS	CHPI	WLI	ICSHC
Galicia	X	X	X		X	X	X	
Navarre	X	X	X	X			X	X
Aragon		X	X		X	X	X	
Extremadura	X	X	X	X				X
C. Leon	X	X	X	X				X
La Rioja	X	X		X			X	X
Cantabria	X	X	X				X	X
Murcia	X	X		X				X
C. Mancha	X	X		X				X
Valencia		X						X
Andalusia		X						
Madrid		X						
Basque C.							X	
Balearic I.		X						
Catalonia								
Canary I.		X						
Asturias		X						

Notes: (X) indicates the presence of regulation in the AC's provisions. HPI: health programmes information; SWBA: services and welfare benefits available and requirements of access; QMI: quality mechanisms implemented; EQCHS: evaluation of the quality of the centres and health services; EINHS: efficiency indicators of the NHS; CHPI: coverage of health programmes; WLI: waiting list indicators; ICSHC: information on the characteristics of services and health centres, facilities, and technical resources.

Public Character

Eight ACs have a high level of formalisation (Andalusia, Cantabria, Castile-Leon, Extremadura, Galicia, La Rioja, Murcia, and Navarre) since they stipulate that health information is 'public' and identify the means by which such information will be made accessible (electronic means, internet, user guides). Five ACs (Aragon, Castile-La Mancha, Valencia, Basque Country, and Balearic Islands) have a medium level of development because, although their provisions set out that the information is public, they do not specify the procedures to make such information public. The remaining ACs (Asturias, Catalonia, Canary Islands, and Madrid) have a low level of formalisation, since they do not explicitly mention the public character of this information.

Accountability for Health Policy Resources

The central state legislation includes some general mechanisms related to the accountability of the budget allocated to the implementation of health policies. For example, the Health Information System (HIS) provides public information on the 'financing' of the NHS. However, HIS regulation does not specify the contents and the procedures to give information about the resources allocated to health policy. The central state regulation also contemplates the Court of Auditors (Tribunal de Cuentas), a 'supreme body' responsible for the external auditing of public sector financial and economic activities. However, it does not have formal specific rules for accounting for the budget specifically allocated to health. In the following section, the analysis of the level of formalisation in the ACs is presented.

Specific Character

From the analysis of the regulatory framework of the 17 ACs, it was found that there is no specific legislation to inform/justify regarding the implementation of health spending. Since there is no such specific development, this study analyses whether there was a certain degree of formalisation in broader sections of health legislation. For example, this study analyses whether the right to know how the budget of this policy is spent is included in the 'information rights', finding that such a right is not recognised in the laws of the ACs. This study also analyses whether the regulation on 'health plans' – in which health systems' planning and evaluation is developed – includes some rules to inform/justify health spending. However, the only mentions found were generalisations such as the following: health plans should consider 'an analysis of existing resources', and 'the description and evaluation of resources for the attainment of the objectives, in coordination with the general budgets of the autonomous community'. These general references did not permit one to discern different levels of formalisation.

Finally, since all the ACs have the competences to establish health care contracts with the private sector, this study analyses whether associated centres and services are subject to the same rules for the accounting of public expenditure. The health laws of nine ACs (Andalusia, Asturias, Balearic Islands, Cantabria, Castile-La Mancha, Extremadura, Galicia, Navarre, and La Rioja) establish that the associated centres and state-assisted services are also subject to public accounting rules, which is why a medium level of formalisation has been assigned to them. Although the remaining eight ACs also incorporate health care contracts with the private sector in their health laws, their level of formalisation is considered low, since they only make general references to the accounting of these health care contracts.

Binding Character

The analysis of the binding character was carried out by examining if the state-assisted centres and services are required to report on the health expenditure incurred and if the contents of the contracts they conclude with the public sector are specified by law. The health laws of four ACs (Asturias, Castile-La Mancha, Navarre, and Extremadura) establish this obligation and regulate the contents of the information on health expenditure, and the contents that such contracts should have, for example, the timing of payment of financial contributions, the inspection regime to verify the compliance with economic and accounting rules, the price of arranged services and a report justifying the execution of the budget by the state-assisted centre or service, which is why a high level of formalisation was assigned to them. The health laws of five ACs (Andalusia, Balearic Islands, Galicia, La Rioja, and Cantabria) also establish this obligation of state-assisted centres and services, but have only general references relating to the information of health spending that such contracts should have, which is why they achieve a medium level of formalisation. Finally, eight ACs (Aragon, Basque Country, Canary Islands, Castile-Leon, Catalonia, Madrid, Murcia, and Valencia) have a low level of formalisation, since neither the obligation nor the contents mentioned above are made explicit.

Public Character

The legal framework of the Spanish regions establishes two formal mechanisms to make public certain information on health spending. The first is the referral of the public accounts of the ACs to their respective councils/chambers/courts of accounts. However, the purpose of these auditing bodies is not to inform how health spending is executed, but rather to undergo a process of accounting and control of the general budget execution of the AC. For this reason, this study focuses on the analysis on the second formal mechanism identified, which is the information on public spending that the economic affairs body [*Consejería/Departamento de Economía*] of each AC provides. This mechanism aims neither to account for the execution of health spending, nor explicitly establishes the public nature of this information. However, a certain degree of formalisation can be identified as it is pointed out that spending information will be published in their official gazettes.

The laws on finances of eight ACs (Andalusia, Aragon, Canary Islands, Cantabria, Castile-Leon, Catalonia, Extremadura, and Galicia) stipulate the provision of information to regional parliaments on the execution of public spending – which includes information on health spending – and its publicity in its official gazette, which is why a medium level of formalisation was assigned to them. For their part, the nine remaining ACs do not make a provision for publicising this information. This is reason why a low level of formalisation was assigned to them.

Accountability Index and Conclusions

From the assessment of formalisation in the ACs, a basic valuation scale was assigned to each of the identified levels of accountability: $v = 1$, if the variable of accountability has a high level formalisation; $v = 0.5$, if the variable has a medium level of formalisation, and $v = 0$, if the variable has low or no formalisation. This basic valuation allows us to observe, in a synthetic and quantifiable manner, the levels of accountability for each AC. After assigning these values, an index – on a scale of 0 to 100 – of accountability for each of the three policy elements analysed was obtained, where each aspect has an equal weight in these indexes. Finally, from these scores, an overall index of accountability for the informative/justifying dimension of health policy was obtained.

The overall index of accountability in Table 4.2 shows 17 heterogeneous systems of accountability for health policy across Spanish ACs. Six ACs (Galicia, Navarre, Extremadura, Andalusia, Castile-La Mancha, and Cantabria) have achieved the highest scores on the informative/justifying dimension of accountability, while Murcia, Valencia, and Madrid obtain the lowest. Furthermore, the levels of accountability of the responsible actors, the resources and the policy results present not only significant variations across regions, but also inside each AC. For example, a higher level of accountability for the results is not always associated with a higher level of accountability of the resources and of those responsible for the policy, as is the case of Murcia and Aragon. Finally, some relevant variables that in the context of this study could explain the variation in accountability and whose empirical verification would require further investigation are outlined below: presence of governments led by non-state-wide parties, public/private management and length of decentralisation of health policy.

Firstly, the analysis of the influence of governments led by non-state-wide parties would be relevant since the party system in Spain is characterised by the existence of two main state-wide parties (SWPs) – the Spanish Socialist Workers' Party (PSOE) and the Popular Party (PP) – and the presence of various non-state-wide parties (NSWPs), like the Basque Nationalist Party (PNV) or Convergence and Union (CiU) in Catalonia, among others, (Barrio et al. 2010: 7; Pallarés and Keating 2003).

Table 4.2   Accountability index for the informative/justifying dimension

	AC	Accountability: The responsible actors	Accountability: Results	Accountability: Resources	Accountability: Index
1	Galicia	73%	100%	50%	74%
2	Navarre	65%	75%	63%	67%
3	Extremadura	67%	81%	46%	65%
4	Castile-Mancha	60%	67%	56%	61%
5	Andalusia	60%	65%	50%	58%
6	Cantabria	58%	73%	44%	58%
7	Castile-Leon	33%	81%	27%	47%
8	Balearic I.	44%	54%	42%	47%
9	Mean	40%	58%	33%	44%
10	La Rioja	58%	48%	17%	41%
11	Basque Country	46%	50%	13%	36%
12	Canary I.	35%	40%	27%	34%
13	Asturias	15%	27%	56%	33%
14	Catalonia	44%	31%	21%	32%
15	Aragon	0%	65%	27%	31%
16	Murcia	8%	69%	0%	26%
17	Valencia	8%	42%	13%	21%
18	Madrid	0%	21%	13%	11%

Source: Author.

In the case of Spain, NSWPs range from pro-independence nationalist parties which 'define themselves as belonging to a nation other than Spain' (e.g., Basque and Catalan), to regionalist parties that 'do not question the Spanish state or nation but aspire to represent and defend certain particularities or interests of their communities (e.g., PAR, PA, and UV)' (Pallarés et al. 1997: 139). In any case, the declared core mission of these parties is the defence of the interests of the autonomous region. Following this argument, one might expect that regional governments that have been led by non-state-wide parties have greater accountability on policies over which they have competences, in order to differentiate them from those carried out by the central government. However, the empirical analysis shows that ACs that have a high presence of governments led by this type of party, which in the case of Spain are mainly nationalist right-winged parties such as CiU in Catalonia, PNV in the Basque Country, or CC in the Canary Islands, have not developed stronger mechanisms for accountability.

Secondly, one of the main arguments in favour of public management highlights that there are more formal controls for accountability of public managers than for private ones (Rainey and Chun, 2005). In this sense, Minow (2003) emphasises that 'privatisation creates possibilities of weakening or avoiding public norms' (1246), which carries the risk of loss of control of such private operators by the government (Donahue and Zeckhauser 2008: 507). At the same time, Palley et al. (2011) suggest that in the absence of a public regulatory framework, increased privatisation could lead such private entities into becoming part of an 'increasingly inequitable class- and income-based asymmetrical health care delivery system' (90).

From the above, one would expect that, if public health policy is implemented by private operators, the weakening of accountability mechanisms would follow. Unfortunately, data on the percentage of private expenditure on health in each AC are not available. However, a way to monitor the involvement of private management in the implementation of this policy is to observe the percentage of the health budget allocated by each region to contract their health services with private entities.

Table 4.3   Health budget allocated by each region to contract health services with private entities (2002–2010), and hospital beds managed by private organisations that receive public funding (2004–2008)

	ACs	Health budget allocated to contract health services with private entities (%)	Hospital beds managed by private organisations and funded with public funds (%)
1	Andalusia	4.7	0.13
2	Aragon	3.8	0.13
3	Asturias	6.7	0.18
4	Balearic I.	4.6	0.06
5	Basque Country	68.0	0.18
6	Canary I.	9.6	0.21
7	Cantabria	5.1	0.27
8	Castile-Mancha	5.6	0.00
9	Castile-Leon	4.5	0.16
10	Catalonia	31.3	0.68
11	Extremadura	4.3	0.05
12	Galicia	5.6	0.05
13	Madrid	6.3	0.21
14	Murcia	7.4	0.10
15	Navarre	5.4	0.40
16	La Rioja	5.0	0.06
17	Valencia	5.8	0.09

Source: Author's research, based on Ministry of Health, Social Services and Equality data, and Spanish National Hospitals catalogues.

Table 4.3 shows that some ACs, such as Catalonia, Canaries, or Murcia, have greater private management in the implementation of public health policy, together with a low level of formal accountability. For example, although Catalonia has a high percentage of private management through 'health agreements' (*conciertos sanitarios*), its level of accountability is below the ACs' average. Moreover, another way to assess the involvement of private management is the percentage of hospital beds that are not directly managed by regional governments or by the NHS, but by other managers who receive public funding (e.g., by health consortia, private foundations, and charitable institutions). As Table 4.3 shows, we can again observe that the ACs that have lower levels of private intervention are those that have higher levels of accountability. From these findings further studies should be developed in order to test the hypothesis that management of health services by the private sector lead to less formal mechanisms for accountability.

Finally, regarding the length of decentralisation, some scholars have emphasised that '[d]evolution of political power makes politicians less remote, more visible and more accountable' (Pollit 2005: 381). As mentioned, the decentralisation of health policy in Spain started with the 'historical nationalities' and was then expanded to all other autonomous governments in 2002. If decentralisation of public policies can make governments more visible and accountable, one might expect that the regional governments that initiated the process of decentralisation of health policy at an earlier date would have further developed their mechanisms for accountability. The results obtained in Table 4.2 do not allow identifying a clear association between the early/late decentralisation of this policy and accountability. If we take into account the six ACs that have higher levels of accountability, we see that in three of these there was an early decentralisation of the policy (Andalusia in 1984, Galicia and Navarre in 1990), while in the other three regions this policy did not become decentralised until 2002 (Extremadura, Castile-La Mancha, and Cantabria). In order to identify the possible existence of a relationship between greater accountability of health policy and early or late decentralisation, it would be necessary to extend the analysis beyond the length of decentralisation for this policy, including other indicators such as the strength of regional authorities (Hooghe et al. 2010).

Chapter 5

Italy

Federico Toth

Introduction

The National Health Service (*Servizio Sanitario Nazionale* or SSN) in Italy was established in 1978 and is mainly financed through general taxation. The SSN is committed to guaranteeing people resident in Italy (not only Italian citizens but also foreigners who hold a permit to stay in the country) a broad range of health services. The benefits package provided by the SSN includes preventive services, hospital care, family doctors, and specialist services. Dental care, rehabilitation, and vision care are, on the contrary, largely excluded. Two thirds of the healthcare funded by the SSN is issued by public suppliers (belonging to the SSN), while one third is provided by private suppliers holding special agreements with the public service.

During the last two decades, Italy, along with other European countries (Saltman et al. 2007; Adolph et al. 2012; Costa-Font and Greer 2012), has been experiencing a progressive transfer of competencies in the health sector from the centre to the regions. Since the early 1990s, every Italian regional government has autonomously planned and organised the healthcare services in its own territory. The autonomy enjoyed by Italian regions is such that some consider it no longer appropriate to talk of a single national health service, but rather of a federation of 20 different regional systems (Mapelli 2012).

The aim of this chapter is to offer a rough description of the regionalisation of the health service underway in Italy. We start from the reconstruction of the regulatory framework, focusing specifically on the dynamics triggered by this process. The individual regional governments are making different use of the independence granted to them. As a result, significant differences are emerging between regions, and the gap between the north and south of the country is particularly worrying.[1]

The 'regionalised' arrangement of the Italian SSN is also generating constant friction between central and regional governments. The federal government is required to guarantee a certain uniformity of the services throughout the whole country. It must also ensure that the regional governments do not exceed the

---

1   In this work, the Italian regions are grouped as follows: centre-north (Valle d'Aosta, Piedmont, Lombardy, Veneto, Friuli–Venezia Giulia, the autonomous provinces of Trento and Bolzano, Liguria, Emilia–Romagna, Tuscany, Umbria, and Marche), and centre-south (Lazio, Campania, Molise, Abruzzo, Puglia, Basilicata, Calabria, Sicily, and Sardinia).

budget assigned to them. The regional governments, on the other hand, accuse the central government of failing to allocate sufficient resources to funding the SSN. The distribution of the healthcare budget is also generating disagreements from region to region. Regional governments that manage to stay within their allocated budgets have no desire to take on the debts of those regions that are financially less disciplined, and they argue for criteria for the breakdown of the national health fund that rewards the better managed regional systems.

Institutional Description: The Regionalised Arrangement of the Italian National Health Service

Italy is divided into 20 regions. One of these, Trentino–Alto Adige, is made up of two autonomous provinces (Bolzano and Trento) each of which manages its own healthcare system independently. The Italian Constitution, which came into force in 1948, assigns five regions (Friuli–Venezia Giulia, Sardinia, Sicily, Trentino–Alto Adige and Valle d'Aosta) the status of 'special statute region'.[2] Compared with 'ordinary statute regions', special statute regions enjoy greater legislative and financial independence. The special statute regions were the first to be established, during the late 1940s (with the exception of Friuli–Venezia Giulia, established in 1963). The remaining 15 regions, on the other hand, came into being only in 1970 (Cotta and Verzichelli 2007).

Law 833 of 1978, which established the SSN, should have involved – at least on paper – a substantial transfer of responsibilities to regions; however, during the 1980s, the regionalisation process advanced slowly. The regions still depended entirely on transfers from the central government, and had weak administrative structures that were largely in a build-up phase (Mosca 2006; Helderman et al. 2012). They ended up, therefore, exercising their prerogatives only to a small extent, limiting themselves to a role substantially subordinate to the central government.

The health care reform of 1992–1993 proceeded to change the balance. This reform granted broad discretion to the regions in planning, organising, and financing health care services in their own territory. The regional governments acquired the control – earlier a concern of municipalities – over the local health agencies whose general managers they could appoint. All things considered, the 1992–1993 reform had the effect of considerably increasing the powers of the regions, which became the level of government having the most responsibility for health care (Tediosi et al. 2009).

A further step forward in the process of regionalisation was represented by the constitutional reform of 2001. On the basis of this amendment, health care

---

2   These regions obtained special conditions of autonomy because of their geographic isolation (this is the case of Sicily and Sardinia) and their linguistic-cultural peculiarities (linguistic minorities are present in Trentino–Alto Adige, Valle d'Aosta, and Friuli–Venezia Giulia).

has become the object of 'concurrent' legislation between (the central) state and regions: this means that the regions have full autonomy in organising and managing health care services in their own territories, while the state must confine itself to formulating general principles and to distributing health care funding. The constitutional reform of 2001 represents then the final stage of an intense process of regionalisation that in less than 10 years has transformed the SSN from a substantially centralised system into a highly regionalised one (Fiorentini et al. 2008).

Organisation of the SSN on Three Levels

The Italian National Health Service is currently structured on three levels: the *national* level consists of the Ministry of Health, the *intermediate* level is represented by the regional governments, and the healthcare agencies provide service at *local* level. Each of these three levels is assigned specific functions.

At the *national level*, despite the fact that reforms over the past 20 years were intended to promote accentuated decentralisation, the Ministry of Health still plays a central role in the coordination of the SSN. Firstly, the Ministry of Health is responsible for determining the overall budget for the SSN. Despite years of talks about fiscal federalism, the purse strings are still held by the central government (Ferrario and Zanardi 2011). A second strategic task assigned to the Ministry of Health is the definition of the so-called 'essential levels of assistance' (*Livelli essenziali di assistenza* or LEA). LEAs are the services that the public health system undertakes to provide for everyone in the country, on a uniform basis.[3] In other words, LEAs correspond to the 'package' of services guaranteed by the SSN to all those assisted free of charge or in exchange for a prescription charge.[4] The definition and update of the list of LEAs is a crucial activity in the relationship between central and regional governments in that the amount of resources allocated by the state to fund the SSN should be based on the determination of the essential levels of assistance (Torbica and Fattore 2005).

The next level is *regional*. As mentioned earlier, the Italian Constitution places health care among the matters of 'concurrent' legislation between state and regions. Basically, this means that the autonomous provinces and regions, while observing the general principles laid out by the national government, can establish the priorities and the objectives to pursue in the health care sector, and decide how to divide resources among the various spheres of assistance. The regions are

---

3   The LEAs are defined on the basis of two schedules: a positive schedule of services that each region must supply to its residents; and a negative schedule listing the services considered 'non-essential' following criteria of efficacy, efficiency, and clinical advisability (Torbica and Fattore 2005; Fiorentini et al. 2008). The list of essential services is very long and currently comprises over 5,700 types of service.

4   When compared with that envisaged by other countries, the contribution payable as prescription charges by patients in Italy is not particularly high. To receive services provided by the SSN, every Italian citizen pays an average of less than 60 euros a year.

able to implement the most diverse strategies and models arranging their regional health care system in the way they see fit. This means that each individual regional government is responsible for identifying hospitals to turn into hospital agencies and determining the total number of local health care agencies within their jurisdiction. The appointment of the general managers of the health care agencies is also the responsibility of the regional council, and it is at regional level that the criteria for crediting and remunerating both public and private suppliers are established.

Last, but by no means least, is the *local level*. The health care agencies, set up following the 1992–1993 reform, operate at this level. They are split into two categories: local health care agencies (*aziende sanitarie locali* or ASL) and hospitals. The local health care agencies are required to guarantee that people receive all the services included in the essential LEA. In saying that the ASL have to guarantee specific services does not means that they necessarily have to be provided directly by the ASL, which can assign the provision of part of their services to independent suppliers. Italy as a whole is currently divided into just over 140 ASL, with an average number of about 412,000 people served by each agency.

Some hospitals have been separated from the respective ASL and transformed into independent hospital agencies (*aziende ospedaliere* or AO). In most cases, it is the larger and most specialised hospitals that have been transformed into AO. There are currently about 80 AO throughout Italy. Public hospitals that are not independent agencies continue to be productive establishments within the respective ASL: they enjoy limited independence compared to the hospital agencies. Every health care agency is headed by a general manager who is appointed by the regional government.

Economic Description: Budget Restrictions and the Future Sustainability of the SSN

For several years now, the Italian government has been committed to reducing the public debt, partly in order to fulfil the obligations undertaken at the European level. The budget restrictions imposed upon the countries belonging to the Eurozone became even stricter with the entry into force, from 1 January 2013, of the Fiscal Stability Treaty (the so-called Fiscal Compact). This imposes upon countries in severe debt, like Italy, the obligation not only to keep the public deficit below 3 per cent (as already envisaged by the Stability and Growth Pact signed in 1997), but also to reduce the public debt by 5 per cent every year.

In recent years, Italy has succeeded, through considerable effort, in reducing its public deficit, which fell progressively from 2009 to 2013 from 5.5 per cent to 3.0 per cent of the gross domestic product (GDP). The progress made in terms of the public deficit has not however made it possible to reduce the public debt, which – on the contrary – continued to grow. In 2013, in Italy, the ratio between public debt and gross domestic product has risen above 132 per cent. Of all the member states of the European Union, Italy has the highest public debt after that of Greece (Eurostat 2014). If we also consider that the growth forecasts relating to the Italian economy for the near future are not particularly positive (a 1.8 per cent drop in GDP has been recorded in 2013), it is easy to see how important it is for the Italian government to keep public spending under control.

This is where the health care sector comes into play. The Italian National Health Service accounts for over 16 per cent of Italy's public spending, and provides jobs for over 670,000 employees, corresponding to 20.8 per cent of all public employment. The health care sector easily represents the main sector subject to regional intervention. If we look at the budgets of the ordinary statute regions, we can see that they allot over 80 per cent of said budgets to health care.

The health care sector cannot, however, be considered as nothing more than a public spending item. The health care system – which includes not only outpatients and hospital services, but also the pharmaceuticals sector and the medical device industry – plays a leading role in the Italian economy. It is worth over 11 per cent of the GDP (*Confindustria* 2012). Health care provides employment for over 1.5 million people, and this figure rises to 2.8 million if we also consider collateral activities. In view of the data supplied by the Ministry of Economic Development (*Ministero dello Sviluppo Economico* 2012), health care is the country's fourth most important production sector after construction, farming and ICT.

The Debate on the Future Sustainability of the SSN

The public health service is crushed in the grip of two opposing needs: on one hand, the need to keep public spending down and, on the other, the need to avoid holding back the development of an important productive sector. This is why the debate on the future sustainability of the Italian National Health Service has been raging for some time in Italy. The crux of the matter is basically the following: will there be sufficient resources to maintain the SSN at its current levels of intervention in the future? Concerns relating to the future sustainability of the Italian National Health Service are based upon two forecasts, both of which are quite plausible. The first is that, in the future, the demand for health services by the population will tend to increase; the second is that, in the years to come, the resources allotted to fund the SSN will probably be cut and, in any case, will not be increased in proportion to the growing needs of the people.

It is easy to predict an increase in the demand for health care in the near future due not only to the continuing progress of medical techniques, but especially to the progressive ageing of the Italian population. The life expectancy of Italians is becoming longer and longer, and consequently people are being increasingly affected by chronic and degenerative illnesses. It is expected that over-65s, who currently account for 20 per cent of the population, will represent about 33 per cent of the entire Italian population in 2050 (*Ministero del Lavoro e delle Politiche Sociali* 2011). The demographic trend is a source of concern also because it will be accompanied, in the years ahead, by a more than likely reduction in the financial resources available to the public health service.

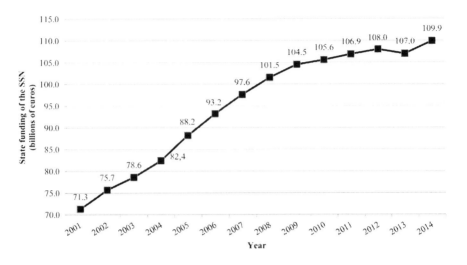

Figure 5.1   State funding of the SSN

Source: Ministry of Health, Department of Health Planning.

Let us consider the trend in state funding of the SSN portrayed in Figure 5.1: until 2012, the central government was able to accumulate more and more resources every year to fund the public health service. Between 2001 and 2012, the average growth rate of the national health care fund was 3.9 per cent per annum. Things have changed since the beginning of 2013. In 2013, for the first time, the state funding of the SSN has fallen in absolute terms compared to the previous year, from 108 to 107 billion euros.

The effects of the austerity policy are starting to become evident in Italy, too: as in other European countries, Italy is responding to the economic crisis by cutting social spending, comprising expenditure for health care (Mladovsky et al. 2012; Karanikolos et al. 2013).

One of the first consequences of cuts to the SSN could be the increase in spending for private health care. As a result of the reduction in funding of the public health service, families inevitably end up spending more for health care (*Censis* 2012). Remember that spending for health care in Italy is divided between the SSN, which takes on about 78 per cent, and the people, who pay the remaining 22 per cent (OECD 2014). The overall cost of the Italian health care system corresponds to 9.1 per cent of the GDP.

Of the total spent on private health care, over 82 per cent is out-of-pocket. The high incidence of private spending – particularly with regard to the out-of-pocket component – can be attributed to the fact that certain categories of health care services are not adequately covered by the public service and are, therefore, left largely to the private market. Today, 92 per cent of dental treatment, 64 per cent of gynaecological treatment and 57 per cent of diet-related treatment

(Collicelli et al. 2012) is carried out by the private sector without intervention by the SSN. If the state reduces its funding of the SSN, these percentages risk further increases.

Political Analysis

In order to understand the dynamics triggered by the regionalisation of health care and the relationships that are created between the different levels of government of the SSN, it is worth concentrating on the mechanisms used for the funding of the entire system. The methods via which financial resources flow in are particularly good at revealing the tension that exists between the various stakeholders.

The Determination and Breakdown of the National Health Care Fund

The SSN is funded according to a typical sequential process. First of all, the total amount of resources to be allotted to the National Health Service is determined. The budget allocated at national level is then split among the regions. In turn, every region splits its budget among the health care agencies and, lastly, the ASL use the resources assigned to them to pay the public and private suppliers of the health services. The first step in the funding process is the responsibility of the national government, which has to decide the extent of the resources to allot to the SSN every year. Since 2001, efforts had been made to plan the budget on a three-year basis. In negotiating the so-called Health Pact [*Patto per la Salute*][5] with the regions, the government developed the habit of indicating the amount of resources it was going to allot to the SSN in subsequent years. This planning was, however, subject to review and the government was often forced to cut the agreed amounts. These national government rethinks were, naturally, cause for complaint by the regional presidents.

The disputes between the state and the regions regarding the extent of the national health care fund go back a very long way. Since the early 1990s the regions have been accusing the government of systematically allotting insufficient resources to the SSN. Some scholars claim that the underfunding of the SSN has been a deliberate strategy by the national government pursued, also recently, with the hope of keeping the increase in spending for public health as low as possible (France et al. 2005; Mosca 2006; Mapelli 2012).

After establishing the total amount of the resources to be allotted to the SSN, the next step consists in dividing these resources among the regions. We ought to point out that the matter of splitting up the budget is very different from sourcing resources. The structure of the conflict changes dramatically depending on the

---

5   The Health Pact is an agreement, signed by the national government and by the regions every three years, outlining the strategic orientations relating to the planning and funding of the public health care system.

stage of the process. During the phase in which the decision is made regarding the amount of resources to allot to the SSN, the regions join forces against the national government, exerting pressure on it so that as much money as possible is allotted. Then, when they move on to discussing the criteria to be applied to the division of the budget, the regions find themselves competing against one another, with each one pressuring for the criteria that will afford it the greatest benefits during the division of the available funds. The methods used to divide the health care budget are subject to heated debate.

In recent years, the division of the health care fund has taken place mainly on the basis of the number of residents in every region. In addition to the number of residents, the age of the regional population has also been taken into partial consideration (Caruso and Dirindin 2012). This means that regions with a higher average population age have been assigned more resources than those with a younger population. It is a well-known fact that consumption for health care rises considerably as people age. It seems, therefore, understandable that the regions with an older than average population insist on the implementation of a distribution formula that takes into account the age of its residents. Obviously those regions (mainly in the centre-south) with a younger population have precisely the opposite perspective.

Law 42 of 2009 provides that, from 2013, transfers to the regions shall be calculated on the basis of the so-called 'standard costs'. In short, some benchmark regions that stand out from the others in terms of efficiency and appropriateness in the disbursement of health care services are identified. The standard cost corresponds to the spending per capita sustained by the *benchmark* regions to ensure that the essential levels of assistance are provided. The financial resources transferred by the central government to the single regions are calculated on the basis of these standard costs. The introduction of the standard costs should, therefore, encourage less efficient regions to fill the gap that separates them from the benchmark regions. We will see whether or not it works.

The Regional Deficits and the Balanced Budget Plan

On the basis of the above procedure, every region will be allotted its share of the national health care fund. The division has nothing to do with the fiscal capacity of the individual regions which receive more or less the same amount per capita with which they are required to guarantee the essential levels of assistance throughout their regional territory. Some regions manage to stay within the budget allotted to them while others do not and spend more. For several years now, it has become standard practice – among those operating in the sector – to separate the 'virtuous' regions (whose accounts are in line with expenditure guidelines) from the 'undisciplined' regions (whose accounts are characterised by heavy and recurrent management deficits). The operating result becomes an important criterion for assessing the ability of the regional governments to manage their own health care system.

Table 5.1   The regional health care deficit (2001–2012)

	Health care deficit accumulated per capita, millions of euros (2001–2011)	Operating result per capita, in euros (2012)
Piedmont	216	+4
Valle d'Aosta	936	+8
Lombardy	38	0
Bolzano	424	+14
Trento	127	+4
Veneto	81	+1
Friuli V.G.	-163	+8
Liguria	892	-19
Emilia–Romagna	86	0
Tuscany	122	-13
Umbria	136	+20
Marche	273	+14
Lazio	2,470	-111
Abruzzo	922	+39
Molise	2,083	-101
Campania	1,500	-21
Puglia	490	+3
Basilicata	461	-29
Calabria	723	-33
Sicily	860	-3
Sardinia	1,120	-127
Italy	*652*	*-17*

Source: Ministry of the Economy and Finance, General Report on the Economic Situation in Italy (various years).

As Table 5.1 illustrates, many regional health care systems find it difficult to reach a financial balance. The third column indicates the operating result for 2012 (in euros per capita) for every region: the '+' and '-' signs indicate a positive or a negative balance. All the health care systems of the central-northern regions, with the exception of Liguria and Tuscany, reach a financial breakeven. The health care systems of the centre-south regions, on the other hand, with the exception of Abruzzo and Puglia, are in the red. The regions in the most severe conditions are Sardinia, Lazio, and Molise.

The table also indicates the health care deficit accumulated, once again per capita, with reference to the period from 2001 to 2011. In this case, it being an accumulated debt, the negative sign indicates an operating asset. We ought to acknowledge that, alongside certain 'good' regions (particularly Friuli–Venezia Giulia), there are others (especially Lazio, Molise, Campania, and Sardinia) that, in recent years, have accumulated a very large health care debt. Remember that, in absolute values, the deficit accrued during 2012 by all the regional health care systems was 1.04 billion euros. This can also be considered as positive: in 2001, the overall deficit amounted to 4.1 billion euros. This means that, from the early 2000s onwards, many (but not all) regional governments have considerably reduced their operating deficit.

Northern and southern regions have, however, contributed differently to rebalancing the accounts. From 2001 to 2012, the central-northern regions reduced the average deficit per capita from 46 to 0.1 euro, almost reaching a breakeven. The southern regions have progressed less than their northern counterparts. In the period from 2001 to 2012, the average deficit per capita of the centre-south regions – most of them are all still in the red – has gone from 104 to 39 euros.

The gap between north and south emerges even more clearly if we assess the extent by which the single regions contribute to the overall deficit. If we consider the deficit accrued by all the regional systems on a scale of 100, in 2001 the northern regions accounted for 35 per cent of the total deficit, while the southern regions accounted for the remaining 65 per cent. In 2012, the northern regions are responsible for a mere 6 per cent of the total deficit, 94 per cent of which is generated by the southern regions. Campania and Lazio alone are responsible for 64 per cent of the overall deficit of all the regions put together.

To gain a better understanding of the trend in regional health care deficits from 2001 to the present day, we should take a look at the so-called 'balanced budget plans'. We can date the beginning of the story back to the August 2001 agreement between federal and regional authorities (Tediosi et al. 2009). According to this agreement, the government made additional resources available in order to settle the debts accrued up until then by the regional health care systems. In exchange, the regions made a commitment to cover any deficits generated from 2001 onwards using their own resources. In subsequent years, some regions respected the commitment undertaken. This was possible thanks to the reorganisation of services and a reduction in expenditure (cutting the number of hospital beds, closing small hospitals, reorganising territorial services, limiting the use of private suppliers and unifying purchases). Nevertheless, some regions, particularly in southern Italy, continued to accumulate significant deficits.

Consequently, a few years after the 2001 agreement, the central state and the regions had to negotiate a new agreement. The aim of the central government was to interrupt, once and for all, the vicious cycle according to which the less disciplined regions were always saved by the national government, which agreed to cover their debts after they had been run up. In autumn 2006, the first Health Pact [*Patto per la Salute*] was drawn up and the national government made a commitment to find new resources to settle previous debts. From then onwards, the financial support for regions in difficulty was to be conditional upon the signing of a specific budget balance plan, aimed at settling the balance.[6] If a region were to be unable

6   A budget balance plan is an agreement, which a single region that finds itself with a considerable deficit enters into with the Ministry of Health and the Ministry of the

to respect the balanced budget plan, the government would have had the power to take away the regional government's power to manage the health care system, entrusting it to a compulsory administrator appointed by the national government.

Upon the implementation of the Health Pact in 2007, the regions with the greatest deficits were forced to draw up strict budget balance plans in agreement with the Ministries of Health and the Economy. This applied to Lazio, Abruzzo, Liguria, Campania, Molise, Sicily, and Sardinia in 2007. The other regions that followed them in the signing of a budget balance plan were Calabria (2009), Piedmont, and Puglia (2010). As was to be expected, some of these regions were unable to fulfil the obligations entered into in the balanced budget plans. Therefore, the government had to intervene, appointing a compulsory administrator for the regions in greatest difficulty. The first to be placed under compulsory administration were Lazio and Abruzzo (in 2008), followed by Campania, Molise (2009), and Calabria (2010). Naturally, the signing of a balanced budget plan (especially when this involves compulsory administration) implicates a loss of sovereignty by the regional government, which is obliged to observe the restrictions and the instructions imposed mainly by the Ministry of the Economy.

It is important to point out that profound differences among the 20 regions already existed even before the reforms of the 1990s. The Italian regions have always been different in terms of size, economic development, civic culture, and institutional performance, with a sharp cleavage between the north and the south of the country (Banfield 1958; Putnam 1993; Cotta and Verzichelli 2007). From an economic point of view, the northern regions are, in fact, traditionally more developed than the southern ones. Today they still have a higher per capita income: it exceeds 27,500 euros in the northern regions, while it is 18,200 euros in the southern regions. However, such a disparity at the economic level is not reflected in the public health spending of the Italian regions. In fact, an equalisation fund at the central level aims at guaranteeing roughly the same resources per capita to all regional governments.

Why did the regions of the south not adopt the same strategies undertaken in the north? Leaving aside the influence of organised crime and the widespread political corruption (problems that particularly affect the southern regions), the answer can probably be found in the fact that, in Italy, the resources intended for health care have traditionally been utilised for patronage and political consensus purposes (Ferrera 1995). The creation of new jobs justifies the recruiting of personnel in excess of the real needs. Awarding rich contracts to suppliers outside the SSN responds to the wish to stimulate the private sector. The appointment of managers and the hiring of new employees often take place on the basis of patronage considerations or political affiliation. These conditions are shared, to some degree, through the entire country, but they flourish especially in the southern regions, economically backward and affected by unemployment rates much above the national average.

Economy. The plan, which has a duration of three years, aims to re-establish the economic and financial balance of the region concerned.

Interregional Health Care Mobility

In addition to budget-related tensions, another interesting phenomenon that characterises health care regionalisation in Italy is the mobility of patients from one region to another. All users of the Italian National Health Service can, once in possession of a prescription from their GP, choose the hospital at which to have their treatment. They can choose from all the public institutions as well as those private institutions that have special agreements with the public service, including those outside their region of residence. This freedom of choice given to patients is responsible for what is known as interregional health care mobility, on the basis of which, every year, hundreds of thousands of people receive treatment in a region other than that where they are resident.

Sometimes admission to hospital outside the region is not a decision made by the patients. It may be that they find themselves in another region for work, study or pleasure and have to be admitted to hospital in an emergency. In any event, admissions considered 'emergencies' represent less than 10 per cent of all admissions outside the region (*Censis* 2012). If we exclude emergency admissions and also mobility just beyond the regional boundaries, in most cases it is the patient's deliberate choice to leave the region, in the hope of finding a better service, of reducing waiting times, or of receiving treatments – such as highly specialised care – that are not available in the hospitals within their home region (Collicelli et al. 2012).

This is why the phenomenon of health care mobility can be classed as an indicator of the perceived efficiency and quality of the regional health care systems (Messina et al. 2008; Glinos et al. 2010). We have to assume that if people are happy with their regional health care service, they will not seek admission to a hospital further away from home, and that, once a patient decides to move, they will choose the region where they think they are going to receive the best care. It is particularly interesting to analyse the flows of interregional health care mobility, because it allows us to understand which regions' patients 'escape' from, and which regions are their preferred destinations (Table 5.2).

We notice immediately how there are particularly attractive regions. This is the case of Lombardy and Emilia–Romagna. If we calculate the relationship between incoming patients (from other regions) and outgoing patients (residents in regions who go elsewhere for treatment), these two regions have been confirmed for several years now as the regions that are best able to treat their own patients and to accept many more from outside. The regions that attract[7] fewest patients, on the other hand – partly due to their geographic isolation – are Sicily and Sardinia, followed by Campania and Calabria.

---

7   Reference here is being made to the *index of attraction*, which consists in the percentage of non-residents admitted to hospital in the region out of the total number of patients admitted to the regional hospitals.

Table 5.2   Interregional health care mobility (2012)

	Admissions of patients from outside the region	Residents admitted to hospital in other regions	Balance of mobility, in no. of admissions	Balance of mobility, millions of euros
Piedmont	40,965	47,473	-6,508	-7,508
Valle d'Aosta	2,409	4,199	-1,790	-10,752
Lombardy	142,930	66,563	76,367	555,183
Bolzano	6,482	3,813	2,669	10,629
Trento	9,490	12,531	-3,041	-15,488
Veneto	54,426	49,306	5,120	75,790
Friuli–V.G.	22,979	12,719	10,260	30,076
Liguria	34,021	38,608	-4,587	-56,743
Emilia–R.	110,944	43,750	67,194	336,690
Tuscany	69,869	35,875	33,994	132,294
Umbria	24,107	19,655	4,452	9,411
Marche	24,931	29,366	-4,435	-33,677
Lazio	90,000	68,260	21,740	32,739
Abruzzo	26,197	38,424	-12,227	-69,559
Molise	16,875	13,429	3,446	30,109
Campania	26,028	81,744	-55,716	-310,810
Puglia	26,281	58,454	-32,173	-180,058
Basilicata	14,146	22,342	-8,196	-19,111
Calabria	7,248	59,279	-52,031	-251,654
Sicily	15,514	49,416	-33,902	-188,774
Sardinia	4,391	15,027	-10,636	-68,787
Italy	*770,233*	*770,233*	*0*	*0*

Source: *Ministero della Salute* (2013).

Moving on to passive mobility (this expression is used for residents who are treated outside the region), patients exit[8] particularly from smaller regions, like Basilicata, Valle d'Aosta, and Molise, with about one patient out of five from these regions leaving to go to hospitals outside the regional boundaries. It is, however, also true that some small regional systems, such as those in Molise and in the Autonomous Province of Bolzano, succeed in attracting more patients than those that leave. Consequently, these systems present an active mobility balance. At this point, it should be said that every regional health care system is required to reimburse the cost of admissions of its patients to hospitals outside the region.

---

8   The *escape index* corresponds to the percentage of residents admitted to hospitals in other regions, compared to the total number of residents in the region who have been admitted to hospital during the year (both inside the region and elsewhere).

Outgoing mobility is, therefore, an expense borne by the regional finances. Incoming mobility, on the other hand, is a source of income for the regions. The economic balances of interregional mobility are indicated in Table 5.2 (last column on the right).

All the centre-south regions, apart from Molise and Lazio, have recorded a negative balance. The worst situation is that of Campania (-311 million), followed by Calabria (-252 million), and Sicily (-189 million). A negative balance, albeit of a more modest entity, is also recorded in some of the centre-north regions: Valle d'Aosta, Piedmont, Province of Trento, Liguria, and Marche. If this is the overall picture, it is interesting to make a more detailed analysis of the flows among the single regions. In this way, we discover that in central-northern Italy, most of health care mobility takes place between neighbouring regions. About half of the residents of Marche who seek treatment outside of the region head for Emilia–Romagna. Of the Piedmontese patients that 'emigrate', 60 per cent go to hospitals in nearby Lombardy, and Emilia–Romagna and Lombardy also exchange several thousands of patients every year. The situation is partly different for the southern regions. When patients from most of these regions decide to move, they prefer to travel to the north. The favourite destinations of people from Sicily, Puglia, and Sardinia who decide to seek treatment outside their region are Lombardy and Emilia–Romagna. Those from Calabria head mainly for Lazio and Lombardy, and so on.

The figure that most clearly highlights the imbalance between northern and southern Italy, however, is the financial transfer between these regions. In 2012, 221,000 patients residing in the southern regions headed north for treatment. Only 43,000 travelled in the opposite direction, from the north to hospitals in the southern regions. In economic terms, this means that the southern regions pay their northern counterparts about one billion euros a year.[9] This financial transfer from south to north has a twofold effect. On the one hand, southern regions end up paying a huge amount of money. In this way, they find it difficult to stay within the budget. On the other hand, many northern regions would hardly be able to balance their operating budgets without the additional income generated by patients' mobility.

Conclusions

A first conclusion that emerges from the data given above is the wide gap that separates the north and south of the country. For those familiar with the Italian situation, this contrast does not come as much of a surprise. The fracture between the regions of the centre-north and those of southern Italy is highlighted by numerous socio-economic indicators and is found in numerous policy sectors. From this point of view, health care is simply no exception. However, this does not make the

---

9   With reference to the year 2011, the southern regions paid those in the north 1,147 million euros, while the latter transferred just 169 million euros to those in the south.

problem less serious. It is as though a line has been drawn, cutting the peninsula in two. The regions north of Rome have a more or less balanced financial situation and attract patients from other regions (leading to the assumption that they offer better quality services, for otherwise patients would not move). Conversely, the regions south of Rome, in most cases, have negative accounts and offer poorer quality services (at least this is the perception of the residents of the southern regions, many of whom prefer to travel to hospitals in the north for treatment).

The disparities among the various regions are a source of concern for the national government, as the Italian Constitution assigns the central government the task of guaranteeing uniformity of health care services throughout the entire country. Particularly alarming to the national government are the operating deficits accrued at regional level. In recent years, some regional health care systems (especially in southern Italy) have accumulated considerable deficits and are unable – even today – to stay within the budget assigned to them. This lack of financial discipline shown by certain regional governments naturally risks annulling the considerable efforts made by the Italian government to keep public spending down, representing a serious problem for the competitiveness of the whole country. From this point of view, certain experts in health care policies believe that the regionalised arrangement of the SSN is becoming an obstacle on the road to rebalancing the public accounts. Many hold that, if Italy were to return to a more centralised system, it would be easier to keep health care spending under control.

This situation is understandably generating tension among the regions. Those in the north – which not only have healthier finances but also boast a much higher income per capita – are tired of having to take on the debt deriving from the poor management of others. The 'virtuous' regions feel that they are being damaged and are asking for acceleration on the road to fiscal federalism and for the adoption of criteria for dividing the national budget that reward the most efficient regional health care systems. The introduction of the 'standard costs' method should take this direction. Conversely, the strategy implemented up to now by the national government has been – in contrast with the requests by some regions – to slow down the fiscal federalism process, continuing to hold the purse strings. As mentioned earlier, the national government still determines aggregate national health care funds and the criteria used to share it among the regions. Through its key financial lever, the central government is able to limit the autonomy of the regional governments whose accounts are in the red. This is achieved by signing strict budget balance plans.

Today, the Italian regions can be split into two groups, which proceed at different speeds (Tediosi et al. 2009; Helderman et al. 2012). Those whose accounts are balanced continue to enjoy the autonomy acknowledged to them by the Constitution (albeit within the restrictions imposed by recent cuts to spending for health care). The regions with financial difficulties, on the other hand, are stripped of their full autonomy in relation to health care. These regions are initially kept under close observation and, if they fail to respect the balanced budget plans agreed to with the government, they risk being placed under compulsory administration.

Chapter 6
The United Kingdom

Gwyn Bevan, Sheelah Connolly, and Nicholas Mays

Introduction

The argument developed in this study is that understanding subnational governance is a vital but largely absent element in comparative health care policy analysis. It is vital because descriptions at the national level using traditional archetypes, such as the Beveridge and Bismarck models, fail to capture differences in subnational governance that have emerged over the past 20 years. At the national level, both Italy and the UK follow the Beveridge model, and in these countries there were attempts, in the 1990s, to introduce provider competition across the regions of Italy (France and Taroni 2005) and the countries of the UK (Bevan and Robinson 2005). Although this model is still being tried in Lombardy (Brenna 2011) and England (Boyle 2012); the region of Tuscany (Nuti et al. 2013) and the country of Scotland (Steel and Cylus 2012) have abandoned provider competition for systems of performance management. Theories of comparative federalism ought to enable us to provide richer descriptions of subnational systems of governance and hence more powerful comparative health care policy analysis.

This chapter aims to contribute to this new kind of comparative health care policy analysis by analysing the impacts of political devolution in the United Kingdom (UK) on the publicly financed health care systems of the UK's constituent countries. Powers were transferred to the Scottish parliament and Welsh Assembly on 1 July 1999, and to the Northern Ireland Assembly on 2 December 1999 that allowed each to varying degrees to set policies for public services including education and health care. This has resulted in four different national public health systems in England (Boyle 2011), Scotland (Steel and Cylus 2012), Wales (Longley et al. 2012), and Northern Ireland (O'Neill et al. 2012). Devolution in the UK provides a particularly interesting case study to test the value of theories of comparative federalism. This is because although following devolution the UK ceased to be a unitary state in the governance of health care, as we explain below, it lacks key elements of federal governance. So the UK might be described as a hybrid between a centralised and federal system or, as having elements of both: with a strongly centralised system of governance within England and a relatively loose federation of the three devolved territories in relation to the devolved public services in including health (Bevan 2014). The UK is an example of one type of what Bogdanor (2001: 233) describes as 'asymmetric devolution', in which there is a very large unitary state (England) and much smaller ones (Scotland, Wales, and Northern Ireland): other examples are in Denmark with the Faroe Islands and Greenland, and Portugal with Madeira and the Azores. The other type is where some regions enjoy greater powers than others: in Italy, five special regions were created in 1948 (Valle d'Aosta, Trentino–Alto Adige, Friuli–Venezia Giulia, Sardinia, and Sicily), 22 years before the other 15 were created, and those five special regions have 'exclusive legislative powers in economic social and cultural matters'; in France, 'Corsica and the overseas territories have special status'; in Spain, 'seven of the seventeen "autonomous communities" have a greater degree of autonomy over their health and education services'. The inherently unstable 'asymmetric devolution' of the UK has shifted from being largely a concern of constitutional experts to being the subject of mainstream political and public debate following the 'No' vote in the September 2014 Scottish independence referendum.

The next three sections of this chapter outline the historical and political influences that have shaped governance of health care in each country of the UK, the constitutional arrangements of the devolution settlement, governance of health care before and in the first phase after devolution and the outcomes of asymmetric devolution. The chapter concludes by discussing these outcomes and subsequent developments.

Historical and Political Influences

Tuohy (1999) argued that history matters in understanding policies as these tend to follow paths influenced by the 'accidental logics' of political settlements. We see such 'accidental logics' at play in making sense of the constitutional arrangements of devolution and also the policy responses of governments for their national health systems following devolution. Before devolution, legislation passed by the UK parliament was different for Scotland and Northern Ireland, and the same for England and Wales. These differences were reflected in the initial devolution settlement: the Scottish parliament and the assembly in Northern Ireland had a wider range of legislative powers and were free to legislate on all matters except those reserved for the Westminster parliament; the powers of the assembly in Wales were more circumscribed and initially limited to the executive matters that the former government department for Wales (the Welsh Office) had had responsibility for before devolution. We now describe the contexts that have shaped government policies in the four territories.

The political context of England makes it the odd man out in the UK. Only in England is there a strong Conservative party; significant independent provision of health care and education; persistent advocacy from think tanks and academics to implement public service reforms that challenge producer 'capture' and support the development of provider competition involving the private sector; a large and critical, predominantly right of centre press; and political debates that regularly put 'the operation and even the existence of the NHS in question' (Greer 2004: 103). Furthermore, the much larger scale of England means that it is more complicated to run public services including the NHS in England than in the devolved countries, with the consequence that its 'civil service policy and administrative capacity [...] far exceeds that of the devolved administrations' (96) and 'The decisions of the government can be turned into policy and implemented far more quickly and with less hazard' (Greer 2004: 97).

Of the devolved territories that united with England to form the UK, argues Bogdanor (2001: 144), only Scotland remained a 'historic' nation 'which succeeded in retaining the institutions of statehood'. Greer (2004) argues that the geopolitics that made Scotland a separate successful state before the union with England in 1707 also allowed it afterwards to assemble and develop an imposing and distinctive civil society and social institutions. The legacies of these distinctive Scottish institutions meant that, of the three devolved territories, Scotland had 'the most complicated, competitive and well-worked out policies' (64). In relation to the pre- and post-devolution Scottish NHS, Greer argued that the key players were the Scottish medical elite that had a significant national presence with its own royal colleges of physicians and surgeons, and historic university medical schools.

Wales, following its union with England, in two Acts of 1536 and 1543, ceased to be a 'historic' nation and failed to retain the institutions of statehood (Bogdanor 2001). Prior to devolution, Wales was treated in terms of governance of its public services as an English region in all but name, although some differences did emerge in education related to teaching in Welsh (Bogdanor 2001: 157). Greer (2004: 130) observed that 'Wales has historically been, and for many purposes still is, part of a unit called "England and Wales"'. McClelland (2002) states that the pre-devolution NHS in Wales was perceived as 'forming an adjunct to the English health service'. Greer (2004) contrasts the existence of the powerful medical elite that influenced NHS policy in Scotland with its absence in Wales. The royal colleges based in London cover Wales, which also lacks its own powerful and distinctive academic centres. The principal political influences on the Welsh Assembly were from local government rather than from professional elites.

In Northern Ireland, the objective of devolution following the partition of Ireland in the 1920s was not to give Northern Ireland greater autonomy within, but to ensure that it stayed part of, the UK (Bogdanor 2001). In Northern Ireland, following devolution in 1999, there has been relatively little distinctive policy development. Greer (2004: 159–61) attributes this to its small size, history of direct rule from Westminster, and the nature and intensity of its sectarian rather than Left–Right political conflict. Indeed because of that conflict, devolution was suspended four times between 2000 and 2007 (O'Neill et al. 2012: 5). Greer describes its style of policy-making as that of 'permissive managerialism', which he defines as 'a combination of minimal policy activity (such as quality improvement, new public health, or acute care redesign) and an emphasis on running services' (159).

Constitutional Arrangements of Asymmetric Devolution

The Westminster parliament acts as the legislature and provides political accountability for public services in England, and for UK-wide issues (such as the economy, spending on social security, and defence and foreign policy). Hazell (2000) has called the absence of an elected body for England 'the hole in the devolution settlement', but argues that this is a necessary outcome from the structural arrangements of devolution with one giant, England (with a population of 52 million), and three pygmies, Scotland, Wales, and Northern Ireland (with populations of five million, three million, and 1.8 million respectively). This is because 'as a rule of thumb, there is no successful federation in the world where one of the parts is greater than one third of the whole; England with four fifths of their population would be hugely dominant, even more dominant than Prussia in the old Germany' (35). Bogdanor (1999: 267) also argues that an English parliament would unbalance the devolved system of governance because of England's size. He cites the Report of the Royal Commission on the Constitution (Kilbrandon 1973) on the subject of an English parliament, which stated that it 'would rival the United Kingdom Federal Parliament' and any such federal parliament would be abnormal as it would not be possible democratically to scale down the representation of England so that it could be outvoted by the combined representation of Scotland, Wales, and Northern Ireland, as would be the norm in any truly federal parliament. Hence, Bogdanor argued that '[d]evolution in England, therefore, if it is to serve the same ends as devolution in Scotland, Wales and Northern Ireland must be devolution to English regions' (268), which he judged to be quite unrealistic. Indeed, when the option of elected regional government was piloted in 2004 in northeast England, it was rejected so heavily in a subsequent referendum that it was generally regarded to have been removed from the political agenda for a generation as a result (BBC News 2004a). This may be changing rapidly in the aftermath of the 2014 Scottish independence referendum and the majority vote for Scotland to stay in the UK, which has revived serious discussion of political devolution within England, as Scotland stands poised to receive increased devolved powers. The 'accidental logics' of the asymmetric devolution settlement have created problems because of the absence of an English parliament and of true federal arrangements for governance to which there are no easy solutions.

The absence of an English parliament has resulted in two particular problems. The first is what is known as the 'West Lothian question' (after Tam Dalyell, the former MP for the Scottish seat in the Westminster parliament of West Lothian): why should MPs from non-English constituencies be able to vote on policies for England's public services (which include health care, education, and transport) when English MPs cannot vote on the policies for these services in each devolved country (as these are matters for their own parliament and assemblies) even though their finance comes from the budget of the UK as a whole? Second, whilst in each devolved territory, the governments are responsible for public services only and politically accountable for these to the parliament in Scotland and assemblies in Wales and Northern Ireland; in England, political accountability for English public services is via the UK government to the Westminster parliament in the same way as for UK-wide policies.

The lack of arrangements for federal governance in the UK means that there is no constitutional basis for agreeing what should be the UK-wide elements of policy for public services versus those that should be determined by the legislatures of the devolved territories and the Westminster parliament on behalf of England. Greer (2004: 197) observed that the UK after political devolution was 'an international outlier because of its lack of frameworks constraining the regional governments. The various mechanisms by which the central government constrains decentralised jurisdictions by law in other territories is simply lacking in the UK's formal constitution'. In the UK, for health care, there is, for example, no analogy to the Canada Health Act (Flood and Choudhry 2004), which sets out five key requirements that provincial governments must meet through their public health care insurance plans in order to qualify for the full federal cash contribution under the Canada Health Transfer. Greer (2004: 179) states that 'the UK, almost uniquely in the world does not constrain substantive policy divergence in health'.

Devolution has so far been essentially a political arrangement with virtually no fiscal devolution (though, again, matters may be about to change after the Scottish independence referendum of 2014). The only constitutional change in the finance of public services in 1999 was to give the Scottish parliament limited powers (under Part IV of the Scotland Act) to vary the basic rate of income tax applying in Scotland by up to plus or minus three pence in the pound (Commission on Scottish Devolution 2009). These powers, however, have not yet been used and so these services continue to be financed through the Barnett formula, which began to operate in Scotland and Northern Ireland in 1979, and in Wales in 1980, when political devolution was first being considered. The principle of the Barnett formula is that 'growth' in total resources for public services in the UK is allocated to each country in proportion to its share of the UK's population. The Barnett Formula has been criticised over many years, most recently by a Select Committee of the House of Lords (Select Committee on the Barnett Formula 2009) and the Independent Commission on Funding and Finance for Wales (Holtham 2009), among other things, for failing to take account of differences in need between the populations of the UK countries. The UK government's response to the report from the Select Committee on the Barnett Formula was to reject the call to incorporate a weighting for relative need in the formula (HM Treasury 2009). The Commission on Devolution in Wales (2012: 30) recognised that the Barnett formula 'must ultimately be superseded by a needs-based formula', but pointed out that reaching an agreement on such a change would be politically difficult. One obvious obstacle to doing so is the absence of any overarching federal arrangements for public services.

The continuation of the Barnett formula after devolution (and in September 2014 all three main Westminster political parties pledged to retain it for the foreseeable future) means that only in England are government departments effectively accountable to HM Treasury for their spending. In principle, the substantial increases in the funding of the NHS in England from 2000 were contingent on performance that satisfied the Treasury's Public Service Agreements (PSA) targets. For the other governments, the increases in the global funding allocation for their public services were largely determined by the Barnett formula regardless of performance. Connolly et al. (2011) showed how, before devolution, in 1998, the Treasury's PSA targets applied to health services in England, Scotland, Wales, and, to a lesser extent, Northern Ireland. But after devolution, from 2002, there were no PSA targets for the governments of Scotland and Wales. Although PSA targets continued to apply in Northern Ireland, Timmins (2013: 13) observes that, when these were reviewed in 2011 and showed that Northern Ireland had performed comparatively poorly, 'it is not clear that any penalties were incurred, or indeed that much action followed, as a result of that poor performance'. Another form of accountability that applied to the Department of Health in England only, from 2000, was scrutiny by the Prime Minister's Delivery Unit, which reported directly to the prime minister on the progress of the NHS in England in reducing long hospital waiting times (Barber 2007).

Governance of the National Health Systems Before and After Devolution

We describe differences over time and across the four territories in managing the performance of their national health systems by using four archetypal models of governance (Barber 2007; Le Grand 2009; Bevan and Wilson 2013; Bevan and Fasolo 2013). First is Trust and Altruism, which assumes that providers are 'knights' (Le Grand 2003, 2007) and, hence, that there is no need for external incentives to overcome organisational inertia to use comparative information on performance to understand how performance needs to change to deliver better outcomes, and to encourage implementation of the necessary changes (Berwick et al. 2003). Furthermore, in this model, as it is assumed that poor performance can only be due to difficult external circumstances, it follows that poor performance ought to result in extra resources, thereby generating perverse incentives that run counter to prospect theory (Kahneman 2011: 278–88). Second is Choice and Competition, which aims to create external incentives through a quasi-market system in which there is choice of providers and 'money follows the patient'. Third is Targets and Terror, which holds providers to account for performance against a limited set of public targets that clearly signal priorities to those responsible for providing services, with clear threats of sanctions for failure and rewards for success. Fourth is Naming and Shaming, which is a system of performance measurement that satisfies criteria specified by Hibbard et al. (2003) such that providers' performance is ranked so that the public can easily see which providers are performing well and poorly on a regular basis, and so that those shown to be performing poorly are under pressure to improve to remedy damage to their reputations.

The NHS in each country was, and is, mainly publicly financed, with access free at the point of delivery (except for the subsequent introduction of various charges for prescriptions in primary medical care, optometry and dentistry, with variations after devolution see below) and typically via a general practitioner (GP) as gatekeeper to specialist medical services (Webster 1988). From the creation of the NHS in 1948 to devolution in 1999, policies for the English NHS essentially applied across the four territories of the UK with the default model of governance being that of Trust and Altruism (Le Grand 2003). This was controversially abandoned by the Thatcher government, from 1991, for one of Choice and Competition with the introduction of an 'internal market' in which providers would compete for public funds (Secretaries of State for Health, Wales, Northern Ireland, and Scotland 1989). After winning the 1997 election, the Blair government temporarily abolished governance by Choice and Competition in favour of a 'third way', which was in effect a return to the model of Trust and Altruism. A 'crisis' of 'underfunding in the winter of 1999–2000 (Bevan and Robinson 2005) resulted in the UK government's commitment, in January 2000, to increase spending on the NHS in the UK to the European Union average on health care as a percentage of gross domestic product (Smee 2005). This resulted in annual real increases in NHS expenditure of 5 per cent for five years in each UK country. In England only, did the government link these increases in funding to targets for NHS organisations to achieve ambitious reductions in hospital waiting times through the regime of annual 'star ratings'. This regime, which applied from 2001 to 2005, combined the models of Naming and Shaming, and Targets and Terror (Secretary of State for Health 2000; Bevan and Hood 2006; Bevan 2009). Although all governments in the UK countries introduced targets for waiting times for hospitals (Auditor General for Wales 2005: 16), and for ambulance response times to potentially life-threatening emergency calls (Bevan and Hamblin 2009), the Trust and Altruism model of governance continued in Wales (National Assembly for Wales 2003; Auditor General for Wales 2005a), Scotland (Farrar et al. 2004; Propper et al. 2008, 2010) and Northern Ireland (Appleby 2005).

The following three sections consider three different outcomes of asymmetric devolution deriving from the lack of an English parliament; the lack of federal arrangements for constraining the policies of the different governments; and differences in governance.

Three Outcomes from Asymmetric Devolution

Outcomes of the Lack of an English Parliament

From 2002, the Blair government began implementing its policy to develop a second internal market in the NHS in England with competition between hospitals. This justified freeing 'high performing' NHS trusts that had 'earned autonomy' from central regulation and converting them into NHS Foundation Trusts. The governments in Scotland (Steel and Cylus 2012) and Wales (Longley et al. 2012) moved in the opposite direction, in 2004 and 2009, respectively: abandoning the purchaser/provider split and going back to organising the NHS largely as it had been before the 'internal market' of the 1990s. Greer and Trench (2008: 21–2) describe how the Blair government secured a majority in July 2000 for the vote on NHS Foundation Trusts, which was opposed by the majority of English MPs, by relying on the party loyalty of Labour MPs from Scotland and Wales, who would not face any hostile constituency reaction as their (Labour-led) devolved governments at that time were against the policy. They also point out that 'the Scottish National Party, which normally abstains on England-only policies, chose to vote against foundation hospitals, with the declared justification that it might have Barnett formula implications' (Greer and Trench 2008: 21).

Outcomes of the Lack of Federal Arrangements

Following devolution, there are differences between countries in charges for health and social care. Charges for prescriptions have been abolished in the devolved countries (Timmins 2008). In England about 90 per cent of patients are exempt from these charges, but for those who do have to pay, the charge is over £8. The governments in Scotland and Wales have also, where contracts allow, abolished fees for parking cars at NHS hospitals (Timmins 2008). The most important policy divergence is the introduction in Scotland only, from 2002, of free long-term personal and nursing care for people aged 65 years and over. As Greer (2004: 87–90) argues, this is a striking example of what can happen from the combination of the Barnett formula and the absence of any constitutional arrangements for governing policies within the different territories of the UK. Although the Royal Commission on Long Term Care (Sutherland 1999) recommended free universal provision of personal care for the elderly, the immediate policy responses of the different governments in the UK were instead to opt to continue with means testing. In January 2001, however, a majority of Members of Scottish Parliament (MSPs) 'united to assert the supremacy of the parliament over the executive' (Ritchie and Dinwoodie 2001) and voted for free universal provision. The government in Scotland could afford to do this as the Barnett formula made available, untagged, its share of the large increases in spending on the NHS in England. Greer (2004: 88) reports one Scottish Labour politician being told 'angrily' by English colleagues that the higher funding of public services was 'because of the deprivation you have in Scotland, not so you can do things we can't do'.

Outcomes of Differences in Governance

By comparing the NHS in England and the national health systems in the devolved territories, we can begin to test hypotheses relating to the consequences of asymmetric devolution. There is a 'natural experiment' underway between the UK countries because, following devolution, each government has allocated a substantial increase of funding to its NHS and has pursued common policy objectives such as reducing hospital waiting times, but has chosen different models of governance as the means of achieving those common objectives. The first hypothesis is that 'small is beautiful' (Schumacher 2010); that is, that assuming equitable levels of funding per capita, the performance of the three national health systems in the devolved countries should outstrip that of the NHS in England. The reason for this is that the devolved countries of Scotland and Wales are of a size typically seen as the natural level for effective regional governance of health care: they are big enough to have an extensive range of health care services from basic to highly specialised, yet small enough to be capable of being well governed. In contrast, managing an organisation as big as the English NHS poses serious problems. The second hypothesis is that 'big is beautiful' in that it allows the development of a market large enough to support competition between providers, or one with effective sanctions for failure, or both; and that this advantage outweighs any disadvantages of its greater scale of operation. Hood (2007) has suggested that in federal systems that result in small jurisdictions (like Scotland, Wales, and Northern Ireland), in which governments are relationally close to service producers, it becomes difficult for them to abandon a model of Trust and Altruism. This can be an issue in much larger countries. For example, Barber (2006) emphasised the problems of 'producer capture' of government departments and regulators even in a country the size of England, and hence the importance of locating his Delivery Unit outside those departments and in the prime minister's office.

We report here a snapshot of the consequences associated with this 'natural experiment' using data (where these were available and comparable) for 2006, taken from Connolly et al. (2011), who pointed out that the northeast England region is a better comparator with the devolved countries than England as a whole in terms of size and socio-economic composition. Hence, the comparisons include the northeast of England alongside the four countries. This gives indicators over the period from 2000 to 2005, when the English NHS was subjected to the 'star ratings' regime with high-powered incentives and sanctions for failure to achieve government targets (a combination of the models of Naming and Shaming, and Targets and Terror), but the NHS in each devolved country was governed by Trust and Altruism, in which failure to achieve government targets was likely to be rewarded with extra resources. For the inputs, activity and crude productivity, given in figures 6.1 to 6.3, the values are standardised with England at 100. Figure 6.1 shows Scotland having the highest rates of inputs per capita in terms of spending, and hospital medical and dental staff and nursing staff. Figure 6.2 shows that Scotland did not, however, have the highest rates of activity, which raises questions over whether the extra funding of the NHS in Scotland was justified by its extra needs. Figures 6.3 and 6.4 show that rates of crude productivity in terms of rates of treatment of different types of hospital care by medical and dental, and nursing staff (where comparable data were available) were highest in northeast England. Figure 6.5 shows shorter hospital waiting times for inpatients and day cases in England and North East England in the period compared to Wales and Northern Ireland. Although no comparable data were available for waiting times in Scotland, Propper et al. (2008 and 2010) have shown that England also performed significantly better than Scotland in reducing waiting times over the period 1997/1998 to 2003/2004.

Supplementing Connolly et al.'s (2011) efficiency and productivity analysis, Sutherland and Coyle (2009) examined various dimensions of quality of care across the four territories at around the same time and found that the only systematic difference was in hospital waiting times. They found no evidence to suggest that the poorer performance of the devolved countries, compared with England, in terms of lower crude productivity of hospital staff and longer hospital waiting times, was offset by gains elsewhere. Hence, insofar as the limited available data allow, our conclusion is that the outcomes of the 'natural experiment' in the initial period following devolution in the UK suggest that the performance of the NHS in England was better in 2006 than in the devolved nations.

Discussion

The devolution settlement in the UK has resulted in a strongly 'asymmetric' form of devolution, marked by the lack of an English parliament, the fact that the NHS in England has different kinds of accountability from the three devolved countries and the absence of a federal system to agree on major health care system policies that should apply across the UK, such as those governing funding levels and user charges. If anything, current trends are moving the UK further away from developing federal-style mechanisms to agree policy fundamentals across the UK in favour of emphasising the policy autonomy of each country. For example, there are currently proposals to restrict voting rights in the Westminster parliament on policies that only affect England to MPs from England, and to give the Scottish parliament greater powers over taxation and the Welsh Assembly its first limited powers over taxation (Bevan 2014). These proposals can only gain further weight following the Scottish independence referendum which has heightened awareness of these issues. We have presented some limited evidence on the UK's natural experiment of asymmetric devolution over the period 2000 to 2006, which suggests that 'big was beautiful', to some extent, at least at that time: in that the large scale of the English NHS seems to have brought the advantage of enabling a form of governance with sanctions for failure, which appears to have been more important than the disadvantage of managing its much larger organisation. But we now know that, since 2006, the performance of the NHS in each devolved country in terms of hospital waiting times, in particular, has improved (Bevan et al. 2014). So, it looks as if scale alone is not the explanation for differences in governance and performance. So how do we explain changes in governance and performance over time across the four countries?

In 2000, a 'window of opportunity' for policy change opened in all four countries in the form of the combination of the demand crisis of the winter of 1999–2000 and the UK government's commitment to sustained unprecedented increases in NHS funding from 2000. Across the four countries in 2000, the Department of Health in England was best placed to formulate new policies to transform its NHS, as it had always been the driver of policies for the national health system in England that had largely applied throughout the UK before devolution. For the Blair government, it was vital that the massive increases in funding, most of which would be spent on the English NHS, did indeed deliver a transformation in its performance. Greer (2008) quoted a Labour special political adviser saying, in July 2006, that an unsatisfactory NHS will make the 'middle classes first vote against the NHS with their feet, and then with their votes'. So, in England, the combination of the 'NHS crisis' and the extra funding both required and justified tough new systems of accountability: on the Department of Health from the Treasury's PSA targets and the Prime Minister's Delivery Unit; and on providers from the Department of Health's regime of 'star ratings' that applied to English NHS provider organisations. The devolved governments, however, faced threats neither from middle class exit nor their voters: Hood and Dixon (2010) point out that the poorer performance of the devolved nations across their public services compared with England from 2000 to 2006 brought no political costs. Furthermore, the Treasury's PSA targets did not apply to Scotland and Wales, and seem to have had little impact on Northern Ireland. Nor were the devolved governments subject to scrutiny by the Prime Minister's Delivery Unit. So for each devolved government there was nothing like the same level of pressure to achieve a transformation in performance of its NHS in return for its extra funding. Furthermore they were presented with a second 'window of opportunity' for policy change: to use the opportunity of devolution to demonstrate their autonomy by *not* following English policies. Hence the attraction of sticking with the model of governance based on Trust and Altruism, which was popular with providers, and enabled each devolved government to show the benefits of devolution to its population in terms of not needing to follow the new English regime of 'star ratings'.

The problem with the 'star ratings' regime, however, was that it brought opprobrium on the government since it could be portrayed by the health professions and the public as punishing 'knights'. Barber (2007: 335) observes that Blair described such policies as akin to 'flogging' the system. As a result, Hood and Dixon (2010) found that the policies of strong performance management in England, which had delivered a transformation of waiting times, had brought no political benefits. So it seems that the policies of strong performance management could only be justified in response to the 'crisis' in 2000, and, as those policies proved to be effective and the sense of 'crisis' passed, so did their justification. From 2002, the government in England emphasised a shift to governance by Choice and Competition (Secretary of State for Health 2002). This has the attraction of, in principle, putting pressure on providers by an 'invisible hand' (Le Grand 2009) and thus avoids the government being seen to be 'flogging' the system. For the devolved countries, it looks as if the comparative success of the NHS in England in the first phase of devolution put pressure subsequently on their governments to match that performance (Timmins 2013). Given the history of the devolved countries, we would expect Scotland to have been best placed to do so. Steel and Cylus (2012: 113) observe that, in Scotland, in 2005, following '[u]nfavourable cross-border comparisons […] particularly on waiting times' and 'a change in Minister, a tougher and more sophisticated approach to performance management' with a 'new delivery group [... was] established within the Health Department to ensure a sharp focus on the delivery of key priorities and targets' (Steel and Cylus 2012: 114). The outcome has been that, since 2006, the performance of the NHS in Scotland in terms of hospital waiting times has improved so that it is now similar to that of the NHS in England; and although there have also been significant reductions in NHS waiting times in Wales and in Northern Ireland, their performance lags behind that of England and Scotland (Bevan et al. 2014). As the devolved governments faced no prospect of being penalised at the ballot box, the reasons for changing policies are likely to have been to remedy damage to their reputations or to show that they could match anything that could be achieved in England. Thus it can be argued that the 'Naming and Shaming' of hospitals within the English NHS from 2000 to 2005 improved its performance, which in effect 'named and shamed' the governments of the devolved countries to implement weaker forms of governance with sanctions, which resulted in improvements after 2006. This may reflect the likely long term dynamic between the four countries in terms of indirect and delayed cross-country policy and practice learning, but without any of the devolved countries wishing to admit to learning from England and vice versa.

Ham (2014) reviewed the different approaches to reforming the NHS in England that had been tried over the past 25 years to identify lessons for the future from evaluations of those reforms. He also analysed a set of high performing health care organisations in Sweden (Jönköping County Council), US (Intermountain Healthcare and the Virginia Mason Medical Center), New Zealand (Canterbury District Health Board), and England (Salford Royal NHS Foundation Trust). He concluded that high performance generally derives from quality improvement efforts developed from *within* organisations. By contrast, the various reforms to which the NHS in England had been subjected in the last 25 years were largely imposed from without as a political response directed at tackling poor performance. Yet, there does not appear to be any effective system of external incentives that can generate sustained internal incentives for high performance throughout systems of health care; this despite the hope that the model of choice and competition would do so (Le Grand 2007; Barber 2007). Indeed, there is little evidence of that model having been effective in the English NHS (Mays et al. 2011; Bevan and Skellern 2011). Long ago Hirschman (1970: 44) observed in relation to Nigeria 'the prolonged incapacity of the railroad administration to correct some of its more glaring inefficiencies, *in spite of active competition*' (emphasis in original) where the conditions for effective markets were much better satisfied than in health care. So perhaps the crucial lessons for the future are: greater realism in terms of what we can hope to achieve through imposing 'external' models of governance; greater recognition that such models can only aim to set the terms of quality assurance and a focus on seeking to minimise the harms they can cause and on creating the environment in which 'internal' initiatives for quality improvement can flourish. It looks as if those governing the NHS in Scotland have learned these lessons as shown by the continuity and consistency of their policies following the abolition of the purchaser/provider split in 2004. By contrast, in England, the increasing emphasis since 2002 on provider competition has been accompanied by successive wholesale structural reorganisations as governments have striven to make the NHS quasi-market work better. Timmins (2013: 6) observed that this has reached the point at which "'organisation, re-organisation and redisorganisation" almost might be dubbed the English NHS "disease"'.

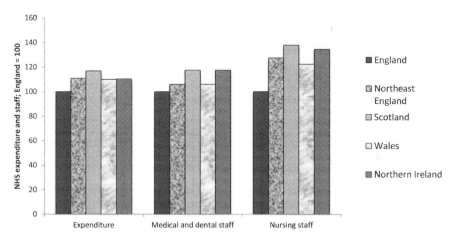

Figure 6.1   **NHS expenditure and staff in England, northeast England, Scotland, Wales, and Northern Ireland (2006) indexed to England = 100**

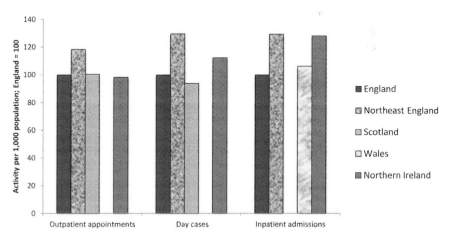

Figure 6.2   **Activity per 1,000 population in England, northeast England, Scotland, Wales, and Northern Ireland (2006) indexed to England = 100**

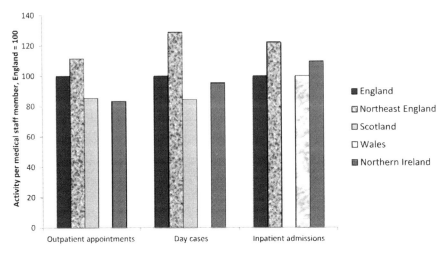

Figure 6.3   Activity per medical and dental staff member in England, northeast England, Scotland, Wales, and Northern Ireland (2006) indexed to England = 100

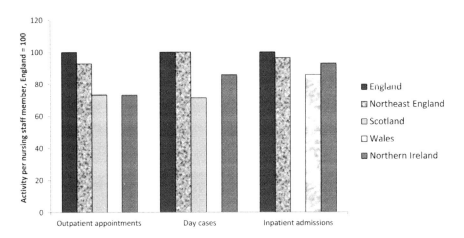

Figure 6.4   Activity per nursing staff member in England, northeast England, Scotland, Wales, and Northern Ireland (2006) indexed to England = 100

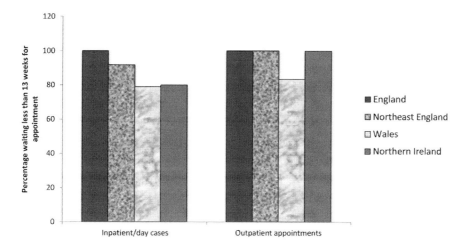

Figure 6.5   **Percentage of the population waiting less than 13 weeks for inpatient or day case admission or outpatient appointment in England, northeast England, Wales, and Northern Ireland, March 2008**

Chapter 7

European Union

Scott L. Greer

Introduction

The European Union (EU) is in the midst of a period of extraordinary turbulence and constitutional creativity. All sorts of options are open – from the failure of its complex new structures to the creation of a new kind of EU that essentially determines member state priorities and spending. For decades, the EU has been easy to characterise for its 'constitutional asymmetry' in which its design favours market-making deregulation and reregulation over social policy (Scharpf 2002). This is certainly case for pharmaceuticals and medical devices. Public health and health care services fit neatly into this schema, with the EU deregulating access to health care by obliging it to comply with the free movement and competition rules of the European market while reregulating, with greater or lesser success, to promote public health and encouraging health policy change in member states.

As ever with meaningful EU health policies, the policies discussed here that matter most were not made with health in mind or a health justification in the enumerated powers of the EU. Rather, the EU is at heart an economic creature, a common market and single currency, and health is a very expensive and complex sector with which it must contend. To study the EU's health policy is to study a happy story of minor public health interventions. To study the rest of the EU in health is to watch the incorporation of health into other areas of law and policy where other actors with other priorities engage with the protectionism and expense they see in health.

Institutional Description

The European Union has grown somewhat haphazardly, in a process of sedimentation and political change that resembles the process that created many modern federations but set atop much more institutionalised and diverse states. It began with three specialist communities among six Western European nations (France, Germany, Luxembourg, Belgium, the Netherlands, and Italy) for common management of coal and steel, then atomic energy and a common internal market. From the relatively humble beginnings of a coal and steel community in post-war Europe, it has grown to encompass 28 member states, constitute a larger population than the United States and a larger economy than China, and an enormous body of shared law known as the *acquis communitaire* (Hix 2005; Rose 2013).

While the geopolitics of Cold War and the post-Cold War Europe undoubtedly made European integration possible and desirable, the structure of the EU itself has made a significant contribution to European integration. The EU's basic structure has four components (Greer 2009c). The first is the European Commission, which has two roles: as the executive of the European Union and as the initiator of legislative proposals. Its political heads – commissioners – are appointed by member states and have some oversight from the European parliament. The rest of the Commission is a fairly classic bureaucracy, with departments (directorates-general) for specific issues, staffed by permanent civil servants. Combining executive functions and the right of legislative proposal concentrates quite a lot of energy and strategic manoeuvrability in the Commission, which can encourage lobbies and member states to give it authorisation to pursue a given policy direction. Its budget and staff are small, but quite a lot of the budget provides grants for networking, research, and 'civil society' activities that frequently call for more EU action, while its staff has almost no actual responsibilities for programme implementation and can concentrate on policy formulation and promotion. There are a variety of theories suggesting that Commission activism and manipulation are behind the growth of EU health policy (Martinsen 2009; Heard-Laureate 2013). In a sense, this is always true in the EU, but it is important to counterbalance this with the Commission's legal and political dependence on authorisation (Page 2012) from member states (and the central services of the Commission itself): Commission officials can always point to the member state or parliament resolution permitting their project. Perhaps the best way to put it is that the Commission acts with authorisation, but authorisation affords it a great deal of discretion that it usually uses to promote European integration.

The next two branches of the EU are representative, legislative organs. The Council is where member states meet to amend and decide on legislation. It is made up of the relevant ministers from member states, so the Employment and Social Policy Council is made up, depending on the topic, of labour, health, and social affairs ministers, and the Economic and Financial Council is made up of finance ministers. Given this disaggregation, the EU has a variety of coordinating mechanisms to create some coherence between Councils, including an elected president, a six-month presidency that rotates between member states, and coordination within member states and the Commission. The European Council is the meeting of the heads of state of the EU, which has tremendous political force (and the Council of Europe is a wholly separate organisation that shares the EU flag). The European parliament is directly elected and increasingly powerful; it has gained power and competency, as well as become an increasingly attractive target for lobbyists, but it still tends to be a 'second-order' elected body, which voters use to express discontent rather than vote for changes or parties. The importance of the Council and the parliament vary with voting procedures, which are laid out in the treaty and vary by policy area.

The Court of Justice of the European Union (CJEU) is the final part of the core EU institutions. Over the decades, it has taken on a major role in law and policy, notably by enunciating the doctrines of 'direct effect' and 'supremacy'. These mean, respectively, that EU law is law regardless of whether member states have implemented it; and that EU law trumps member state law (though a few member state constitutional courts, such as the German, try to demarcate core areas of democratic national sovereignty over which EU law is not supreme). The CJEU is the most powerful supranational court in history (Stone Sweet 2005) and it has shaped the EU (Burley and Mattli 1993; Alter 1998; Vauchez 2013). Without the CJEU, and EU law, it is hard to imagine the EU that we have today. Notably, it is possible to invoke EU law in member state courts, which can then refer questions that they see as being of EU law to the CJEU. In the case of health, for example, this mean that individual litigants could sue in member state courts for access to health care abroad, the member state courts could refer the question to the CJEU, and the CJEU could hand down decisions applying EU law to health care issues that the member states never sought to have under EU jurisdiction (see below) (Kelemen 2011).

Finally, there is an extra institution whose tremendous power has been visible since the start of the 2008 financial crisis: the European Central Bank (ECB), the central bank of the Eurozone. Continuing the trend throughout the creation of the monetary union, German preferences were dominant (Dyson and Featherstone 1999), and German policymakers preferred a central bank that would be strictly rule-governed, not accountable to politicians, and strongly anti-inflation.[1] The problem is that, once the sovereign debt crisis hit the Eurozone, autonomy trumped rigidity in the ECB's behaviour – limited political accountability meant that the ECB could step outside its rigid rules to take decisions that were by no means Keynesian but did keep the Eurozone banking system operational and show the broad range of ECB discretion. The ECB's actions, which made manifest the latent ECB-centrism of Eurozone governance (Dyson 2001), are discussed in more detail below.

---

1 It is facile to say Germans have a cultural horror of inflation, and silly to attribute German inflation aversion to interwar inflation, which had more to do with French occupation of the Ruhr than bad central banking (Maier 1975). Germany is a manufacturing export economy, and in such economies inflation and bubbles do not play the positive role that they can in other European and world economies – they tend instead to threaten export competitiveness. German experience of Keynesian expansion is consequently inflation without additional growth, which naturally gives German policymakers a different orientation than policymakers from countries such as the US or UK where easy money more effectively stimulates the economy (Hall 2012). Dyson and Featherstone give a lucid account of the ordoliberal thinking this produced (Dyson and Featherstone 1999) and which converted useful rules of thumb for export economies into an ostensibly universal economic philosophy (not a problem unique to German thought). It is worth noting that this German perspective seems to be largely elite; Eurobarometer suggests that the German mass public does *not* have much of an aversion to inflation compared to other Europeans (LeMay-Bouchet and Rommerskirchen 2014).

The interlocking effects of these institutions are dramatic and encourage European integration. In the terms of art of European integration, the result is the neo-functionalist expansion of a regulatory state (Greer 2006; Haas 1958; Majone 1996). Neofunctionalism refers to a theory of European integration that suggests activity in one area 'spills over' into another area – for example, the activity of the CJEU in health spills over into Commission, lobby, and member state activity on health policy in Brussels (Greer 2012b). It is also a 'regulatory state': the EU has very little money and very few staff relative to what it does, but it has a powerful legal system. It therefore relies on deregulation and reregulation as its nearly exclusive policy tools. That makes it in a sense a very cheap organisation – the Commission's bureaucracy is supplemented by member state officials at every stage, and member states and courts bear the costs of implementing and compensating losers (Page 2001). Put together, this produces a very distinctive form of forward momentum, in which the Commission or Court (or sometimes member states) set up a problem to which the solution always seems to be more European Union action. It is also a system that in many ways is less comparable to member states than it is to the United States. Its legalism, vast lobbying system, fragmentation and complexity all give it characteristics more akin to American than to French or German or UK politics (Mahoney 2008; Kelemen 2012).

For social policy purposes, what this all cumulates into is a 'constitutional asymmetry' in the EU: market-making is easy, compensating for the effects of markets is hard (Scharpf 2002). The EU has extremely limited ability to redistribute between people or territories. As a regulatory state, the EU has a powerful legal system but a budget that pales in comparison to health – the whole EU budget, including agriculture and structural funds (aid to poorer areas) is capped around 1 per cent of the EU gross domestic product (GDP), while according to the Organization for Economic Cooperation and Development (OECD), the average health expenditure as a percentage of GDP among the EU member states was 9 per cent in 2012. European Union money gets attention and helps to strengthen networks and European debates, but it does not compare to the expenditure on health or redistribution in member states. Comparing EU policies to member state policies is always tricky because member state policies can be and frequently are redistributive and direct in ways that regulatory EU policies are not (Dehousse 1994). What passes for social policy in the EU is more often than not more regulation, e.g., a Working Time Directive that limits the hours people can work, or research and networking expenditures leading up to exhortation, as with the Social Investment Package, which amounts to hundreds of well-researched pages of advice to member states on how they might spend far more money than the EU will ever have.[2]

Furthermore, the CJEU introduces its own views; it is common in EU legal circles to speak of the treaties as constitutional law, and the 'four freedoms' as

---

2   http://ec.europa.eu/social/main.jsp?catId=1044&langId=en&newsId=1807&more Documents=yes&tableName=news.

constitutional principles of the EU. These four freedoms are not those of Franklin Delano Roosevelt,[3] but rather those of the internal market: freedom of movement of goods, capital, services and people. The effect is that in EU law a policy that interferes with the four freedoms needs a very good justification in the eyes of the CJEU, while it is relatively hard to challenge liberalising law under EU law.

Economic Description

The European Union is a large closed economy, roughly in trade balance with the rest of the world, that is made up of small states with open economies and in many cases serious imbalances.[4] It also, notably, has a currency union (and rules associated with the currency union that apply to states outside the common currency). As has been much noted since the first steps toward monetary integration, and as has become inescapable since the financial crisis of 2008, there are fundamental instabilities in the Eurozone.

The effect of entering a currency union without any fiscal union (redistribution between people or territories) and without a shared banking regulatory structure has become very visible since the launch of the Euro. The financial sector crash of 2008 triggered a variety of different problems across Europe. Most states responded in essentially Keynesian ways until 2010, which seems to have broken the fall of the markets, but they also saw serious vulnerabilities exposed.

Contrary to the many moral tales being told, there was no one kind of European crisis (Bastasin 2012 is probably the best one-volume account to early 2012). The list of countries, and their complexities, is long, and few stories place blame in one place, but all too often they are obscured by national stereotypes, political prejudgement, and misplaced morality. The common denominator was the threat of a sovereign debt crisis, starting in 2010 with the discovery of Greece's situation and extending through the time of writing. Whatever the combination of revenue shock, assumption of private banks' losses, and pre-existing fiscal vulnerability, the effect was to leave bond markets concerned about governments' creditworthiness. Starting with Greece, countries that could not reliably roll over their public sector debt entered into a form of receivership with the 'Troika' of ECB, Commission and IMF – an ad hoc arrangement with no basis in the EU treaties or, for that matter, in the theory of central banking. The relationships, formally known as Economic Adjustment Programmes (EAPs) kicked off a period of constitutional innovation in the EU whose end, or consequences, we have yet to see.

Member states had been signed up since Maastricht to a 'Stability and Growth Pact' (SGP) that was intended to make sure member state laxity would not interfere with the stability and economic success of the whole Eurozone. The SGP

---

3   Freedom of speech, freedom of worship, freedom from want, and freedom from fear.

4   A point made and explored by Wolfgang Muenchau: 'Europe's tragic small-country mindset', *Financial Times* 13 June 2010.

extended Euro accession targets into law for Eurozone countries. This means that states trying to join the Eurozone, or in the Eurozone, had to hit numerical targets including a maximum 3 per cent budget deficit and 60 per cent debt to GDP limit. The SGP turned these targets into law and arranged to fine member states that breached them. Fairly quickly, France violated the SGP and Germany began to come close – and worse, both member states had reasonable arguments for their policy decisions. The result was a 2005 'softening' of the SGP. The 2005 reforms did indeed reduce the automaticity of the SGP process, but also constructed a substantial apparatus of 'soft' oversight over member state finances, including constant dialogues between finance ministries and the Directorate General (DG) Economic and Financial Affairs (ECFIN), and between member state statisticians and the EU's statistics agency EUROSTAT. In principle, this eased the rules to reflect reality (and admit Keynesian arguments), and built a large new policy review process to gather information about member state policies in more detail (Schelkle 2006, 2009).

The crisis created an appetite for more determined enforcement of a rigid SGP in order to make sure there was no future equivalent to Greece, or the macroeconomic imbalances of many EU member states. Strengthening the SGP means changing the voting rules of the Council to make it harder to avoid punishing member states that deviate, and also changing the process of managing SGP violations, thereby reducing the discretion of the Commission. Reaching into member state policymaking means several things: creating tough new standards for independent statistical agencies, asking (in the TSCG) for member states to entrench SGP targets in their budgets, rather like states in the US, and above all creating a large process known as the European semester, parallel to a Macroeconomic Imbalances Procedure, in which the Commission (functionally, DG ECFIN) scrutinises member state budgets *on a shared schedule, and before they are presented to member state legislatures*. In other words, member state governments' accountability to each other, as personified in the Commission, is antecedent to their accountability to their own legislatures – since accountability to domestic voters had patently failed to ward off a European crisis in 2010. It turns DG ECFIN into a kind of European finance ministry. It is a special kind of finance ministry, though – one tasked not with making the complex decisions necessary to ensure re-election, but rather dedicated to making elected governments comply with the SGP and pursue the kinds of budget and microeconomic policies conducive to such discipline. The UK and Czech Republic refused to accede to the Fiscal Compact, which means that it is technically an intergovernmental agreement serviced by the Commission (insofar as the European Semester and Macroeconomic Imbalances Procedure provide the data) that further entrenches the new fiscal rigor of EU law and also affords signatories access to a new bailout fund called the European Stability Mechanism.

While books and articles about austerity and crisis in European welfare state go back at least 30 years now, the current crisis is remarkable – and the expansion of the EU's claim to a role in member state policymaking is also remarkable.

While there are major questions about every component of the EU's actions – from the compromised position of the ECB to the cobbled-together Troika and its problems to the effectiveness of the new fiscal governance architecture – it is clear that the EU institutions, particularly the ECB and Commission, have been given a major new role in every aspect of member state domestic policy. And given that health is very expensive – both in terms of health care expenditure and in terms of the costs to business of public health policies – it is no surprise that it is suddenly the focus of much EU activity.

Political and Policy Analysis: What Did This Mean for Health?

The combination of the EU's longstanding constitutional asymmetry with the new economic governance system means that there are now three faces to European Union health policy (for accounts, see Greer 2013b, forthcoming). This section treats them in ascending order of likely importance, and duration of their impact on health in the EU. What should become clear is that EU policies focused on the health sector are almost always less important than EU policies from some other sector, with stronger treaty bases and greater elective affinity with the basic political structures of a neo-functionalist regulatory state. This should not be surprising in light of the basic workings of the EU.

Health Policies

The first is its enumerated public health powers, contained most notably in Article 168 of its constitutive Treaty on the Functioning of the European Union. EU health policy has a long history, dating back to the 1980s, with the Europe Against Cancer programme agreed by the European Council (Briatte 2013; Trubek et al. 2011). There are a number of books spanning the wide range of EU health policies (Steffen 2005; 'European Union Public Health Policies: Regional and Global Perspectives' 2013; and parts of Mossialos et al. 2010). Broadly, they find that the effect of the EU is limited. Sometimes it is deep but narrow, as in the Europeanisation of blood and blood products regulation (Farrell 2005). Sometimes it is broad but very shallow, as in the commitment of the EU to pursue a high level of human health in all its endeavours (Koivusalo 2010), a commitment not at all visible in the EAPs or fiscal governance (Karanikolos et al. 2013).

These activities are as diverse as health policy, from communicable disease control to structural funds for healthcare facilities to workshops on patient safety to health research to work on protocols for electronic patient information sharing. What they have in common is two kinds of limitations. First, there are the structural limitations of the European regulatory state. The EU cannot provide much by way of actual services; Commission staff lack expertise and are busy, and the budget is nowhere near adequate to actually supply services (even if they are transferred to an agency, a classic technique for increasing the budget).

Second there is the structural limitation that Article 168, the health policy article, is a weak treaty base. It not only limits EU activity outside blood and organ regulation to strictly supporting measures, but also makes it clear (since the Lisbon Treaty) that the organisation and finance of health care systems is up to member states.

What should stand out about EU health policy (Article 168 – justified policies) is actually the amount that it gets done despite a tiny budget and derisory legal authority. The reason is one well rehearsed in studies of European Union governance: the EU, by financing European networks and research, can prime the pump for both more member state action, and more EU action. In communicable disease control, for example, an increasing number of EU projects created networks and projects across Europe that could be converted into a European agency when a variety of crises showed the weakness of communicable disease control in most states (Greer 2012a). Likewise, investment in the apparently benign topic of Health Technology Assessment (HTA) (which infuriates industries who depend on selling health technologies) led almost inexorably to inclusion of HTA and a network of agencies in the Directive on Patient Mobility (Loblova and Greer, forthcoming). It is easy to be dismissive of endless EU projects, and some do indeed have lamentable results (Ernst et al. 2010; Charlesworth et al. 2011), but they create networks and demand for further European integration as well as, in many cases, specialist capacity and data that would not otherwise exist (Steffen 2012). In short, the EU has spent its small health budget and used its small public health in ways that have contributed to greater awareness and capacity in public health issues and low salience areas of health care policy, despite the fact that networks and research are at best uncertain ways to change member state policy.

Internal Market Policies

The second face is the market-making face of the EU. The EU was rightly known for decades as the 'Common Market'; while the old coal and steel and atomic energy communities declined with their industries, the mechanisms of integration detailed above turned the common market into a political triumph of free markets and European integration.

Some areas of health care were textbook cases of spillover. In pharmaceuticals the relationship between increasingly networked European regulators, Commission entrepreneurs, and multinational drug companies led to an increasingly European market access regime for medicines that is partially extended to medical devices (Hauray 2006, 2013; Greenwood 2003; Permanand 2006). European integration seems to advance, increasingly just an ordinary policy issue on which those who speak for payers, those who speak for generic or branded firms, and those who regard drugs as an industrial policy issue have their arguments at an EU level.

Second, there are health care services. It should not have been any surprise that the EU legal machine eventually turned to health care. A legal system that prized the four freedoms and whose top court had made it clear that health care was a service (Lawson 1994) was one that would see an eventual bid for application of internal market law to the workings of health care systems through its extensive decentralised enforcement. That is exactly what happened: in 1998 the European Court of Justice decided two cases, Kohll and Decker, that created EU health care law and spawned a substantial legal and policy literature (McKee, Mossialos, and Baeten 2002a, 2002b; Mossialos et al. 2010; Busse, Wismar, and Berman 2002; Hancher and Sauter 2012; van de Gronden 2008; Van De Gronden et al. 2011; Greer 2009c; Lamping 2005; Martinsen 2005; Martinsen and Vrangbaek 2008; Hervey and McHale 2004; Hervey 2011) as well as much litigation and policy activity leading up to a directive on cross-border patient mobility that was to be at least formally implemented in 2012.

It is wrong to see a directive as bringing 'legal stability', of course. Passing a law has effects well known to scholars of law and society, none of which would stop further European activity. It educates policy advocates, bureaucrats, and lobbyists of all sorts; it gives judges firmer ground on which to make more judgements; and it validates legal challenges. Both American and EU evidence, discussed extensively by Kelemen, and the composition of the new EU law suggest that it will produce more legal activity, not more legal stability (Greer 2013a; Kelemen 2011).

Looking only at health care services law might leave the impression that EU law has been wholly deregulatory, even 'neoliberal'. There are two reasons why this is not entirely the case. First, the actual effects on health care systems are rather limited by the simple fact that patients do not want to exercise their right to free movement under internal market and have good reason to use the older social security coordination mechanisms when they do (Glinos 2012). It was never about the patients (Greer 2008); it was about European integration. Without lobbies willing to use EU legal challenges in pursuit of business objectives (Greer and Rauscher 2011; Greer 2009a), it was relatively easy to come to a pragmatic bargain (if one with administrative costs) between the claims of EU law and the operation of health systems. The CJEU, meanwhile, has been increasingly deferential to national health systems, in part as it learns just how complex health really is (Hatzopoulos and Hervey 2012; Hancher and Sauter 2012).

Second, it is wrong to focus just on the relationship between health care services and internal market law. The EU's internal market affects public health in many ways, and the benefits from its environmental laws, for example, might have had a tremendous effect on morbidity and mortality (Jordan and Adelle 2013). The substantial differences between the EU and United States approaches to endocrine disruptors, for example, could have effects on population health, happiness, and productivity for decades (balancing demonstrably convenient plastics for the US against potentially much healthier lives for Europeans). Likewise, its health and safety legislation, and its consumer protection laws, have often times disappointed advocates but nonetheless made advances over the status quo ante in many member states (Studlar 2012; Kurzer 2012; Cisneros Ornberg 2012).

Economic and Fiscal Governance

The third and newest face of the EU in health is the economic governance mechanism detailed above. In the short term, it means above all the economic adjustment programmes for Cyprus, Greece, Ireland, and Portugal, as well as the EU's less dramatic interventions into troubled non-Eurozone states such as Latvia and Hungary. The EAPs are filled with detailed health policy recommendations (Fahy 2012) and a sort of learning is even visible as the second Greek EAP (after the failure of the first) included far more detailed prescriptions for Greece's very corrupt health system (Greer 2013c). The Troika has taken onto itself reforms of these countries' health systems every bit as thoroughgoing as its reforms of their labour laws and banking systems. To read the EAPs is to read a very long set of detailed policy conditionalities – which were unlikely to be fulfilled, and are not all being fulfilled, but which nonetheless breach a frontier between the EU and member states.

In the longer term, it means fiscal governance will impinge on member state policymaking, and the Commission–member state dialogues are already making that clear with detailed recommendations to all member states (Jarman and Greer 2013). In principle, the SGP has been conditioning the budgeting of all EU states for 20 years, and there are cases in which it has indeed affected the structure of health expenditure through expenditure cuts, reforms, or reorganisation (as in Italy and Spain in the 1990s). But the ferocity of bond markets, and the effort to constitute equally ferocious but more nuanced implementation mechanisms within the fiscal governance system, have given it a new cast. While member states are responsible under the SGP for the quality of their statistics and their fiscal balance (should the fiscal governance architecture be enforced and credible), the outworkings of that architecture immediately enter the health policy world for one reason: health care is so costly. On one hand, the endless battle between public health and short-term economic interests is joined on a new front as labour market and other member state regulations justified (spuriously or not) on grounds of health are critiqued in the European Semester as forms of inefficiency that impede growth. On the other hand, the vast expenditure of member state health systems means that they are automatic targets for reform plans in the Semester. Health systems are just that expensive.

Conclusion

In the early 1990s, it was common to point to the weakness of the EU treaty bases on health as evidence that the EU institutions neither had nor wanted health policy powers and responsibilities. In a sense, that was right; member states have repeatedly amended the treaties to enable the kinds of health policies that constitute the first face of EU health policy – meliorist, integrative, technical, and benign. But that has never been the core of EU health policies; those were always to be found in the politics and law around the internal market and latterly the fiscal governance mechanisms. The constitutional asymmetry toward deregulation and market making rather than social policy has long been known; the credibility and impact of a new constitutional asymmetry towards SGP compliance rather than, possibly, growth or social investment is yet to be seen.

In the terms of this book, the European Union's structure and current policies might be good in theory for health policy – if we could actually imagine a plausible world in which the current diverse states of the EU could find a way to move their economies back into structural balance, with some level of economic growth, and act according to the rules of the fiscal compact. Given the implausibility of this vision for the actually existing economies of Western Europe, and the suitability of the rules for only a few high – value export economies, the judgement on the EU is negative. The fact that the credibility of the reformed SGP, and therefore of the whole machinery of fiscal governance, is not yet established should not be too cheering; unenforced problematic law is not a good outcome, even if that is better than rigorous enforcement.

Is the EU experience evidence about problems with federalism at large? No – rather it suggests the usefulness of the thesis that the character and institutions of a federal polity are crucial to its sustainability and innovation. The European Union is in many ways imitating the worst aspects of federations with regard to health and social policy. If the basic rule of fiscal federalism is that activities should be conducted at the lowest level that permits the internalisation of externalities (Wetzel 2001; Adolph, Greer, and Massard da Fonseca 2012), then the EU is violating a very sensible rule by pooling risk at a low level (member states) while regulating, without interterritorial or interpersonal redistribution, at a very high level. The logic of insurance would suggest a redistributive EU in some form, rather than rules seemingly designed to make poorer member states make smaller social investments forever in a kind of replay of the processes that kept the American South in its position of relative underdevelopment (for which see Bensel and Sanders 1990).

Rather, the EU experience suggests that the impact of decentralisation depends on institutional factors (Greer 2009b). While the intergovernmental-into-federal nature of the EU means that its specific characteristics and policies are somewhat eccentric, the basic situation resembles nothing so much as the growth of federal power in the United States, with its combination of judicialisation (Kelemen 2011), acceptance of territorial inequality, and demand that state and local governments provide substantial funding (Rodden 2005).

Beyond those peculiarities, it is worth focusing on one distinctive European situation (which if it has any analogue, is the relationship between American federal states and their local governments): the combination of high-level fiscal oversight, with increasing intrusion into policy areas such as health. In most federations, the central government must buy its way into an area where it has very limited powers. In the EU, the innovation of its fiscal governance architecture is that it claims to have a say, but does not pay. It is an extension of the European regulatory state *par excellence*, focusing on law and its enforcement as the only tool, even if it has no credible way to compensate losers (as seen in the exhortations of the Social Investment Package, all very sensible but all directed at the member states). Likewise, an academic focus on 'social investment' is at best a contribution to a better policy debate, since advising member states on how they might spend money is weirdly beside the point when they are mostly trying to constrain expenditures under the erratic dual discipline of the Commission and bond markets. This is a mismatch in powers and responsibilities far beyond most other federations, and its effect on health is a combination of top-down priorities unmatched by money or expertise, and overall budgetary squeezes and anti-Keynesian frameworks whose intellectual framework is wholly doubtful (Greer, forthcoming). It is also not clear that the EU fiscal governance regime will work on its own terms: by prompting actions and punishing shirking states, or by promoting growth. It remains to be seen whether the political will exists to reform in line with the European Semester or punish states that violate the SGP. If the political will does not exist, as it did not in 2005, the EU could end up with a large, invasive fiscal policy regime that is not credible.

The question now is whether the EU must necessarily be a problem for health, social policy, redistribution, social democracy and for that matter any compensation to the losers of the world economy. The lack of any redistribution, whether between people, generations, or territories, is easy to take as a fact of European life, but it is still possible to imagine policies that would allow the EU to escape its current trap of viewing essentially every policy as interterritorial redistribution, with all the according national stereotypes and scapegoating. A European basic income, for example, might appeal to all member states and separate the idea of solidarity from indiscriminate bailouts. While such ideas are not on the current policy agenda, the combination of invasive fiscal policymaking, economic stagnation, disillusionment with politics and nationalism are so poisonous, unstable, and undesirable that some more creativity might be the only way out of a bad situation.

Chapter 8
Canada

Katherine Fierlbeck and Howard A. Palley

Introduction

Given that Canada is one of the most decentralised of all federal states within the *Organisation for Economic Cooperation and Development* (OECD), it is noteworthy that one can discuss the idea of a discrete Canadian health care 'system' at all. Despite the fact that Canadian provinces have both the formal constitutional authority and considerable financial ability to determine health care systems at the level of the provinces, there has been remarkable consistency in overall health care design across all of Canada's provinces and territories. This may, however, be changing. The first section of this chapter explains why Canada's 13 health care systems are so homogenous notwithstanding the exceptional level of decentralisation that characterised Canadian federalism in the twentieth century. The second section explains why, despite this historical homogeneity, a far more fragmented health care landscape is emerging. The third section addresses the consequences of such a shift, and examines some of the political actions being undertaken in response.

Establishing and Maintaining National Policy Coherence in an Exceptionally Decentralised Federalism

Determining the level of decentralisation in any federal state depends upon which indicators one chooses to employ. Nonetheless, Canada is usually seen as a highly decentralised state in overarching terms. If one considers the relative level of tax revenues collected by central (as opposed to substate) governments, Canada (at 47.2 per cent) is lower than the United States (54.2 per cent), Germany (65.0 per cent), Spain, and Australia (74.8 per cent); and if one examines intergovernmental transfers as a percentage of substate revenue, Canada (at 12.9 per cent) is again lower than almost all OECD states, including the United States (25.6 per cent), Germany (43.8 per cent), Australia (45.6 per cent), and Spain (72.8 per cent). (Watts 2008: 102, 105) On an aggregative 20-point scale measuring relative levels of decentralisation, Canada (at 16.5) again surpasses the United States (14.5), Switzerland (14.0), Germany (12.0), Australia (12.0), and Spain (10.5) (Requejo 2010: 287; Marchildon 2013: 180; Atkinson et al. 2013: 11–12).

Like constitutional authority over taxation, legal jurisdiction over health in Canada is also situated firmly in a constitutional agreement dating to 1867. In both cases, however, interpretation and circumstance have heavily shaped the nature of contemporary practice. Section 92 of the Canadian Constitution gives authority over 'the Establishment, Maintenance, and Management of Hospitals, Asylums, Charities, and Eleemosynary Institutions' to the provinces, as well as jurisdiction over matters of a 'mere local and private nature'. Key aspects of health care governance such as regulation of health insurance and the health professions later developed from interpretations of the provinces' authority over 'property and civil rights'. Notwithstanding later judicial interpretations that willed specific areas of federal and provincial jurisdiction into 'watertight compartments', the reality of Canadian federalism has been that the national government in Ottawa can claim not only its own powers of taxation, but also residual powers which permit it to engage in areas not explicitly noted as resting under provincial jurisdiction. The federal authority over the regulation of 'noxious substances' has become very pertinent with the increasing utilisation of pharmaceuticals and blood products in contemporary health care; and, while Ottawa is generally considered to be directly responsible for the health care of discrete groups such as the military, the Royal Canadian Mounted Police, aboriginals, immigrants, and convicts in federal penitentiaries, and discrete circumstances such as control of pandemics, there has been increasing concern by the provinces that certain aspects of health-related costs for some of these groups are increasingly offloaded to the provincial governments.

It is useful to keep in mind that, until the middle of the twentieth century, the Canadian health care system was remarkably similar to that of the United States: both were characterised by private health care providers charging on a fee-for-service basis and complemented by a nascent system of private health insurance. Beginning in 1957, however, Canada's federal government in Ottawa began to offer shared-cost funding to provinces willing to establish publicly-insured physician, diagnostic, and hospital services. The financial incentive to the provinces was a very attractive one, and by 1972 all provinces had accepted Ottawa's framework for health care provision, resulting in a national health care 'system' that was quite distinctive from its southern neighbour.

The political explanation for this divergence between the two countries is complex, but several factors can be distinguished. The initial attempt to construct a coherent system of public health care in Canada was grounded in the larger post-war project of nation-building. The most prominent figure in this endeavour was Leonard Marsh, who had developed his administrative expertise in Britain under the direction of Sir William Beveridge, architect of Britain's National Health Service. The need for national presence in the development of a modern welfare state was especially pressing for Canada, given the considerable disparity in the size and the capacity of each of the provinces. At the end of World War II, many of the smaller units simply did not have the fiscal capacity or policy expertise to facilitate the development of an effective and coherent system of social programming. The disparity in size between substate units also underscored another dangerous reality for the country: as Watts (2008) has noted, federal systems characterised by considerable levels of disparity are much more likely to manifest signs of tension and instability. In Canada, where a considerable proportion of the population lived in two of the (then) 12 political jurisdictions, this was a matter of some concern.

Exacerbating the problem was the fact that one of these two provinces, Quebec, was a culturally-distinct region with a long history of political grievances. By the 1960s a potent nationalist presence had emerged, destabilising the country even more. The celebration of Canada's centenary in 1967 created tensions between Canadian pan-nationalism and the nationalism of Quebec. Nevertheless, the fiscal federalism which followed the 1957 Hospital Insurance and Diagnostic Services Act and the 1967 Medical Care Act provided significant oversight functions at the national level. As Bégin (1984) noted, 'Ottawa had the power to define what a hospital or other health institution was, and who was a resident of a province. It calculated costs and defined who was to be included in the bilateral accords. It had extensive powers of regulation and interpretation. The agreements were exceptionally detailed and precise' (55). It was, nonetheless, not a well-defined national plan but rather the sum of 10 provincial plans. This situation was to change significantly with the 1977 Established Programs Financing Act, which stipulated that two thirds of a fixed federal contribution would go to health and the rest to post-secondary education. It also transferred 'tax points' to the provinces. While federal funding was now limited in health, the provinces could use this money as they saw fit, with little federal oversight. As Bégin (1984) notes:

> The "army" of federal civil servants charged with auditing provincial bills and repaying half had been dismantled. The "army" had been reduced to twelve people! All of a sudden the Regulations of the 1957 and 1967 laws were no longer in effect. Among other things, this meant that the user fees were *no longer prohibited – since they were no longer penalized – therefore they were allowed*. No one neither the public nor the health milieu, had known of this procedure, which had been quietly been an administrative practice. Only a few public servants, and the ministers at the time, knew about it [... T]he five basic conditions [of the 1967 and 1977 Acts] still theoretically applied, even though they no longer had any relation to concrete reality and were essentially useless since there application was no longer regulated or sanctioned. (66–7; original emphasis)

By the 1980s Canadian health care had become quite distinct from that of the United States. The iconic status of public health care was not immediately recognised by the long-governing Liberal administration in Ottawa (Bégin 2002); but when the immense public affection for the Canadian health care 'system' was understood, the federal government capitalised on this sentiment by reinventing itself as the protector of public health care. The federal–provincial agreement on funding public health insurance became codified in a very public manner in 1984 with the articulation of the Canada Health Act, which specified precisely which conditions provinces would have to honour in order to receive an already-diminishing level of federal funding. The Canada Health Act (CHA) of 1984 sought to restate and clarify the social rights of national citizenship with regard to health care.

In sum, Canada's constitutional framework clearly favoured the decentralised development of health systems at the provincial level. This was exacerbated by provincial politics, and especially Quebec nationalism. Because of Canada's specific political challenges, however, the federal government attempted, for over five decades, to shape provincial policy across regions into a coherent and compatible national 'system' of health care. But by the late 1980s the impact of global forces on the Canadian economy became an increasingly prominent concern to decision makers at the national level, and issues of international competitiveness began to exert a counterforce to the nation-building project of the Canadian state. Other perspectives on the advocacy of commercial activities within provincial health systems reflect the political acceptance of some political leadership of a 'business' or 'private' corporate model. This was openly advocated by former minister of health and wellness, Ron Liepert, in Alberta, who advocated a fixed funding model under which seniors who could no longer care for themselves would receive limited funding and would have to turn to the private market to locate a for-profit or not-for-profit facility or a supportive community-based living space. Under this proposed arrangement, seniors would receive a provincially-provided 'flat rate' and could shop around for chronic care services. If the flat rate was not comprehensive enough they would need to pay additional amounts out-of-pocket. In advocating for this model, Liepert noted: 'Quite frankly, it's a business. And the numbers haven't justified the business case. What we want to do is open some of that up' (Palley, Pomey, and Adams 2012: 128). While this proposal would have opened up a market for commercial groups, it would have also lowered the level of provincial obligation to provide necessary services to the poor and frail elderly.

The tension between the competing ideals of Canadian nationalism (with public health care as a cornerstone) and economic prosperity (based upon international trade, and the presentation of health service innovation as a commercial activity) were brought into sharp focus in the 1987 election, when the national Conservative party began to define itself as the force which could facilitate Canada's competitive entry into global markets. The era of health care as a form of pan-Canadian nation-building was on the wane. Rather, health care was represented in a number of public statements as an expensive budgetary cost to be contained by increased federal limitations on health care spending, rather than an investment in social capital benefitting a healthy workforce and a vigorous citizenry.

At the provincial level, too, support for private commercial activity within health care delivery systems was articulated. The former Liberal Premier of British Columbia, Gordon Campbell, argued that health care had reached a level of 40 per cent of British Columbia's budgetary costs, and that the Canada Health Act's qualification that provinces adhere to the principles of accessibility, universality, portability, comprehensiveness, and public accountability needed to be supplemented by a sixth principle, 'sustainability', in order to '[…] guarantee that our public health care system does not implode for lack of innovation and action' (Smith 2007: 2). This perspective led Campbell to indicate support for the idea of private medical/hospital health insurance to supplement British Columbia's public medicare system and to implement public/private partnerships with respect to hospital construction projects. Critics of this approach claimed that these initiatives undermined the efficiencies of single-payer public medicare systems (Smith 2007).

The Fragmentation of Canadian Health Care

If the task of the preceding section was to explain why a country with a constitution granting authority to health care to the provinces was able to develop such a nationally-coherent system of health care, albeit with a degree of decentralisation, the business of the current section is to explain why the current health care system is becoming more decentralised. Again, the analysis must begin with the Constitution as its reference-point: because the federal government has no constitutional responsibility to fund health care, it can decide to step back from this task when it chooses. What this observation fails to explain, however, is why Ottawa would decide to do so now, when it has gained so much from its role as 'defender of public health care' in the past. One reason for this federal reversal is that the evolving international economic context has had a significant impact on federal–provincial relations. Another reason is that health care has evolved considerably, both in complexity and expense, from what it was when the federal government became involved in the health care arena in 1957. Together, as the final section of this chapter will explain, these changes have led to a palpable shift in the dynamic of Canadian federalism.

If the sea change in thinking about the role of the federal government in Canadian politics came in the 1987 debate over free trade, the full implications of this shift were felt in the following decade. To be competitive, as the 1985 Royal (Macdonald) Commission on the Economic Union and Development Prospects for Canada argued, businesses could not be protected and subsidised; taxes would have to fall; and national debts and deficits would have to be addressed. The 1990s, at the federal level, was a time of 'getting the house in order' to prepare for a future based upon free trade. Unfortunately, this meant that federal deficit reduction was, as many premiers complained, built on the backs of the provinces. The most dramatic instance of this was the substantial reduction in federal spending to the provinces in the 1996 federal budget which, without warning, cut transfers to the provinces for social spending by over 6 billion dollars. The move was successful fiscally, but disastrous politically. Provinces were obliged to make severe cuts to their spending programmes, and public ire was thus directed at the provincial governments far more than at the national one. A notable 'vertical fiscal imbalance' developed in which the provinces, with the constitutional responsibility to provide specific social programmes, could not easily afford to do so; while the federal government, with a reinvigorated economic capacity, and greater elasticity in collecting revenues, had no direct constitutional obligation to do so.

Canadian health care federalism in the early 2000s was characterised no longer by nation-building, but by bridge-building. In an effort to address the political damage done over the previous decade, the federal Liberal government negotiated a series of health care accords with the substate governments in 2000, 2003, and 2004 which infused large amounts of health care funding into the provinces and territories. The 2003 Accord on Health Care Renewal alone provided C$36.8 billion over five years, while the 10-Year Plan to Strengthen Health Care introduced in 2004 committed an additional C$41.3 billion over 10 years. These agreements had two objectives. The first was to smooth political relations between the federal and substate governments; and, while the funds kept flowing, this strategy enjoyed a moderate degree of success. The second objective was to fund a radical shift in the way in which health care was provided; and, in this respect, the exercise was a notable failure. The 2002 Romanow Commission had advocated for such a release of federal funding, arguing that this would facilitate the rapid change of health care to a more sustainable system. It did not. With the demise of the 2004 Accord, it became apparent that the vast majority of the new money went into the salaries of physicians and other health care providers. While national salaries have remained relatively constant since 2000, average physician income has increased from 3.5 times the average Canadian income to 4.5 times more over the same period (Grant and Hurley 2013). At the same time, health care indicators such as wait times, hospital utilisation, and the implementation of electronic record systems do poorly compared to other OECD states (Thomson et al. 2013). When a Conservative federal government was elected in 2006, the new government articulated a commitment to rethink the federal relationship between governments according to the principle of 'open federalism'. According to this tenet, Ottawa would concern itself only with matters under federal jurisdiction, leaving all areas of provincial authority (like health care) to substate governments. Ottawa would continue to supply the provinces with some degree of health care funding (under 20 per cent) but did not state any intention to make this conditional upon the provinces' willingness to cleave to a common commitment to universal health care. Harper, early in his administration in a letter to Alberta premier, Ralph Klein, had indicated that he would maintain the principles of the CHA (Harper 2006). Nevertheless, Ottawa's subsequent policies showed no willingness to engage in debates of whether the principles of the CHA were effectively honoured at the provincial and territorial level or to see that these principles were actually implemented.

Unconditional federal funding for provincial health care had historically been a long-standing objective for most if not all of the provinces. Yet the response by the provinces to this move ranged from muted to disparaging. It was not lost on the provincial governments that the federal government had finally agreed to cede largely unconditional authority, with increasingly limited federal financial contributions, when it became apparent just how onerous health care costs had become. By 2013, provincial governments were channelling between 30 to 47 per cent of their respective budgets to health care (CIHI 2013). Part of this cost increase was due, as noted above, to the ability of health care professionals, and particularly physicians, to capture salary increases when Ottawa offered huge funding increases to the provinces in the 2003 and 2004 Accords. But cost increases were also due to the changing nature of health care itself: sophisticated diagnostics, next-generation pharmaceuticals, complex surgeries, and state-of-the art medical devices have improved the health of Canadians considerably, as they have across the world. Survival rates and treatment options are better than ever before; but they are also considerably more expensive than ever before.

This unprecedented, but costly, capacity for quality health care presents a particularly difficult political problem for highly decentralised states comprised of units of vastly disparate sizes when those substate governments have significant jurisdiction over health care. While all provinces are concerned about their technical and financial capacity to provide a high level of good quality health care, smaller and poorer provinces clearly struggle harder to do so. The issue is not simply one of paying for goods and services. Larger political units also have an advantage in the regulatory, organisational, and political aspects of public health care management. The management of modern health care systems is largely regulatory, and requires a very sophisticated understanding of how such regulatory frameworks ought to be designed and run. Another important task for governments is the coordination of discrete components of the health care system. A focal point for modern health care reform is integration between the health service 'silos', but the precise means of doing so is complicated and uncertain. Again, larger substate units have devoted more resources to the task of health service integration. Finally, larger political units have a much better capacity for bargaining with the providers of health care goods and services. This includes health care professionals, who have a technical expertise that they can strategically employ not only when bargaining for salaries but also when rate-setting for fee-for-service schedules. But it also includes negotiating with private businesses in the construction of large enterprises such as hospitals and other treatment centres, which are increasingly financed on the basis of public–private partnerships (P3s).

The extent to which such partnerships work to the advantage of either government or business depends largely upon the experience and acumen of those involved, as well as the political disposition of the political office holders, and smaller jurisdictions often simply do not have the resources or experience to take advantage of these funding models (Vining and Boardman 2008). Neither is it clear that public–private partnerships necessarily benefit the larger provinces; much depends on the degree of public accountability that these provinces can exert over such involvement (Minow 2003). An example of this problem was revealed by Ontario's auditor general's review of a Private Financing Initiative with respect to the construction of the William Osler Health Centre. The auditor general's review indicated that the estimate of risk transferred to the private sector amounted to a

13 per cent cost overrun. Furthermore, the cost estimates for the government to complete the project by itself were significantly overstated. Finally, Ontario's cost of borrowing at the time of the agreement was considerably lower than the cost of capital charged to Ontario by the private sector consortium (Auditor General of Ontario 2008).

The political fragmentation between the provinces has been exacerbated by Ottawa's declaration that it was changing the formula through which it was delivering federal health care funds. Beginning in 2014, not only were federal health transfers capped to the rate of economic growth, but they were allocated according to a strict per capita basis. In the past, provinces' income levels were considered when health transfers were calculated: this has now been eliminated. The strict equality of the new funding formula, however, ignores the reality of considerable disparity between provinces. Poorer provinces with high numbers of elderly citizens will have to spend a disproportionate amount of their resources on health care, as will provinces with large rural areas where the provision of health care services is quite expensive. Under the new formula, for example, the province of Nova Scotia will lose C$23 million in 2014–2015, while the province of Alberta will gain C$954 million. This may well be a deliberate political strategy on the part of the federal government. In the mid-1990s, when Ottawa reduced health care funding to provinces across the board, the usually-querulous provincial governments understood clearly that they had a common political purpose, and were able to unite effectively in order to pressure Ottawa into providing substantial funds for health care in the 2003 and 2004 Accords. Unlike the mid-1990s, however, the federal strategy of ensuring both winners and losers under the new funding formula increases the difficulty for provinces decisively to unite in opposition to the federal funding strategy. The long-term projection for provincial health budgets is especially grim for the poorer provinces. Canada's Parliamentary Budget Office (PBO) projects overall health spending to grow by an average of 4.9 per cent annually from 2012 to 2050; yet federal health transfers to the provinces are projected to decline considerably, 'averaging 17.9 per cent of other levels of government health spending over the first 25 years of the projection horizon, 13.7 per cent over the next 25 years, and 12.0 per cent over the remaining years' (Office of the Parliamentary Budget Officer 2013: 17–18).

What are the Consequences for Health Care of this Increasing Political Fragmentation in Canadian Federalism?

The stated intention of the federal government no longer to be an active player in health policy has significant consequences for the shape of health care in Canada. These can be grouped into two separate but related categories: the pressure on provinces to seek alternative means of funding health care costs (potentially through greater privatisation), and the lack of coordination between provinces in planning and regulatory frameworks.

The Move Away from Public Funding

The 'national' character of Canadian health care has largely been based upon the provision of universal public health insurance, a policy that was encouraged and underwritten by the federal government since 1957. While each province has its own public insurance plan, the conditions under which Ottawa would assist in funding these plans were formalised by federal statute in 1984 as the Canada Health Act. This legislation, however, is not binding upon the provinces; it applies only to the federal government. The terms of compliance to this agreement have been largely financial, as the legislation calls for cuts in health transfers should provinces deviate from these terms. Canada is the only OECD country which, in most cases, does not permit supplementary private health insurance for publicly-insured services. Yet the reasons for this have nothing to do with national policy-making, for each province has its own regulatory mechanisms for limiting the presence of private health care.

The provinces have dealt with the pressure for inclusion of commercial initiatives within provincial medicare prior to the Conservative administration elected in 2006, and returned as majority government in 2011. Nevertheless the period of minimal national implementation of the Canada Health Act has led to initiatives before the judicial system to try to maintain the Canada Health Act, sometimes in spite of federal non-enforcement and sometimes directly through the provincial political process. In the early 1990s, private for-profit clinics (particularly eye surgery clinics) were billing patients for facility fees while professional fees for services rendered by surgeons under the Alberta Medical Plan were paid publicly. These facility fees amounted to about C$1,000 per day. A number of other units were also charging facility fees in Alberta. These units included two women's health centres providing abortions and a small number of multipurpose surgical centres in Calgary that offered minor ear, nose, and throat (ENT) procedures (Palley, Pomey, and Adams 2012). In the face of federal penalties imposed for these apparent violations of the Canada Health Act by the federal government, in 1996, the Alberta government backed down from open defiance of federal implementation of the Canada Health Act and put a plan in place ending these facility fees as of 1 July 1996. Nevertheless, it indicated a 'politics' evolving with respect to defiance of the implementation of the Canada Health Act in some provinces.

An 'opening' which challenged restrictions on the right to supplementary medical and hospital insurance for services beyond Quebec's Régie was the case of *Chaoulli vs Quebec* (Supreme Court of Canada 2005). In spite of subsequent supportive legislation, however, no insurance companies in Quebec have offered such a supplementary insurance policy. A more recent judicial/political initiative to undermine the implementation of the Canada Health Act is the 2009 case of *Canadian Independent Medical Clinics Association vs British Columbia*. Dr Brian O'Day, past president of the Canadian Medical Association, and other owners of for-profit private medical clinics challenged the provincial government's prohibition against charging patients fees for essential medical services. The suit before British Columbia's Supreme Court argued that, given the constraint of undue waiting times, the Supreme Court of Canada's earlier Chaoulli decision would hold that such constraints deprive British Columbians of medically necessary health care services and therefore constitute a violation of British Columbia's human rights law. The writ of summons brought by Dr Day's Cambia Surgeries Corporation, and four other private firms, as well as the Canadian Independent Medical Clinics argues that patients are entitled to medical treatment at over 50 independent surgeries in British Columbia and that the restrictions regarding fees to patients imposed by the provincial Medical Protection Act violated Section 7 of the federal Charter of Rights and Freedom which guarantee a person's right to life, liberty, and personal security, as well as Section 15's right to equality (Writ of Summons 2009).

British Columbia's health minister, as well as the attorney-general and the Medical Services Commission, noted in a counterclaim that the Charter did not provide for a 'freestanding' constitutional right to health care and that furthermore the private billing of patients for insured services violated British Columbia's Medical Protection Act as well as its obligations under the Canada Health Act. Furthermore, they noted that such 'extra-billing' placed the province in serious risk of financial penalties which could be imposed by the federal government – and thus, the province sought to enjoin such activities by private clinics (Collier 2009; Statement of Defense and Counterclaim 2009). Following a ruling by the British Columbia Court of Appeals, British Columbia's Medical Services Commission instituted injunctive proceedings against the Cambie clinic in August 2012 (*Canadian Independent Medical Services Association vs British Columbia* 2010; Chao and Martin 2012).

Nevertheless, private commercial clinics, operating either in purchase-of-care arrangements with provincial medicare plans or independent of such plans continue to expand in the Canadian context. By 2011, British Columbia listed 66 private commercial clinics which provide only one type of surgery, such as cataract eye surgery, and 12 that provide a variety of services. In Alberta there were 60 listed private commercial clinics. These numbers did not include private corporate executive health programmes or diagnostic imaging clinics (Glauser 2011). The president of the Canadian Independent Medical Clinics Association has estimated that there are about 300 private commercial health clinics in Quebec. A spokesperson for *Médicins Québécois pour le Régime Public*, a pro-medicare group in Quebec, indicated of these facilities that they are 'becoming mini-hospitals' where cataract, as well as knee and hip surgeries, are increasingly performed (Glauser 2011: E437–8). Moreover, as of 13 July 2013, there were 300 physicians practicing medicine in Quebec who were non-participants in the Health Insurance Plan of Québec [*Régie de l'Assurance Maladie du Québec*] (*Régie de l'Assurance Maladie du Québec* 2013).

Given the constraints of federal health funding, the incorporation of for-profit clinics into provincial medicare systems makes, as former Quebec premier, Lucien Bouchard, indicated, 'common sense' [*le gros bon sens*] (Yakabuski 2004: B2).

Such 'publicly regulated' participation by the commercial private sector may be needed in this circumstance for, as Raisa Deber has noted (in citing the observation of Deng Xiaoping), 'it does not matter if a cat is black or white as long as it will catch mice' (Deber 2002: 2). The cost of high-tech health care services in Canada places an increasing burden on the delivery of health care services in Canadian provinces and territories. In a variety of ways that differ across provinces and territories (ranging from the acceptability of commercial diagnostic centres to delivery of radiation therapy and to provision of in-home chronic care services), for-profit health care organisations have contributed to the financing as well as the delivery of health care services in the provinces, either with public authorisation or outside the framework of provincial health care plans. Nevertheless as Palley, Pomey, and Adams (2012) observe:

> [...] the downside of these efforts is the possibility that private (commercial) care may contribute to an asymmetrical, increasing inequitable, class- and income-based health care delivery system. Nevertheless, the enactment of proposals to expand publicly regulated private commercial services in some instances both as necessary health services and as extended health services within the framework of the CHA could result in increased health care services in an equitable manner. (142)

Overcoming this increased fragmentation and the equity and access issues accompanying this situation would require an active national public-regulatory framework (Minow 2003; Starr 2011). Increased privatisation must be held publicly accountable through the development of management and political regulatory procedures that prevent the benefits to the health delivery system from 'spilling out' excessively into the profits of commercial providers. Such national public regulation of private commercial 'competitive' initiatives has effectively taken place in the Netherlands as well as the federal republic of Switzerland (Reinhardt 2004; Rosenau and Lako 2008). More problematically, however, this solution does little for cost containment: the Netherlands and Switzerland are amongst the most expensive health care systems in the OECD at US$5,099 and US$5,643 per capita expenditure, respectively, compared to the OECD average of US$3,322 per capita (OECD 2103: 155).

The Problem of Fragmentation between Regions

There has never been much formal coordination between Canadian jurisdictions in health care. Informal discussions between provincial health departments are common, and annual meetings of health ministers permit some exploration of pressing policy issues. Beyond this, there is little structured coordination of Canada's health care systems. However, because of the requirements imposed on the provinces as preconditions for federal funding, separate but similar systems have arisen across the country. As the previous section has discussed, refusal by recent federal governments to enforce the Canada Health Act have allowed provinces more leeway to develop distinct policy paths. From a theoretical perspective, such divergence is often seen as useful as it permits greater policy innovation at a regional level (Boessenkoel 2013). Yet this practice rarely acknowledges the considerably disparity in size and capacity between provinces, and has also led to considerable difficulty in achieving regulatory and policy coordination between the country's regions as well as the related matter of unequal accessibility to the delivery of health care services on a provincial and territorial basis. The passive federal encouragement of health policy decentralisation has at least two broad consequences.

The first is the loss of potential positive-sum gains to be made through greater coordination across jurisdictions. The training and hiring of health care professionals is one example: provincial colleges of physicians, dentists, pharmacists, and other self-regulating health care workers have jurisdiction over the training and licensing of members within their professions, but there is still insufficient effort made to connect projected health human resource needs across the country with the capacity of provincial training facilities to meet them (Tomblin Murphy 2013). Also, to the extent that a quarter of Canada's physicians (and a substantial proportion of nurses) is foreign-trained, provinces (with jurisdiction over health care service provision) need to coordinate this aspect of health human resource provision with the federal government (with jurisdiction over immigration). Another potential area of constructive policy coordination across jurisdictions is the development of a national pharmacare programme, which could reduce the cost of pharmaceuticals considerably (Morgan, Daw, and Law 2013). In broader terms, a permanent forum for discussing national health care issues, measuring progress across regions, and highlighting 'best practices' across the country would be very useful in developing innovative and sustainable health care at a national level. In April 2013, however, Ottawa announced that the single institution Canada had to perform these objectives – the 10-year-old Health Council of Canada – was to be discontinued. Six provinces have Health Quality Councils, but there is little interaction between them, leading both to the duplication of research and the failure to communicate positive research results.

A second potential consequence of greater decentralisation in health care across regions is the loss of equity in the provision of health care across the country. Despite polls that continue to show considerable public support for 'single tier' health care, there is no way of determining whether Canadians' commitment to the redistribution of health care resources extends *across* or simply *within* provincial boundaries. The concept of a 'social union' in which resources were distributed to permit all provinces to provide similar social programmes was an implicit but key aspect of Canada's nation-building strategy in the latter half of the twentieth century, but the national vision of the Harper administration has focused instead upon the achievement of an economic union permitting greater movement of capital and labour across provincial boundaries.

Why, given the advantages of policy coordination across jurisdictions, would a national government choose *not* to maintain a strong presence within the field of health care? One explanation is based on the federal administration's principled articulation of 'open federalism', in which governments are expected to concern themselves only with matters within their own clearly-articulated constitutional authority. To the extent that Ottawa has shown a willingness to overstep its constitutional authority in attempting to forge a strong economic union, however, or to engage in policies that produce significant negative externalities to the provinces (Fierlbeck 2014), the concept of 'open federalism' is in practice little more than political window-dressing. Another, more plausible, explanation is simply that it costs too much: an administration with an ideological focus upon deficit reduction will not willingly become more involved in expensive policy areas over which it has no formal constitutional jurisdiction. But it may also be the case that strengthening the economic union while dismantling the social union is a more concerted effort to achieve cost containment in health care by forcing provinces to make hard decisions with limited funding.

According to some economists, providing federal health care payments to provinces that cannot meet current health care expenditure through the direct taxation of their citizens leads to a form of moral hazard in which provinces engage in excessive spending relative to what they could otherwise afford (Kneebone 2012). By reducing transfer payments and by facilitating the ready movement of both capital and services, the federal government imposes 'hard constraints' upon substate governments, obliging them to trim their expenditures or face the economic and political repercussions of carrying a heavy debt. And, to the extent that substate governments compete with each other within a common market, they must keep taxes low or face the exodus of businesses moving to jurisdictions with more competitive tax rates. The most effective way to bend the cost curve within substate governments, argue proponents of market-preserving federalism, is to modify the overarching federal relationships themselves (Weingast 1995). This model has been a sharp contrast to the established view that the national government should initiate or encourage health care reforms enforced through a regulatory framework in return for fiscal transfers (Vladeck and Rice 2009). In any event, the current system of health care federalism in Canada by no means reflects a pure model of market-preserving federalism: federal transfer payments, while diminishing relative to provincial expenditure, will certainly not be eliminated; and some of Ottawa's efforts to solidify a common market (including the establishment of a national securities commission) have been stymied by the courts. But there is no doubt that the current federal administration has been attempting to prod the country in this direction (Fierlbeck 2014).

Conclusion

What are the consequences of greater decentralisation for Canadian health care? Once again, the country is facing a vertical fiscal imbalance in which provincial governments face high expenditure costs for programmes under their jurisdiction, while the federal government enjoys higher revenues but shows no inclination to use them to alleviate the provinces' fiscal pressures. As described above, this has led provinces more seriously to consider engaging with the private sector in various funding options. Interestingly, however, the strategy has not made provinces more competitive with each other within the field of health care itself; to the contrary, the response by provinces has been to initiate more horizontal collaboration between substate governments in the absence of federal leadership. This has resulted in some policy coordination, including the establishment of provincial drug alliances facilitating the negotiation of competitive pricing for pharmaceuticals and the sharing of 'best practices' developed within particular jurisdictions (such as the adoption by Saskatchewan of Nova Scotia's 'collaborative emergency centre').

Theoretically, what this indicates is that committing to a particular policy direction does not simply congeal the policy context so that the costs of moving away from the path become prohibitively expensive politically. We should not lose sight of the possibility that pushing forward in one direction can also mobilise interests to push harder in the opposite direction. Institutional factors will always be substantial, but they are not necessarily decisive in explaining political outcomes. This may be the single most important lesson that current dynamics of Canadian health care federalism have to teach us. By shifting the contours of federalism to force provinces into a more competitive mode, Ottawa has given them reason to think harder about the utility of collaborative undertakings. And by refusing to acknowledge Canadians' passionate, albeit sometimes limited, support for public health care, the current federal administration has opened a political space for competing parties to present a palatable and clearly-defined policy alternative to voters. The political directions of the moment are often subject to change with the assumption of power of a new political regime with a different disposition to act. Greater fragmentation and increasing privatisation of Canadian health care are possible, but they should not be seen as inexorable.

The trend to decentralisation, in Canada as elsewhere, was built upon the belief that a centralised process lacked the capacity to respond imaginatively to diversity and transformation. Advocates of decentralisation support the administrative paradigm of New Public Management, which emphasised the flexibility and responsiveness of greater regional control. And, certainly, this fragmentation has afforded the opportunity to explore a number of different concepts and procedures on a limited scale. But when considering what the net result of this experimentation has been over the past two decades, the results are sobering. Regardless of regional innovation, Canada's standing in national league tables has fallen dramatically across a number of indicators (Thomson et al. 2013). The country has lost the capacity to address critical issues in a systematic way: it cannot efficiently implement electronic health systems, or develop pharmacare at a national level, or coordinate health human resources, or effectively communicate best practices across jurisdictions. Even a decentralised federal system can benefit from imaginative national political leadership. As Atul Gawande (2012) has noted, we must, at some point, be able to implement such innovative measures effectively, or their impact is limited. Decentralisation has allowed a proliferation of inventive processes but, without a way of translating them systematically into widespread practice, Canada has remained little more than 'a nation of perpetual pilot projects' (Bégin et al. 2009).

Chapter 9
Australia[1]

Stephen Duckett

Introduction

Australia is a federation with six states, two territories (collectively here called 'the states'), and a federal ('Commonwealth') government based in the national capital, Canberra. With 22.5 million people (2011 census), it is one of the world's least densely populated, though heavily urbanised, countries. In three of the states, more than 70 per cent of the population lives in the capital city while about two thirds of New South Wales lives in the capital. Most of the population lives on the eastern seaboard, with a pocket around Perth in the southwest of the continent.

Like the hybrid platypus, Australia's health system is also a curious hybrid of public and private financing and provision with federal and state roles in governance and provision. There is still an ideological divide between the main political parties (Labor in the Centre or Centre-Left, Liberals on the Centre-Right) in terms of their attitude to key health policies at the federal level (Duckett 2008). There is no clear delineation of federal and state responsibilities in most areas of domestic public policy, including health care, with Wiltshire (2008) using the term 'marble cake federalism' being applied to characterise the interwoven jurisdictional responsibilities 'where the functions of government swirl around, engulfing two or three levels'. As Sharman (1991) puts it:

> The operation of state and national governments involves such a degree of interpenetration that it is hard to find either an area of Commonwealth activity that does not impinge on state policies, or state administration that does not entail some Commonwealth involvement. (23)

One claimed virtue of federal systems is that they allow policy experimentation, and this has certainly been the case in Australia. Unfortunately, the one health sector example typically cited, the introduction of activity-based funding (Twomey and Withers 2007), took 20 years between its introduction in Victoria and national adoption. Commonwealth–state friction is regularly cited in public commentary as a significant problem in Australia – because of overlapping responsibilities, it can

---

1 This chapter draws on a presentation to the 1st International Conference on Public Policy, Grenoble, June 2013. Unless otherwise specified, all dollar values are in Australian dollars.

lead to cost shifting with one level of government implementing policies which force the other to incur costs (Buckmaster and Pratt 2005) and blame shifting where each level of government attempting to shift political responsibility for system faults to the other (House of Representatives 2006).

Pressure on government budgets from escalating health expenditure is increasing, requiring adroit responses which are made more difficult by the messy context. Over the last decade, spending on health care in Australia doubled; spending by state and territory governments grew even faster almost tripling, and consuming a larger and larger proportion of state budgets (Daley et al. 2013). For all but two years of the last decade health spending grew faster than the gross domestic product (GDP), markedly so in the last few years as the global recession cut into Australia's GDP growth. Australia now spends about one in every 11 dollars of its national wealth on health care, up from just under one in every 12 dollars a decade ago, an increase from 8.2 per cent to 9.3 per cent of GDP.

It is the thesis of this chapter that the peculiar division of responsibilities in the Australian federal system hinders the development and implementation of effective policies to respond to contemporary health issues, including this escalation of health costs. Recognition of this issue, however, does not mean that there are any easy or feasible solutions to address it.

The Australian Constitution and Governments' Responsibility for Health Services

The problems of Commonwealth–state relations in the health sector stem in part from the nature of the Australian Constitution. The Australian Constitution is based on the principle that the Commonwealth parliament does not have power to legislate in a policy area unless that area is specifically mentioned in the Constitution as an area of Commonwealth power. In the absence of a specific mention, governance of that area is deemed to be the responsibility of a state. Although originally the Commonwealth's health-related power was limited to quarantine, post-World War II reconstruction policies of the Commonwealth Labor government saw a constitutional amendment (Mendelson 1999) to give the Commonwealth power to make laws with respect to

> [t]he provision of maternity allowances, widows pensions, child endowment, unemployment, pharmaceutical, sickness and hospital benefits, medical and dental services (but not so as to authorise any form of civil conscription), benefits to students and family allowances. (Section 51, xxiiia)

Outside of specific 'health powers', the Constitution grants the Commonwealth government explicit power over corporations and foreign affairs including matters covered by treaties and conventions that Australia has signed. The Commonwealth government has used the 'corporations' power' to regulate a range of health-related issues (for example, to prohibit advertising of tobacco products). Health policies can be based on several of the other constitutional provisions (such as insurance).

Financial Power and Intergovernmental Relations

While the introduction of Section 51 (xxiiia) significantly expanded the Commonwealth's direct constitutional power in health care, other factors have been even more significant in explaining the growing dominance of the Commonwealth's power in the health system. Of particular importance has been the Commonwealth's power under section 96 of the Constitution to make grants to states in areas over which it would otherwise have no power. Section 96 grants have traditionally been known as 'tied grants' or Specific Purpose Payments as the Commonwealth has the ability to set conditions on their use. Tied grants are particularly prevalent in the health sector. Although section (xxiiia) gives the Commonwealth power over 'hospital benefits', Commonwealth funding in this area has been through a Section 96 grant (Scully 2009), currently under the National Healthcare Agreement. This health funding agreement represents the largest flow of funds from the Commonwealth to the states across any portfolio or agreement (excluding the arrangements for the goods and services tax, which is a Commonwealth tax, the revenue for which is passed to the states). Section 96 grants account for about one quarter of state revenue.

The Constitution also grants the Commonwealth the sole right to impose excise duties (including sales tax). The High Court has interpreted excise quite broadly, and in 1997 ruled invalid state business franchise taxes on tobacco and petrol as illegitimately imposing an excise (*Ha vs New South Wales* [1997] 189 CLR 465). However, all revenue (after administration costs are deducted) from a federal excise tax, the goods and services tax, is allocated to the states and between them by a complex equalisation formula (Williams 2012). This revenue (accounting for about one quarter of all state revenue) has no conditions attached.

In 1942, the Commonwealth, using its wartime powers, assumed responsibility for income tax. Although this decision was challenged in the immediate post-war period, the Commonwealth's pre-eminence in taxation was upheld. As a result, both income tax and excise have become the preserve of the Commonwealth. As these are the most significant growth taxes in the Australian economy, this has limited the states' ability to impose taxes to meet burgeoning demands to provide for state services, including hospitals. The Commonwealth control of both income tax and excise means that Australia has a significant vertical fiscal imbalance and this exacerbates Commonwealth–state tensions in the health sector. In 2012–13, personal and company income taxes, together with the GST accounted for more than $300 billion of total Commonwealth revenue of $376 billion (Daley et al. 2013). Total state own-source revenue was $114 billion, just over half of which was non-tax revenue. Fuel is thrown onto this fire because of overlapping constitutional and political responsibilities. Australia has the greatest degree of vertical fiscal imbalance of comparable federal nations (Twomey and Withers 2007), with the imbalance between states' revenue raising capacity and their spending patterns bridged through transfer payments made by the Commonwealth to states including the GST and specific purpose payments.

The Australian Health System

Design of Australia's universal health insurance scheme, Medicare, was heavily influenced by the peculiarities of the Australian federation and service provision: historically 'public hospitals' had been creatures of the states, whilst the states had little interest in medical services outside hospitals (Scotton and Macdonald 1993). Australia also has a dense network of 'private' hospitals, run by for-profit chains, Roman Catholic religious orders and other not-for-profit groups, and smaller, independent entities. Although the system parameters have evolved marginally over time, the 1970s elements are still there:

- Public hospitals are provided by state entities (although there are a few Catholic hospitals which function as public hospitals), with the Commonwealth government providing payments through the states toward the costs of their operation. Although initially covering around 50 per cent of costs, the proportion of costs covered federally is now around 45 per cent. All Australian residents are entitled to hospital services without charge from public hospitals. About two thirds of all hospital beds are in public hospitals and these hospitals provide the most complex care and are the site of most acute-care teaching and training.
- Medical services (outside public hospitals) are mostly provided by private practitioners remunerated on a fee-for-service basis who can set their own fees but with the Commonwealth government setting a fee schedule and providing rebates. Medical practitioners can choose to bill a Commonwealth government agency directly and accept the rebate as full settlement of the account. This practice varies in direct relation to market power, both by geography and specialty (Young et al. 2000; Essue et al. 2011). Over the last 30 years, an increasing proportion of medical practice has been corporatised (White 2000). Public 'safety-net' arrangements have also been introduced by the government to cover annual accumulated gaps between patient payments to practitioners and government rebates, with private insurers legislatively prohibited from offering products to meet gap payments for medical services provided outside hospitals. A proposal to introduce capitation payments into the medical remuneration mix (National Health and Hospitals Reform Commission 2009) was opposed by medical organisations, with a softer 'trial' of new payments arrangements introduced instead (Leach et al. 2013).

- Other aspects of primary health care are provided through market arrangements (dental care, allied health care) and by state governments (community nursing services). The organisational arrangements for primary health care services vary between the states, with Victoria having a continued strong system of government funded but independently managed community health centres whereas most other states have absorbed primary health care services (to the extent they exist) into area health authority structures.
- Insurance against the cost of private hospital treatment is available on a regulated modified community rated basis by a number of private (and one publicly-owned) insurers, with premiums increasing by 2 per cent per year above age 30, based on age from which coverage has been maintained continuously. In the 1990s, the Liberal government introduced a 30–40 per cent subsidy against the cost of insurance. There are tax incentives for middle to high income earners to take out health insurance. The age-related community rating, combined with limited access to elective surgery in public hospitals is the most significant incentive leading to approximately 45 per cent of people maintaining private hospital cover. (Although all Australians can access public hospitals without charge, about 40 per cent also take out private insurance which covers – generally with a deductible – the costs of private hospital care. Private insurance also provides rebates for visits to dentists and allied health professionals).
- Due to a combination of mandatory co-payments (e.g., for pharmaceuticals), limited public coverage and provision of allied health services and dental care, and market based co-payments for medical services, Australians meet a higher proportion of health care costs out of their own pocket than is the case in most other developed countries (Duckett and Kempton 2012). And indeed, out-of-pocket costs meet a larger share of total health costs than private insurance. Out-of-pocket costs account for about 20 per cent of all health expenditure with higher income families paying higher amounts out-of-pocket, but a lower proportion of income, than lower income families (Yusuf and Leeder 2013).

Australia's Federalism Problem

In this chapter I make a narrow claim: that Australia's marble cake federalism hinders its ability to respond incisively and consistently to emerging health problems. The claim is not that federalism, per se, is the problem, but rather that the peculiar nature of the Australian system militates against swift (or, sometimes, any) action. Despite these structural problems, Australia performs well internationally on most measures of health system performance. Its per capita health spending is below the average of Organisation of Economic Cooperation and Development (OEDC) countries, as is the percentage of GDP spent on health care. Similarly, Potential Years of Life Lost are below the average, and average life expectancy is in the top quartile of comparable countries. There may be demographic reasons for this good performance (e.g., Australia's age distribution is younger than Europe's), and the relatively good system performance has not led to complacency in terms of desire for system improvement. Health expenditure growth and projections of growth have been used to justify claims that the health system is 'unsustainable' and to drive system reform. Australia's federal structure is often seen to inhibit such reform. Examples of poor management of health policy due to federalism usually centre on 'fiscal squabbles', 'waiting', and 'waste'.

This section draws on Swerissen and Duckett (2007). Fiscal squabbles break out between different levels of government when one level tries to shift costs to another or, alternatively, seeks to minimise its contributions to funding health services. Much of the politics and negotiation between the Commonwealth and the states involves deciding who has fiscal responsibility for various health functions and programmes and then developing mechanisms to ensure that each level of government meets its agreed responsibilities for funding.

'Waiting' drives much of the politics of health. The public, through the media, is primarily concerned about access to services (particularly acute hospital services). When indicators of access suggest services are unavailable, unaffordable and very distant or require a long wait, governments come under pressure. Not surprisingly, professional groups and service providers often fuel these debates. Given that the Commonwealth and the states share responsibility for service provision, they then share responsibility for criticisms over access to services. As with cost shifting, there is a tendency for each level of government to blame the other for access problems. In addition to the fiscal rules, health agreements between the Commonwealth and the states often have a heavy emphasis on defining responsibilities for demand and access to services.

'Waste' is a proxy for inefficiency, fragmentation and duplication in the delivery of health programmes. At its worst, this leads to significant concerns about quality. Often discontinuity and conflict between the Commonwealth and the states is blamed for poor health outcomes and inefficient use of resources. A significant drive to improve the productivity, quality and effectiveness of the health system underpins Commonwealth–state negotiations.

There are three main sources of federalism's inhibiting effect: vertical fiscal imbalance (discussed above), diffuse power, and programmatic discontinuities.

Distribution of Power

Australia's messy allocation of responsibilities means that there is no central control point for policy initiatives, and this creates myopic policy development and multiple veto points. Blame shifting is endemic. The Commonwealth government is clearly the *primus inter pares* (or first among equals) in health policy in Australia. Central governments in federal systems have typically increased their relative roles since their foundation (Wheare 1963). Oates (1972) goes so far as to suggest that these centripetal tendencies are inevitable and that central power will continue to increase. This is certainly the case in Australia and is as prophesised by Alfred Deakin, one of the architects of Federation (James 2000). The introduction of a goods and services tax (GST) from 1 July 2000 was heralded as a counterbalancing force to the centralisation trend. For the first time, it provided states with a growth tax, with the negotiations leading up to the GST ensuring that the states collectively accrued all the revenue of the GST. However, the GST has not been the windfall it was first thought, as a slowdown in consumer spending has diminished state receipts from this source.

Commonwealth government now dominates critical aspects of health policy in Australia and funding sources. Health insurance policy is set by the Commonwealth government, which in turn means that the Commonwealth exerts a major influence over the demand for private hospital care. Medical fees policy is also the preserve of the Commonwealth government. But the Commonwealth government is not the centralised control point for health system reform in Australia: states are the 'system managers' for public hospitals.

Until the most recent round of system reforms, the Commonwealth was not directly exposed financially to increases in costs of public hospital care, and hence had no financial incentive to use levers it controlled to reduce demand for hospital care. Cost shifting between the states and the Commonwealth (and vice versa) is institutionalised as a way of life, and each party blames the other for system shortcomings. The significantly different shares in funding responsibilities have implications for policy formation. The Commonwealth government clearly dominates in the area of medical services, but state governments dominate funding of community health services. These funding splits result in separate policy responsibilities organised by level of government which do not encourage integration of primary health care services.

One of the weaknesses of these shared funding responsibilities is that government (be it Commonwealth or state) may see the health system simply as those parts of the health system that it funds. For example, the Commonwealth may equate primary health care with primary medical care because of its dominance of funding of medical services and the fact that its expenditure on medical services is orders of magnitude greater than its expenditure on community and public health services. This then creates further weaknesses in policy design. Until the recent system reforms (see below) there were no national autonomous governing bodies in the health sector. Almost all national authorities involved multi-jurisdictional membership and often became paralysed by lowest-common-denominator politics. Finally, multiple loci of power create multiple veto points, hindering implementation of new policies (Pressman and Wildavsky 1973).

Programmatic Discontinuities

Australia's 'marble cake' federalism is also characterised by extensive and problematic programme discontinuities. These discontinuities inevitably create problems at each margin. With income support schemes, rules can create poverty traps and very high effective marginal rates of taxation if a low income person earns additional income. Service delivery programmes create equivalent gaps and perverse incentives and so it is not possible to design a service system with no problems of service coordination and transitions across boundaries.

Programmatic boundary issues can be characterised as being of two kinds:

- Where a programme 'silo' is tightly defined and creates an all or none discontinuity in programme provision, with a 'cliff' created at the edge of the programme boundary.
- An alternative overlap discontinuity where programmes are substitutes with different funding sources creating perverse incentives for services to be provided under one scheme or another depending on the relative available of funds or who is the payer.

These programmatic discontinuities can cause problems in terms of continuity of care or efficiency, schematically creating a 2 × 2 table.

Of course, programme boundaries can create problems for service delivery even in unitary countries and where a single level of government has sole responsibility (Pritchard and Hughes 1995). In Australia, single-level discontinuity occurs in aged care where the Commonwealth is responsible for residential aged care and its direct substitutes and has a number of tightly designed programmes to fulfil this responsibility. Two such programmes provide support in the community for people assessed as requiring residential aged care. There is a significant gap in the level of support provided under the programmes, whereas support needs vary as a continuous function. This dichotomous nature of the design of support programmes creates a programmatic discontinuity in a programme area in which the Commonwealth has sole responsibility. But an additional layer of complexity is involved when there are multiple players.

Table 9.1 provides four examples of alignment problems caused by Commonwealth–state programmatic discontinuities. The first row, identifying problems associated with continuity of care, is becoming increasingly important.

Table 9.1   Examples of problems of programmatic boundary alignment

System attribute affected	Programmatic discontinuity	
	Silos and cliffs	Overlaps: price at the margin for substitutes
Continuity of care	Failures of MBS chronic disease design	Long stay in hospital residential care interface
Efficiency	Workforce	Hospital out-patient specialist rooms interface

In a system characterised by chronic disease, the patient journey crosses a number of different funding programmes. At each programmatic boundary, problems of continuity of care can emerge, exacerbating handover problems associated with institutional provision. The example used in the table is one of missed opportunities. From a state government perspective, managing the increasing costs of chronic disease requires a significant investment in prevention programmes. But the key to enhancing investment rests with changing the behaviour of medical practitioners, the levers for which are in the hands of Commonwealth government through its responsibility for the Medicare Benefits Schedule (MBS). The benefits of better designed chronic disease programmes fall in part on the Commonwealth (through reduced use of medical and pharmaceutical services) but also significantly on state governments through reduced use of hospital services. The Commonwealth may emphasise that significant benefits fall on states, reducing its incentive to redesign the MBS arrangements to reflect the contemporary reality of chronic disease. This is all the more important because of the economics of the Medicare Schedule: the time of medical practitioners is limited and the cost of incentive payments to redirect medical practitioner time from one activity to another is thus quite low. In contrast, for the state to design an incentive programme to apply to medical practitioners it would need to create an infrastructure for paying doctors and it would face the full costs of any programmatic design.

A second example of problems in terms of patient flow is the second cell in the first row of the table. People in need of long stay care can be accommodated in either residential aged care facilities, provision of which is funded and rationed by the Commonwealth government, or they can occupy a hospital bed after the conclusion of an acute stay episode. Because the services are substitutes, failure to provide adequate residential aged care will cause a backup of people inappropriately accommodated in acute hospital beds. Here the Commonwealth makes the savings from under-provision and the costs fall on the state government through its provision of hospital services. The political and economic costs of back-ups of patients in acute wards fall on states, while the benefits of reduced expenditure falls on the Commonwealth. State hospitals provide rehabilitation services after strokes and other conditions. Inadequate rehabilitation may mean patients are unable to be discharged home and may increase their need for a residential aged care bed. The cost of this failure in state services falls on the Commonwealth.

The residential aged care-hospital interface provides an example of yet another complicating factor in health care in Australia: reciprocal interdependence. Thompson (1967) argued that reciprocal interdependence, where the outputs of one system are the inputs into another and vice versa, is the most complex form of interdependence and requires the most complex coordination strategies.

Other examples of programmatic discontinuity occur in terms of realisation of the efficiency goal of public sector management. Two examples are provided in the table, one of problems of programmatic silos and one of pricing at the margin. In the first place, the Commonwealth has a large degree of control over workforce supply through its control of immigration and the university sector. But the cost of tight supply controls fall in part on state governments through inability to staff public hospitals. The second example relates to specialist outpatient services in public hospitals funded by state governments and specialist services in the community funded through the Medicare Benefits Schedule, clear service substitutes. Assuming that a local hospital is committed to providing access to ambulatory specialist services, there is strong incentive on the hospital to have those services provided through the uncapped fully Commonwealth funded Medicare arrangements rather than through state government funding arrangements (which may only have weak incentives for outpatient provision given the typically poor recording in this sector).

These problems of programmatic discontinuity are also affected by problems of programmatic design. The principal objects of direct Commonwealth expenditure are through the Medicare Benefits Schedule, Pharmaceutical Benefit Scheme, health insurance subsidies and residential aged care. In contrast, state governments' principal objects of expenditure are for hospitals, community health care and prevention. As discussed earlier, these different foci of expenditure tend to create a similar set of foci of policy interventions. The concept of bounded rationality is relevant here: managers cannot be totally 'synoptic' and so they tend to limit their consideration of policy options to ones that emphasise incremental change to existing programmes (Lindblom 1965). Thus state officials addressing problems of chronic disease might tend to focus on community health provision rather than involvement of general practitioners.

For similar reasons, there is a tendency towards 'programmatic isomorphism': programmes at a single level of government tending to evolve to look similar in basic design (DiMaggio and Powell 1991). The vast bulk of Commonwealth expenditure is allocated through payments to private sector (and non-government sector) agents: Medicare to doctors, pharmaceutical payments to pharmacists, residential aged care payments to residential aged care facilities. The states are much more involved in direct service delivery. This is in part because of the wording of section (xxiiia) of the Constitution which limits Commonwealth power in some of the specified areas to providing benefits i.e. payments where the benefit to an individual recipient can be identified. Governments thus tend to develop new programmes (or change old programmes) in ways that align with the dominant provision type of the relevant government. All of this means that states and the Commonwealth approach the health system with very different eyes and very different inclinations in terms of programme design. This in turn means that programmatic alignment can be quite difficult. The problem of programmatic discontinuities is exacerbated by the tendency of the Commonwealth government to introduce micro-programmes: highly targeted programmes to address the needs of a specific constituency. The number of such programmes has mushroomed and policy development has been likened to sprinkling 'programmatic confetti' with 'narrow programmatic responses disconnected from a broader strategic purpose, and from measurable outcomes' (Moran 2010).

The 2007–2013 Attempted Fix

The stimulus for the most recent wave of health reform in Australia was the election of a Labor government in 2007, which had highlighted in the election campaign the problems inherent in the health system, particularly the confused responsibilities between the Commonwealth government and the states. The prospects for a renegotiation of Commonwealth and state roles was good as at the time of its election, as all state and territory governments were of the same political persuasion (Labor). During the election campaign, Labor's leader (Kevin Rudd) committed to eliminate the blame game in the health sector. The new government moved swiftly to appoint a commission (the National Health and Hospitals Reform Commission) with broad ranging terms of reference to review the health system. The media release announcing the commission identified its task as addressing:

- the rapidly increasing burden of chronic disease;
- the ageing of the population;
- rising health costs; and
- inefficiencies exacerbated by cost shifting and the blame game.

The Commission focused on health financing, maximising a productive relationship between public and private sectors, and improving rural health. There were two main federal–state issues before the Commission: should there be a realignment of Commonwealth and state responsibilities in health care, and what should be the relative financial shares paid by the Commonwealth and states. The Commission received many submissions relating to the problems of Commonwealth state relations and the complexities caused by Australia's federal system, with most advocating a greater Commonwealth role in funding, principally driven by a perception that, absent reliable growth taxes, states would not be able to fund future health needs adequately. Despite advocacy from many in the health sector, the National Health and Hospitals Reform Commission's (NHHRC) recommendations were aimed at clarifying and rationalising responsibilities rather than transforming them (NHHRC 2009). In brief, the NHHRC's recommendations kept states in the leadership role for inpatient care but attempted to deal with programmatic discontinuities in primary care by transferring full responsibility to the Commonwealth. The Commission proposed locking in the contemporary public hospital funding share but exposing the Commonwealth to the costs of activity growth in the sector for the first time (previous funding arrangements sheltered the Commonwealth from activity growth as the growth formula was principally based on population growth). Prime Minister Rudd embarked on an extensive 'listening tour' across Australia as part of his consideration of the NHHRC recommendations. This traversed the same territory as the Commission's consultations and led to a government response which rejected the Reform Commission's somewhat cautious approach. Prime Minister Rudd announced a dramatic proposal: that the Commonwealth would become the majority funder of public hospitals. Given the historical funding context, this proposal to assume responsibility for 60 per cent of (the efficient) costs of public hospitals met by governments was clearly a 'game changer'. The Commonwealth proposal to become the dominant funder of public hospitals was dependent on states returning about one-third of GST revenue to the Commonwealth. Hence, the Commonwealth proposal would worsen vertical fiscal imbalance and continue the trend towards greater centralisation that has been evident in the Australian federation over about the last 40 years.

At the time the proposal was put forward, most states had Labor governments and, despite misgivings, those states eventually signed up to the Rudd initiative. Only one state held out against this deal (Western Australia, where a newly-elected Liberal government was in office), implementation was delayed as negotiations continued. Shortly after this deal was announced, Rudd was replaced as prime minister by Julia Gillard, and Labor lost government in the two larger states (New South Wales and Victoria), increasing political opposition to the deal partly negotiated by the former prime minister. Prime Minister Gillard negotiated an alternative proposal which was less dramatic: the Commonwealth still agreed to share the risk of hospital cost growth, but not as majority funder, the states would continue as the majority funder for the foreseeable future and were formally designated as the 'system managers' for public hospitals. There would be no claw back from the goods and services tax, but the Commonwealth would fund 45 per cent of the cost of additional activity in public hospital (at the efficient cost) from 2014, rising to 50 per cent from 2017. The Commonwealth also pulled back on assuming full financial responsibility for primary health care.

The Rudd proposal (carried over into the Gillard implementation) also required states to establish local governance arrangements for groups of hospitals (called 'networks'). In parallel with these changes to hospitals, 61 new local organisations (Medicare Locals) were established with very broad expectations about reforming local primary care arrangements.

In parallel with the discussions on responsibility realignment and funding, negotiations were proceeding on establishing an alphabet soup of 'national' agencies to govern the health system. A weakness identified by the Reform Commission was that pre-existing national agencies tended to be either Commonwealth agencies (and were thus distrusted by the states) or were jurisdictional fora, often without a capacity to make decisions given the consensus-oriented (or more accurately, multiple veto based) approach adopted in these arenas.

New bodies were established to:

- establish the National Efficient Price to be used in hospital funding (refereeing between Commonwealth and state interests in this regard);
- ensure transparency of hospital funding flows;

- report on the performance of public and private hospitals on a range of dimensions (waiting times, readmission rates) and also on primary health care services in geographical areas; and
- advise the Commonwealth on a new prevention agenda.

The then-Liberal Opposition (now government) has criticised the new bodies, arguing they create an expensive and unnecessary overburden. It is unclear what the fate of the new bodies will be if there were to be a change of government.

The National Health Reform Agreement which gave effect to the Gillard-negotiated reforms described the changes as being designed to achieve 'a nationally unified and *locally controlled* health system' (emphasis added). The local element involved a commitment from the states to introduce local governance for 'hospital networks'. Most states (the notable exception being Victoria) had abolished local governance of hospitals in favour of direct accountability of areas/districts (which incorporated multiple hospitals) to the state department of health. Area/district chief executive officers' (CEOs') performance accountability was either to the state Director-General of Health or his/her deputy.

The other change in local structures was the creation of 61 'Medicare Locals', independent organisations primarily funded by the Commonwealth government charged with:

- improving the patient journey through developing integrated and coordinated services;
- providing support to clinicians and service providers to improve patient care;
- identification of the health needs of local areas and development of locally focused and responsive services;
- facilitation of the implementation and successful performance of primary health care initiatives and programmes; and
- being efficient and accountable with strong governance and effective management.

These organisations replaced previous 'Divisions of General Practice' which were general medical practice dominated and aligned. The rhetoric surrounding Medicare Locals created expectations out of all proportion to the funding allocated. They are expected to 'coordinate' primary health care and improve the general practice–hospital interface, but were given no policy levers to induce either private medical practices or hospitals to change their ways.

Unfortunately, the Medicare Locals did not have the power to achieve the changes expected of them. The 2014 Budget (see the next section) defunded the Medicare Locals and foreshadowed new, larger organisations called Primary Healthcare Networks. Whether they will suffer from the same problems of diffuse goals and unrealistic expectations is unknown at the time of writing (August 2014).

The Medicare Locals also represent a major intrusion of the Commonwealth into what was once a state domain. Although the Commonwealth had clear responsibility for primary medical care, states had carried responsibility for public funding of non-medical primary care services.

The 2014 Budget

The Labor government was defeated at the 2013 election and a new Liberal–National coalition government elected. Its first budget (May 2014) introduced sweeping changes to Commonwealth–state arrangements in health care. In addition to proposing a new co-payment for general practitioner visits, which was expected to increase demand for state-funded hospital emergency department attendances, it unilaterally terminated a range of grants to the states. It also effectively tore up the National Health Agreement which the previous government had negotiated with the states and changed indexation arrangements for hospital grants from being based on a share of the costs of activity growth to being a parsimonious formula based on population and Consumer Price Index growth. These changes significantly reduced funding to the states and represented the largest cost-shift between governments seen in recent decades. As a result, trust between the Commonwealth and the states largely evaporated. As part of the Budget announcements, the Commonwealth government foreshadowed reviews of Australia's federalism arrangements and tax powers. The reviews are expected to be finalised in late 2015.

Discussion and Conclusion

The settlement of the division of responsibilities between Australia's Commonwealth government and the states agreed at Federation survived 50 years before it was amended to increase Commonwealth responsibilities as part of the then Labor government's post war reconstruction policies. The existing division of responsibilities has a number of problems:

- significant vertical fiscal imbalance;
- overlapping roles leading to cost and blame shifting, fiscal squabbles, and multiple veto pints; and
- evidence of poor coordination of programme design leading to cliffs and programme discontinuities.

There are many different types of federal systems. Australia's marble cake federalism provides a particularly poor example of how a federal system might work. The overlapping responsibilities and absence of clear control points inhibit policy development.

Recognition of Australia's federal problem does not mean that it will be changed. Even Australia's muddled federalism serves a political purpose. Although residents of Australia's populous southeast corner might be comfortable about a shift of power from their state capitals to Canberra, residents further afield have a stronger states' rights tradition.

Reagan and Sanzone's (1981: 170) description of the role of federalism in the United States has some resonance in Australia:

> [Federalism is] now best described as that states [...] have won the right to be heard in the design of programs and a right to share in their implementation.

The extent of consultation between the Commonwealth and states varies with personalities (at both bureaucratic and political levels) and political affiliations.

There are two broad directions to mitigate the adverse effects of federalism: functional separation and improved coordination. Although health professionals regularly call for a Commonwealth takeover of responsibility for health care, such proposals have never progressed despite threats by previous Labor Prime Minister Rudd to initiate a constitutional change to effect it and musings by current Liberal Prime Minister Abbott that it was 'a debate we have to have' (Griffith 2006: 1).

The alternate functional separation strategy is to expand the role of the states. The condition present for this is for the states' tax base to be expanded significantly, although the politics of this suggest that it is unlikely to be achieved. The prospect of the Commonwealth handing full responsibility to the states, and their accepting that, must be seen as remote.

The real action in terms of reforming federalism in health care has been on improving coordination. As outlined above, the Reform Commission recommended a number of new national bodies to reduce the policy paralysis that had been associated with Commonwealth–state mechanisms. Although these recommendations were implemented, the 2014 Budget proposed abolishing or merging many of these so the prospects for national coordination are unclear. The Commonwealth's 2014 Budget represented a step backward in the development of mechanisms and incentives for cooperation between the Commonwealth and the states in health care. Nothing tangible was proposed to replace the nascent structures established through the 2007–2013 reforms.

Coordination is not a neutral concept. As Peres (1974: 151–2) pointed out:

> Coordination is one of the most fraudulent words of politics and administration. It dresses neutrally to disguise what nakedly is pure political form. Coordination is a political process by which the coordinated are made to change their value positions, their policy conceptions and their behaviour to conform to the conceptions and expectations of the coordinator.

In Peres's world, the coordinator needs to have some basis of power (Lukes 1974) to be able to exercise coordination. In the Australian context participation in coordination discussions by the states has been achieved by the Commonwealth allocating funding to buy involvement. The junior participants must feel that the costs of participation are worth the benefits. Coordination also requires trust and a collaborative mindset. The 2014 Budget undermined trust in Commonwealth–state relations and took money off the table. The prospects for trust-based cooperative arrangements were thus also undermined.

Another basis for coordination is a partnership of equals where the participants have clear and explicit financial incentives to participate and cooperate, akin to what Lindblom (1965) called partisan mutual adjustment. The National Health Agreement led to a new settlement which exposed the Commonwealth to the costs of growth in public hospital costs, through their assuming responsibility for 50 per cent of the costs of growth (at the National Efficient Price) from 2017. This created a better alignment of incentives on the Commonwealth relating to provision of hospital care (but does nothing to change incentives on states to improve primary care). The 2014 Budget abolished this provision leaving no incentive on the Commonwealth to use its policy instruments to reduce future growth in hospital costs. The shared financial incentive that the previous policies about sharing the cost of growth in hospital activity created gave the best prospect for facilitating cooperative working between the Commonwealth and the states. Future progress on improved Commonwealth–state working will probably require these policies to be restored.

The 2014 Budget was thus a watershed moment in Commonwealth–state relations. Trust was undermined, national coordinating structures merged or abolished, and the financial incentive to work in concert was thrown out. In summary, as of August 2014 the future of Commonwealth–state relations in Australia is uncertain, to say the least, and problematic. There is no sign that their manifold weaknesses will be reduced.

It is therefore likely that Australia will continue to muddle through with its marble cake federalism, and pursue a non-strategy of lamenting the adverse consequences of its federal structure but taking no positive action to change the status quo.

Chapter 10

The United States

Kieke G.H. Okma and Theodore R. Marmor

Introduction

This contribution takes a comparative perspective of health care reforms in the United States (US) and Western Europe in the broader context of the welfare state changes of the last quarter of the twentieth century. The widespread claim that the modern welfare states and health care had become unaffordable and ungovernable fuelled a movement of ideas across borders that met, we argue, with too little evaluative scrutiny. We summarise key features of health care in the US and Europe and discuss the main elements of the 2010 health care legislation enacted by the Obama administration. We next turn to two central questions: is the US health domain 'unique' – and if so, is that uniqueness related to US federalism? While federal states have formal delegation of fiscal and social policy making to regional levels of government based on constitutional division of powers, there are tensions between central governments and regional and local authorities over health policy decisions everywhere. Our brief answer to the first question is yes, to some extent, and to the second one, no.

The Five Worlds of American Health Care Funding

European policy analysts regularly depict the United States as the ultimate 'market model' (Kane 1995; Rothgang et al. 2005; Wendt 2009), with few limits on consumer choice. That label is misleading. US health care is actually a complex mix of public and private funding and provision. The major social programmes – Medicare for the elderly and disabled, Medicaid for particular groups of the poor, and the Veterans' Health programme – reflect strong solidarity with particular population groups. Public funding contributes more than 50 per cent of the nation's 2.7 trillion dollar medical economy. And, notably, public polls continue to show that most Americans favour government action to insure universal access to health care (NASI 2013), though opinions differ sharply about the way that should be done. None of this supports the portrait of American health care as a market-driven sector.

When comparing US health care funding with that of Europe, differences seem prominent at first. The United States was the only major industrial nation without a universal or near-universal health insurance by 2010 (see discussion about the effects of the 2010 Patient Protection and Affordable Care Act below). Most adult employees had insurance coverage sponsored by their employer, some families have individual plans, and there were several public programmes targeted at specific population groups. Some of those are very similar to health funding arrangements in Europe.

There are, in fact, five 'Worlds of Health Care' (Okma and Marmor, forthcoming). The first is Medicare, America's form of European social insurance. The hospital insurance part of Medicare (Part A) covers more than 50 million retired persons over 64, as well as disabled persons and patients suffering from renal failure. Here, the Center for Medicare and Medicaid Services (CMS) sets the rules, but decentralised, private insurers administer hospital payments. Social insurance contributions during work bring entitlements to health care when ill during retirement. There is no link between health status and payment (or of service), core marks of social insurance. The second 'Health America', Medicaid, is a close cousin to the European Poor Law tradition. The states administer Medicaid, with largely federal funding, but access is limited to poor families who meet income and asset tests and demographic eligibility criteria. Third, most families (over 60 per cent of adults under 65) get employer-sponsored health insurance at work. Workers and their families can sign up for health plans offered by private insurers. The rates reflect group characteristics as a common feature of private insurance. The fourth 'Health America' is the 'socialised medicine' represented by the Veterans' Health Administration (VHA), where disability after service to the country brings entitlement to medical care for life. The VHA is a national system of public hospitals, clinics, and affiliations with medical schools under general direction from Washington, but with considerable autonomy for VHA's regional offices. Lastly, there is the insecure world of the uninsured, estimated at almost 45.5 million Americans in 2012 (www.CDC.gov). They depend on private charity in hospitals and physician offices, as well as federal law that requires hospitals to admit and stabilise anyone who shows up at the emergency room. The public funding includes the major programmes noted above, and other federal programmes like care for Native Americans and the Armed Services, local health clinics and, importantly, the tax expenditures that subsidise the employment-based coverage for working Americans.

The problems of access worsened in the past two decades, with growing numbers of uninsured and underinsured (peaking at 50 million in 2010). The estimated number of uninsured sometime within a two-year period was almost 58 million persons in 2012 (CDC 2012). Medical inflation (the difference between the growth rate of health expenditures and general price increases) in the US has exceeded any other industrialised country since the early 1970s, and medical bills remain the second major cause of personal bankruptcy (kff.org 2008).

The most striking features of America's health care, then, are its fragmentation, high costs and continued high level of medical inflation, uneven access to health care and unfair distributive consequences (Marmor 2008; Elhauge 2010). Those features are not directly linked to America's federal structure, but reflect a complicated mix of national and regional state responsibilities, and state and markets controls. In the last three decades, facing high rates of medical inflation, employers have become more reluctant to offer (private) insurance to their employees. They cut costs by offering lower-priced plans with restricted coverage and high deductibles. Private insurers, too, imposed more and more restrictions on the choices of their insured. Federal and state governments sought ways to restrain medical care expenditures that have persistently out-distanced their revenue growth.

Comparing the US experience with that of its northern neighbour, Canada, highlights its distinctive features. In 1970, both nations spent about 7 per cent of their national income on medical care. By 1990, the US share had risen to 11.5 per cent of gross domestic product (GDP), and Canada had risen to 9 per cent. The gap widened to 14 and 10 per cent respectively in 2000, and while US health expenditures increased to 17 per cent in 2012, Canada's expenditures remained constant as a percentage of GDP (www.OECD.org). Those divergent growth rates highlight, above all, the cost restraining capacity of Canada's health financing policies. Whereas the US discovers the total of its national expenditures after the fact, Canadian federal and provincial governments decide what to expend on hospital and physician services (prescription drugs outside hospitals are not included in the national health insurance, but most provinces offer separate schemes). Canadian provinces set limits on hospital budgets and outlays for physicians. As in Europe, those overall spending limits were more powerful in restraining medical expenditure than the fashionable parade of cost control instruments celebrated (and then largely abandoned) in the US since the 1970s.

Contracting Health Care

Both North American and European countries have regularly altered the methods of contracting and paying hospitals and physicians during the past three decades. In the mid-2000s, several European countries followed earlier experiences of Australia and the US with set amounts for specific patient groups (diagnosis-related groups or DRGs). England introduced 'performance-based payment' for general practitioners (GPs), offering additional income for reaching certain targets. On a modest scale, the NHS also allowed physicians to practice in for-profit clinics, whether financed from public or private sources. But the pay for performance did not replace traditional fee for service payment for GPs. The common experience across Europe has been an increasing hybridisation – or mix – of payment modes: fee for service per activity or office visit, per episode of care, amounts for specific patient groups (DRGs), salary, per diem, reimbursement for actual costs, or annual budgets based on historical expenditure. Interestingly, the fact that mixed systems had become dominant across Europe did not prominently figure in American discussions of payment innovation.

Most change in US health care contracting and payment occurred in private health insurance rather than in Medicare or Medicaid. Private insurers experimented with ways to reduce physician and hospital payment. Often under the rubric of 'managed care', they 'bundled' payments for the treatment of certain categories of patients and limited reimbursement. The early 'health maintenance organisations' (HMOs) of the 1970s at first combined health insurance with the responsibility to actually provide care to their insured. Over time, however, HMOs limited themselves to contracting health professionals and hospitals (shifting financial risk to providers and limiting choice of patients). With that came an explosion in the proper names and acronyms for different types of insurance coverage like Preferred Provider Organizations (PPOs) or Independent Provider Organizations (IPOs) (Hacker and Marmor 1999).

HMOs next restrained the use of medical care in other ways: pre-authorisation of treatment, ex-post denial of reimbursement, and, in some cases, cancellation of insurance once patients with chronic illness or other 'pre-existing conditions' were identified (Marmor, Okma, and Rojas 2008). Those changes caused great distress for providers and patients. Providers took their insurers to court and convinced US state legislatures to restrain the restrainers and ban selective contracting, gag rules (the prohibition to publicly discuss the terms of contracts) and other restrictions imposed by health insurers. By the late 1990s, there was widespread scepticism about the cost-containing capacity of the new forms of paying doctors and hospitals.

Changes in Ownership in Health Care

In the US, as in Western Europe, the majority of hospitals remained independent, non-profit institutions, although for-profit ownership increased more in the US than in Europe. During the last three decades of the twentieth century, hospital mergers and takeovers led to accelerated market consolidation. Private chains bought a number of publicly owned county hospitals, and a few university medical centres sold their hospitals to large medical companies like Columbia-HCA and Tenet. Those private medical centres – concentrated in the south and the west – comprised about 20 per cent of all hospitals in 2012 (AHA 2013). (In general, private hospitals have fewer beds than non-profit ones, thus the share of bed capacity is somewhat lower). The transformations received substantial media attention, especially over some financial scandals in the above two companies that had urged physicians to falsify results of their departments to boost profits. Both settled major fraud cases. Some hospitals started purchasing the offices of local general practitioners and internists in the 1990s, but soon dropped this practice when they realised the limited financial benefits (by 2012, there was renewed interest in this practice).

American physicians largely remain independent professionals, with separate offices and staffs, affiliations to hospitals and remuneration from a variety of sources. The number of physicians employed by hospitals (with the new specialty 'hospitalist') increased and by 2012, one third of American physicians were employed by hospitals, clinics, and group practices. There was considerable change in methods of payment and the balance of power among physicians and those paying for their services. As in Europe, payment methods became more mixed, with fee-for-service supplemented by sessional payments, capitation, and salary.

The never-ending struggles over income levels and payment methods, which in many European countries are the subject of extended negotiation with the organised parties, take place in the US in a decentralised and unorganised way. American doctors and hospitals face scores of separate payers, each with their own rules and conditions – but absent overall budget restraints set by central and regional governments. That administrative fragmentation helps to explain the high administrative costs of American health care. While federalism in Canada fortified the position of provinces, hospitals, and physicians as the core players in the health care bargaining arena, the US decentralised and fragmented authority weakened collective negotiations.

Health Care Administration

The term 'health care administration' refers to decision-making over the allocation of resources. In all industrialised countries, there is a public–private mix in the administration of health care and health insurance. Reflecting historical patterns of governance, as noted above, both US and European hospitals and health facilities remained non-profit, and the administration of social health insurance remained in the hands of legally independent, non-profit sick funds in the majority of continental Western European countries. Reflecting historical patterns of larger power distribution between central (federal or non-federal) and regional (and local) levels of government, however, there are substantial differences in the roles of governments and other parties.

The fiscal and budgetary pressures of the 1970s and 1980s prompted widespread efforts to reduce the direct role of (central) governments and decentralise health care administration. The decentralisation efforts went into two directions: first, *regionalised decentralisation* with a shift from central (federal) levels to regional and local authorities as in Spain and Italy or, as in the UK, to parts of the country (Wales, Scotland, and Northern Ireland). Scandinavian countries strengthened the role of regional and local governments. The assumption is that on those levels, there is strong 'community involvement' of local citizens, who will hold elected officials accountable, voting them out of office if they fail to deliver on their promises. This decentralised administration comes with potential conflicts of interest (Anell 2005). Local and regional officials carry the budgetary and administrative responsibility for health care services, but also represent the interests of the general population, including patients, tax-paying families and health care providers. Those roles present many opportunities for conflict and blame-shifting. For example, in Spain and Italy, large-scale tensions reappeared over the regional allocation of budgets – similar to the tensions in Canada's federal–provincial annual budget negotiations.

The United Kingdom (UK) and France, both non-federal countries with strong centralised traditions, governments engaged in efforts to decentralise administration in a model of deconcentration (e.g., regional offices of central departments) as well as genuine shifts in budgetary powers to regional levels – at least on paper. It remains to be seen how in those two states the central powers are really able and willing to shift decision-making powers and financial risks to the regional level. Critics observed that the decentralisation efforts have, in fact, often resulted in strengthening central controls.

The second form of decentralisation (*functional decentralisation*) entails shifts in decision-making and financial risks from governments to independent (both non-profit and for-profit) health services and health insurers. This shift – with marked variation – was more common in the social health insurance countries like Austria, Germany, Belgium, Luxembourg, and the Netherlands. The 'Bismarckian' policy-making tradition of those countries includes permanent platforms for policy debate where governments and stakeholders discuss policy change. The US and Canada – both federal states – do not have such neo-corporatist traditions. But Canada has developed its own 'home grown corporatism' (Okma 2002b). There are quasi-permanent consultations by ad hoc (federal and regional) expert committees or countrywide royal commissions. While not as crucial in legislative reforms as in, for example, the UK, those Commissions nonetheless have more influence on agenda-setting than the presidential commissions in the United States.

The overall fragmented and complex institutional arrangements of American government disperse power and authority over federal, state and local authorities as well as over the three branches of government. This power fragmentation provides many veto points for opponents to reform in any sector – as illustrated by the extraordinary difficulty in enacting both financial and health care reform during 2008–2010. The fragmentation also shows up in diverging views about administrative responsibilities and the large number of institutions that administer and regulate American medical care. In fact, each of the separate 'worlds of health' we described above, entails a different set of administrative responsibilities of federal and state governments, employers and employees, private health insurers and insured, and public and private providers of health care. That fragmentation is both complex and costly to public and private players. It also creates substantial barriers to change and reform that are not explained by federalist structures.

US Health Reform of 2010: Patching Up the Patchwork

The patchwork features of America's health care described above are crucial in understanding the complex character and scope of the Patient Protection and Affordable Care Act (PPACA or ACA) of 2010. The ACA, enacted after a bitter ideological debate, is in fact a quite limited challenge to the five 'Health Americas'. Indeed, it can be regarded as patches on a patchwork, with four major elements (Marmor and Oberlander 2010).

First is the expansion of health insurance to the uninsured, with mandates to buy private insurance (and fines for non-compliance) as the regulatory stick and means-tested subsidies as the financial carrot, as well as federal subsidy to the states for expanding access to Medicaid. The ACA reform model borrowed substantially from the Massachusetts reform of 2006 (enacted by Republican governor Mitt Romney) that encouraged uninsured to seek private coverage by offering premium subsidy.

The second feature of ACA is extensive insurance regulation to prevent practices characteristic of commercial insurance that create access barriers for elderly or persons with 'pre-existing conditions'. This regulation also requires insurers to accept anyone seeking insurance, without charging higher risk groups higher premiums, and limits the profit margin of insurers by imposing minimum 'loss ratio' rules (minimum amounts for spending on health costs of the insured). Illustrating the fact that reforming health care systems is not a one-shot effort (Okma and Crivelli 2010), the effort to secure minimum standards for health insurance meant that by early 2014, many insured were forced to change plans (sometimes to more expensive plans) as their earlier coverage did not meet the standard. This prompted widespread outcry and heated debate.

The third feature of the reform is the long list of new programmes and initiatives aimed to improve the quality of medical care and control costs: increased attention to prevention, expanded research on the comparative effectiveness of medical innovations, and expanded use of information technology such as electronic medical records. Other rules focus on the organisation of medical care by encouraging physicians to work in group practices (labelled 'accountable care organisations'). Those instruments, in our view, are unlikely to be effective in reining in expenditure. No doubt helpful in improving the organisation of health care and the quality of medical care decision-making, none seriously confront medical inflation.

The fourth crucial feature of the reform is the political strategy and its implications for comparing US and European reform experience. First and foremost, the Obama administration sought to obtain bipartisan support by embracing a reform model that to a considerable degree reflects Republican value preferences on health insurance. The new law builds on the patchwork of present arrangements, rather than transforming those. It does not bring a single overarching model of medical care financing and provision. Rather, the reform aims to gradually expand insurance, both public and private, hoping to substantially expand insurance coverage (or even reach universal coverage) over time, and offers coverage that is catastrophic in character (leaving considerable financial risks to families in the form of high deductibles and co-payments). The reform thus tolerates great differences in how the care of similarly ill Americans will be provided, financed, and regulated.

The irony is that, while reflecting Republican preferences, ACA failed to secure a single Republican vote in the US Senate. So, explaining the reform requires an understanding of the institutional structure of American politics. Dispersion of authority marks American politics, especially prominent in the sharing of power among the executive, the Congress, and the courts at the national level, and, next, the federal, state, and local levels of administration. Added to that are rules – like the filibuster – that permit minorities within the Congress (41 votes in the Senate) to block legislation. Facing that context, the Obama administration decided to expand two of the five worlds of health care (private coverage and Medicaid) rather than rationalising and overhauling the system, hoping to realise major change during the first term in office.

The details of the episode are less central than the character of the reform that emerged. The reform model borrowed heavily from the idea of 'regulated competition' among health insurers, creating wider market of subsidised and non-subsidised citizens. It reflected not only the dominant interests of major insurance firms and medical care providers, but also the growth of pro-market thinking in health care among policy elites since the stagflation of the 1970s, both in the US and in Europe (but there, as we noted above, it never gained much popular support). It is at that level – the dissemination of policy ideas – that parallels between the US and EU reform experiences are evident. One also needs to emphasise the limited impact of these ideas in European countries where norms of universal or near-universal coverage and equal treatment enjoyed strong popular support. In the US, the recent reform did not arise with a comparable commitment to equal access of equally ill people to health care.

Conclusions

In many ways, the United States remained exceptional after the introduction of the 2010 Patient Protection and Affordable Care Act (ACA). It still is the only OECD nation without universal or near-universal health insurance, though the ACA seeks to reduce the number of uninsured. The current system is highly fragmented and offers health insurance coverage to different population groups – elderly, (very) poor families, veterans, working families – with widely divergent distributional consequences. By 2012, almost 15 per cent of the population, 45.5 million persons, had no insurance and another 15 per cent or so is underinsured or has been without coverage in the last few years. They have to pay themselves for medical care or depend on charity care and public subsidy. While there is strong public support for Medicare, the social insurance for elderly, and most Americans support the notion of universal health insurance, there is not agreement on the form of such scheme. Moreover, the fragmented political system in the US has created many veto positions that all but block major change. The 2010 mid-term elections brought a Republican majority in the House, and Republican leaders announced that they continue their efforts to repeal all or part of the legislation, and weaken or reverse it in the years ahead. That means that president Obama has faced strong and continuous opposition in the actual implementation of the ACA.

Our overall conclusions are as follows. First, transformative change in public policy is rare, and the health policy domain is no exception. There are not that many 'windows of opportunity' for 'big bang' reforms (Kingdon 1984). The passage of the 1935 Social Security as well as Medicare and Medicaid (in 1965) in the US, the introduction of the British NHS in 1948, the passage of Holland's 2006 universal health insurance mandate – these are all examples of major change.

Second, values matter. Over time, dominant social values shape political institutions and policy making. Reversely, once in place, institutions themselves fortify and shape values as well (Marmor, Okma, and Latham 2006). For example, America's Social Security and Medicare reflect the idea that retired elderly are especially 'deserving' of income protection. Over time, both programmes became very popular. Likewise, the British NHS of 1948 expresses support for universal and fair access to health care for all Brits, publicly funded and administered. The NHS itself has added to the sense of common values in the UK, and so has Canada's medicare. In Europe (as in Canada), strong popular support for universal access to health care without undue financial barriers constrains government efforts to shift costs of medical care to families.

Third, reforming health care is not a one-shot effort (Okma and Crivelli 2010). Unexpected and unwanted side effects, public dissatisfaction and strong opposition by organised stakeholders commonly force governments to change policy or abandon their plans altogether. Actors in the health care arena anticipate policy change and react strategically to gain or defend their market positions. In fact, 'after-reform maintenance' seems to be a more or less permanent feature of health reforms. In the United States, the ultimate fate of the 2010 reform bill is far from secure after its passage.

And finally, institutions matter. In a narrow sense, political institutions (defined as the political decision-making structure) not only enable or prevent reforms, but also determine the speed of change. For example, 'neo-corporatist' decision-making in Austria, Belgium, Germany, or the Netherlands provides strong veto powers for organised interests over social policy. In the 'Westminster' politics, in contrast, strong political leadership can implement its political agenda more easily. Nonetheless, there are limits to that power. Certain programmes or entitlements, once in place, create their own constituencies that resist change if seen detrimental to their positions (Pierson 1994). The American reform of 2010 is a striking example of how political institutions shape and limit governments' abilities to address widely-acknowledged problems. Typically, final legislation is distinct from and typically less far-reaching than popular demands for reform or political rhetoric. The gap between the rhetoric of the Obama administration and the reality of the ACA is large, but largely explained by American politics with numerous veto points – not so much by it particular federal governance structure.

When studying 'federalist' policy making, it is important to assess whether the conflicts between central and regional governments are related to the federalist structures per se. We found that in fact, such conflicts occur in all states where central or federal authorities share budgetary and decision-making responsibilities in health policy. In that sense, the US is not unique.

Chapter 11
India

James Warner Björkman and A. Venkat Raman

Introduction

This chapter explores relationships between the provision of health care in India and its federal structure of government. Governmental institutions are not neutral; they shape the behaviour and decisions of political actors that directly impact on policy development. In particular, a federal system influences and constrains any government activity – including a public health system – through multiple veto-points, interregional tax competition and regional jurisdictions (Jordan 2008). Sixty-plus years of federalism in India have produced a disorganised health system with mismatched funding among levels of government and a concentration of health care professionals in urban areas. Patterned on the 1946 Bhore Report with its tiers of integrated responsibilities and logical structures, the health system in India is simultaneously centralised and a patchwork of programmes.

As contextual background, India's population of 1.3 billion is governed by a democratic federal system that includes the central government of India, 29 constituent states, seven union territories, 593 districts, and, in most states, three levels of local rural government (*panchayati raj*) at district, block, and village levels. Of the 29 states, 19 each have a population of more than 25 million – and one state, Uttar Pradesh, with over 200 million inhabitants, is approximately the population of Brazil. With 17 per cent of the total population of Earth, one of every six people lives in India. The annual demographic growth is 1.6 per cent; half of all Indians are below 25 years of age, and almost two-thirds below 35. By 2030 India is predicted to have more than 1.53 billion people.

To understand India's political system, a brief sketch puts its institutions in perspective. During the Raj, India's princely states had considerable discretion over their internal affairs but remained under British rule (Rao and Singh 2005). In the early twentieth century, a system of 'dyarchy' evolved in which provinces of British India had responsibilities for domestic functions while the empire retained overall control. Even the Indian nationalist movement developed a federal structure based on regions and linguistic lines. In 1928 the Motilal Nehru Committee of the Indian National Congress stated that an independent India would be parliamentary, bicameral, and federal (Stepan et al. 2010: 55). India has a legacy of central planning and a concentration of power that has left governments at state and local levels in a subordinate position.

Historical legacies are important in the shaping of any polity. Centuries of colonial rule facilitated the development of communication and the spread of the English language that underpinned mass mobilisation. But given the trauma of partition and its aftermath, the post-independence Constituent Assembly focused on the unity and integrity of India. The fear of excessive federalism and the risks of centrifugal forces were cogently articulated. The constitutional framework finally adopted departed significantly from all existing models of federalism. Self-rule and shared rule were combined in unorthodox ways that produced a hybrid termed quasi-federalism. Unlike the 1869 US Supreme Court ruling in *Texas vs White* that confirmed the United States as 'an indissoluble union of indestructible states', India's Constituent Assembly created an indissoluble union of destructible states.

Institutional Description

In order to manage geographic size and social complexity, the founding fathers of the Indian Constitution established a network of constituent units analogous to geographic divisions in the United States. At the same time, they adopted the parliamentary system of government used in the United Kingdom (Austin 1999). India thus has a quasi-federal parliamentary system of government. Its strong Centre has proved resilient and, given social diversities and cleavages, is considered indispensable for maintaining social harmony. Even during the current era of economic liberalisation, the Centre retains control over all macroeconomic levers. Proponents of state autonomy in India do not challenge a strong Centre but want stronger states within the same framework.

Federalism in India differs from other federations in the world because it is not a group of independent entities (states, cantons, provinces) that joined together to form a federation by conceding a portion of their rights of government. Rather it is a distributional entity that derives its power from a single source. Sovereignty and governance are distributed and shared among several entities and organs. Dr Bhimrao Ramji Ambedkar, chair of the Drafting Committee of the Constituent Assembly, stressed the importance of describing India as 'Union of States' rather than a 'Federation of States': 'Though the country and the people may be divided into different states for convenience of administration, the country is one integral whole, its people a single people living under a single imperium derived from a single source'.

The Indian constitution defines the distribution of federal powers between the Centre and the states. Unlike the federal governments of the United States, Switzerland, or Australia, residual powers remain with the Centre. Strongly biased toward the Union government, features of federalism in India include:

- Both houses of parliament based on population: Lok Sabha (House of the People) directly; Rajya Sabha (Council of States) indirectly.

- Consent of a state is not required by the parliament to alter its boundaries.
- No state, except Jammu and Kashmir, can have its own constitution.
- No state has the right to secede.
- No division of public services between Centre and states.

As defined by the Constitution, powers of the states and the Centre are divided among three lists. The Union list consists of 99 items, on which parliament has exclusive power to legislate. Among these are defence, armed forces, atomic energy, foreign affairs, citizenship, extradition, railways, airways, communications, currency, foreign trade, interstate trade, and commerce, banking, insurance, income tax, export duties, etc.

The state list consists of 61 items in which uniformity is desirable but not essential. The state legislature has exclusive power to make laws on these subjects but, under certain circumstances, parliament can also make laws on subjects in the state list. However, parliament then has to pass a resolution with two-thirds majority that it is in the national interest to legislate on this state list. Selected items in this list include law and order, police forces, *health care*, transport, land policies, and electricity. Though states have exclusive powers to legislate on items in the state list, several articles in the Constitution identify situations in which the Centre can legislate on these items.

The Concurrent list consists of 52 items where, again, uniformity is desirable but not essential. Items on this list include marriage and divorce, transfer of property other than agricultural land, education, trustees and trusts, civil procedure, contempt of court, drugs and poisons, adulteration of foodstuffs, contracts, bankruptcy and insolvency, economic and social planning, etc.

Constitutionally, except in a few cases, union law trumps state law. If any provision of a law made by a state legislature contravenes any provision of law made by parliament on which parliament is competent to enact, or contravenes any provision of an existing law with respect to one of the matters enumerated in the Concurrent List, then the law made by parliament, whether passed before or after the law made by the legislature of such a state, will prevail and the law made by the legislature of the state is void. However, even in the heyday of Congress dominance and the command economy, the states sat at the bargaining table with the Centre with enough political clout to scuttle policy initiatives of the central government and to introduce their own (Sinha 2005: 83–8).

Although the 1950 Constitution of India outlines the allocation of central and state-level responsibilities for health care, these have never been matched with political commitment or substantial resources. While responsibilities are theoretically decentralised, the system is centralised in practice. Although constitutionally responsible for health care, state governments in India lack policy autonomy and capacity (John 2010; Reddy et al. 2011).

The same limitations apply to local governments in India. Based on recommendations of the 1958 Balwantrai Mehta Committee, most states introduced a three-tier system of rural local government: district council (*zila parishad*), intermediate level (*panchayat samiti*), and *gram panchayat* at village level (Björkman 1979: 19–26). Although charged with such activities as community development, plans, and oversight of health and education, the panchayat system had no independent role due to lack of resources coupled with vaguely defined responsibilities. Lacking financial resources and clearly defined powers, the panchayat bodies became mere agents for state authorities.

Despite the constitutionally enabling amendments of 1992, local finances remain under the strict control of state-level departments or their subordinate offices at district and subdistrict levels (Mahal et al. 2000). Personnel in schools and primary health facilities rarely report to, and are not accountable to, elected local representatives. Their salaries are directly payable by the appropriate state department. Senior political representatives such as members of parliament and the state legislature are often appointed to these local bodies, further curtailing their limited role (Bjorkman and Chaturvedi 1994). The fact that elections to panchayats have been held infrequently, or not at all, has further eroded their legitimacy and credibility.

In 1983 the Union government of India appointed the Sarkaria Commission to examine relationships and the balance of power between state and central governments and to suggest changes in the constitutional framework of Centre–state relations. After eliciting information and conducting deliberations, the Commission in 1988 submitted a 1,600-page report with 247 specific recommendations. While the commission concluded that the Centre had too much power and recommended greater decentralisation by allowing states more autonomy (Ray 1988), in practice it endorsed the status quo in Centre–state relations. It is widely agreed that the changes recommended by the commission have not been implemented (Bagchi 2003).

After the Sarkaria Commission and the onset of Indian liberalisation in the 1990s, greater decentralisation had been expected. In reality, transition towards a decentralised form of political and fiscal federalism proved to be difficult. States continue to rely on the Centre for direction and resources, and the limited powers devolved to the states have not been extended to rural and local bodies of government. Unsurprisingly, in 2002 the National Commission to Review the Working of the Constitution reported that centralisation is the root cause of India's institutional problems.

A step towards decentralisation occurred in 1992 when the 73rd and 74th amendments to the Indian Constitution were adopted. Enacted in response to calls for more responsibility in local governments, the amendments sought to increase the autonomy of municipalities and Panchayati Raj institutions at district, block, and village levels by granting them constitutional status (Johnson 2003; Rothermund 2008; Singh 2008). The amendments gave local bodies the responsibility for 28 development activities including health and sanitation, family welfare, women and child development, drinking water, poverty alleviation, and the public distribution system. These amendments were intended to provide local governments with greater autonomy and generated hopes for improving the quality and effectiveness of public spending by pushing decision-making about local public goods down to the local level (Bagchi 2003).

Despite the 73rd and 74th amendments, however, little autonomy has been given to local governments. Reforms anticipated after the Sarkaria Commission and the constitutional amendments have not occurred; power remains centralised at national level and, relative to local bodies, at state level. This centralisation has been exacerbated in the area of fiscal matters where local governments have no influence and rely on their respective state governments to finance health services. To compound matters, state governments have limited funds to allocate to local governments because they too are disadvantaged in fiscal powers (National Commission on Macroeconomics and Health 2005; Singh 2008).

Since the 1980s, decentralisation has been frequently debated in India. Recommendations of the Sarkaria Commission, the 73rd and 74th Amendment Acts, and the 2002 National Commission to Review the Working of the Constitution exemplify this debate. However, with significant implications for health policy, power has not been delegated downwards. The political centralisation of powers has distorted incentives at all levels of government in India, including its health system. Although local governments have responsibilities for health services, they have not been allocated the authoritative power or the funds to carry out these responsibilities.

While not constitutionally specified, political parties operate the structures of government in democratic polities. For more than a century, India's political history has been shaped by the Indian National Congress that emerged from a nineteenth-century association of political amateurs into a twentieth-century mass nationalist movement and then into a political party that dominated the first two decades of post-independence politics. The impacts of federalism on Indian health policy and performance are due in no small measure to the changing fortunes of the Congress Party that remains one of India's two national political parties, the other being the Bharatiya Janata Party (BJP). 'National' refers to the number of parliamentary constituencies throughout India in which a political party nominates its candidates; in contrast, 'regional' parties field candidates in a relatively limited area of the Indian Union – usually confined to a single state or a small region of the country.

The last election in which the Congress Party obtained a majority of seats in parliament was in 1984. Domination by one party gave way to a coalition system in which no single party has been able to achieve a majority in the parliament. Electoral politics in India is characterised by coalition building among political parties in order to form a majority and thus to form the government (Mathur and Björkman 2009). Other than a few exceptions in the 1990s, the pattern has been for multiparty coalitions led by the Congress or by the BJP – respectively the 'United Progressive Alliance' (UPA) or the 'National Democratic Alliance' (UDA). But technically these 'airbus' coalitions remain minority governments because each requires support in the parliament by political parties outside (not members of) the respective coalition.

The year 1989 was a watershed because, for the first time since independence, a national election resulted in a hung parliament; no party won a majority. An era began of coalition governments in a multiparty system. The multiparty system was further 'federalised' by the rise of regional parties. State parties like the Dravida Munnetra Kazagam (DMK) in Tamil Nadu and the Telegu Desam Party (TDP) in Andhra Pradesh began to play a key role in forming coalition governments at the Centre and in making policy (Rudolph and Rudolph 2010: 152).

One feature of 'national' political parties has been their top-down centralising tendencies in government policies. Regional parties, on the other hand, favour maximum discretion or decentralised autonomy. The Members of Parliament in the 15th Lok Sabha (2009–2014) represent 38 political parties, all but two of which are ethnic or regional enterprises. In the foreseeable future, it is unlikely that a single party will be able to form the Union's central government in New Delhi but single political parties do form the governments in many states and union territories. The emergence of regional parties as centres of power in India is one of the most important developments in the country's post-independence history. In the 2014 general elections required for the 16th Lok Sabha, regional parties will play a pivotal role in the formation of the next union government. It is even possible that India's next general elections will produce a 'third front' government headed by the leader of a regional party.

Economic Description

Dramatic shifts in India's economic policy help account for the changing nature of Indian federalism. By 1991, when India changed course from a command economy to a market economy, the system was literally broke. The central government's Planning Commission no longer had public funds to invest; India could not pay its current account balance. The radical reduction of public investment by the Centre created a need for private investment to replace it that was quickly met by the more enterprising state governments. State chief ministers began to play leading roles in India's emergent 'federal market economy' as they sought to convince both domestic and foreign investors about the opportunities and incentives available in their respective states (Rudolph and Rudolph 2010).

India has a chronic imbalance between its government revenues and expenditures as well as a growing trade imbalance. Its fiscal deficit in FY2011–2012 was 5.8 per cent, sharply higher than the 3.5 per cent four years earlier, and it will rise in the near future due to new obligations. Initially promulgated as a presidential ordinance in July, the National Food Security Act became law in September 2013. Based on eligibility, this 'Right to Food' guarantees five kilos of subsidised grains monthly to approximately two-thirds of India's population. The fiscal deficit may well exceed its target of 4.8 per cent of GDP due also to imports of oil (because India imports 80 per cent of its oil) depending upon the price of oil at any given point in time.

India's balance of payments crisis in 1991 generated radical economic reforms in which tariffs were reduced, foreign investors were allowed in Indian markets, and procedures were simplified. The impending economic crisis, however, is more dangerous. The IMF has warned India that the fall in the growth rate since 2008 may engulf it in the same trap that once plagued Latin America and then countries in Southeast Asia.

While India is among the world's most rapidly growing economies, its growth rate has slowed considerably and it remains one of the world's poorest countries. Although it has relatively large amounts of foreign currency reserves, the current account deficit has recently deteriorated. Excluding remittances from workers overseas, India's current account deficit is just over 4 per cent of GDP. Rising wages, property, and food prices fuel inflation. In October 2013 the Union Ministry of Commerce and Industry reported a 7 per cent inflation rate. Between 1969 and 2013 the inflation rate averaged 7.7 per cent with an all-time high of 34.7 per cent in September 1974 and a record low of -11.3 per cent in May 1976.

Subsidies have helped to create a rudimentary social safety net in India but poor targeting of subsidies and an ineffective physical and social infrastructure contribute to fiscal stress with limited progress in poverty alleviation. Having tripled since 2006, food subsidies are driven by increasing costs of procurement and transportation that are the main drivers of the higher cost of food grains. Subsidised food and fuel such as kerosene and LPG are intended for those below the poverty line who have a ration card to prove their economic status. However, data reveal that about half of poor rural households do not have a BPL card. A large share of subsidised items are sold illegally, hoarded, or diverted to non-household use. The current structure of subsidies in India is regressive in the long-term and not sustainable from both fiscal and growth perspectives. The solution lies in gradually moving to a more effective direct cash-transfer system that is better targeted, eliminates profits by middlemen, and creates space for investment in infrastructure (Deorukhkar and Herrero 2013).

Other issues that challenge India's economy involve education, sanitation, inequality, and labour laws. Although India has a large number of English speakers (important for the call centre industry and for world trade), high levels of illiteracy exist – especially in rural areas and among women, one-third of whom remain illiterate. Likewise many Indians lack basic amenities such as access to running water. According to the 2011 census, 59 per cent of Indian households have a mobile phone while only 47 per cent have a toilet on the premises (including pit latrines that do not use running water). Limited access to toilets is a major problem that puts drinking water for millions of people at risk. India has the worst of the problem. With approximately 600 million practicing 'open defecation', the country has more than twice the number of the next 18 developing countries combined.

Inequality has risen in India rather than decreased. While economic growth was expected to pull India's poor above the poverty line, economic growth has been uneven with its benefits accruing disproportionately to the skilled and the wealthy. Many of India's rural poor are yet to receive any tangible benefit from the India's economic growth. With the spread of television in villages, they are increasingly aware of the disparity between rich and poor. But as India has one of the largest budget deficits in the developing world there is little scope for increasing investment in public services like health care and education.

Policy Analysis of India's Health System

India spends five per cent of its GDP on health care, a proportion in line with developing countries at similar income levels, but the portion of health spending undertaken in the public sector is about 20 per cent – well below most other countries. The private sector provides the vast bulk of health care services. In India, almost nine-tenths of all health expenditures are out-of-pocket and paid to the private sector. India has one of the world's highest levels of out-of-pocket financing with debilitating effects on the poor. Poor and socially marginalised communities depend on the public health system for their health services, but deficiencies in public systems in terms of lack of capacity and insufficient resources force the poor to seek health care in an unregulated private sector, borrowing money or selling assets (land, cattle, even children) to pay for such services. It has been estimated that each year one-third of Indians who are hospitalised will the fall below the poverty line because of hospital expenses (Mahal et al. 2000). Inequities in the health system are aggravated by the fact that, until very recently, public expenditures on health in India never exceeded one per cent of GDP.

The private sector, however, has greatly expanded over the years, due partly to failure of the public sector health system and partly to policies of economic liberalisation. India's private sector accounts for 93 per cent of hospitals, 85 per cent of doctors, 80 per cent of outpatients, 64 per cent of hospital beds, and 57 per cent of inpatients (Venkat Raman and Björkman 2009). Although unregulated and inequitable, the private sector is perceived to be easily accessible, better managed and more efficient than its public counterpart.

Each state has its own set of actors that influence the policy processes in the state. How different states have dealt with the private sector is one example of divergent approaches and results. Recognising the dominance of the private sector (including both for-profit and non-profit providers), several states have drafted legislation to regulate private hospitals. Given the limited capacity of state governments to enforce such laws, however, it is doubtful that these can significantly improve quality of care and may instead be misused to harass private providers (Peters et al. 2003: 254).

To review problems in India's health system, the national Ministry of Health and Family Welfare periodically releases a National Health Policy Report. While its 2002 report recommended improvements in the system, the central government ignored state actors – another example of the dominance by the Centre (Gupta 2002). Acknowledging the need for greater civil society integration and for increased public investment, the 2011 report made policy recommendations but did so without a plan for implementation. The latter report vaguely hints at allocating health funds to states based on performance indicators and notes that states must start contributing independently to primary health care.

But these reports on national health policy do not adequately address basic health needs. They appear to be window-dressing or prophylactic pronouncements full of suggestive movements but without any embarrassing consequences. On the contrary, since the early 1990s 'fiscal profligacy and mismanagement by state governments, and imbalances in the sharing of resources and constitutional responsibilities, have made them more dependent on the central government for financial resources' (Peters et al. 2003: 250). While the states account for 75–90 per cent of public spending on health, about 80 per cent of the funds are committed to human resources such as salaries and wages, which make the states depend on the Centre for critical inputs such as drugs, equipment, and other non-wage items.

Centrally sponsored schemes have become a powerful instrument for intervention in the states. They are changing the federal balance of power by making it possible for the Centre to shape state policies and priorities even in fields that are constitutionally under state jurisdiction, such as education and health. State ministries and departments, local bodies, and externally funded NGOs become de facto agents of the Centre in ways that subvert state autonomy policy (Rudolph and Rudolph 2010: 157). While the states prefer block grants that they can control, the Centre favours specific purpose assistance that implements its priorities.

India's framework for public health policy is weak, a problem that is compounded by a restrictive interregional fiscal transfer system (NCMH 2005). Local governments have no appreciable fiscal autonomy because they rely on funding through grants from state-level agencies. These grants are characterised by restrictions and are often wasted through the inefficiencies of bureaucracy (Wyke 2009). Expenditures by local governments depend on their respective state governments that retain constitutional responsibility for health. States that fund local governments through a State Finance Commission have devolved limited fiscal power to local governments largely because these states fall short in terms of their own revenue.

Horizontal fiscal inequalities refer to disparities among constituent units within the same federation; vertical fiscal inequalities refer to disparities in fiscal capacity between the central government and the constituent states. In federal systems, equalisation policy concerns horizontal redistribution aimed at tackling fiscal inequalities among constituent units (Bird and Tarasov 2004; Boadway and Shah 2007; Stark 2009). The goal is to find a balance between preserving the autonomy of constituent units and ensuring relatively equal access to public benefits and services across an entire country despite the institutional decentralisation inherent to federalism. Australia's goods and services tax (GST) is a good example because some of the revenues generated by its 10 per cent tax-rate are allocated to its states on a per capita basis and the balance is distributed on the fiscal capacities and expenditure needs of each state in order to reduce horizontal inequalities among them (Morris 2002). Discussions about GST have been underway in India since

2000; the 2007–2008 central budget of the Union Finance Minister announced that GST would be introduced in April 2010 and preparatory committees were duly appointed that produced a series of reports but to date (February 2014) nothing has yet been decided.

Like other federal systems of government, India has problems of imbalances within and between its federal components. Vertical imbalances occur when states incur expenditure disproportionate to their sources of revenue while attempting to fulfil their constitutional responsibilities. Horizontal imbalances occur among states due to historical backgrounds and differences in resource endowments. To address imbalances, the Indian Constitution provides measures to bridge the financial gap between the Centre and the states. In order to facilitate intergovernmental transfers, a Finance Commission is appointed every five years to recommend ways to share resources between the Indian Union and its states. In 2012 the 14th Finance Commission was established; chaired by Yaga Venugopal Reddy, former governor of the Reserve Bank of India, it will operate during 2015–2020. After assessing India's financial scene in terms of revenues and expenditure, it will recommend allocation of tax-resources to the states of the Indian Union to balance equity and growth.

The major responsibilities assigned to the states include agriculture, irrigation, public order, and public health. However, the most profitable taxes, such as taxes on income from non-agricultural sources, corporation tax and customs duty, are assigned to the central government. While a long list of taxes is assigned to the states, only the tax on the sale of goods is significant for generating revenues. In turn, the states provide limited revenue autonomy to local governments that have little legislative autonomy. In practice, revenue authority and legislative autonomy in India have not been increased to match the political decentralisation mandated by federalism.

The combination of constitutional assignments of tax and spending authority in India produces vertical fiscal imbalances. In 2006, the states raised 38 per cent of all combined government revenues but incurred 60 per cent of expenditures. Transfers from the Centre made up most of the difference. The Planning Commission makes grants and loans for implementing development plans as well as coordinates central ministry transfers that account for almost one-third of Centre–state transfers. There are over 100 such schemes, but attempts to consolidate them have failed. Local governments are even more dependent on transfers from higher levels. Aggregate local government spending was only about 5 per cent of total government spending at all levels, while local revenue from own sources was only 1 per cent of total government revenue (Singh 2008).

Because states have the constitutional authority to determine their own health systems, decentralisation of powers over health care in India varies by state. Since constitutional amendments in 1992, the three tiers of institutions for Panchayati Raj have the bulk of health care responsibilities for their constituents. But Primary Health Centres operate in an underfunded and weak public health system while the private health system dominates in terms of facilities, skilled professionals and resources – and it is concentrated in urban areas (Bansal 1991; NCMH 2005; Reddy et al. 2011).

In 2005 the National Rural Health Mission (NHRM) began to revamp the public health care system 'by increasing funding, integration of vertical health and family welfare programs, employment of female accredited social health activities in every village, decentralized health planning, community involvement in health care, strengthening of rural hospitals, providing united funds to health facilities, and mainstreaming traditional systems of medicine into the public health system' (Reddy et al. 2011: 763). The programme covers all of India but focuses on 18 states with poor infrastructure. Although NHRM is centrally funded and vertical in organisation, its implementation and execution are at state and local levels. In the state of Karnataka, decentralisation of power was one of the first initiatives to reform its health system by integrating communities and people into the planning process (Sudarshan and Prashant 2011).

As a federally supported strategy to strengthen the capacity of states to provide rural primary care, NRHM epitomises the dilemmas of federal versus state control over health systems. Launched in 2005 with a focus on 18 underperforming states in order to correct systemic flaws (e.g., shortages of financial and human resources, lack of community ownership, lack of integration with national programmes, and managerial deficiencies), NRHM provides insights into the consequences of federal intervention.

Several of its components benefit state health systems. One core component is to improve health infrastructure and resources for primary care in rural areas; another is to provide reproductive and child health services including immunisation and newborn care. Local rural health facilities have been upgraded to become first referral units, unconditional (untied) allocation of funds allows greater flexibility in usage, and skilled health workers (Accredited Social Health Activists or ASHAs) have been deployed at village level. Other components include more funds for resource-strapped state health systems, disbursements directly to autonomous institutions at state and district levels, and the introduction of a uniform system for financial accounting. Introduction of professional financial accounting includes the electronic transfer of funds, tracking the flow of funds, and tracking expenditures. In addition, NRHM launched an unprecedented countrywide campaign for health awareness that brought health issues into the public limelight.

Central government intervention through NRHM has been financially significant. From 2005 to 2012 the Union government released 607 billion rupees for health programmes. Overall funding from government sources for the health sector in India was raised from 0.9 per cent of GDP in 2005 to 1.4 per cent in 2009. Since 2005 there has been a fourfold increase of central assistance to states for health programmes. Capital expenditures to improve health infrastructure account for most of the funds but NRHM has added over a million workers to the health system (860,000 ASHAs; 148,000 skilled service providers appointed on contract). There has been a 46 per cent increase in medical colleges (mostly in the private sector) and a fourfold increase in the number of training institutes for Auxiliary Nurse Midwives. While rural health infrastructure, especially the numbers of primary health centres and community health centres, has increased, results are mixed in terms of hiring doctors and specialists for these facilities.

While it is difficult to attribute a direct correlation between the centrally supported NRHM and improvements in rural health indicators across the states, reports since 2005 suggest significant improvement in rural health indicators compared to urban areas. Nonetheless, poorly performing states are a 'drag' in the pursuit of MDGs and create regional imbalances. Federal support is essential for poorly performing states that lack technical, managerial, and resource capacity even though such interventions pose the classic conflict between uniformity for managerial efficiency versus flexibility for meeting contextual service delivery needs. In a diverse country like India, states must eventually assume greater responsibility for meeting local demands in synergy with national health objectives. Yet in 2013 the central government in India assumed even greater authority by launching the National Urban Health Mission.

In May 2013 the Union Cabinet approved the National Urban Health Mission that is to be implemented in 779 cities and towns with more than 50,000 inhabitants. Focused on the urban poor, NUHM is expected to cover approximately 80 million Indians in slums and disadvantaged urban areas by facilitating equitable access to quality health services through a revamped primary public health system. The government proposes to set up one Urban Primary Health Centre for every 60,000 people; one Urban Community Health Centre for 5–6 Urban PHCs; an Auxiliary Nurse Midwife for 10,000 people; and a community worker or Accredited Social Health Activist for every 200–500 households.

The cost of NUHM for five years is estimated at 225 billion rupees or US$3.5 billion so about US$700 million per year. While the Centre will fund 75 per cent of the mission and each state 25 per cent, the funding ratio for the seven states in north-eastern India and the special category states of Jammu and Kashmir, Himachal Pradesh and Uttarakhand will be 90:10. The NRHM mechanisms now operating in rural India will be strengthened to meet the needs of NUHM.

Because India is a 'Union of States', its states and union territories administer internal affairs. Yet the government of India has sponsored a proliferation of schemes. While it may seem odd for the Centre to run central schemes in and for states when it need only transfer money for specific purposes, central schemes are used as 'vote-buying' machines by whatever political parties are in power. Centralisation of financial and economic power leads to increasing dependence of the states on the Centre. Three examples follow in the policy domains of education, health, and employment.

Sarva Shiksha Abhiyan (Education for All Movement) is a programme of the government of India aimed at the universalisation of elementary education that had been mandated in 2002 by the 86th amendment to the Constitution of India. The amendment established free compulsory education as a fundamental right for all children between 6 and 14 years of age. The roots of Sarva Shiksha Abhiyan can be traced to 1994 when the District Primary Education Programme was launched with the aim of universal primary education (Björkman and Mathur 2002) and eventually covered 272 districts in 18 states of India. On 1 April 2010 the Right to Education Act came into force so some educationists and policymakers believe that Sarva Shiksha Abhiyan has now acquired the requisite legal force for its implementation.

Janani Suraksha Yojana (Safe Motherhood) is a central government scheme launched on 12 April 2005 to promote the institutional delivery of babies and thereby decrease neonatal and maternal mortality. Financed 100 per cent by the central government, the scheme integrates cash assistance with delivery and post-delivery care. The success of the scheme is measured by the increase in institutional deliveries among poor families. Accredited Social Health Activists have an important role to encourage women in families below the poverty level to go to institutions (clinics or hospitals) for the birth of their babies. The scheme has differential incentives for rural and urban areas based on whether a state has a low rate of institutional deliveries (Uttar Pradesh, Uttaranchal, Jharkhand, Bihar, Madhya Pradesh, Chhattisgarh, Rajasthan, Assam, Orissa, Jammu, and Kashmir) or a high rate (all other states). Currently conditional cash benefits are as follows:

Around 70 per cent of India lives in villages, but agriculture contributes only 14 per cent of its GDP. According to the Eleventh Five-Year Plan (2007–2012), 300 million Indians live below the poverty line (less than one dollar per day) – an absolute number that has barely declined since 1973 although their proportion in India's population decreased from 36 per cent in 1993 to 28 per cent in 2005. The Mahatma Gandhi National Rural Employment Guarantee Act (MGNREGA) guarantees the 'right to work' in rural India by providing 100 days of guaranteed wage employment per year to every household whose adult members volunteer to do unskilled manual work. Under the 2005 act, people are entitled to employment, or else the government is liable to pay an unemployment allowance.

Table 11.1   Conditional cash benefits in rural areas

Category	Mother's package	ASHA's package	Total package (rupees)
Low	1400	600	2000
High	700	–	700

Table 11.2   Conditional cash benefits in urban areas

Category	Mother's package	ASHA's package	Total package (rupees)
Low	1000	200	1200
High	600	–	600

The law is the culmination of efforts to ensure security of livelihood for the poor. While employment generation through rural works has a long history in India, no prior programme had promised employment as a legal right. Previous top-down schemes of India's central government included Food for Work (FWP) in 1977, the National Rural Employment Programme (NREP) in 1980, the Employment Assurance Scheme (EAS) in 1983, Jawahar Rozgar Yojana (JRY) in 1989, Jawahar Gram Samridhi Yojana (JGSY) in 1999 and Sampoorna Grameen Rozgar Yojana (SGRY or Universal Rural Employment Programme) in 2001. In contrast to the earlier schemes, MGNREGA is a rights-based demand-driven employment programme that is supposed to be implemented mainly by village-level local government (*gram panchayats*). However, local governments are markedly ill equipped for effective performance in any field, whether employment or education or health care.

Commonly cited as the source of operational problems, government-run rural health services in India are centralised with little local autonomy over programmes or resources. Services are unresponsive to local needs as the population has few alternatives. Despite low coverage of services, there is excess capacity in 'bricks and mortar' infrastructure with corresponding shortages of supplies and sometimes of staff. Staff are assigned, rotated, and paid without consideration of output or client satisfaction; staff members are inadequately trained, ill-equipped, and commonly indulge in private practice. Referral systems do not work so patients bypass the rural health infrastructure and, when they can, go directly to hospitals, thereby raising costs and leading to more investment in hospital facilities. In contrast, private and NGO services are usually decentralised and more accessible, reasons that are often mentioned by clients who use them despite the average quality of such services as well as their fees that are higher than in the public sector (Gupta and Gumber 1999).

Kerala in south-western India provides an intriguing example of federal–state issues in the health sector. Constitutional amendments adopted in 1992 required the states to delegate some administrative functions and taxation powers to local governments in rural and urban areas. In the forefront of decentralisation of powers was Kerala (Narayana and Kurup 2000), which has achieved 'some of the highest indicators of social development in the developing world' (Chaudhuri 2003: 5). Kerala has an impressive history of public engagement as well as local management of public services despite political polarisation between two ideologically opposed parties (Communist and Congress).

Yet despite these achievements, Kerala in the 1990s faced a 'health crisis' triggered by outbreaks of contagious disease, increased numbers of HIV/AIDS cases, the rise of parasitic and infectious diseases, and a decline in longevity. Given deterioration in health conditions, the Left Front state government in 1996 launched a People's Campaign for Decentralised Planning that gave local governments about 38 per cent of development expenditures. By empowering local actors, Kerala sought to motivate community participation. In the second year of the campaign, there was a dramatic increase in the participation rates of marginalised people while women and child development services improved significantly (Chaudhuri 2003; Elamon et al. 2004).

In summary, the two constitutional amendments of 1992 provided legal recognition, increased political status, and greater expenditure responsibilities to local governments. The amendments changed the assignments of taxes and expenditures to local governments by more fully specifying their authority and responsibilities. They also instituted a system of state–local fiscal transfers as well as periodic State Finance Commissions patterned on the national variant. But during the two subsequent decades, classic problems have appeared in the implementation of these amendments including lack of clarity, mismatches between revenue and spending authority, and lack of local administrative capacity. Federalism on paper is not federalism in practice.

Conclusions

Poor quality and inefficient delivery of public services in India are pervasive problems that are not restricted to health care. Part of the problem lies in weak mechanisms of accountability for individuals (politicians and government employees) and organisations (ministries and public enterprises). Evidence suggests that decentralisation has improved local responsiveness and service delivery in some cases but, unless accompanied by the decentralisation of funds and functions, political decentralisation is likely to have limited benefits. Heterogeneous services like health care require building local capacity as a critical prerequisite for successful decentralisation that might then improve the delivery of services. And some components of health care that are subject to economies of scale or spillovers are not candidates for decentralisation. In the complex field of service delivery, one size does not fit all.

The impact of decentralisation on service delivery is not straightforward. Its usefulness as a tool varies between poor countries and emerging economies. Where a state lacks the capacity to fulfil its basic functions, there is a risk that decentralisation will exacerbate problems rather than reduce them. But in countries where a state is committed to the devolution of power to local tiers of government, decentralisation can enhance service delivery. Given the ambiguous link between decentralisation and service delivery, decentralisation could complicate matters in countries characterised by weak institutions and political conflict. The impact of decentralisation depends less on a country's physical setting – its size or the quality of its infrastructure – than on the capacity of policymakers. In an environment where a government is not fulfilling basic functions, decentralisation could be counterproductive. But in countries that fulfil these functions, decentralisation may be a powerful tool for targeting the delivery of services (Jütting et al. 2004).

As India demonstrates, government is not one homogeneous entity. Government consists of layers at central, state and local levels that interact with one another as well as operate separately. The efficacy of public expenditures depends not only on their magnitude and composition but also on the layer of government that makes decisions about financing and spending. 'Too much' centralisation may inhibit efficiency; 'too little' may endanger coherent delivery of services and exacerbate disparities. For more than a century, India has been a laboratory for experimentation on this topic ... and the jury is still out.

Chapter 12
China

Michael K. Gusmano

Introduction

In 2009, China adopted a major health reform designed to expand health insurance to the entire population. The adoption of this plan, and the subsequent efforts to implement it, reflect the priority that the Chinese government has placed on health in the wake of the Severe Acute Respiratory Syndrome (SARS) outbreak in 2002–2003. SARS exposed the weakness of the Chinese public health and health care systems and embarrassed the Chinese leadership.

Despite recent government investments in health, China's overall spending on health is still relatively low by international standards. In 2011, China spent 5.2 per cent of gross domestic product (GDP) on health care compared with an average of 9.3 per cent among countries in the Organisation for Economic Cooperation and Development (OECD). Among the BRIC countries (Brazil, Russia, India, China, and South Africa), only India spends less per capita on health than China (Ivins 2013). Efforts to improve the health system and address inequalities are limited by China's extensive system of fiscal federalism. China is a unitary state, but it has several layers of local and regional government. Economic reforms first adopted in the late 1970s not only increased the role of markets in the Chinese economy, they shifted responsibility for financing a range of public services, including public health and health care, to local governments and individuals. Because provinces in western China have far fewer resources than the country's wealthy coastal cities, the reliance on local governments for the administration and financing of health care creates large regional disparities in access to care with substantial gaps between needs and resources in the poorer provinces of the country. There have been modest efforts by the central government to equalise financing for health care by providing additional resources to poorer provinces, but inequalities in access to care and affordability among and within the provinces have grown during the past decade.

This chapter begins with a review of China's political organisation and the role of provincial and other local governments. The second section reviews the economic reforms started by Deng Xiaoping in 1978, the decentralisation of financial responsibility for public services and the transformation of the Chinese health system. In this section I also review the consequences of economic liberalisation and decentralisation in China for geographic inequalities in health and health care. The third section of the chapter provides an overview of health reform in China and documents the persistence of geographic inequalities. The problems faced by the rural provinces of China are contrasted with the remarkable success of the city of Shanghai, not only to reveal the scope of geographic inequality, but to demonstrate the promise of greater health investment in China. Finally, I conclude with reflections on the implications of fiscal federalism for the capacity of China to respond to the growing health challenges associated with non-communicable disease and population ageing. Administrative and financial responsibility for health and social services are highly decentralised in China. Under some circumstances, decentralisation can strengthen the welfare state. In China, however, local government officials remain dependent on central government leaders for their power and authority and the central government has not significantly redistributed resources among its provinces. As a result, decentralisation has undermined, rather than strengthened, the capacity of the country's health system.

China's Fiscal Federalism in a Unitary State

The People's Republic of China, established in 1949 following the victory of the Chinese Communist Party (CCP) led by Mao Zedong, is a unitary system of government ruled by the CCP. Although formal power is centralised and the system is dominated by the CCP, there are four levels of government administration under the central government. Since the mid-1980s, there has been a significant decentralisation of fiscal authority and local responsibility for implementing policy (Ong 2012). In recent years, China has been characterised as a political system that has embraced federalism in practice even though it has no constitutional basis (Feng et al. 2013). In fact, a study by the World Bank actually called China 'the most decentralized country in the world' because of the extensive local government contributions to public services (Ong 2012). While there is broad recognition of the extent to which many public services, including health, rely heavily on local government contributions, others argue that the political autonomy of local officials is severely constrained by the CCP (Ong 2012). Both features of the Chinese political system have implications for regional variation in health care.

China's fiscal federalism arrangements are particularly crucial for understanding the distribution of health care resources and the capacity of the government to implement policy change. As Greer reminds us, extra-constitutional features of political systems like 'intergovernmental relations and intergovernmental finance' are often more important factors for explaining the size of welfare states and the distribution of resources among subnational units of government than the mere fact of decentralisation (Greer 2010). The extraordinary power of the CCP and the unitary nature of the Chinese political system have facilitated the adoption of sweeping changes in health policy – with one set of changes occurring in the late 1970s and another since 2009 – but the reliance on local government units as sources of funding results in the uneven implementation of policy and the perpetuation of striking geographic inequities. There are large income inequalities within and across regions of China and interregional differences increasing over time (Candelaria et al. 2013). Recent changes in health care financing have attempted to address this situation but, to date, these efforts have not been sufficient to reduce the trend of growing regional inequalities in the affordability and accessibility of health care (Long et al. 2013).

Formal Organisation of Government in China

According to the constitution of the PRC, the National People's Congress (NPC) is the foremost political institution in the country (english.peopledaily.com). The NPC has responsibility for enacting legislation, approving budgets and personnel appointments. The NPC has formal responsibility for oversight of the president, the Supreme People's Court, the public prosecutor and the People's Liberation Army (PLA). The State Council, which controls the ministries of the central government and other levels of government, also reports to the NPC and is responsible for the operation of government. The national government also includes two types of institutions that play a consultative role, but have little power. These are the People's Political Consultative Conferences and China's eight minor political parties. The minor political parties were all established before 1949, but are loyal to the Communist Party (china.org).

The formal constitution notwithstanding, real power in China continues to rest with the CCP. Although it does not have a specific role under the constitution, the preamble to the constitution states that '[u]nder the leadership of the Communist Party of China and the guidance of Marxism-Leninism and Mao Zedong Thought, the Chinese people of all nationalities will continue to adhere to the people's democratic dictatorship and follow the socialist road' (english.peopledaily.com). The CCP controls the PLR, the People's Armed Police, all personnel appointments and the media (Fisher 2010). It nominates all candidates for political office and the provincial level People's Congresses and the PLA elect candidates from among the party nominees, so officials at all levels of government owe their positions to the support of the CCP.

The top-down control over appointments is important for understanding limits to the autonomy of local government officials. As I discuss below, critics of fiscal federalism as a mechanism for addressing social and economic inequality in China argue that local officials often place an emphasis on economic growth, rather than health and social welfare policy, in an effort to be responsive to the leadership of the CCP (Hipgravel et al. 2012). This contrasts with some of the theoretical arguments about federalism based largely on western democratic institutions and a more autonomous political base for local officials. Many theorists claim that federal arrangements, particularly the reliance on fiscal federalism, are helpful for aligning policy with local preferences of citizens who can 'vote with their feet' and move to an area with policies that best align with their views (Brennan and Buchanan 1980; Hayek 1939; Tiebout 1956; Weingast 1995). These theorists argue that this will often result in greater focus on market performance, but they claim this is a reflection of greater local government understanding of, and responsiveness to, local preferences, and of a willingness to resist the imposition of regulatory and redistribution policies enacted by the national government (Rao and Singh 2005; Théret 1999). Critics argue that local officials may be subject to 'capture' by local elites and fail to be responsive to other local constituents (Rao and Singh 2005). Beyond the question of capture, local expenditures on health care services for the poor (or the lack thereof) may conflict with the view of many urban political theorists that cities, and other local governments, are 'limited' by their need to attract business (Peterson 1981). According to this view, an economic imperative prevents cities and other local governments from spending on health care and other redistributive programmes. Decentralisation alone is not sufficient to guarantee responsiveness to local concerns. Because provincial and other local Chinese officials owe their loyalty to the CCP and not to local constituents, neither the positive nor the normative arguments from this branch of the federalism literature are persuasive in the Chinese political context.

Provincial, Municipal, County, and Township Government

Below the national government, China has four levels of regional and local governments. There are 34 provincial-level governments. These include the 'special administrative districts' of Hong Kong and Macau, as well as the island of Taiwan, over which the PRC claims sovereignty but does not exercise control. Below the provincial level governments are 333 prefectures and prefectural cities and four cities with direct control: Beijing, Chongqing, Shanghai, and Tianjin (Oizumi 2010). The third level includes 2,859 counties and the fourth is made up of about 40,000 townships and towns (Saich 2011).

The structures of local government are similar to the national level with the exception of prefectures that have administrative agencies rather than people's congresses. They may adopt their own laws and regulations as long as they do not conflict with national policy, and the CCP encourages local governments to experiment with policies that lead to economic growth. The central government is responsible for national defence, but local governments have their own sources of revenue and are responsible for financing a large portion of public services (Ong 2012). By the mid-1990s, local government revenues financed 80–90 per cent of social services, including health care (Hipgravel et al. 2012; Wong et al. 1995). As I discuss below, the adoption of health reform in 2009 has increased central government contributions to health care, but local government and out of pocket payments still represent the vast majority of health spending in China. As of 2012, local government (provincial level and below) revenues financed

> 70 per cent of local expenditures, 90 per cent of general public service expenditures, 76 per cent of public security, 84 per cent of education, 8 per cent

of social security and employment, 78 per cent of health care, 59 per cent of environmental protection and 49 per cent of science and technology [programmes]. (Guilhem 2013)

Like the 'new federalism' policies adopted during the Reagan administration in the United States, devolution of financial responsibility in China since the 1980s has been coupled with efforts to shrink the role of government in financing public services (Conlan 1988; West and Wong 1995). As West and Wong (1995) explain, this trend means that regional disparities are often even larger than official budget statistics might indicate because a great deal of spending for services was shifted off budget and depended on private spending and led to income-based inequities. This approach exacerbated the large economic differences between the wealthier coastal provinces and poorer rural provinces in western China (ibid.). The national government has attempted to address the country's rural–urban disparities, but with limited success (Jian 2010).

China's Economic Reform and the Transformation of its Health System

Between 1949 and the early 1980s, the Chinese economy was dominated by state owned enterprises. In the context of the health care system, China's central government provided public funding for an extensive system of 'first level' hospitals, which are often community clinics with a modest inpatient capacity that offer access to basic primary care services and engage in public health interventions, including vaccination and health education. First level hospitals were the initial point of contact with the health care system for most people living in cities and they offered relatively equitable access to both western and traditional Chinese medicine (TCM). In rural areas health care was provided by communes, which provided housing, education and other social services, as well as basic medical care. An important feature of the communes' Cooperative Medical System was the staff of paraprofessionals known as 'barefoot doctors' (Rosenthal and Greiner 1982). Most of the barefoot doctors were young peasants who received a few months of training in anatomy, bacteriology, diagnosing disease and prescribing western and Chinese herbal medicine and could offer basic primary and preventive care, including health education (Hesketh 1997; Valentine 2005). If the needs of patients were more complex, they would refer them to physicians at the commune health centres or, if necessary, the closest hospital (Valentine 2005).

The available data suggest that this system was effective and, by the mid-1970s, the World Health Organisation considered this programme as a less expensive alternative to traditional Western health care (Valentine 2005). Overall, life expectancy increased from 35 years to 68 years between 1949 and 1978, although much of this can be attributed to the end of military conflict and investments in basic infrastructure, including sanitation (Hesketh 1997; Lee 1974). More directly attributable to the health care system, however, is the elimination or reduction of specific diseases during this 30-year period. Throughout the country, a number of fatal communicable epidemic diseases, including plague, cholera, and smallpox were successfully eliminated and mortality associated with others like diphtheria was greatly reduced (Ge and Gong 2007; Lee 1974). Even though measurement of the programme's success was limited, it did provide access to care, and barefoot doctors served as patient advocates (Valentine 2005). As Dr Philip Lee observed in 1974 after a visit to China as part of a medical delegation to the PRC in 1973, 'progress has not always been smooth' and it is important to recognise that health programmes were discarded and medical schools were closed during the cultural revolution from 1966–1969 (Lee 1974). Overall, however, health and health care improved dramatically under Mao and the government made health improvements a priority.

In contrast to the success of the public health and health care systems under Mao, the economy grew slowly during this period and production was barely able to keep pace with the demands of a rapidly growing population. Before 1978, the average annual growth rate was 6 per cent a year, with notable dips, including famine following the Great Leap Forward, in which the government adopted a programme of rapid industrialisation (Hu and Khan 1997). By the late 1970s when Deng Xiaoping assumed power, the Chinese economy had stagnated at the same time Hong Kong, Singapore, South Korea, and Taiwan were booming. In response, Deng called for economic reform, believing that the use of markets were the key to economic growth (Naughton 1993). These reforms, known as 'socialism with Chinese characteristics', included opening up the country to direct foreign investment, ending the system of collectivised agriculture and allowing entrepreneurs to create new start-up businesses (Vogel 2011).

Following the political unrest associated with the democracy movement in China and the global outcry against the government's crackdown on the Tiananmen Square protests in June 1989, the government accelerated economic reforms (Vogel 2011). Today, the private sector accounts for 70 per cent of gross domestic product, although much of the banking, communications and energy industries are still controlled by state owned enterprises. In addition to reforming state owned enterprises and increasing the role of markets in the economy, the Chinese government further decentralised responsibility for economic growth. Under the tax-sharing reform of 1994 there was a large transfer of resources to the central government and local governments were given much greater responsibility for economic development and financing public services. These policies created a 'mismatch between revenues and expenditures at the local level, partly covered by transfer payments subject to government discretion, and mainly covered by the income of the land use rights transactions for a period of 40 to 70 years' (Guilhem 2013). At a party summit held in November 2013, Chinese leaders expressed concern about the growth of local government debt (Bloomberg News 2013). Investors are concerned that the use of bad loans from state-controlled banks to alleviate the problems of local government may crowd out access to capital for small firms (Bloomberg News 2013).

The economic reforms since 1978 have resulted in major changes in the Chinese health care system. Following the adoption of market reforms, the central government decided to minimise its role in financing health care and other public services. 'From 1978 to 1999, the central government's share of national health care spending fell from 32 per cent to 15 per cent' (Blumenthal and Hsiao 2005). The government slashed subsidies to public hospitals and introduced market mechanisms into the health care system resulting in rapid growth of out-of-pocket payments characterised by income-based inequities. These changes and subsequent reforms during the 1980s shifted greater responsibility for public health financing from the central to local governments, reduced funds available for public health, and created large geographic disparities in the availability of health care. A much greater share of health care services had to be financed from local government taxes and out of pocket payments from patients. 'That had the immediate effect of favouring wealthy coastal provinces over less wealthy rural provinces and laid the basis for major and growing disparities between investments in urban and rural health care' (Blumenthal and Hsiao 2005).

Even in wealthier cities, e.g., Beijing and Shanghai, first-level hospitals reduced their provision of public health services (such as immunisation) because they did not generate sufficient revenue from patients (Wang et al. 2010). Instead, first-level hospitals focused on profitable services with a new emphasis on selling pharmaceutical products at marked-up prices. Since the 1980s, these institutions have developed a reputation for poor quality care with inadequate staff and many patients stopped using them (Wang et al. 2010).

As a substitute, patients started using 'second' (regional hospitals that provide general medical services, mostly on an outpatients basis) and 'third' (large tertiary hospitals that provide a wide range of health care services, including specialty and surgical care) level hospitals for primary care and the management of chronic illness. Although these are inappropriate settings for primary care, patients often assume that the quality of care in these facilities is superior. Between 1997 and 2001, the number of first level hospitals declined from 51,535 to 48,643, while the number of second- and third-level hospitals increased from 10,789 to 11,194 (Wang et al. 2010).

The challenge in rural China is even greater. Rural Chinese citizens often have to travel to the nearest large city to receive specialty or surgical care. Few rural residents have health insurance, so they often have to deplete their savings to pay for their care. In 2003 13.8 per cent of urban and 15.8 per cent of rural households incurred catastrophic medical spending – and 15.1 per cent of urban residents and 21.6 per cent of rural residents went without medical treatment because they could not afford it (Liu 2009).

Along with aggravating economic inequalities between rural and urban provinces in China, the decentralisation of funding for health decimated the country's public health system. To help local governments make up for the loss of health subsidies, the central government allowed local public health agencies to charge 'for certain public health services, such as inspections of hotels and restaurants for sanitary conditions and of industries for compliance with environmental regulations' (Blumenthal and Hsiao 2005). Just as first level hospitals shifted from providing primary care to selling pharmaceuticals, local public health agencies also shifted their focus to 'revenue-generating activities and neglected health education, maternal and child health, and control of epidemics' (Blumenthal and Hsiao 2005). The impact of these policies varied greatly within the country. Because the economies of coastal cities are much stronger than rural areas in western China, decentralisation of responsibility for public health resulted in public health expenditures that were 'more than seven times higher in Shanghai than in the poorest rural [regions]' (Blumenthal and Hsiao 2005).

The health reform adopted in 2009, which involved the creation of three health insurance funds, has helped this situation, but access to care is still limited and geographic inequities are still significant. Even with an infusion of additional resources from the central government, the pressure on local government leaders to grow the local economy and produce revenue for the central government creates large regional disparities in the health care system. Because wealthier provinces have greater access to off-budget government revenue there is 'deeply unequal, regressive capacity of local governments to fund social services' (Hipgravel et al. 2012).

Fiscal Federalism, Geographic Inequalities, and Health Care Reform

By the late 1990s, Chinese officials took steps to increase investment in public health and to address growing disparities between rural and urban areas. Starting in 1997, the central government made the reduction of rural and urban inequalities a focus of policy. It adopted rural assistance programmes and since 2003 the CCP has listed targets for making health care more affordable in rural areas in its 'No. 1 Central Documents', which announce the government's priorities for the year (Jian et al. 2010).

Government efforts to improve the public health and primary care systems throughout China accelerated after the outbreak of SARS in late 2002. By the end of 2003, more than 5,000 people were infected in China and 349 people died (Smith 2006). SARS exposed the weaknesses of the existing public health and health system (Eckholm 2007). The decentralisation of the public health system had 'significantly undermined China's ability to mount an effective, coordinated response to potentially pandemic infectious illnesses' (Blumenthal and Hsiao 2005). This episode, following closely on the World Health Organisation's (WHO) 2000 report on health system performance, which was highly critical of China's health care system, led to lengthy public debate about the need for health reform. The initial response to SARS was greater central government investment in public health infrastructure. These included the development of a district level electronic disease surveillance system and the establishment of dedicated infectious disease hospitals in every district. These efforts were criticised, however, for failing to improve surveillance below the district level and for the lack of investment in public health education and personal hygiene (Blumenthal and Hsiao 2005).

After years of discussion and the development of multiple proposals, in 2009 the State Council of China enacted extended public health insurance and called for the development of community health organisations (CHOs) and establishment of a stronger public health and primary care system (Wang et al. 2010). In 2009, the central and local governments allocated RMB 15 Yuan ($2.46) per person for public health programmes and by 2012 this increased to RMB 25 Yuan ($4.10) per person, but the level of investment across the country has been uneven (Tang 2013).

Along with efforts to strengthen the primary care and public health systems, Chinese health reform involved two major components. It expanded three insurance schemes that had been started a decade earlier as pilot projects: the Urban Employee Basic Medical Insurance (UEBMI); the Urban Resident Basic Medical Insurance (URBMI) and the New Cooperative Medical Scheme (NCMS) (Lin et al. 2009). UEBMI is a health insurance scheme for people in the paid labour force in cities. It is financed through contributions by employers and employees and risks are pooled across each city or district (Li et al. 2012). Both URBMI and NRCMS are financed through a combination of central and local government funds and individual premiums. Central government contributions vary based on the economic status of the region, with central government financing a larger share in poorer regions.

In 2010, although local governments contributed roughly half of total fiscal revenues, they financed 82.2 per cent of total expenditures, notably for health and social services which has created, despite central government transfers to match the discrepancies between revenues and expenses, enormous inequalities among cities and regions in their capacity to provide for their residents (Aglietta and Bai 2012). The total subsidy available through the schemes noted earlier depends on the income of the individual, although the government allows poorer central and western regions to provide as little as RMB 25 Yuan ($4.10) per enrolee per year (Tang 2013). Nationally, the URBMI and NRCMS insurance schemes cover inpatient hospital care, but many cities, including Shanghai, use local funds to include coverage of outpatient care in the URBMI benefit package (Li et al. 2012).

Health care reform in China also involved the establishment of an 'essential drug list', which includes about 205 Western medicines and another 102 traditional Chinese medicines (Wang et al. 2010). The law regulates the price of drugs on the essential drug list and prohibits health care facilities from marking up the price of the drugs on the list for the purpose of making a profit. One of the goals of this reform was to strengthen public trust in so-called 'first-level' hospitals by shifting the focus of these facilities from sale of pharmaceuticals to providing primary care.

An evaluation of public satisfaction with the reform based on a survey of Shanghai residents indicates that, while most people believe the reforms have improved the quality of care in health care facilities, including first level hospitals, fewer are satisfied with the adequacy of the essential drug list or the new insurance schemes. People who reported lower incomes and lower levels of education were less satisfied with the results of health care reform than other residents of Shanghai (Li et al. 2012). This is consistent with the finding that, although health insurance coverage grew from just under 20 per cent in 2003 to almost 96 per cent by 2011, out-of-pocket costs faced by most Chinese citizens continue to be a burden because of the rapid escalation of health care costs (*The Lancet* 2012).

In 2009, the central government committed RMB331.8 billion ($54.4 billion) over three years to help financing expanded insurance coverage and improvements in health system delivery. Despite this important investment, local governments were expected to financing more than RMB518 billion ($84.9 billion) (Hipgravel et al. 2012). In 2012 the State Council announced in new phase of health system reform with an unspecified commitment to increasing central government funds (Hipgravel et al. 2012). Critics argue that public financing of the health sector between and within China's provinces as regressive and that the new 'insurance schemes and broader health resource allocation across urban–rural and regional boundaries ignore community needs' (Hipgravel et al. 2012). Because of the pressure on provincial and lower level officials to improve economic performance, 'poorer provinces and counties neglect co-funding of health despite national priorities and earmarked allocations' (Hipgravel et al. 2012). An analysis published in 2013 found that, even with a substantial increase in funding for health care from the central government since 2009, health care affordability for residents of rural China is getting worse (Long et al. 2013). The new insurance schemes describe above offer limited benefit packages focused on inpatient care. The limits of this coverage, coupled with the rapid escalation of health care costs in China, means that poorer residents face large and growing financial burdens (Long et al. 2013). Between 2000 and 2011, 'out-of-pocket payment increased 10.5 per cent annually among the urban population and 15.6 per cent among the rural population' (Long et al. 2013). To some extent, these problems reflect China's inflationary fee-for-service health care financing system, but the regional disparities reflect the central government's limited efforts to equalise financing among the provinces.

The problem of uneven regional capacity is a challenge for all federal systems. The degree to which national governments redistribute financing among regions varies substantially (Pahwa and Beland 2013) and has a profound effect on the impact of federalism on the welfare state. When central governments redistribute resources among regions and local government officials have the authority and incentive to respond to local needs, 'decentralisation can have positive social policy consequences' (Pahwa and Beland 2013). Of course, the equalisation of financing often varies within countries over time, but this can result in policy innovation at the local level if local officials are motivated to respond this way. As Richard Nathan explains, during more conservative political periods in the US when the national government is focused on welfare state retrenchment, more liberal states pushed back against this trend. He claims that, over time, the aggregate impact of the state-push factor has been to expand health and social welfare programmes by demonstrating their value at the state and local level. Although it is not yet clear that provincial and other local government innovations have led to the future expansion of the welfare state at the national level in China, evidence from its more innovative cities could be used to make this case. Below I present evidence from Shanghai's recent investments in health to illustrate this point.

Demonstrating the Value of Public Health Investment: Shanghai

Since 1999, Shanghai has launched a series of major efforts to improve its public health and health care delivery system. Shanghai has experienced remarkable economic growth during the past three decades and is considered one, if not the, leading global city in Asia. Since the 1990s, it has experienced the fastest economic growth of any global city in the world (Chen 2009). In 2008, Shanghai's economy slowed, slightly, as a result of the global economic downturn, and recorded a growth rate of less than 10 per cent for the first time in 17 years (ibid.).

The health implications of these economic changes are unclear. On one hand, rapid urbanisation poses important public health challenges. Along with concerns about the deterioration of air and water quality, urbanisation is associated with changes in lifestyles that contribute to non-communicable diseases (Gong et al. 2012). On the other hand, Shanghai's economic success has allowed the city to make significant investments in health and social programmes. During the past decade, Shanghai has adopted several major health initiatives. These include implementing an employment-based social medical insurance system, establishing Shanghai Metropolitan Centre for Disease Control and Prevention, investing significantly in medical research, developing, standardising, and providing additional financial support to community health care centres. In 2000, Shanghai implemented a community health reform designed to improve access to and continuity of care for older people (Wei et al. 2005).

In the wake of the 2009 national health care reform, Shanghai has increased efforts to improve its primary care and public health systems even more aggressively. While the central government has worked to ensure a minimum of RMB 25 Yuan ($4.10) per person in central and western China, the Shanghai Municipal Government allocated RMB 70–80 Yuan ($11.48–$13.12) per person for public health initiatives (Tang 2013). While Shanghai's substantial investment in public health raises important questions about regional equity within China, the improvement in Shanghai's urban infrastructure and health care services, coupled with health reform at the national level, have contributed to a significant decrease in the avoidable mortality rate in Shanghai (Gusmano et al. 2014).

Shanghai has experienced rapid economic development, with a double-digit annual GDP growth rate over the past two decades. Although economic growth is associated with challenges to public health, it is also associated with improved nutrition status, living conditions, and public health infrastructure. Shanghai has been a leader in Chinese health reform, establishing a basic medical insurance system for employees in 1999 and expanded the insurance system to unemployed urban residents in 2007. At the same time, Shanghai strengthened its ability to provide better community-based health services, including immunisation, preventive services for women and infants, and chronic disease management. These services are now widely available in community health centres, medical clinics, and infirmaries. Following the outbreak of SARS, Shanghai government increased investment in public health services, including public health surveillance, medical research, and the expansion of the health care workforce. It also improved its emergency medical response capacity and chronic disease management. The substantial decrease in cerebrovascular disease between 2000 and 2010 reflects great improvements in the Shanghai health care system. In particular, these reductions in cerebrovascular disease most likely reflect improvements in primary care, emergency care, and intensive care unit (ICU) services (Shanghai Municipal Health Bureau 2010). At the same time, a host of studies have found that that rates of non-communicable disease (NCD) are increasing in China as a whole (*The Lancet* 2012), rates of diabetes, ischemic heart disease and hypertension have actually fell in Shanghai between 2000 and 2010 (Gusmano et al. 2014). Given the growth of NCD in the rest of the country during the past decade, Shanghai's performance has been remarkable.

Even in its wealthy eastern cities, concerns about the affordability and quality of health care remain. For example, it is important to note that Shanghai's large (9.4 million in 2010) population of 'unregistered' migrant workers does not benefit from the expansion of health insurance and it is not clear how much they benefit from other investments in public health and primary care. Zhao et al. (2012) provide evidence that migrant women in Shanghai face significant access barriers to prenatal care. As policy makers in China strive to contain health care expenditures, the experience of Shanghai demonstrates that further investment in the country's public health infrastructure may produce substantial gains in health. Whether this will happen outside wealthy coastal cities like Shanghai, however, will depend on getting the incentives 'right' (Pahwa and Beland 2013).

Conclusion

China is an example of a unitary political system that relies heavily on the mechanisms of federalism to implement health and social policy in the context of government retrenchment. Starting in 1978, the government has encouraged foreign investment, the reduction in state-owned enterprises and collectives, the growth of private industry and the use of market competition to spur economic growth. Although the pace of growth slowed considerably after the worldwide recession of 2008, China has enjoyed rapid economic growth during the past 30 years, with a particularly remarkable rate of growth during the past 20 years. Many question whether this growth rate is sustainable, particularly now that standards of living and the demand for better wages have increased, but even if the health of the economy stabilises, it is clear that the benefits of economic growth have not been distributed evenly. The eastern portion of the country is far wealthier than the provinces to the west.

Because of China's large regional inequalities in wealth, heavy reliance on provincial and local governments to administer and finance health and other social services contributes to enormous inequalities in access to care and health outcomes. Although China will continue to need local feedback about health care needs both formal and informal coordination at the local level, there is a need for greater national funding for health to meet the requirements of regional and municipal health care delivery systems in underserved areas. Since the outbreak of SARS in 2002–2003, the central government has placed a higher priority on public health and health care. It has increased investments in this domain and, in 2009, enacted a sweeping health care reform plan that has extended modest levels of health insurance to most of the population. Nevertheless, the continual reliance on local financing without more aggressive efforts to redistribute resources from wealthier provinces to poorer provinces makes it unlikely that China will be able to address large and growing inequalities in health and health care. China's population is aging at a rapid pace and there has been a well-documented increase in non-communicable diseases. The recent success of wealthy cities like Shanghai demonstrates that with sufficient resources, China can address the health needs of its population. Unless the country is willing to substantially increase spending on health overall, enhance the financial capacity of local governments, and provide incentives for local officials to invest in health, rather than focusing myopically on short-term economic development, China will not cope successfully with its current health policy challenges.

Chapter 13

Brazil

Lenaura de Vasconcelos Costa Lobato and
Mônica de Castro Maia Senna

Introduction

Brazil is a complex federal system involving three levels of government, 27 states and over 5,000 municipalities. The public health system is a responsibility shared among the three levels of government, each with specific responsibilities. The system is unified and national, but states and municipalities have a reasonable degree of autonomy in managing their own systems of health care. On the other hand, as there are large disparities between regions, and between municipalities within each state (both in terms of funding capacity and in the provision of health services), cooperation is not only a guiding principle, but also a necessity for achieving health goals. However, there are important constraints which impede the balance between autonomy and cooperation that should govern health systems in Brazil's federal state.

This chapter explores current issues in Brazil's health care federalism. The first section describes the main aspects of the Brazilian federation. The second section analyses the development of health policy within the context of Brazil's political history. The third section highlights specific characteristics of the current health care system, focusing on the particular development and obstacles that have arisen as a result of federalism. The conclusion highlights the relevance of 'agreement mechanisms' created within the health sector arena and their importance in tackling the constraints inherent in federalism. It also argues that the health sector's internal decision-making process is a crucial element for understanding Brazilian health care federalism.

Brazilian Federalism

As suggested by Souza (2013), Brazil – unlike most federal countries – was not constituted as a federal state in order to address ethnic, religious, or language problems or to respond to external threats (61). Rather, the federal structure was developed in order to accommodate conflicting demands in the search for financial resources arising from the tax inequities always prevalent among its substate units. In this sense, Brazilian federalism developed various characteristics influenced by the social context within which it grew.

Federalism was officially adopted in 1891, and until 1930 the federal government was generally quite weak as political power belonged primarily to oligarchies within each state. The presidency of the country alternated between the two most powerful oligarchies (from the states of São Paulo and Minas Gerais). All of Brazil's states enjoyed a great deal of autonomy, especially as they were still mainly rural; and being the state governor meant being the centre of a powerful oligarchic system (Leal 1986; Abrucio 2002). Consistent with such a power structure, the tax system of Brazil was quite decentralised.

After 1930, federalism in Brazil focused upon reinforcing the federal executive power in order to facilitate greater industrial progress. The federal government became strengthened not only because of the need to establish and industrial base, but also to mediate the competing social demands arising from corporatist and patronage practices (Abrucio 2005). This new centralisation was also the result of President Vargas's 1937–1945 dictatorship. During this period, many negotiated concessions were granted from the federal government to the states in form of debt redemption. But the main intent of the centralising project was to delegate to the federal government the right to regulate taxation in the states. This made it possible to complete the unification of the domestic market and strengthen the foundations of industrialisation (Souza 2013).

During the 1946–1964 democratic period, the federal model reverted back to a more decentralised structure. This time, however, the decentralisation focused on municipalities, which had the advantage of preserving and strengthening the role of the federal government. State taxes were transferred to the municipalities and, for the first time, financial resources were sent to the country's poorest regions. Although not achieving substantial results, this would be the first attempt to reduce the federal fiscal imbalance (Souza 2013).

The process of centralisation intensified once more during the military regime from 1964 to1985. The federal structure during this stage has been termed a 'unionist–authoritarian model' by Abrucio (1998). It was characterised by a vertical and highly authoritarian relationship between the national level and substate units which demanded that these units obey and cooperate with national federal decisions. Failure to do so meant losing bureaucratic and financial support. The unionist–authoritarian model may be characterised broadly by the curtailment of the power of states' elites due to the adoption of indirect elections for state governors, tax changes resulting in strong income centralisation and the imposition of standardised national public policies for state administrations (Abrucio 1998).

Despite the concentration of resources at the federal level, subnational governments were compensated by the creation of exclusive taxes for states and municipalities, and by a formal mechanism for the regular transfer of resources – the States and Municipalities Allocation Funds – which had a strong redistributive impact, favouring the poorest states and aiming to reduce tax inequities (Souza 2013). The criteria for the distribution of these funds have changed a few times but they are still a source of major conflict between national and regional governments. Some states filed a lawsuit at the Supreme Court claiming that the current criteria are unconstitutional as they were defined in 1989 and valid until December 2012. The Supreme Court agreed with the claim and called for a deadline for the parliament to change them.

Those favouring democratic transition have sought a greater substantive federalism in place of the ersatz federation in force during the military regime. The new model defined by the 1988 Constitution emphasises a decentralisation based on increased regional tax capacity and freedom for states and municipalities to have greater control over resources, and, in the same way, the reduction of the fiscal role of the federal government. New policy initiatives were developed at subnational levels, with an emphasis on the role of municipalities in social policy (which, in turn, improved their share in the distribution of public resources). Substate units, because of the focus upon municipalities, lost a significant degree of control over social policy and, unsurprisingly, became the loudest opponents of this new form of decentralisation. Under this new model of federalism, the federal government (which had previously experienced less control over the distribution of resources) began to see the broadening of its competencies (Souza 2013). This shift became visible during the 1990s, when several structural reforms conducted by the federal government received little reaction from subnational levels, demonstrating that the loss of national power had been episodic. In fact, as Arretche (2013) notes, the federal government's authority is an undeniable characteristic of Brazilian federalism.

The extension of this central authority has led to considerable debate in Brazil. On the one hand, Stephan (1999) has noted that Brazil's regional authorities have considerable ability to constrain the federal government. The political strength of substate units rests in such political mechanisms as the strong veto power of regional senators in the Senate. The application of these political mechanisms by substate units means that there is increased decision-making paralysis and blocking of federal government initiatives. On the other hand, Arretche (2013), among other authors, refutes Stephan's thesis, showing that predictions of decision-making paralysis are largely unconfirmed, as numerous laws of interest to the federal government restricting subnational levels have been approved (Arretche 2013).

General Aspects of the Brazilian Economy and the Place of Health Policy

Brazil is one of the countries characterised by late industrialisation. Until 1930, its economy relied on the export of primary products. From 1930, the import-substitution industrialisation (ISI) model began to be implemented, as was the case in several Latin American countries. Before 1930 it had been a country characterised by less state intervention in the economy; after 1930, the state started to develop an important role in economic modernisation and industrialisation, a role it still plays today. The drive toward modernisation received the support of a broad coalition of labour and corporate interests. It was characterised by the construction of a modern state bureaucracy and polices to stimulate industry

(Fonseca and Souza 2009). However, this first stage of capitalist expansion occurred under a dictatorial regime. Health care benefits were granted to formal and urban workers under the social security provisions, but most of the population (around 70 per cent) had no right to health care. A parallel structure unrelated to this first benefit system was established as a public health system, and remained a separate system until 1993.

The import-substitution industrialisation process experienced a new boom with the focus on 'developmentalism' adopted after 1950, and it showed great dynamism and significant industrial growth. The military regime maintained the development model characterised by state intervention, and heavily centred on international capital. Economic growth was significant until the early 1970s when, following the global crisis, Brazil went into a long period of economic recession, facing the falling of exports, public debt growth and, particularly, increasing inflation rates. Economic growth was no longer able to reduce levels of economic inequality that, on the contrary, worsened during the military regime. The economic recession generated a dramatic social upheaval, showing the exhaustion of the import-substitution model (Mattei 2013).

The health care arena, as well as the entire social sector, was an important part of the military regime's strategy concerning economic development and political legitimacy. The structure that remained relatively unchanged since the 1940s substantially changed after 1964. Coverage was broadened following the stimulus for private sector expansion in order to widen the provision of health services. The private network expansion was largely due to public funding by means of subsidised loans for construction of hospital units with the further granting of services to be hired. This was accomplished via incentives to secure agreements between social security and medium- and large-sized private companies, which then became responsible for their employees' health care in return for a subsidy. It also occurred via incentives to private hospitals to provide assistance to those insured through social security based on the payment of units of service. These agreements with private health providers companies became the embryo of Brazil's new health care system.

The mechanism of payment per unit of service (similar to fee-for-service), however, led to deliberate service misuse and also generated a powerful system of fraud due to the low effectiveness of supervision (Lobato and Burlandy 2000). The health system was centralised at the federal level, granting little power to states and municipalities. This generated a bureaucratic apparatus that expanded in a disordered way, showing little administrative accountability and a low capacity to resolve administrative disputes. The economic crisis of the 1980s directly impacted social security and health. Several initiatives at rationalisation were taken at this point, including government regulations requiring the lowering of prices for services provided by the private sector. In response, the private sector, already responsible for most of the services provided by the public system, drastically reduced services to the public sector or selected services and clientele. Expenses were also reduced within public services, directly affecting the population's health care.

The military regime, which relied on economic growth as one of its pillars, lost considerable legitimacy as a result of the crisis. Pro-democracy civil movements arose, giving birth to a long and complex process of transition to democracy throughout the 1980s. From the economic point of view, Brazil called the 1980s the 'lost decade' due to the combination of negative growth and hyperinflation. Yet, from a political perspective, it was one of the most fruitful decades of Brazilian history. And it is within this context of democratisation that changing strategies for health sector are now being created. The materialisation of these changes has been situated in the 1988 Constitution, where health care has been formally institutionalised as a universal right through the establishment of the 'Unified Health System' (SUS).

Economic recovery initiatives came in the 1990s, when Brazil was already under democratic rule, following the recommendations of the so-called Washington Consensus to peripheral countries (including economic deregulation as a way to attract new foreign investments, economic liberalisation to broaden international trade, and incentives to programmes of public companies to privatise in order to tackle fiscal problems) (Mattei 2013). Inflation control and price stability were achieved by means of a new currency created in 1993, but the high interest rate policy hindered development (Bresser Pereira 2003) which would only be resumed in the following decade. The adjustment phase was accompanied by changes in the organisation of public bureaucracy with significant reduction of public companies' personnel and reduction of public sector activities, part of which entailed transfer to the private sector. One of the most important fiscal balance measures taken during this period was the approval of the 'Fiscal Responsibility Law'. The law defines several mechanisms for fiscal and budgetary discipline in the public sector and creates limits for spending on personnel. This measure has a powerful impact on health policy as it inhibits the broadening of the professional staff necessary for service provision, principally in the municipalities, which traditionally had difficulties in contracting and retaining qualified staff and which must now meet a greater demand for services resulting from the move toward universalisation.

From the early 1990s, it has been possible to observe in Brazil a major conflict between economic and social policy. Health policy was one expressions of this conflict. In the transition to democracy, civil society demands focused upon the reduction of inequalities and the expansion of citizenship-based social rights. The 1988 Constitution defined health as a universal right, breaking with the contributive model of social insurance that had prevailed since the 1930s. As noted above, it was under the 1988 Constitution that a national system called the Unified Health System (SUS) was created. SUS is a public system, unified throughout the country, characterised by decentralised management among the three government levels and supported by funds from the social security budget, as well as additional funding by states and municipalities.

This new institutionalism had, as an important premise, expansion of the state similar to the European welfare state model. However, the implementation of the new system occurred at the same time as the economic adjustment policy. So, in addition to the problems inherent in the construction of a national public health care system in the face of past policies and organisational structures, the development of a universal public health care system in the 1990s had to address constraints resulting from economic stabilisation programmes and the development options subsequently adopted.

The poor economic performance during the macroeconomic adjustment period was characterised by low growth and high unemployment, leading to the inauguration of a new political project. Through the articulated economic strategy, the new government would hold to the principles of monetary policy, adopting a model some authors term 'the new developmentalism' (also known as 'the Brazilian model' in international domains). Essentially, this is a model that respects the foundations of macroeconomic policies adopted during the 1990s adjustment period, except that it has poverty reduction as well as economic growth as a core concern. The model was responsible for recent changes in the economy, characterised by low unemployment and positive and continuous growth rates (although these latter followed an irregular path).

Between 2003 and 2013 the level of employment increased by 24.8 per cent, with the creation of about 4.5 million jobs; the current unemployment rate is 5.3 per cent, the lowest in 10 years, and informal employment has been reduced by an average of 15 per cent (IBGE 2013). Job creation has been followed by a real appreciation of the minimum wage, positively impacting household income and, by consequence, the expansion of the internal market and the reduction of income inequalities. The GINI coefficient fell from 0.587 in 2002 to 0.527 in 2012 (IPEA 2013). This reduction was supported by cash transfer programmes, which now serve about 25 per cent of the poor or extremely poor at a relatively low cost (about 0.46 per cent of GDP).

This model also opted for subsidising the investment of large national companies, and for counter-cyclical policies to protect the economy from the 2008 recent crisis, reducing taxes of high-employability sectors and maintaining and even expanding public funding in infrastructure. These policies do not have a wide consensus of support, and are criticised for a number of reasons. A key factor concerns the decline of industry's share of the GDP (Cano 2012), a factor which prevents the model being characterised as a developmental model (Gonçalves 2012). Also, the maintenance of high interest rate policy as the only mechanism of inflationary control weakens the economy and discourages further investments.

Health has not been incorporated into this model of development. In fact, health in Brazil has always been considered a service rather than a mechanism of economic development. And, despite constituting a high GDP percentage and generating jobs, the productive and technological aspect of the health sector in Brazil is still fragile. This is also true of the relationship between industrial and health policies (Gadelha et al. 2012). Progress has been made in the area of vaccines, but Brazil is dependent on imports throughout the health production chain, reporting growing deficits in the trade balance in this area since 2003 (Gadelha et al. 2012). In fact, investments in health represent a very small portion of the Ministry of Health's budget, staying below 6.3 per cent (Machado et al. 2014).

On the other hand, there have been changes in the state structure, such as the strengthening of the administrative apparatus, as opposed to previous state reduction policies. However, the state is still very much bureaucratised, and its structure serves the accommodation needs of governments' partisan composition, generating particularisms and discontinuity within the administration. This situation is more visible in the federal administration, but is nonetheless currently much more serious in the states and municipalities. In a number of social areas, Brazil currently counts on robust service systems. However, significant problems remain regarding access and quality of care. This also clearly applies to health.

Health Federalism

In Brazil, the relationship between health and federal policy is not a new issue. During the First Republic (1898–1930), a period of strong regional autonomy and considerable state power, the need to provide answers to public health challenges of that time stimulated a joint solution between the national government and the states. This strengthened the federal government's power throughout the country without prejudicing the states' autonomy (Hochman 1998). In this way, public health played the peculiar role of integration in a young federation characterised by isolation and the existence of few communication channels between the levels of government. This public health role lasted throughout the post-1930s period of modernisation and industrialisation, supporting a more centralised model of federalism that controlled investments in the states and which encouraged negotiation and coordination between the government levels (Fonseca 2007).

Health care itself developed in a centralised way, not directly through the federal government but through the national institutes of health and medical care of the various occupations. These institutes granted retirements, pensions, and health care to formal urban workers under a contributive model. These rights however were restricted to occupations recognised by the state, leaving out the majority of workers (e.g., rural, informal, domestic workers). The military regime, adopting a policy of extreme centralisation, then unified all of these institutes into a sole agency of the federal government (Machado and Viana 2009). Subnational governments were left with the implementation of public health actions. In some cases, emergency services with very low or almost zero technical and managerial capacity became a feature of the overwhelming majority of these governmental entities.

This pattern had important repercussions for the institutionalisation of health policy. With the escalation of conflicts in the second half of the 1970s and the weakening of the authoritarian regime, health policy was also part of the process of intense federal bargaining, contributing to further regional inequalities. From the 1980s on, with the democratic transition, the question of federal relationships in health care became a central concern. Several pioneering municipal experiences with respect to the reorganisation of health services have been undertaken since the 1970s and these strengthened the reform proposals of the health sector in terms of greater decentralisation. Machado and Viana (2009) define decentralisation during that period as 'a mechanism of increasing speed of the country's democratization in a cooperative intergovernmental environment' (43), in which different spheres of government came together for the drafting of the wording that would be part of the 1988 Constitution. Particularly noteworthy here are instances of negotiation performed by national councils of state and municipal health secretaries, who would act as essential political actors throughout the process of re-establishing the federal bases of Brazilian health care.

The 1988 Constitution represented an important legal boundary for health sector reform in Brazil. The Constitution defined SUS principles and guidelines with the aim of building a national and universal public system that, at the same time, would be decentralised, integrated and hierarchical, and able to meet the regional diversity of the country. Grounded on constitutional wording, SUS implementation unfolded in two main movements: the unification of the national command by the Ministry of Health, previously divided into two ministries (Health and Social Security), and political and administrative decentralisation, in which states and (mainly) municipalities took on responsibilities for the provision and management of health services in a way that was unprecedented in the country and unparalleled in international experience.

As a unified system, SUS follows the same organisational basis in all federative levels: a single command (the Ministry of Health and state and municipal secretariats), a single health fund, and a single health council (that includes the participation of government, professionals, providers, and users). Three agencies are responsible respectively for health surveillance, sanitation, and the private insurance sector. The system is the responsibility of all three federal levels and is funded by fiscal resources. All levels have to meet a minimum level of health funding in their budgets. Municipalities surpass this minimum but many states are still below it. The transfer of financial resources has basically two forms: a per capita transfer to municipalities for primary health care and public services, and a DRG payment to states and municipalities for medical procedures. Recently, new forms of transfer have been introduced based on some health need indicators and the compromise of states and municipalities on selected health outcomes (e.g., reduction of maternal mortality). These new forms are attempts to surpass the traditional logic of funding based only in the production of health services to cope with disparities and persistent inequities among municipalities. The amount of money to be transferred is decided by joint commissions ('Inter-Managers Commissions') coordinating all three levels of government. Another important variable regarding the financing of the system are the incentives of the Ministry of Health targeting a large range of specific national policies.

The delivery of health services is a responsibility of the municipalities but is supported by the national and state governments. What municipalities actually deliver nationwide is primary health care. The majority offer some secondary care but not hospital care, which is offered by states or medium and large municipalities. There is also an important highly-specialised network, owned by the federal government, which includes public university hospitals. The role of the municipalities is to manage, control, and regulate the services needed and used by their citizens. Consequently, the agreements concerning the utilisation of services among municipalities and among those and their state are very important.

The SUS service network is comprised of both public and private providers contracted by the SUS. To take one example, Brazil's health care system currently has over 500,000 beds. Among the beds under the purview of the SUS, around 52 per cent are private (mostly owned by philanthropic organizations), and 48 per cent are public (23 per cent municipal, 20 per cent state, and 5 per cent national) (Brasil 2014).

In early 1990s, the SUS faced strong political and financial constraints which severely impacted intergovernmental relations. Brazilian health policy was characterised by institutional and decision-making paralysis within the federal government. Municipalities were delegated the responsibility for the provision of health services based mainly on fiscal and sectorial transfers. The role of states remained undefined, which favoured state governments participating in politics only if funded by the federal government. Otherwise, substate governments chose to exempt themselves from functioning or to transfer the assignments to local governments (Abrucio 2005).

This reality contributed to the deepening of inequalities between Brazilian municipalities because of the responsibilities assigned to them. Although municipalities received greater allocation of resources and autonomy to manage the organisation of health services, those with greater operational, technical, and managerial capacities were the ones to respond more effectively to the demands of the health sector. This disparity has been reinforced by the existence of a huge number of small municipalities with a low tax-based income capacity.

SUS management during this period was highly dependent on existing local conditions, reflecting the municipalities' distinct technical, financial, political, and managerial capacities in the provision of health care. Furthermore, it was influenced by the distinct political dispositions of governors and mayors (Souza 2002) and their electoral mathematics. This framework was further worsened by the adoption of neoliberal policies stimulating competition among federated entities. To attract private investment, states and municipalities resorted to exemptions and subsidies to private companies and negotiated the transfer of their debts to the federal government. Abrucio (1998) termed this tax war a form of 'predatory federalism', where cooperative initiatives are subsumed by major conflicts between levels of government.

Attempts to strengthen the federal pact took place in 1993 with emphasis on the expansion of municipal health secretaries' councils and the institutionalisation of joint commissions in each state (with the participation of state and municipal managers) called 'Bipartite Inter-Managers' Commissions' (CIBs). At the federal level, a 'Tripartite Inter-Managers' Commission' (CIT) was created. It was a political joint composition involving the Ministry of Health representatives and state and municipal health secretariats. The Commissions are regarded as an innovation in the SUS (Lima 1999) because they are based on the creation of a permanent centre of negotiation, planning, and intergovernmental decision-making regarding shared management. The purpose of these Commissions is to discuss measures that concern all three levels of government (the responsibility of the 'Tripartite Inter-Managers' Commission' [CIT]), or those relevant to the municipalities and the state government in a certain state unit (the responsibility of the 'Bipartite Inter-Managers' Commissions' [CIBs]). All the states have a Commission. They hold formal meeting on a regular basis, and any decisions must be made by consensus. The Commissions also focus on building partnerships aimed at the consolidation of municipal, regional, and state health systems. As an example, the meeting of the CIB of Mato Grosso State in April 2014 agreed, among other matters, on the criteria for the distribution of the resources transferred from the Ministry of Health for influenza vaccination, on the accreditation of a rehabilitation unit at one of the municipalities, and on the minimum number of medical doctors to be in charge of the supervision of the centres of medical regulation throughout the state.

Despite the construction of an intergovernmental environment more favourable to federal coordination by means of the joint mechanism of CIB and CIT, the following years experienced minor advances in the process of SUS decentralisation. The agenda of social policy reform became subsumed to the imperatives of macroeconomic adjustment. Upon the success of the 1993 currency stabilisation plan, significant changes in intergovernmental relations in Brazil occurred regarding a number of public policies. The decrease in inflation allowed for more stable intergovernmental transfers, favouring the process of decentralisation to the extent that the federal government could bargain the transfer of taxes and functions to subnational governments in a more rational and programmed way.

The new standardisation of SUS in 1998 triggered major changes in intergovernmental relations regarding health care. New funding mechanisms were set up by establishing per capita intergovernmental transfers and by adopting strategies of financial induction so that municipalities could take charge of primary health care management by means of a comprehensive programme called the 'Family Health Strategy' (ESF). Initially deployed as an expansion programme to cover the poorest and most vulnerable populations, the ESF became a priority, reorganising the mechanisms of health care towards primary care.

Changes in funding mechanisms created a fairer model of resource allocation as, until then, transfers favoured municipalities with a larger capacity of service provision and prevented the expansion of those with less capacity. A direct transfer based on per capita calculation was introduced, allowing poor municipalities with weak service networks to invest in primary care and basic health needs. The change favoured northern and north-eastern regions, precisely the regions experiencing the most impoverishment and the greatest difficulties in the management of health policies (Lima 2007). Such advances, however, were not sufficient to address the structural inequalities throughout Brazil, as the majority of services were still concentrated in medium or large (and richer) urban centres.

Since the early 2000s, there has been a larger attempt to redefine the role of the state governments, especially as they were largely subsumed in the past by the greater presence of municipalities in SUS implementation. The logic connecting the federal government directly to municipalities was not able to resolve the huge weaknesses in implementing coordinated health services. It failed to stimulate integration among municipalities, which in turn continues to hamper the rational use of resources and the efficient organisation of services at a regional level.

The attempt to strengthen a regional presence, in which states would play a central coordinating role, was pursued through different strategies. The latest one is the 2006 'Pact for Health'. This agreement calls for new guidelines governing SUS regionalisation based on the principles of strengthening the political relationship between federated entities, and recognising economic, cultural, and social diversity in the redesign of health regions. One might say, following Lima and Viana (2011), that the 'Pact for Health' also reflects the way the federal government operates in SUS federal relations, expressing the commitment between managers to strengthen SUS shared management, and emphasising both the need for intergovernmental cooperation on health policy and a major role for states and municipalities in operationalising greater regionalisation. The 'Pact for Health' has also created an incentive to institutionalise intergovernmental negotiation and cooperation within regions by means of regional committees of agreement – the 'Regional Management Committees' (CGR). The logic here is the same of the Bipartite Inter-Managers' Commissions' (CIBs), but focused on regional matters.

The agreement is essential for regionalisation since the autonomy granted to federated units does not oblige them to adhere to specific programmes and policies. Moreover, electoral logic sometimes prevents coordination between municipalities located in the same region whenever partisan opposition among mayors exists. In these cases, either municipal managers create new services that could more efficiently be offered in association with other municipalities, or they transfer services to private organisations, often tendering services to specific interests or constituencies (or simply not providing the required services to their inhabitants). This, in turn, means the citizens of these regions must search for the services they need, at their own risk and expense, in other cities. This is the case, for example, of two close cities in Rio de Janeiro state. One has a quite regular health system and the other has not, despite being a rather wealthy municipality. Patients from the latter try to access medical services (especially diagnostic exams and specialist doctors) at the former. However, as the former does not get paid for the services, it blocks the entry of those patients. The latter city chose not to invest properly in health care, and has the autonomy to do so. The first city resolved to block the population (despite the system being universal in principle), and it, likewise, has complete autonomy to do so.

Another common situation is that of poor municipalities that depend almost totally on the resources transferred from the national government. Even applying the minimum of their budget in health (15 per cent), this is not sufficient to pay other municipalities for the health services their citizens need. Sometimes a single cancer patient or a neonatal ICU can take a large proportion of the money. On the other hand, municipalities which offer the services are not obliged (and usually cannot afford) to pay for the health care of their poor neighbours. That is why the participation of the state is crucial to search for a financial and managerial balance among all. And the best way to do so in Brazilian health federalism is through cooperation.

The 'Pact for Health' has improved direct transfers of resources from the federal level to states and municipalities. However, this did not mean greater autonomy for subnational levels in the use of these resources. A major part of federal transfers are bound to specific federal programmes, meaning that despite the progress with respect to agreements among governments, the federal government still maintains the power to decide where the money is to be spent (Machado et al. 2014: 190).

Despite advances, major problems and challenges remain regarding health care federalism in Brazil. The regional disparities and social inequalities that permeate the more than 5,000 Brazilian municipalities are a result of the quite divergent regional capacity for the management and provision of health care services. This wide disparity in capacity has not yet been resolved, reinforcing the need for federal coordination.

Traditionally, the overwhelming majority of Brazilian municipalities depend on constitutional transfers from supranational levels, especially from the Union, and the situation remains the same in the current decade. Data obtained from the Public Health Budget Information System (SIOPS) for the year 2012 show that 80 per cent of municipal revenues derive from transfers, with half of this amount (51 per cent) coming from the Union.

It is worth noting that from the more than 5,500 Brazilian municipalities, about 70 per cent have less than 20,000 inhabitants; approximately 25 per cent have between 20,000 and 100,000 inhabitants; and the remaining 5 per cent have more than 100,000 inhabitants. But the reliance on intergovernmental transfers is observed even in large municipalities with considerable economic strength, despite the differences in transfer percentages.

Parallel to that, when analysing the municipalities' per capita revenues, Lima (2014) identifies the persistence of great disparities: the system ends up favouring both the capitals, comprising 23 per cent of the country's population, compared to the municipalities whose population varies from 10,000 to 100,000 inhabitants (representing 41 per cent of the Brazilian population). In some capitals, the per capita income is 80 per cent higher than in medium-sized municipalities. For their part, small municipalities (with less than 5,000 inhabitants) have a per capita income higher than the capitals, especially due to the Municipalities Allocation Fund (FPM) and to other intergovernmental transfers, and in particular those coming from specific sectorial policies, such as the health care sector.

Another aspect concerns the question of health financing. Despite the increase in resource allocation based upon the so-called 'Constitutional Amendment 29' (which establishes the gradual increase in the percentage of resources destined to health care in the three levels of government), the system remains underfunded. The constitutional amendment increased SUS funding from 2.89 per cent of GDP in 2000 to 3.91 per cent in 2011 (Piola et al. 2013). However, as can be observed, public expenditures on health in Brazil are considerably below those of countries with public and universal systems. The same applies when they are compared to other countries in Latin America, impacting the possibilities of establishing cooperative actions in a context of scarce resources. The Union stays as the main responsible provider of health spending, although its share has remained stable since the years 2000, corresponding, in 2011, to 1.75 per cent of GDP (IBGE 2012). That spending increase is mainly due to the efforts undertaken by the states and cities over time. According to a survey carried out by Piola et al. (2013), states and municipalities more than tripled the volume of resources allocated to health between 2000 and 2011.

In this context, one cannot underestimate the redistributive effects of federal transfers to SUS, in particular regarding the northern, north-eastern, and mid-western regions of the country, where the transfers from the Union to the sector far outweigh many municipalities' own fundraising, especially for the smaller ones. Such redistribution is mostly provided by the resources linked to the Primary Health Care financing system (*Piso de Atenção Básica* – PAB). These are calculated on a per capita basis, and incorporate incentives for specific actions. The transfers are given on a regular and automatic basis to the municipalities to promote measures strengthening the Primary Health Care system. But the amount of sectorial resources has not been sufficient to overcome inter- and intraregional inequalities, colliding with the differences in the direct tax collection and in the appropriation of other non-exclusive health transfers from the Union and states.

Another aspect that deserves attention is the relationship between various public and private segments of the Brazilian health care system. The SUS is composed of a combination of public and private services (of different modalities) and is impacted by strong private and corporate interests that make the delivery of health services an exceptionally complex enterprise. In this sense, a challenge to the SUS in its various related spheres of government lies in regulating these relations, guided by public demand and the health needs of the population. The difficulties of SUS financing and technical management have forced municipalities to transfer services and public health units' management to private organisations. In several cases, the Public Ministry tried to prevent this practice without much success due to the expansion of these organisations.

While there is no evidence of such privatisation at the national level, in important states like Rio de Janeiro, São Paulo, and Bahia they have been adopted by several hospitals and also, to some degree, in primary care. There are indications that privatisation has increased difficulties in coordinating service networks since hiring rules vary among services, states and cities. If this is true, inter-federative coordination for managing the health care system could well be jeopardised.

A brief review of the SUS's 25-year operation allows us to identify significant changes in intergovernmental relations in health, especially with regard to advances in the ways in which negotiations and conflicts have been conducted among federated entities. However, the challenge remains to build a new logic of federal coordination that connects the promotion of citizenship and the fight against social inequalities, on the one hand, to the flexible formulation and implementation of public policies for distinct territorial and social realities.

Conclusion

Decentralisation in Brazil has always been linked to democracy. Authoritarian periods corresponded to constraints upon federalism, concentrating power in the federal government, while democratic periods stimulated greater decentralisation. Following this pattern, the 1988 Constitution reaffirmed the federal approach and deepened decentralisation, which carried more visibility in social policies. Health policy was the most radical case, and the one to experience most advances in this regard. This was a largely technical strategy to deal with the significant regional differences and the problems that had been caused by the tradition of centralisation. It also acted in a way as a political strategy to democratise the system and consolidate health as right. But the autonomy and cooperation referred to as principles for the success of health system decentralisation nonetheless conflicted continually with the structures of federalism.

Tax and fiscal decentralisation did not follow logically from the decentralisation of responsibilities. Despite greater tax autonomy of states and municipalities, the federal government controls the largest share of public resources and, in consequence, the decision-making power over the sectorial transfer of subnational levels. The same occurs in the fiscal area, where the federal government prevails in the decision-making process and adopts guidelines of maintaining high surpluses in public accounts and high interest rates to control inflation. This severely restricts the options of states and municipalities. Although some increases in social expenditure by the federal government are visible, universal health and education policies are not among them.

SUS underfunding is a consensus among experts. Public expenditure currently corresponds to less than half of total health expenditure as a proportion of GDP. Brazil is in a unique situation since it is the only country providing a universal and comprehensive health care system in which public spending is less than private spending and where about 25 per cent of Brazilians have private health plans.

Federal government control over public resources consequently generates control over the policies to be adopted. This control also unbalances sectoral federalism to the extent that it hinders the autonomy of states and, even more importantly, of municipalities. Municipalities directly provide many health care services and, as most of them are small units with little technical and financial capacity, they rely on federal resources to manage the system, submitting themselves to the central authority guidelines.

Nonetheless, while this level of federal control undermines the autonomy of subnational levels, one may also say that it contributes to the maintenance of a unified health care system. And that is due to problems also in the area of sectorial federalism. SUS decentralisation in the mid-1990s was, in fact, a 'municipalism', i.e., the shifting of responsibilities to the municipalities. This transfer of responsibilities and resources pushed the states to the sidelines, even while they were already playing an indirect and less consequential role in the system. Because of the focus upon municipalities over states, the formal regionalisation of services did not evolve. The strategy of decentralisation that was implemented did consolidate SUS in the municipalities, which responded positively with regular and growing increases in resources as well as the evolving organisation of their local systems. But it has become evident that this model would not solve (and in some cases even increased) regional inequalities.

To remedy the problems related to constraints on sectorial federalism, the instances of formal agreement in health care collaboration should be highlighted. As joint mechanisms of consensual decision-making and broad participation in the three government levels, the CIBs and the CIT have succeeded in breaking (though slowly) the political and technical constraints that have hindered SUS management. The exposure of conflicts and the implicit need for cooperation have eased the decision-making process. Power imbalance is still present among members, but the principles of equal representation and consensual and effective decision-making hopefully will be able to generate trust among the members.

These agreement mechanisms have no ability to resolve federative conflicts outside the sectorial arena. But when discussing and deciding on health policies, criteria of resource allocation, coordination among government levels, and so on, they strengthen the system with regard to government policies as a whole. The process of mutual learning with respect to mechanisms of agreement regarding health policies in Brazil is perhaps the most significant development in contemporary Brazilian health care federalism. Ideally, it may indicate the possibilities for consensus at regional and municipal levels which can serve as a basis for an integrated and effective federal health care system.

Chapter 14

The Russian Federation

Tatiana Chubarova and Natalia Grigorieva

Introduction

The particularity of Russian health care federalism rests in the dramatic shifts in the relationship between the national and subnational units that arose due to the collapse of the Union of Soviet Socialist Republics (USSR). This event led to the recognition of the Russian Federation as an independent state, and to the transition to a market economy.[1] Historically, problems of federalism in Russia have been determined by geographical and socio-economic factors, and specifically by the disproportionate development of Russian regions and a low level of interregional cooperation on strategic joint projects. Significant regional disparity in economic as well as social and health indicators exacerbate difficulties in providing the population with accessible, good quality health services.

Currently, health care federalism in Russia has two distinct features. On the one hand, the federal government is attempting to transfer considerable decision-making power regarding social policy, including health issues, to regional and municipal levels. At the same time, there has been a gradual but steady reduction in federal support for the financing of regional health services as a share of gross national product (GNP), and the obligations that arise in dealing with difficult and intractable social problems are thereby shifted to regional budgets. On the other hand, the influence of the federal government is still visible in the articulation of general social objectives. It is, unsurprisingly, extremely difficult for regions to address these problems given the budget shortfall experienced by almost two-thirds of the regional governments within the Russian Federation.

This chapter first provides a brief general overview of the development of federalism in modern Russia. This is followed by a description of how these recent changes have impacted the health care system. Problems related to federalism in health care are subsequently discussed in more detail, including the modes of federal intervention in health care, the regional dimension of health status indicators, and the formation of federal–regional relations in drug supply. Some tentative conclusions are offered that summarise the main points developed in the chapter.

---

1   It should be noted that Russia was a federation when it was a part of the USSR.

The Development of Federalism in Modern Russia

Russia, a large country with a centuries-old history, is located athwart two quite distinct parts of the world (Europe and Asia) It shares borders with 18 different countries and, in consequence, is characterised by great ethno-cultural variety. The population of Russia by the beginning of 2013 has been estimated as 143 million (the 9th most populous in the world), with a geographic territory of 17,098,246 square miles. As a federal state, Russia is comprised of 83 discrete regions (officially referred to as 'subjects of the federation') including 46 oblasts (regions), 21 republics (mostly formed along ethnic lines), nine territories, four autonomous regions, one autonomous territory, and two cities, Moscow and Saint Petersburg, which have the formal constitutional status of 'subjects of the federation'. Regions have their own administrative division as well. For instance, the Moscow oblast is divided into 72 municipalities; Novosibirsk oblast into 40, and Kaliningrad oblast into 15. The regions are in turn grouped into eight Federal Districts, each of them headed by a representative of the president of the Russian Federation.

The legal structure of the Russian Federation is based upon both its Constitution and federal statutes. Regions, in turn, have their own charters and legislation. In mutual relations with federal bodies of the government all regions are equal in rights. Researchers (e.g., Lapina 2006) generally identify three basic periods in the history of federal relations in post-Soviet Russia:

- spontaneous decentralisation (early–mid 1990s);
- asymmetric federalism (mid 1990s–early 2000s);
- re-centralisation (early 2000s to the present).

During the first period, established relations between the federal and regional governments became quite destabilised: the federal government lacked sufficient administrative and other resources to control the regions but, at the same time, there was no uniform institutional and political framework for their development. International organisations were also active in promoting the decentralisation of political powers based on the principle of subsidiarity (Vereschagina 2008). In August 1990, then-president Boris Yeltsin called regional governments to 'take as much sovereignty as you want', which led inexorably to the growth in power of regional elites. As a result, many of the regional jurisdictions, especially republics, adopted their own constitutions and elected their own presidents. Federal authorities, during this period, made a political compromise with regional elites which amounted to a trade-off between political loyalty and greater sovereignty.

The second period was marked by the formalisation of relations between the federal centre and the regions. The creation of a working Constitution of the Russian Federation in December 1993, which assigned to the subjects of the federation the right to form their own legislative base and system of governance, was a notable reference point in the development of Russian federalism. At the same time, the regions started actively developing their own international trade relations despite differing widely in their export and investment potentials, based, in turn, on their geographical location, natural resources, industrial base, and financial infrastructure (Vardomskij and Skatershchikova 2002). By the end of the 'Yeltsin era', asymmetric federation had become pronounced. This period was particularly characterised by a bilateral interaction between federal and regional leaders that, in effect, led to quite unequal relations between regions and the federal centre.

The third period saw the beginning of the redistribution of resources and powers back to the federal government. This included the formation of a uniform legal, economic, and administrative space. By the mid-2000s the federal government had strengthened its position, but it failed to get completely free from the political influence of regional elites. To overcome this situation a new order of elections for federal and regional bodies was authorised. This period, which began with Putin's election as president to the Russian Federation in March 2000, can be characterised as the period of re-centralisation (Lapina 2006) or 'unitary federalism' (Larina 2006).

At the same time, interestingly, local self-governance grew increasingly sophisticated, albeit with a large degree of variation between municipalities. The 1993 Constitution of the Russian Federation formalised the institutional structures of local self-governance. But in the early 2000s centralised control over municipalities became much more pronounced, their powers crippled by the lack of financial and economic resources. While there has been a more recent tendency to strengthen local self-governance, the scope of municipal power is now subject to regional governments' respective policies, goals, and strategies.

Budgetary transfers are very important for local governments: in 2012 they amounted to 46.6 per cent (1,045 billion roubles) of municipalities' total revenues. Significant resources within the framework of budgetary transfers go to social needs. The main focus of the federal policy is to maintain certain common social standards, although regions can adopt higher standards based on their capacity.

Health Care Federalism in Russia

Federalism has had a significant influence on the formation and implementation of health policy in Russia. The Constitution of the Russian Federation stipulates three levels of health services in the country: federal, regional, and municipal. It clearly reflects the aspiration for the division of powers and active engagement of all levels of government in health care. Federalism in Russian health care has several important features in terms of the financing and provision of health care. Health care is a sphere of a shared responsibility between different levels of power in Russian Federation, and it is fixed in law. This means that, on one hand, all jurisdictions are responsible for the health care of their respective populations and, on the other hand, each has its own area of responsibility in health care.

The health services are divided into federal, regional, and municipal levels. Accordingly, they are regulated and financed by the relevant authorities and are supposed to provide treatment to the relevant populations. At present 75 per cent of health services are regional, 22.6 per cent are municipal and 2.4 per cent are federal (the latter provides sophisticated tertiary treatment to all Russian citizens regardless of what region they come from).

As in all federal states, health care financing is a particularly important aspect of Russia's health care federalism. The 1991 law on statutory medical insurance (SMI) embodies the shift towards a new system of health care in the country from a general tax-based model (Semashko) to a social insurance model. As a result, the federal SMI fund and regional SMI funds were established as independent bodies. Regional SHI funds can act as insurers themselves (establishing direct relations with health services) or via special medical insurance companies. This has led to variations between regions in CHI models that have been adopted across the various regions. At the outset of this transformational stage, the federal SMI fund did not act as insurer and was responsible only for technical support and for providing money for regional SMI funds for certain targeted programmes.

By the late 1990s a complex double-channel system of health care financing via both CHI and general tax revenues was formed. As a result, health services were financed through two sources (budget appropriations and CHI), each financing certain defined expenditures. Budget appropriations went to cover expensive hi-tech treatments, major renovations, and equipment, gas, and electricity, and so on, while SMI money covered only some operational expenditures (including soft material and catering salaries). Accordingly, budget funds came from the relevant budgets, either federal, regional, or municipal.

Regional SMI funds in turn collected money from two sources. First, they accumulated payments made by employers, which are fixed legislatively at 3.6 per cent of payroll (this money was streamed into two channels: 0.2 per cent to the federal CHI fund, and the rest to regional CHI funds). Regional authorities paid for the non-working population; these amounts were not fixed, and were determined by the regions themselves. It is necessary to note the diversity in the scope of regional authorities' control over governance of SMI funds. Research indicated that in 2005 only 24 out of 89 regions' health care departments participated in control over quarterly and/or monthly SHI fund reports on a regular basis (*Public Health Care in Regions of the Russian Federation* 2006). The relations between regions respecting SMI funds transfers were very poorly developed. As a result, the CHI policy issued in one region was often ignored in another.

Modes of Federal Involvement in Health Care

Several federal regulatory mechanisms have evolved to regulate health care across Russian regions. First, the federal government sets a *conceptual framework* for the development of the health care system in Russia. It adopts major laws that lay down the basic principles of its functioning. This, in general, leads to the universality of *institutional* structures of health care system in regions that are more or less the same (for example, SMI). Problems that arise here are mostly of a financial nature. Second, federal authorities provide *normative-legal regulation* (including the introduction of treatment standards, financial norms, and licensing). For example, a federal programme of basic guarantees of free medical care stipulating a certain level of medical services for the entire population was adopted annually starting from 1999. Regions are obliged to execute these obligations in full. Third, the federal government *directly participates* in solving health care problems in regions, the most common tool being special targeted programmes that include financial transfers from federal to regional budgets. It should be noted that the programme approach is gaining momentum in Russian budget policy-making in general. There are several types of federal programmes in health care. These include special federal target programmes (e.g., 'Diabetes', 'Urgent measures for tuberculosis', 'Prevention of diseases through vaccination', 'High medical technologies', 'Against AIDS', etc.). In September 2005, the so-called 'National Health Care Project' was one of four high-priority projects started with the aim to develop primary health care, preventive care and improve access to tertiary care. One of the objectives was to build 14 centres with advanced technological health services in regions covering various types of diseases (Table 14.1).

In 2011, a health care modernisation project was launched that had a clear regional dimension. It was aimed at improving equipment supply in health services, introducing electronic health systems, and developing comprehensive quality standards in health care. To receive federal funding, all regions were required to work out special regional modernisation programmes based on their health system audits. It should be noted that pilot projects are today quite common in Russia, and are first introduced in a few target regions before being established as federal guidelines. The utility of these pilot studies, however, is often limited given the poor evaluation of the results obtained.

Table 14.1   Financing of the National Health Project (billion roubles)

	2009	2010	2011	2012	2013
Total	*126.6*	*144.1*	*134.9*	*139.5*	*100.5*
Promotion of healthy life style	0.731	0.820	0.820	0.820	0.820
Medical services to patients with vascular diseases	3.1	3.1	3.4	5.88	5.88
Medical help for road accidents	2.5	3.3	2.8	5.48	5.48
Health services to cancer patients	6.8	5.9	6.9	6.9	6.9
Tuberculosis	2.7	4.1	2.6	2.8	3.1
Hi-tech medical services	30.3	37.2	42.2	43.2	43.2
Development of blood services	4.2	4.5	4.2	5.0	5.0
Development of network of prenatal centres	7.2	6.0	0.257	0.8	0.8

Fourth, federal involvement in health care includes the *coordination of public health care policies between all interested federal and regional bodies.* In addition to the federal Ministry of Health, there are many governmental bodies that participate in the management of health issues at the federal level, including the Ministry of Finance, the Ministry of Regional Development, the Ministry of Economic Development, the Ministry of Labor and Social Development. It seems to be widely acknowledged that health care requires an interdisciplinary approach. However, coordinating all the parties concerned is still a difficult task, and in the end it is Ministry of Health that is usually responsible for issues directly related to health, including healthy lifestyles.

Fifth, the federal government has a role in the *provision of information.* This involves collecting and disseminating information on health care issues at both federal and regional levels with the aim of improving the quality of decision making. Development of the state register of patients with diabetes is one example of this. As a result of this federal programme, regions greatly improved their capacity to monitor the epidemiological status of diabetes (its complications, supply of drugs and self-checking tools) and to evaluate the concomitant economic expenses involved.

Sixth, *training and/retraining of health care professionals* is an important sphere of influence for federal authorities. In 2012 the concept of a system of continuous medical education in the Russian Federation was developed with the aim of introducing new forms of education, and especially those based on information technologies (IT). In October 2013 pilot projects introducing continuous medical education for primary care physicians started in nine regions of the Russian Federation (Skvortsova 2013). Specialised educational centres for professional retraining of the personnel were created in 14 (out of 46) medical schools in the country. These pilot programmes are often designed at the federal level, but occasionally the initiative for the creation of such centres comes from regional Ministries of Health.

The basic financial mechanisms of federal policy are transfers from the federal to regional level. These include transfers from federal to regional budgets and from the federal SMI fund to regional SMI funds. They are typically allocated for specific targets set by the federal government (so-called 'federal mandates'). Within these target areas, the regions have significant powers to influence the municipalities. The special regional commission (which is headed, as a rule, by the governor or vice-governor on Social Issues) makes a further decision on the distribution of these federal budget transfers to health care.

Several observations are important to make here.

1. The federal government sets common standards that all regions are obliged to follow. However, they are also free to realise higher standards if they have the necessary resources to finance them. The problem here is determining whether such higher standards should be applied to the local population only or to everybody receiving treatment in the region in question.

2. Recently, the federal government introduced a new system of subsidies (uniform grants) that give regions the right to redistribute such subsidies at their discretion in accordance with their needs. There is a real risk of under-financing of health services if health care is not included as a priority in the utilisation of these subsidies.

3. Regions certainly have the ability to innovate (both in practice and in legislation), especially in areas where federal guidelines are lacking. The development of public-private partnerships (P3s) is a good example. In the absence of clear federal regulations, some regions started to adopt regional laws on P3s. As a result, a draft federal law on P3s that is now being debated in the State Duma is largely based on norms developed and implemented by regions.

Health Care Indicators in the Russian Federation: A Regional Dimension

The problems of the Russian health care system, and of the health status of the population in general, are well described elsewhere. When evaluating the Russian Federation through the lens of theories of federalism, however, the major issues are clearly the substantial variation in population health status and health services availability across the regions.

Table 14.2   Life expectancy at birth in Russian regions, 2011, both sexes, years

Regions with the highest life expectancy		Regions with the lowest life expectancy	
Russian Federation average – 69.8			
Republic of Ingushetia	76.3	Republic of Tyva	61.4
Moscow	75.8	Chukotsky autonomus okrug	61.6
Republic of Dagestan	74.3	Evreyskaya autonomus oblast	63.4
St. Petersburg	73.1	Amur oblast	64.8
Republic of Karachay-Cherkessiya	72.9	Republic of Altay	65.4
Republic of North Ossetia–Alania	72.6	Sakhalinskaya oblast	65.7
Republic of Kabardino-Balkariya	72.4	Trans-Baikal Territory	65.8
Republic of Chechenskaya	72.1	Irkutsk oblast	65.9
Belgorod oblast	71.7	Magadan oblast	66.0
Stavropol kray	71.6	Khabarovsk kray	66.0

Source: Russian statistic yearbook, 2012 C.107.

Average life expectancy in Russia was 69.8 years in 2011. But there are significant differences in life expectancy across the regions. Table 14.2 demonstrates the data for 10 regions with the highest and the lowest life expectancy. It varies from 61.4 years in the Republic of Tyva to 76.3 years in the Republic of Ingushetia. Thus regional differences in life expectancy in 2011 exceeded 15 years. Age mortality rates (Table 14.3) also differ greatly even within one federal district.

Table 14.3   Age mortality rate coefficients (per 100,000) depending on type and population density of settlements in the Central Federal District of Russia, 2008–2009

	0–14	15–29	30–44	45–59	60 and older
Men					
City type settlements	106.8	365.9	893.8	2265.8	7955.1
Small cities: up to 10 thousand	145.9	271.6	1001.0	2502.3	8349.1
Small cities: 10–19.9 thousand	99.8	331.9	891.4	2326.0	8152.8
Average cities: 20–49.9 thousand	104.5	310.5	896.1	2252.9	8054.5
Average cities: 50–99.9 thousand	117.3	332.9	862.2	2241.0	8252.3
Large cities of 100 thousand and more	79.9	230.0	776.8	2043.1	7431.3
The centre of the subject of the Russian Federation	93.2	243.3	752.1	1932.7	7169.2
Women					
City type settlements	85.8	102.9	273.5	690.9	5321.1
Small cities: up to 10 thousand	53.0	135.8	264.1	807.0	5625.5
Small cities: 10–19.9 thousand	72.4	99.3	291.3	717.1	5471.5
Average cities: 20–49.9 thousand	77.9	91.4	272.7	661.2	5299.0
Average cities: 50–99.9 thousand	69.4	96.3	250.4	678.1	5335.5
Large cities of 100 thousand and more	55.3	54.1	248.8	625.1	4902.1
The centre of the subject of the Russian Federation	73.6	67.5	224.7	577.3	4735.1

Source: Compiled by the authors based on the Report of the Ministry of Health on Implementation of the Programme of the State Guarantees in Providing Free-of-charge Health Care Services to the Population of the Russian Federation, corresponding years.

By the end of 2011, there were a total of 58,600 health services in Russia, a third of them located in cities with a population of more than 1 million residents. The greatest numbers of health services were located in Moscow, Saint Petersburg, and Novosibirsk (9,126, 3,221, and 1,072 respectively). A gradual reduction in the network of municipal health services suggests a reduction in access to treatment for local people all over the country, especially in rural areas and small settlements.

Many of Russia's health care problems are a clear consequence of its federal structure and policy. They can be grouped according to the following considerations:

Conceptual and Political Factors

One of the most pronounced problems in Russian health care federalism is that, politically, the role of regions in general is not well defined. This corresponds with the lack of a clear conceptualisation of 'health system development' throughout the country. In the early 2000s, the draft strategy Developing the Public Health Care System in the Russian Federation to 2020 was articulated and discussed, but it was not formally approved. Nevertheless, in 2010–2011 a number of important acts were adopted, including the new SMI law, Fundamentals of Health Protection of Citizens of the Russian Federation and The Federal Program of Health Care Development. The Presidential Decree signed in May 2012 is the most recent legislation concerning health care.

Pointedly, over this 20 year period of heath care reforms exhibited the tendency towards an insufficient allocation of financing for public health services. This has forced a significant part of the population to pay for health services. The numbers of services-for-fees has been growing constantly, and as a result in 2012 the federal Rules for Health Services to Provide Paid Health Services was approved (commencing in 2013). This is the first indication of substantive state support for private health care services.

The Spatial Factor

The spatial factor that underlines the importance of geographic barriers between those seeking health care, and the provision of health services, significantly influences people's health status and access to health services. It also affects the organisation of health care systems in Russia (Bochkareva 2009). Average population density across Russia is not high (8.3 persons per square km) and it differs significantly across regions. For instance, in the Central Federal District (CFD) density averages 57.14 persons per square km (10 per cent of the population of the country lives in CFD), compared to 1.05 persons in the Far Eastern Federal District (FEFD).

The transportation problem is also acute in Russia. The average density of railways (railways cover almost 50 per cent of all needs in transportation) across Russia is 5–20 times lower, and the average density of highways is 20–50 times lower, than it is in other developed countries (Bochkareva 2009). There is also great disparity in health services between urban and rural areas. In areas outside regional centres there are insufficient numbers of paved roads; the absence of convenient transport system between the settlements is quite common; and there are limited transport schedules (Gnatjuk et al. 2013). This makes it difficult for patients to reach health facilities, especially those providing specialised care. The share of people unable to access health services due to long travel times is also increasing. In many cases, especially in rural areas, health services have limited capacity in terms of equipment and staffing with specialists, and people lack the choice of services or physicians.

In addition, over the past few years the network of health services has been shrinking. For the period 1995–2011 the number of hospital beds was reduced by 511,000. The decrease of health services in rural areas is much more profound than that in urban areas. The number of primary care clinics (*polikliniks*) decreased in rural areas from 9217 in 1995 to 2979 in 2010. This in turn led to a decrease in the number of visits per shift from 133 to 116. Over 8,000 paramedic/midwifery service units (according to regulations one such unit should be open per every 700 residents) and 232 ambulance stations were eliminated. One result of this is that the frequency of calls for an ambulance per 1,000 residents in villages is 2.7 times lower than in cities.

These closures were explained by the need to cut expenses, but in health care such rationalisations often lead to even higher medical expenditures. Only about 400 rural municipal hospitals remained in the entire country after reforms (compared to 4,400 in 1995). This meant, for example, that in order to visit a paramedic one had to travel between 40–60 kilometres, which sharply reduced the availability of health care to those most in need. As a result, only 40 per cent of rural residents visit doctors when sick. Their outpatient numbers are half that of the urban centres, and they are hospitalised only in the most serious cases. According to the National Survey of Household Welfare and Participation in Social Programs, 50 per cent of respondents did not visit health services; of these, 16 per cent mentioned lack of a required specialist, or the necessity of paying for treatment, as reasons for not seeking treatment.

Financial, Economic, and Organisational Factors

There are clear differences in financial and economic opportunities across Russia's regions, as they differ in their respective economic and social development. In many respects this is due to the availability of natural resources, historically developed infrastructure, climate conditions, political culture, and other factors. As a result, only 11 regions out of 83 are considered as 'donor' regions; the others rely heavily on federal subsidies.

For the last three years, the rating agency RIA evaluated Russian regions based on official statistics. In 2012 the most economically powerful regions were Moscow, Saint Petersburg, Khanty-Mansi Autonomous Okrug (Yugra), Tyumen oblast and Moscow oblast. About 40 per cent of the country's GDP is produced by these regions and they are the major contributors to the federal budget. This is where the major export stream of the country begins. The majority of the largest corporations (including all major Russian natural resource monopolies) are located there. Having powerful resource potential, these regions have a great advantage in economic development. Historically, Moscow and Saint Petersburg have been leaders in social and economic development. The concentration of financial resources, highly-trained personnel, well-developed infrastructure, special status, and competitive production capacity create the preconditions for the high rating of these regions. However, the orientation of Tyumen oblast towards oil and gas production makes it highly dependent on the demands of the foreign market.

In the late 2010s, financing of the SMI system changed considerably. First, there was an increase in SMI payments for employers of up to 5 per cent of payroll. Second, payments to the non-working population were for the first time fixed by federal legislation. Earlier, as mentioned above, regional authorities addressed this problem at their own discretion. Third, transition to a single-channel financing system now means that all charges will be gradually included in the payments for SMI. Fourth, since 1 January 2012 all the SMI financing goes to the federal SMI fund which then allocates them among regions using special coefficients to reflect regional situation. As a result, transfers from the federal SMI fund became the main source of funding for regional SMI funds (640.6 billion roubles or 61.5 per cent of total amount of regional SMI fund revenues in 2012) and regional modernisation programmes (229.7 billion roubles or 22.0 per cent in 2012). Regional budget financing for regional SMI funds was only 109.1 billion roubles (or 10.5 per cent). Currently, the SMI funds make up only 35 per cent of total expenditures on public health services; other charges are being carried by federal and regional budgets. The total public health expenditures in Russia are very low and fluctuate around 3 per cent of GDP. In sum, regional budgets play an important role in Russian health care financing (Table 14.4).

As Table 14.4 illustrates, the share of federal health care funding peaked in 2009 and then started to diminish, while regional contributions hit a nadir in 2010 and increased thereafter. The share of SMI was consistently around 40 per cent. There are also differences in the division of responsibilities in health care provision and regulation between regional and municipal governments: some regions centralised the responsibility for health protection at the regional level, while others delegated some powers to municipalities.

Comprehensive assessment of implementation of regional health care programmes allowed for the division of Russian regions into four groups. The first group includes 12 regions (14.5 per cent of the total number of regions) with a high level of success in realising regional programmes targets (Republic of Mordovia, Chuvash Republic, Krasnodar kray, Krasnoyarsk kray, Belgorod oblast, Voronezh oblast, Kemerovo oblast, Penza oblast, Samara oblast, Saratov oblast, Ulyanovsk oblast, and Tyumen oblast). The second group includes 33 regions (approximately 40 per cent of total number of regions) with an above-average level of realisation of regional programmes. The third group consists of regions with a less than average level of success in achieving programme goals (28 regions, or 33 per cent).

Table 14.4   State health care financing in Russia

	Total			Federal budget		Consolidated budgets of subjects of the Russian Federation		SMI system	
	billion	% GNP	%	billion	%	billion	%	billion	%
2001	238.4	2.6	100	18.0	7.5	130.1	54.6	90.3	37.9
2002	311.0	2.9	100	24.8	8.0	162.3	52.0	123.9	40.0
2003	355.6	2.7	100	27.9	7.8	178.4	50.2	149.3	42.0
2004	435.2	2.7	100	31.5	7.3	217.3	49.9	186.4	42.8
2005	559.5	2.6	100	89.3	16.0	253.0	45.2	217.2	38.8
2006	690.7	2.6	100	117.4	17.0	317.2	45.9	256.1	37.1
2007	897.3	2.9	100	162.5	18.1	406.6	45.3	328.2	36.6
2008	1185.1	2.8	100	288.6	24.4	483.7	40.8	412.8	34.8
2009	1378.6	3.5	100	391.6	28.4	481.6	34.9	505.4	36.7
2010	1449.9	3.2	100	393.1	27.1	403.7	25.3	540.4	37.3
2011	1596.9	2.9	100	403.7	25.3	568.3	35.6	624.9	39.1
2012	1718.4	2.7	100	411.4	23.9	580.6	33.8	726.4	42.3

Source: Compiled by the authors based on the Report of the Ministry of Health on Implementation of the Programme of the State Guarantees in Providing Free-of-charge Health Care Services to the Population of the Russian Federation, corresponding years.

Ten regions (12 per cent) have a low level of realisation of regional programmes, namely Kabardino–Balkarian Republic, Karachaevo–Circassian Republic, Republic of Karelia, Republic of Tyva, the Chechen Republic, Republic of Khakassia, Kurga oblast, Pskov oblast, Orenburg oblast, and Chukchi Autonomous region.

The level of financial deficit of regional state health care programmes shows the difference between what is required by federal standards regarding funding amounts, and what actually exists. Regional programmes have no deficit in 17 regions: in the cities of Moscow and Saint Petersburg, Republic of Saha (Yakutia), Nenets, Khanty–Mansiysk, Yamal–Nenets and Chukchi autonomous regions, Krasnodar and Kamchatka krays, Kaluga, Moscow, Magadan, Nizhniy Novgorod, Sakhalin, Sverdlovsk, Tyumen, and Yaroslavl oblasts. The financial deficit of regional programmes in all regions in 2012 reached 164.5 billion roubles (14.4 per cent less than the amount needed). The maximum was observed in Republic of Dagestan (48.2 per cent); large financial deficits still remain in the Republic of North Ossetia–Alania (40.1 per cent), Republic of Mari–El (37.1 per cent), Primorski Krai (34.6 per cent), Tomsk oblast (33.9 per cent), Tambov oblast (32.7 per cent), Bryansk oblast (31.1 per cent), Kurgan oblast (31.2 per cent), the Republic of Kabardino–Balkaria (30.1 per cent).

The comparison of the provision of free-of-charge state health services with the social and economic development of regions allows for interesting observations.

For example, Moscow is a leader in social and economic development but, at the same time, it is only in the third group as to implementation of regional programme of free-of-charge health care, with its indicators being below the Russian average. Only in three parameters out of 17 does Moscow show a high level of meeting programme objectives. There is an interesting paradox here: in a situation of good financing (in comparison with other regions) the programme of state guarantees in Moscow is in fact carried out poorly.

Federal–Regional Relations in Health Care: The Case of Drug Supplies

The problem of the division of responsibilities between federal and regional levels of health care system is well illustrated by the provision of pharmaceuticals. Since the early 1990s, drugs increasingly became out of reach for many Russians, and especially for low income groups, due to the changes in drug production and trade, rising prices, and a complex combination of adverse socio-economic factors including the deterioration of the population's health, reduction in life expectancy, an increase in socially-caused diseases, and a deficit in health care financing. It is important to note that some measures were taken to secure access to drugs. Patients in hospitals and patients with socially significant diseases are provided with drugs without charge within the framework of the SMI system and through special federal target programmes. The new policy of drug provision started in 1994 when certain groups of the population and individuals with certain diseases were to receive drugs prescribed by physicians, either free-of-charge or with a 50 per cent discount. Since 1996, a list of 'vital and essential drugs' has been used for this purpose. The provision of pharmaceuticals formally falls under the responsibility of the regions. However, they have been unable to execute their obligations in providing medicines in full, largely due to financial pressures. Therefore, the problem of maintaining drug quality and availability across the population remains.

There is a strong imbalance in public financing of pharmaceuticals across Russian regions. For example, there are significant discrepancies throughout the regions in per capita public expenses. According to the Ministry of Health Data, the federal financing of drugs for eligible populations (federal programmes) was 918 roubles per person per month, while the *average* regional financing was 513 roubles. In the Central Federal District, however, it amounted to 837 roubles, while in the North Caucasus it only reached 323 roubles.

To address this situation, a target programme of additional drug provision for socially vulnerable groups was launched in 2005. However, this programme was criticised by patients, authorities and legislators which led to a quite significant reform in 2008. Patients with diseases that require expensive treatments (including myeloid leukaemia, haemophilia, multiple sclerosis, Gaucher disease, pituitary dwarfism, and cystic fibrosis) as well as patients in treatment for the transplantation of organs and tissues, were separated into a special sub-programme of so-called 'seven nosologies' (VZN programme). For them, drugs were to be purchased from the federal budget funds. As of 1 December 2013 there were approximately 130,000 patients with diseases requiring expensive treatment and drugs. Responsibility over drug provision for other groups of patients covered by a 'programme of essential drug provision' has been delegated to regional governments. Thus, since 2008, the provision of drugs for those eligible for the state support was divided into two parts: some categories fall under federal responsibility, while others fall under regional responsibility.

According to the Ministry of Health, the total number of people that have a right to preferential drug supplies amounted 24 million in 2011, or about 17 per cent of the population. However, only 11 million people, or 8 per cent of the population, actually received such medicines. Federal budget expenditures on drug provision reached 43.459 billion roubles in 2012. Expenditures from regional budgets on drugs to patients in outpatient care increased from 19.10 billion roubles in 2009 to 25.62 billion roubles in 2012.

In 2013, it was decided to transfer the whole responsibility for the 'seven nosologies' programme to regional governments by 1 January 2015. Purchases of medicines (both federal and regional) are carried out according to the federal legislation through auctions. It is expected that the new framework will clarify the rights and responsibilities of the federal and regional authorities regarding essential drug provision, increase the transparency and predictability of administrative decisions, and strengthen control over the provision of public social services.

Clarification of regional responsibilities has certainly played a role in the stabilisation of drug provision, and delays in the drug supply have considerably decreased. More attention has been paid to administrative and operational issues. However, problems with essential drug supply still remain, including the lack of regional financing, the poor quality of drug needs assessment for state purchases, the auctions procedures, poor management of stocks, financial flows and drug prescriptions, poor cooperation among those involved in executing the essential drug programme, and the incorrect administration of patients' registers in regions.

The main focus of modern drug policy in Russia is to transfer financing for drugs in outpatient treatment from general budgets to SMI, and to replace direct state drug purchases with the reimbursement to patients of costs of prescribed drugs. Taking into account the social importance of the issue, the Strategy for Drug Provision for the Russian Federation to 2025 (and the plan for its implementation) has been developed in cooperation with regions and NGOs. Expenditures on drugs have been distributed between the federal and regional government, and municipal budgets are considered as additional sources of financing

Conclusions

There are two dominant narratives in health care federalism in Russia. On the one hand is the rhetoric that local authorities articulate a list of concerns which federal authorities address in a formal and cooperative manner. On the other hand is the perception the federal government (due to economic, financial, and administrative conditions) interferes with local affairs under the principle of 'manual management' from above. But since 'manual management' can be applied to a relatively small number of issues, the majority of local issues fall into a 'stagnation zone' including issues whose resolution require reforms executed by federal bodies. By law the central authorities should rely on local initiatives, but decision making at the local level often requires more capacity than these jurisdictions have at their disposal. Nevertheless, the responsibility for the public health care system and population health has shifted to the regions of the Russian Federation, while they struggle to find the resources to meet the demand. At the same time, the financial independence of regions is quite limited: only a third of the regions can meet their budgets for public health services. This has led to a political confirmation of the increasing influence of the federal government, which has taken the form of the federal grants-in-aid list of August 2013 (this establishes the uniform federal grants-in-aid to regional budgets). This was one of the first initiatives of the federal government in addressing problems caused by the reduction of many regional budgets (which reflected real fears that regions might fail to carry out the social obligations allocated or transferred to them). The federal measure of August 2013 also mentions the organisation of the system of public health care financing in regions, and notes certain consequences of the failure to carry out regional responsibilities. Regions with numbers of grants exceeding 40 per cent are obliged to sign an agreement with the Ministry of Finance to increase their efficient use of budgetary funds, to increase revenues, and to coordinate budget projects. Such regions can be subject to auditing by the Accounts Chamber or the Federal Agency for Finance and Budget Control. Some regions (approximately 10), that can meet their budgetary obligations, will keep their relative independence, which itself involves an opportunity to gain extra resources.

The general approach of the federal government is formulated very precisely: regions should solve their problems by themselves, within the limits of the uniform grant-in-aid resources allocated. The downside of this approach is the strengthening of supervision by the federal government over regional expenditures. The acceptance of uniform grants-in-aid by the regions has certain consequences. Administrative consequences include a further reduction in the influence of the Ministry of Health on regional health care services in favour of the federal Ministry of Regional Development, which may not be as conversant in the complexities of health care provision as the Ministry of Health. In such conditions, it is a priori more difficult for the Ministry of Health to assist regional governments in the coordination of health care services. More significant consequences include the increased risk of under-financing of certain health services. The reason for this is that uniform grants-in-aid give regions the right to redistribute sources independently. In other words, within the framework of the uniform subsidies the regional authorities can allocate more resources for provision of drugs for patients with rare diseases to the detriment of other patients, or vice versa.

Since the federal government plans to reduce total financing of health services in the coming years while leaving service obligations to regional budgets, it appears that free-of-charge health services are in jeopardy. It is likely that there will be new waves of political criticism of the Ministry of Health as well as an attempt at more careful supervision of activities of health care services at the regional and municipal levels. Another mechanism strengthening federal supervision of regional authorities (and limiting regional independence) is fixed in the Program of the State Guarantees of Free-of-charge Medical Services in 2014 and in 2015–2016. Under this legislation, the federal government has the right to withdraw powers from regional governments which fail to fulfil federal requirements related to CHI.

Modern Russian federalism has been in practice for only 20 years. This is a markedly short period of time for a country with such a complex territorial and administrative structure, and with so many regional governments. Russia manifests perhaps all of the structural difficulties experienced, to some degree, by other federal states: it is an asymmetrical federal state; it has a strongly centrifugal form of federalism; and there are deep ethnic and socio-economic differences between regional governments. One can agree with Elazer (1995) that countries such as Russia would strongly benefit from 'new federalist alternative solutions' although, as with many federal states, exactly what these solutions are, and precisely how they could be implemented, remains elusive.

Like many other federal states, too, Russia struggles to maintain a balance between a decentralised regional system of health care, on the one hand, and the coordinated management of strategic health policy goals, on the other. This balance has been difficult to achieve. A major obstacle to achieving coordinated health care between regional jurisdictions is that the underlying process of the division of powers in Russia is itself far from complete, and is subject to continual revision. The scope of delegated powers is different in various regions across Russia; this, in turn, exacerbates regional disparities within certain Russian states more so than in others. Some regions, for example, have centralised their authority over health care, while others have transferred their authority to municipal levels. In Nizhniy Novgorod oblast and Chukchi autonomous region, powers have remained concentrated at the regional level. In the Kirov oblast, similar powers were transferred *upward* from the municipal to regional level while, at the same time, the Khanty-Mansiysk autonomous okrug (Yugra) delegated the responsibility for providing primary care *downward* to the municipalities.

In order to achieve the coordination of key health policy objectives, the federal authorities thus rely on both regional and municipal initiatives. A serious problem with this strategy, however, is that decision making at the local level often requires more capacity than these jurisdictions have at their disposal. Nevertheless, the responsibility for both health care services and population health has shifted to the regions, while these jurisdictions struggle to find the resources to meet their needs. At the same time, the financial independence of regions is quite limited: only a third of the regions can meet their budgets for health services. As a result, many discrepancies have occurred in the provision of health care. Despite the significant financing that has been allocated to regional health system modernisation, it has simply proven impossible to produce the material and technical bases required to meet the standards of health care services provided to the population under conditions of regional budget deficits (Akchurina et al. 2013).

Up to this point, the results of Russia's evolving federal health care system have not been auspicious. While national-level goals and strategies have been articulated, federal policies have failed to contribute much to overcome the large (and still growing) disparities among regions in population health and access to health care. And, in keeping with the political dynamic played out in other federal states, the debates over 'what ought to be done' and 'who will do what' result in political compromises that hamper the strategic vision of prospective health reforms.

One of the challenges that we faced in writing this chapter was the significant lack of any qualitative studies of Russian health policy focusing specifically on federalism. As this chapter illustrates, however, federalism is clearly an important factor in the development of Russian health care, and one which requires further investigation. Russian health care is especially hampered by the lack of a clear conceptual approach to the problems of health service provision in a federal state. At both the federal and the regional level there exist a tremendous diversity of programmes and projects. This narrows opportunities for health care authorities to carry out purposeful public health care policies in the area of health protection, including structural reforms. Successful projects require both follow-through and the dissemination of key findings. The failure to provide these conditions means that the possibility of developing successful programmes is limited. Unfortunately, this is precisely what happened to many regional pilot projects that were carried out in great numbers, especially in the late 1990s to the early 2000s (partly with international support). At some point there must be a consolidation of results to develop efficient and coordinated health care system but, as the other contributions to this volume show, Russia is not alone in this respect.

Chapter 15

Conclusion

Howard A. Palley and Katherine Fierlbeck

As Frederick W. Riggs noted in his seminal study, *Administration in Developing Countries: The Theory of Prismatic Federalism* (1964), the implementation of programmes and policies tends to be refracted by the history, institutions, and applicable technologies of discrete societies. This notion was further refined to describe federal/subnational relationships in various settings in Daniel Elazar's study of Canadian federalism (1997), while Alain G. Gagnon and Raffaele Iacovino (2007) also utilised this concept in their discussion of the development of Quebec public policy within the Canadian context. In this volume, we have examined the development of health delivery in formal federal systems, the devolved 'functional federal' systems, such as those of Italy and China, and the quasi-federal systems of the United Kingdom and Spain, and found that this notion of prismatic federalism with refracted policies in different national and subnational contexts can be helpful in explaining health service delivery in 'structural' federal and 'functional' federal contexts. As Costa-Font and Greer concluded in their study of European health and social care, 'few generalizations hold well because of the complexity of politics, institutions, powers, and finances in each country […] An observer who expects German federalism to make the Länder powerful actors in health policy, or French decentralization to produce territorial divergence, is inattentive to politics and institutional details and will be accordingly surprised' (2013: 276). But is this all that can be said about the development of health policy in federal states? Beyond the recognition that federal and 'functional' federal systems tend to react to economic and political events in a manner determined by their specific cultural and institutional character, are there any more interesting convergences in the health policy of federal states that underscore either the advantages that federal states enjoy, or the complications that federal states confront, by virtue of their particular structures of governance?

There appear to be few clear substantive patterns regarding the response of federal and federal-like systems to economic drivers having an impact upon health care delivery systems. One obvious variable that affects the thrust of health reform is simply 'politics' itself. As Okma and Marmor note, 'politics' matters and is a variable that may enable or prevent reforms that are aimed at such policy goals as access, equity and efficiency. They observe that '[t]he gap between the rhetoric of the Obama Administration and the reality of the [Affordable Care Act] is large, but largely explained by American politics with numerous veto points […]'. This is also a key point in Duckett's observation that the hybrid complex of commonwealth/state and public and private financing of health care in governance and provision of health care is complicated by the ideological divide between the Labour and Liberal Parties with respect to the organisation and delivery of health care services. With regard to the United Kingdom, Bevan, Connolly, and Mays describe the parliamentary politics leading to the reordering of health care delivery between three devolved 'pygmies' (in terms of small population) – Scotland, Wales, and Northern Ireland – with a unitary England. However, the authors in this volume generally point to a common need that has been noted by Chris Ham for 'complementary approaches to reform, combining top-down and bottom-up, hierarchies and networks collaboration [...] and innovation and standardization as needed' (Creating Strategic Change in Canadian Healthcare: Conference Summary 2015: 5).

This volume examined the nature of policy formulation in the delivery of health care services in structural federal and functional federal systems by addressing an extensive and significant cross-section of such systems. The authors were invited to consider the ways in which the federal or federal-like nature of their respective jurisdictions influenced the nature of health care provision. Overlapping themes discussed throughout most of the chapters included decentralisation, cost control, and access to health care. While contributors were encouraged to identify the constructive aspects of health policy development in federal systems as well as the drawbacks, their analyses – while pointing out some successes – tended to focus on the difficulties of developing rational and efficient policies for reform of health care delivery systems. They also pointed out ways in which in which problems may be addressed to improve the operation of various federal health systems in a variety of national contexts.

A key methodological claim made in this volume is that there is little analytical utility in the traditional division between formal federal and unitary states. Rather, the political dynamics of highly devolved functional federal states closely reflect those of formal federal states. On one hand, an often stated advantage of a federal structure in social policy is its ability to identify and address the particular needs of discrete subnational geographical populations, given that citizens feel more closely attached to a system of service delivery that reflects their specific values and priorities (this is a beguiling aspect of British health care devolution, where the specific natures of the Scottish or Welsh variations of the NHS system are seen not only as policy structures but also as political statements). On the other hand, the main disadvantage of federal systems – formal or functional – is in the way this flexibility facilitates the shifting of blame and responsibility. It is easier to point fingers than to sort through complex policy problems; and both national and substate politicians find it easier to 'play to their constituencies' than to raise taxes or to address imbedded cost drivers. As the acrimonious debates between national and regional authorities in Canada and Australia illustrate, for example, much more political capital can be spent in demanding (or refusing) funding transfers than in addressing the structural inefficiencies underlying health care systems. This is a very basic point, but it is instructive that the literature on decentralisation prevalent throughout the 1980s and 1990s had very little to say on the tendency of federal systems to facilitate political animosity to the point of policy gridlock.

The distinction between 'formal' and 'functional' federal systems has rested primarily upon the recognition that formal federal states are often restricted by a constitutional structure that may act as an obstacle to more efficient policy formation or service delivery. But this is not to say that functional federal and quasi-federal states do not have similar political limitations: while Spain may formally be just a quasi-federal state, greater centralisation of its current federalised structure would be equally difficult because of the collective political memory of the way in which political centralisation and fascism were so irreducibly linked in Spain's recent past. Citizens often feel more strongly about particular values than legal constructs and, in a democratically responsive system, these sentiments become tangible and tenacious enough to take on a political force of their own.

Our studies indicate that general sweeping epistemological claims regarding federalism and the delivery of health care services (such as those made by much of the literature of decentralisation over the past two decades) are not helpful in analysing the processes and outcomes of health care delivery discussed in this volume. This is one reason that this book deliberately avoids evaluating 'federal' versus 'unitary' health care systems per se: the debate over whether federal or unitary states 'do health policy better' is not a new one, and the scope of variety in the health care systems of unitary states is possibly just as vast as the diversity of federal health care systems. To be able to discuss overall unitary health care systems instructively, one would have to delve into the same level of analysis that this volume attempts with federal states; and, while this kind of endeavour would indeed be an intellectually interesting one, such a project is well beyond the scope of this particular book.

Substantively, this volume identifies three specific trends arising from the interplay of political variables and economic constraints in federal health care systems. These themes reveal themselves differently across states, but they are discernible in some manifestation across most of the federal systems examined. These themes – increasing disparity, accountability deficits, and experimentation with new forms of coordination – are aspects of federal governance in contemporary society, and each of these themes is certainly worthy of more sustained analysis than we attempt to offer below.

Growing Disparity between Regions

One of the most striking threads in this volume is the concern that federal states are increasingly experiencing considerable political tensions due to regional inequalities in the provision of health care services. Gusmano, in his chapter on China, and Toth, on Italy, both find that in spite of central government efforts to provide incentives to improve health care delivery in poorer regions, equity between rich and poor areas in terms of the delivery of comparable health services has been a goal that both countries have failed to achieve. Toth acknowledges that, while Italy is not formally a federal system, '[t]he autonomy enjoyed by Italian regions is such that some consider it no longer appropriate to talk of a single national system, but rather a federation of twenty different regional systems'. Similarly, in spite of a system that exhibits a high degree of central control by the Chinese Communist Party, China has adopted a functional federal form of devolution in order to improve health care delivery across the country. Gusmano writes that, despite these recent changes, 'to date these efforts have not been sufficient to reduce the trend of growing inequalities in the affordability of health care'. Rather, these policies have resulted in significant improvements in the delivery of health care through a variety of health insurance systems in the affluent city of Shanghai, while health care has not significantly improved in poorer regions.

Russia and Brazil, both of which are formal federal systems, have attempted similar strategies, with similar results. In Russia, for example, significant improvements in health care delivery and vital statistics have occurred in Moscow and St Petersburg without similar results occurring in poorer areas. Chubarova and Gregorieva observe that, in the face of current financial constraints in federal revenues going to regional governments, there remain 'significant distinctions between regions of the country, both by general social and economic indices, and by basic parameters of their public health systems [causing] difficulties in providing the population with accessible and high quality public health services'. The lack of funding support from the centre has resulted in '[…] almost double the reduction in numbers of municipal health care organisations [… and] the reduction in access to health services for citizens of the country in all municipalities, especially rural areas, small settlements and cities'. Lobato and Senna argue that, in Brazil, where municipal governments assumed a much higher responsibility for both the funding and provision of health care, 'those with greater operational, technical, and managerial capacities were the ones to respond more effectively to industry demands', leading to similarly divergent patterns in health care provision and quality across regions. These trends are by no means limited to states with weaker economies. In Canada, for example, major changes in federal transfer formulae to the provinces are expected to exacerbate the considerable disparity in economic capacity that already exists between provinces.

A more challenging question is the degree to which greater regional disparity in health policy is related to the noticeable trend in the growth of the private sector in health care provision. A common theme that is noted in a number of the previous chapters, for example, is the presence of public/private partnerships (P3s) in subnational units as a strategy for increasing health care capacity which, in turn, is expected to facilitate greater access to health care services. As Elazar's approach suggests, this issue is refracted in various ways across countries such as India, Spain, Germany, Brazil, Italy, Australia, the United States, and Canada. In Canada's case, for example, the question is the extent to which the attempt by a central government to oblige provinces to raise more of their health care revenue from their own tax base, rather than through transfers, is a deliberate attempt to push regional jurisdictions into a position where they feel they have no choice but to embrace greater private sector involvement. Fierlbeck and Palley, as well as Okma and Marmor, note the significant presence of commercial enterprises in the Canadian provinces and the American states although, intriguingly, Canada's federal government has become emphatically disengaged with setting national health care priorities while the American federal government is attempting to do just the opposite. Okma and Marmor point out that, in the United States, the Patient Protection and Affordable Care Act of 2010 is very much characterised by a mixed public/private health care delivery system – but one in which the statute seeks to expand the guarantee of access to health insurance and thus allow for the eventual possibility of greater access to the health delivery system. In the case of Germany, on the other hand, Lang has found that, given constraints on the national government's funding of health care delivery, the use of private commercial sources for funding hospital capital expenditures for diagnosis and treatment as well as the development of private proprietary hospitals have served to increase access to health care delivery and enhance the level of up-to-date technology in the German Länder. However, some of our authors have noted that excessive reliance on commercial organisations in the delivery of health care have resulted in significant inefficiencies as well as difficulties for low income groups seeking access to quality health care services (Björkman and Venkat Raman, Lobato and Senna, and Okma and Marmor).

Accountability Deficits

A major premise of federal systems is that they are more responsive mechanisms of governance because the functional governing units are 'closer to the people'. As Costa-Font and Greer (2013) suggest, however, the exact mechanisms of this purported responsiveness are 'easier to impute than to actually find' (15). In many of the federal states examined in this volume, the purpose of adopting federal structures in the first place focused more upon preventing excessive central control than it was to ensure a vigorous populist dispersal of power. The former does not necessarily entail the latter and, in many of the cases examined here, regionalised health policy becomes quite vulnerable to capture by powerful local interests. In her investigation of which regional health authorities in Spain exhibit greater evidence of public accountability, for example, Pérez Durán finds that the regulatory mechanisms to insure public accountability are more likely to be lacking in regions with 'greater private management of health care'.

A theme that arises throughout the volume is vertical fiscal accountability. A weakness common to all federal systems is the capacity for national governments to download responsibility for health care provision to regional (or municipal) units which simply have neither the fiscal nor the technical capacity to support extensive health care demands and meaningful reforms. Interestingly, the development of serious vertical fiscal imbalance has a number of different explanations, including deliberate political strategising, the inability of national governments to appreciate the local infrastructure available for an efficient operating system, and entrenched institutional fragmentation which makes it difficult for national governments to address such shortcomings even if they wanted to. It goes without saying that federal and federal-like health delivery systems need to be adequately funded to prevent regional disparities, but the reasons that this vertical balance is so difficult to achieve politically vary widely across jurisdictions. Ideally federal health care systems should, as Mätzke and Stöger observe, have both a 'top-down' and 'bottom up' dynamic (see also Katznelson 2014; Palley 2005; Wright 2014) but it often becomes too tempting politically to offload costs and shift blame. (The interesting exception to this, of course, is the American experience, in which – as Okma and Marmor explain – the national government has attempted to assume greater funding responsibilities, a move which has been resisted by some states).

Greer's excellent study of the supranational European Union demonstrates yet another manifestation of this accountability deficit. Despite the fact that the European Union has no direct jurisdiction over individual states' health care systems, and notwithstanding the fact that the European Union does not possess the economic wherewithal to finance reforms of national health care systems, it has been able to influence member states' health care planning through mechanisms that arguably have minimal legal bases. Largely because of the dramatic economic effects following the 2008 recession, the European Commission used its regulatory powers to require formally autonomous states to submit their national budgets – including health policy planning – to the scrutiny of unelected bodies even before national legislatures have had a chance to review them. Other authors are concerned with the degree to which public accountability for implementing laws in democratic societies applies to the delivery of health care services (particularly Pérez Durán; Bevan, Connolly, and Mays; Mätzke and Stöger; and Björkman and Venkat Raman). Such accountability in democratic societies maintains that the execution of laws passed should be carried out in accordance with their legislative mandate (Minow 2003; Stone 2012).

Other perspectives regarding accountability lead to questions of accountability *to whom* and *for what*? All health care systems have complicated relationships of accountability, and the politics of public health care more generally are often simply a matter of trying to sort through the extent to which health care organisations are accountable to their patients, to the taxpayers, to governmental authorities, and to each other (Lowi 1979; Peters 2007). And, to the extent that health care services become increasingly commercialised, the complexity of the accountability process is greatly increased. In federal systems, of course, the complicated lines of accountability become even more blurred. As Bevan, Connolly, and Mays describe, the structure of devolution raises some intriguing questions about the way in which health policy decisions are made; but it also highlights the tension in states where the funding and delivery of health care services are distributed to specific levels of government. In such cases, the debate is often a narrative of blame-shifting where accusations of underfunding are met with accusations that resources provided simply are not being utilised efficiently. Also, Bevan, Connolly, and Mays note that there are difficulties in achieving improvements in health care delivery in the devolved governments in the United Kingdom without an effective accountability process common to England, Scotland, Wales, and Northern Ireland.

Health Care Coordination

The broader purpose of federalism has always been linked to issues of power. The point of establishing a federal system, from the founding of the United States in 1776 to the creation of the Russian Federation in 1991, has been to demarcate the balance of political power between national and regional governments including, in some cases, municipalities. It has also been characterised by shifting dynamics of power between the national and subnational levels. These features of federalism fit well with the rhetoric of decentralisation that overtook health policy planning in the 1980s and 1990s. But, as we have argued in this book, the consequences of centrifugal federalism for health care have not been particularly auspicious. As the complexity, cost, and scope of health care systems increase, so too does the need to connect, communicate, and coordinate. These particular qualities are not easily cultivated in federal systems, and the very structure of federalism in principle presents both obstacles and opportunities with regard to the collaborative development of effective national health policy in the shaping of health care in the twenty-first century.

Duckett's analysis of Australian health care federalism, for example, highlights the difficulty in achieving an effective allocation of financial resources horizontally (across regions and sectors) and vertically (across levels of government). States such as Canada, where regional and national governments have highly segregated responsibilities, cite Australia as a model to emulate in incorporating both levels of government in health policy-making. Yet, as Duckett observes, the mixed financial responsibilities in Australia between the Commonwealth government and state governments ('marble cake' federalism) result in overlapping roles leading to fiscal 'squabbles', 'waiting', 'waste', and poor coordination of programme design.

But regulatory components are also critical aspects of health care systems. Many federal jurisdictions permit health care workers (and often patients) to move freely across regional borders; yet health human resources planning, as well as the training of health professionals, often remain isolated at regional levels. Regional jurisdictions may rely heavily on foreign-trained health care professionals, yet immigration is generally regulated at the national level. The same disjuncture often arises in pharmaceutical policy. In Canada, for example, each province has its own drug formulary, yet the regulation of pharmaceuticals remains strictly under national jurisdiction. The provinces crucially require information on the cost-effectiveness, safety, and efficacy of the drugs that they provide, but it is a federal body which is responsible for determining which drugs are licensed nationally. The data on the adverse side effects of particular pharmaceuticals is collected within each discrete jurisdiction (and recent privacy legislation often impedes the ability of provinces to share this data), yet it is the federal government which has the capacity systematically to analyse and evaluate this data. Canadian provinces pay a very high rate for pharmaceuticals largely because there is no coordinated national pharmacare strategy (as there is in Australia).

An overarching theoretical basis of concern with excessively centralised power is the Montesquieuean insight that the checks and balances comprising the separation of powers can mitigate a dangerous concentration of power. While Montesquieu was mostly concerned with such separation of powers in *The Spirit of the Laws*, he also elsewhere praised the federal principles of the decentralised Gothic system of medieval France (Ward 2007). The theoretical premise underlying the modern decentralisation of public policies has been that innovation is more likely to occur at a regional level where decision-makers, responding to a very specific localised context, and without the constraint of top-down structures of authority, can develop novel and constructive responses to the critical issues of that particular region. This capacity for federal systems to excel at experimentation and innovation has long been an observation of many analysts of health and social policy. There certainly is evidence that this localised experimentation can bear fruit (see, e.g., Costa-Font and Greer 2013). But it becomes clear in this volume that the health care market also must be subject to the oversight of reasonable regulation (Block and Polanyi 2003; Vladeck and Rice 2009; Vladeck 1981). A clear exception to the argument that federalism encourages local innovation is the case where political factors such as 'racial politics' in the American 'deep South' states result in regional obstacles to national level attempts to increase access to the delivery of health care services (Boychuk 2008).

Regarding localised experimentation, this volume also highlights two other cautionary caveats: first, as discussed above, smaller jurisdictions are more susceptible to capture by powerful interests that may either prevent innovative change, or to use change for their own benefit. Second, the capacity to produce innovation at a localised level does not necessarily mean the capacity to reproduce innovation more widely and, in fact, can have the opposite result. The sheer volume of policy responses that have been produced across federal states has been quite remarkable; but the capacity of federal systems to evaluate, implement, and coordinate these policy developments has been much more limited.

Nevertheless, we would also note that the national governments in federal systems may act as significant parties in innovation in the delivery of health care services. Federal grants in the United States have been essential stimulants in significant advances in medical treatment, the development of new anti-cancer drugs as well as related advances in internet technology (Madrick 2014; Mazzacuto 2014). Another factor that is important in considering public policy determination and the operation of health care delivery in federal and other devolved systems is the vertical dynamic between the centre and regional (and sometimes local) jurisdictions. One observation that can be gained from a reading of our contributors is that federal and other devolved systems may suffer when the centre lacks an understanding of local politics and culture and does not sufficiently support the local infrastructure needed for an efficient and equitable operating system (e.g., Russia, Brazil, Italy, Austria, and India). Decentralised health care delivery systems, especially those with limited resources, need to be adequately funded by the centre in order to prevent failures in the public delivery of health care especially to poor and moderate income people (United States, India, China, Brazil, and Russia). Federal and other devolved systems need to distribute sufficient resources from the centre in order to prevent regional inequities, and there needs to be cooperation between the centre and subnational jurisdictions in order for efficient health care delivery to take place equitably (Ingram 1995; Katznelson 2014; Palley 2005; D.S. Wright 2000; G. Wright 2014). As Mätzke and Stöger note, in some situations, greater efficiency will require regulatory action at the national level. Thus, we do not maintain that federal health care systems must be extensively and comprehensively reconsidered. To a large degree, federal systems involve a dynamic which may be fragmented and constrained at various times but at other times also may serve to increase national authority – and reflect the need for vertical and horizontal coordination of efforts in the delivery of health care services. This means that it is necessary for us to begin to think hard about ways in which to address the need to communicate and collaborate both horizontally and vertically across jurisdictions with respect to the delivery of health care. Federal jurisdictions generally employ some form of formal intergovernmental or corporatist bodies. These state-centred mechanisms, however, are often hamstrung by procedural deadlocks such as the 'joint decision trap' (Scharpf 1988; Falkner 2011). This has led to analysis of the potential for 'softer' forms of policy coordination. Such coordination incorporates a multitude of different strategies and mechanisms for policy-making across regional jurisdictions, and includes discursive models (Open Methods of Coordination in the European Union, or Learning Health Care Systems in the United States), lateral (horizontal) mechanisms of governance (reference networks and joint actions), coordination through the private sector (Majone 2010), open-access information (RxISK.org), mutual accountability relationships based upon open transparency and citizens' engagement (such as sunshine legislation and citizen watchdogs), and hybrid hard–soft mechanisms such as shadow-of-hierarchy systems (Heritier and Rhodes 2011). No single approach seems to have a fail-safe formula for overcoming the difficulties and complexities of federal systems for optimising the delivery of health care services in the context of modern policy-making, but each shows potential in addressing the critical need for policy coordination in health care systems within structural federal and functional federal states.

Conclusion

Health policies are obviously embedded in situations that are unique to specific countries and subnational contexts. The specific contexts of such policies include variables such as demographic characteristics, socio-cultural factors, ideological narratives, government organisation and localised and national political dynamics. Such factors, as a whole, refract the trajectory of emerging health policies at the national and subnational levels. History and institutions also play a part in shaping relationships between the centre and subnational units. That health policy is a very specific result of the interplay between local particularities, national particularities and larger exogenous forces is a point made explicitly by a number of authors in this volume, including Bevan, Connolly, and Mays (United Kingdom), Björkman and Venkat Raman (India), Chubarova and Grigorieva (Russia), and Okma and Marmor (United States). That institutional structures and cultural norms remain important mediating features producing different outcomes even within relatively similar systems is a point made particularly clear, for example, when considering Germany and Austria: Mätzke and Stöger, on the one hand, note that in Austria corporatist negotiation leads to public policy decisions that result in a strong public sector hospital structure, while Lang, on the other, observes that corporatist decision-making in Germany has led to the increasing use of private financial capital and the presence of private commercial hospitals due to the limits on available national revenues for the Länder with respect to health service delivery.

But if it is true that the analysis of federal states must, in the end, remain country-specific, what (if any) overarching conclusions can be made about the attempt to understand health policy within federal systems? One very basic observation is that, while structural federal (and 'functional' federal) states have often been analysed from a formalistic perspective, it is also crucial to understand how the fiscal, economic and political bases of health policy are mediated through the fault lines established by each system's constitutional armature. Acknowledging the particular division of constitutional responsibilities in each discrete federal system is of course an obvious starting-point, but federal systems, as noted in some of the studies in this volume, often respond to economic pressures through the specific dynamics of cost-shifting, the downloading of responsibilities, and political blame. The dynamics of offloading costs are generally (but not always) top-down; and where health care costs are downloaded to jurisdictions which simply do not have the capacity to meet their responsibilities, serious regional disparity can be obscured in instances where countries are described and evaluated solely through national statistical averages.

In a world where the distribution of information is global, increased demands for increased equity and access in national health care delivery systems are increasingly reflected through the political process. This is often reflected in the articulation of national policies seeking health care reforms in regional jurisdictions. Unfortunately, demands for reform of health care delivery systems at the regional level are often unaccompanied by necessary funding from the centre for such health care reforms. These economic pressures can, in turn, serve to make regional units lacking in fiscal, technical, or policy capacity more amenable to market-based solutions. Such solutions must be mediated by the kinds of regulatory processes noted by a number of the authors in this volume. In addition, federal states may be stymied by the difficulties of coordinating across jurisdictions the policies, mechanisms, and benchmarks that are increasingly the hallmark of sophisticated health care systems if they do not develop adequate consultation processes. Where federal decentralised systems were once considered to be more flexible than their unitary counterparts, within the context of health care systems, governance, if premised on the utility of barriers and partitions, would be increasingly at odds with the need for the coordination of complex systems, the effective distribution of limited resources, and the dissemination of important knowledge (as noted by a number of the authors in this volume, as well as by Wright (2000) and Ingram (1995)). This has led a number of these authors to indicate that there is a need for more clearly articulated national policies within federal systems in order to create an unambiguous framework of national goals that regional jurisdictions will need to meet in exchange for adequate national funding. The importance of coordination at vertical levels of government, and horizontal public and voluntary aspects of health care delivery, have been noted by many of our authors, and particularly by Lobato and Senna; Duckett; Björkman and Venkat Raman; Chubarov and Grigorieva; and Gusmano. The need for adequate national funding of reforms, particularly for reform in poorer regions, is most clearly emphasised in Björkman and Venkat Raman; Chubarov and Grigorieva; and Lobato and Senna. Nevertheless, as the example of Canada clearly shows, simply directing more money to substate governments is not in itself a solution, as such funding may simply reinforce inefficient cost structures (in the case of Canada, 10 years of increased federal funding to the provinces actually had an inflationary effect that ultimately disadvantaged all jurisdictions).

While centralised 'command and control' health systems (as in the former Soviet Union) were famously dysfunctional (Navarro 1977), federal states' health policy experiences in the past two decades indicate that the answer to these complex problems cannot simply depend upon greater decentralisation itself. Moreover, and more importantly, the problems of equity, accountability, and coordination with which federal states are struggling are increasingly the problems of all health care systems: federal states and federal-like states are, to some extent, merely the canaries in coal mines. As states continue to urbanise, the increasing depopulation of many rural areas will underscore the difficulty of providing comprehensive and equitable levels of health care in sparsely-populated geographical regions, and ensuring social equity and equal access between different economic groups within urban areas as well as between rich and poor regions. As the formal policy capacity of states becomes highly complex, the tasks of policy development, regulation, and coordination will increasingly require us to think more carefully about democratic accountability. Furthermore, as the need to provide integrated health services across sectoral and professional boundaries increases, the attempt to find formal or informal processes and mechanisms of interjurisdictional coordination will not simply be a matter for federal states. The knowledge base of modern health care systems is becoming far more diffuse: due to the sophistication and penetration of modern IT systems, patients have greater access to information on their medical conditions; governments have access to massive data-gathering systems which allow them to determine effectiveness of treatments and procedures through statistical analysis; and non-governmental actors, especially in networked aggregations, may have more capacity to influence formal decision-makers than ever before (though massive data sets, while often very useful, cannot always provide simple solutions to complex or 'wicked' health care problems).

This volume suggests that while perceived economic sustainability is a key factor in health care reform agenda across states, the way in which sustainability can be achieved is quite variable. Institutions, stakeholders, ideologies, and the choices of political leaders lead to a variety of approaches to reform with regard to goals such as access, equity, and efficiency. Ideally, both top-down and bottom-up approaches could facilitate significant reforms. Ideally, as well, such reforms should involve governmental and non-governmental actors at the levels of national, regional, and, often, municipal jurisdictions. It is only through such integrated reform that all regions can achieve effective reforms.

Finally, it may be useful to step back a little bit farther from this particular snapshot in time and ask whether any observations can be made about the progression of health policy in federal states over time. How have federal states tended to think differently about health policy over the past few decades? What has become apparent in recent years in all policy environments is that the role of communication technology has amplified the role of 'ideas' in shaping policy development across all states. The allure of New Public Management theories throughout the 1980s and 1990s, for example, played an important role in creating 'functional' federalism within unitary states, and pushing federal states to become even more decentralised. Nevertheless, the past decade has been a period of disillusionment with such theories and has fostered intellectual reorganisation and, while there has been some discussion about recentralisation, the current trend has been to think harder about how to coordinate the balance between autonomy of regional federal units with the national goals of efficiency, equity, quality care, and access.

This concern has led to an intellectual focus upon 'governance' approaches, in which formal institutions and 'harder' legal constraints have been modified and supplemented by more voluntary, iterative, and flexible attempts at communication and coordination (Levi-Faur 2012). Such ideas have increasingly influenced the way that other federal systems have begun to approach health care policy, from the 'learning health care systems' articulated in the United States to the 'network of networks' being developed in Canada. Such 'soft' approaches may be innovative inputs into the complex process of public policy formulation in health care delivery systems. These approaches are not purely 'informal' but are intertwined with attempts to affect the implementation of national health delivery policy. In the United States, such 'learning health care system' workshops involving federal and state government officials, insurers, health care providers, consumers, and health care researchers have been engaged to influence how the Patient Protection and

Affordable Care Act (ACA) should be implemented. Thus, the knowledge gained seeks to affect reform in the delivery of American health care services (Institute of Medicine 2012). The extent to which it will do so remains to be seen. In the Canadian context, in the absence of political leadership seeking to implement national health care delivery reforms geared to efficiency and accessibility, networks may serve as a device for stakeholders attempting to clarify interests and press for needed reforms. However, it is unclear as to whether such networks will produce 'best policies' (Aral, Hutchison, and Pedlar 2008).

The contributors to this volume have provided an insightful analysis of the need for regional and local governments and voluntary and proprietary organisations to be involved horizontally and vertically in providing accessible and efficient health care in federal and federal-like systems. They also provide examples where devolution without significant national financial commitment and accountable practices has not resulted in increased accessibility and efficiency of health care reform. So both top-down and bottom-up approaches are important in seeking to achieve the innovation and standardisation necessary for meeting the needs of the various national health care delivery systems that have been examined in this volume. The authors also include analyses of the various ways in which the dynamics of the public and private sectors interact in the effort to maximise the delivery of twenty-first-century health care that is efficient, adequate, and equitable – and the successes and failures of such approaches in various national contexts. Additionally, they show a concern with the need for both significant involvement of voluntary 'soft' engagement of network collaboration as well as accountable governmental engagement at all levels in maximizing vertical and horizontal efforts to provide health care delivery that is efficient and accessible within the constraints of national budgets.

Our studies provide no indications that 'newer' federal states systematically behave differently from older ones. The impact of new ideas is always balanced by the institutional context, the financial and policy capacity of a state, the values of its citizens, the initiatives of political actors, and the perpetual calculation of potential gains and losses made by all those with a stake in the change or stasis of a system. The extent to which softer forms of coordination may shape federal health care systems should not be overstated. The vertical and horizontal coordination necessary for effective health care reforms involves clear communication and cooperative interchange. Few jurisdictions can boast of an abundance of any of these qualities. In sum, the ability of states to control and regulate the way in which health care is produced and consumed has become much more complex. Because of this complexity, the difficult issues faced by federal health care systems are also increasingly the problems of all health care systems. By identifying and understanding the tensions in federal health care systems, we can, at the very least, be better prepared to address emerging pressures in health care more widely.

Bibliography

Abrucio, Fernando L. 'A Coordenação Federativa no Brasil: A Experiência do Período FHC e os Desafios do Governo Lula'. *Revista de Sociologia e Política* 24 (2005): 41–67.

—— 'Descentralização e Coordenação Federativa no Brazil: Lições dos Anos FHC'. In *O Estado numa era de reformas: Os anos FHC – parte 2*, edited by Fernando L. Abrucio and Maria Rita Loureiro. Brasília: OCDE, OEA, Ministério do Planejamento, 2002.

—— *Os Barões da Federação: Os Governadores e a Redemocratização Brasileira*. São Paulo: USP-HUCITEC, 1998.

Adolino, Jessica R. and Charles H. Blake. *Comparing Public Policies*. Washington, DC: CQ Press, 2011.

Adolph, Christopher, Scott L. Greer, and Elize Massard da Fonseca. 'Allocation of Authority in European Health Policy'. *Social Sciences and Medicine* 75, no. 9 (2012): 1595–603.

Aglietta, Michel and Guo Bai. *La voie chinoise: Capitalisme et empire*. Paris: Odile Jacob, 2012.

Aja, Eliseo. *El Estado Autonómico. Federalismo y Hechos Diferenciales*. Madrid: Alianza, 2003.

Akchurina, D.R., E.V. Karakulina, V.A. Nigmatulin, et al. 'Modernization of the Health Care System on a Regional Level'. *Health Care Management* 1–2, no. 35/36 (2013).

Alexandrov, O.B. 'Regions in the International Politics of Russia: Role of the North–West'. Moscow State Institute of International Relations: Ministry of Foreign Affairs, 2005.

Alter, Karen J. 'Who are the "Masters of the Treaty"?: European Governments and the European Court of Justice'. *International Organization* 52, no. 1 (1998): 121–47.

American Hospital Association. 'Fast Facts on US Hospitals', 2013. www.AHA.org.

Anell, A. 'Swedish Healthcare under Pressure'. *Health Economics* 14 (2005): 237–54.

Angell, Marcia. *The Truth about the Drug Companies*. New York: Random House Trade Publications, 2011.

Appleby, John. 'Independent Review of Health and Social Care Services in Northern Ireland'. Belfast: DHSSPS, 2005. http://www.dhsspsni.gov.uk/appleby -report.pdf.

Aral, Susan, Paggy Hutchison, and Alison Pedlar. 'Shared Values, Networks and Trust among Canadian Consumer Driven Disability Organizations'. *Disabilities Studies Journal* 28, no. 11 (2008). www.disq-sds.org.

Atkinson, Michael, Daniel Beland, Gregory Marchildon, et al. *Governance and Public Policy in Canada.* Toronto: University of Toronto Press, 2013.

Auditor General of Ontario. 'Brampton Civic Hospital Public–Private Partnership Project'. In *2008 Annual Report of the Office of the Auditor General of Ontario.* Toronto, ON: Auditor General of Ontario, 2008.

Auditor General for Wales. *NHS Waiting Times in Wales. Volume 1 – The Scale of the Problem.* Cardiff: The Stationery Office, 2005. www.wao.gov.uk/ reportsandpublications/2005.asp.

Auel, Katrin. 'Between Reformstau and Länder Strangulation? German Co-operative Federalism Re-considered'. *Regional and Federal Studies* 20, no. 2 (2010): 229–49.

Augurzky, Boris, Andreas Beivers, and Rosemarie Gülker. *Bedeutung der Krankenhäuser in Privater Trägerschaft.* Essen: RWI Materialien, 2012.

Augurzky, Boris, Dirk Engel, and Christoph Schwierz. 'Who Gets the Credit? Determinants of the Probability of Default in the German Hospital Sector'. *RWI Discussion Papers* 54 (2007).

Austin, Granville. *The Indian Constitution: Cornerstone of a Nation* (3rd revised edition). New York: Oxford University Press, 1999.

Australian Institute of Health and Welfare. 'Health Expenditure Australia 2011–12'. Canberra: Catalogue no. HWE 59, AIHW, 2013.

Bachner, Florian, Joy Ladurner, Katharina Habimana, et al. *Das Österreichische Gesundheitswesen im Internationalen Vergleich,* edited by Gesundheit Österreich. Vienna, 2012.

Bagchi, Amaresh. 'Rethinking Federalism: Changing Power Relations between the Center and the State'. *Publius: The Journal of Federalism* 33, no. 4 (2003): 21–42.

Banfield, Edward. *The Moral Basis of a Backward Society.* Glencoe: Free Press, 1958.

Bansal, R.D. 'Health Financing in India: Priorities, Issues, Inter-State Variations and Challenges'. *Health and Population Perspectives and Issues* 22, no. 3–4 (1999): 123–32.

Barber, Sir Michael. *Instruction to Deliver: Tony Blair, the Public Services and the Challenge of Achieving Targets.* London: Politico, 2007.

Barrio, Astrid, Juan Rodríguez, Montserrat Baras, et al. 'Partidos de ámbito no Estatal y Gobernabilidad Multinivel: El Caso de España (1977–2008)'. *Institut de Ciències Polítiques i Socials* WP 291, Barcelona, 2010.

Bastasin, Carlo. *Saving Europe: How National Politics Nearly Destroyed the Euro.* Brookings Institution Press, 2012.

BBC News. 'North East Votes "No" to Assembly'. http://news.bbc.co.uk/1/hi/ uk_politics/3984387.stm. Last modified 5 November 2004.

Bégin, Monique. 'Revisiting the Canada Health Act (1984): What Are the Impediments to Change?' Speech to the Institute for Research on Public Policy. Ottawa, 20 February 2002.

——— *Medicare: Canada's Right to Health.* Montreal: Optimum Publishing Company, 1984.

Bégin, Monique, Laura Eggerton, and Noni Macdonald. 'A Country of Perpetual Pilot Projects'. *Canadian Medical Association Journal* 180, no. 12 (2009): 1185.

Bensel, R. and E. Sanders. *Yankee Leviathan: The Origins of Central State Authority in America, 1859–1877.* Cambridge: Cambridge University Press, 1990.

Benz, Arthur. 'From Unitary to Asymmetric Federalism in Germany: Taking Stock after 50 Years'. *Publius: The Journal of Federalism* 29, no. 4 (1999): 55–78.

Berwick, Donald M., Brent James, and Molly Joel Coye. 'Connections between Quality Measurement and Improvement'. *Medical Care* 41, no. 1 (2003): 1–30.

Bevan, Gwyn. 'Approaches and Impacts of Different Systems of Assessing Hospital Performance'. *Journal of Comparative Policy Analysis* 12, no. 1 (2009): 33–56.

——— *The Impacts of Asymmetric Devolution on Health Care in the Four Countries of the UK*. London: Nuffield Trust, 2014.

Bevan, Gwyn and Barbara Fasolo. 'Models of Governance of Public Services: Empirical and Behavioural Analysis of "Econs" and "Humans"'. In *Behavioural Public Policy*, edited by Adam Oliver. Cambridge: Cambridge University Press, 2013: 38–62.

Bevan, Gwyn and Christopher Hood. 'What's Measured is What Matters: Targets and Gaming in the English Public Health Care System'. *Public Administration* 84, no. 3 (2006): 517–38.

Bevan, Gwyn and Deborah Wilson. 'Does "Naming and Shaming" Work for Schools and Hospitals? Lessons from Natural Experiments Following Devolution in England and Wales'. *Public Money and Management* 33, no. 4 (2013): 245–52.

Bevan, Gwyn, Marina Karanikolos, Josephine Exley, et al. *Comparing the Performance of the National Health Service in the Four Countries of the United Kingdom Before and After Devolution*. London: Nuffield Trust, 2014.

Bevan, Gwyn and Ray Robinson. 'The Interplay between Economic and Political Logics: Path Dependency in Health Care in England'. *Journal of Health Politics, Policy and Law* 30, no. 1–2 (2005): 53–78.

Bevan, Gwyn and Richard Hamblin. 'Hitting and Missing Targets by Ambulance Services for Emergency Calls: Impacts of Different Systems of Performance Measurement within the UK'. *Journal of the Royal Statistical Society* 172, no. 1 (2009): 1–30.

Bird, Richard M. and Andrey V. Tarasov. 'Closing the Gap: Fiscal Imbalances and Intergovernmental Transfers in Developed Federations'. *Environment and Planning* 22, no. 1 (2004): 77–102.

Björkman, James Warner. *The Politics of Administrative Alienation in India's Rural Development Programs*. Delhi: Ajanta Publications, 1979.

Björkman, James Warner and Het Ram Chaturvedi. 'Panchayati Raj in Rajasthan: The Penalties of Success'. In *The Idea of Rajasthan: Explorations in Regional Identity*, edited by Karine Schomer, Joan Erdman, Deryck Lodrick, et al. Delhi: Manohar Publications, 1994: 132–58.

Björkman, James Warner and Kuldeep Mathur. *Policy, Technocracy and Development: Human Capital Policies in India and the Netherlands*. Delhi: Manohar Publishers, 2002.

Blank, Robert H. and Viola Burau. *Comparative Health Policy*. Basingstoke, Surrey: Palgrave Macmillan, 2010.

Block, Fred and Karl Polanyi. 'Karl Polanyi and the Writing of "The Great Transformation"'. *Theory and Society* 32 (2003): 275–306.

Bloomberg News. 'China Vows Bigger Role for Markets as Party Closes Summit'. http://www.bloomberg.com/news/2013-11-12/china-vows-bigger-role-for-markets-as-party-closes-summit.html. 12 November 2013.

Blumenthal, David and William Hsiao. 'Privatization and Its Discontents – The Evolving Chinese Health Care System'. *New England Journal of Medicine* 353, no. 11 (2005): 1165–70.

Boadway, Robin W. and Anwar Shah, eds. *Intergovernmental Fiscal Transfers: Principles and Practices*. Washington, DC: The World Bank, 2007.

Bochkaryova, V.K. 'Spatial Factor in Building an Effective Health Care System'. *Health Care Management* 25, no. 3 (2009).

Boessenkoel, Ken. 'The Future of the Provincial Role in Canadian Health Care Federalism'. In *Health Care Federalism in Canada*, edited by Katherine Fierlbeck and William Lahey. Kingston and Montreal: Queen's University Press, 2013: 159–76.

Bogdanor, Vernon. *Devolution in the United Kingdom*. Oxford: Oxford University Press, 1999.

Böhm, Katharina. 'Federalism and the "New Politics" of Hospital Financing'. *German Policy Studies* 5, no. 1 (2009): 99–118.

Böhm, Katharina and Rüdiger Henkel. 'Krankenhausplanung und Kranken-hausfinanzierung im Wandel'. In *Privatisierung von Krankenhäusern. Er-fahrungen und Perspektiven aus Sicht der Beschäftigten*, edited by Nils Böhlke, Thomas Gerlinger, Kai Mosebach, et al. Hamburg: VSA Verlag, 2009: 83–96.

Bonafont Chaqués, Laura and Anna María Palau Roqué. 'Comparing Law-making Activities in a Quasi-federal System of Government: The Case of Spain'. *Comparative Political Studies* 44, no. 8 (2011): 1089–119.

Boychuk, Gerard W. *National Health Insurance in the United States and Canada: Race, Territory and the Roots of Difference*. Washington, DC: Georgetown University Press, 2008.

Boyle, Sean. 'United Kingdom. England: Health System Review'. *Health Systems in Transition* 13, no. 1 (2011): 1–486.

Bräuninger, Thomas and Thomas König. 'The Checks and Balances of Party Federalism: German Federal Government in a Divided Legislature'. *European Journal of Political Research* 36, no. 2 (1999): 207–34.

Brenna, Elenka. 'Quasi-market and Cost-containment in Beveridge Systems: The Lombardy Model of Italy'. *Health Policy* 103, no. 2 (2011): 209–18.

Brennan, Geoffrey and James M. Buchanan. *The Power to Tax: Analytical Foundations of a Fiscal Constitution*. New York: Cambridge University Press, 1980.

Bresser-Pereira, Luiz Carlos. 'Macroeconomia do Brasil pós-1994'. *Textos para Discussão 131*. Escola de Economia de São Paulo. São Paulo: Fundação

Getulio Vargas, 2003. http://bibliotecadigital.fgv.br/dspace/bitstream/handle/ 10438/1984/TD131.pdf?sequence=1.

Briatte, Francois. 'The Politics of European Public Health Data'. In *European Union Public Health Policies*, edited by Scott L. Greer and Paulette Kurzer. Abingdon: Routledge, 2013: 51–63.

Brown, Lawrence. 'Pedestrian Paths: Why Path-dependence Theory Leaves Health Policy Analysis Lost in Space'. *Journal of Health Politics, Policy, and Law* 35, no. 4 (2010): 643–59.

Bruckenberger, Ernst, Siegfried Klaue, and Hans-Peter Schwintowski. *Krankenhausmärkte zwischen Regulierung und Wettbewerb*. Berlin: Springer, 2005.

Buckmaster, Luke and Angela Pratt. 'Not on My Account! Cost Shifting in the Australian Health System'. In *Research Note* no. 6 (2005–2006). Parliament of Australia.

Bull, Hedley. *The Anarchical Society: A Study of Order in World Politics*. New York: Columbia University Press, 1977.

Bundeskanzleramt. 'Arbeitsprogramm der Österreichischen Bundesregierung 2013–2018'. Vienna, 2013.

Bundesministerium für Gesundheit. 'Die Gesundheitsreform 2013. Bessere Versorgungsstrukturen und mehr Leistungen für die kommenden Generationen'. Vienna, 2013.

Bundesrechnungshof. 'Teilbereiche der Gesundheitsreform 2005 mit Länderaspekten in Tirol und Wien'. Vienna, 2010.

Burkhart, Simone. 'Reforming Federalism in Germany: Incremental Changes Instead of the Big Deal'. *Publius: The Journal of Federalism* 39, no. 2 (2009): 341–65.

Burley, Anne-Marie and Walter Mattli. 'Europe Before the Court: A Political Theory of Legal Integration'. *International Organisation* 47, no. 1 (1993): 41–76.

Buscher, Frederik. 'Bericht zur Lage der Krankenhäuser in Deutschland bei der Einführung der Fallpauschalen'. *das Krankenhaus* 1, no. 4 (2008): 27–30.

Busse, Reinhard, Matthias Wismar, and Philip C. Berman. 'The European Union and Health Services: The Impact of the Single European Market on Member States'. Amsterdam: IOS/ European Health Management Association, 2002.

Büttner, Thiess. 'Fiscal Federalism and Interstate Risk Sharing: Empirical Evidence from Germany'. *Economics Letters* 74, no. 2 (2002): 195–202.

Canadian Independent Medical Clinics Association vs British Columbia Medical Services Commission, 2010 BCSC 927. http//:case law.canada.globe24th. com/0/british-columbia/supreme-court-of-britishcolumbia/2010/07/canadian-independent-clinics-association-v-britishcolumbia.

Canadian Institute for Health Information (CIHI). 'National Health Expenditure Trends 1975–2013'. https://secure.cihi.ca/free_products/NHEXTrendsReport_ EN.pdf.

Candelaria, Christopher, Mary Daly, and Galina Hale. 2013. 'Persistence of Regional Inequality in China'. Federal Reserve Bank of San Francisco Working Paper

Series, Working Paper 2013–16. http:www.frbsf.org/publications/economics/papers/2013/wp2013–06.pdf.

Cano, Wilson. 'A Desindustrialização no Brasil'. *Economia e Sociedade Campinas* 21, Número Especial, dez. (2012): 831–51.

Cantarero Prieto, David and Santiago Lago-Peñas. 'Decomposing the Determinants of Health Care Expenditure: The Case of Spain'. *The European Journal of Health Economics* 13, no. 1 (2012): 19–27.

Caruso, Enza and Nerina Dirindin. 'Health Care and Fiscal Federalism: Paradoxes of Recent Reforms in Italy'. *Politica Economica* 28, no. 2 (2012): 169–96.

Castles, Francis G., Herbert Obinger, and Stefan Leibfried. 'Bremst der Föderalismus den Leviathan? Bundesstaat und Sozialstaat im internationalen Vergleich, 1880–2005'. *Politische Vierteljahresschrift* 46, no. 2 (2005): 214–37.

Censis. *Quale sanità dopo i tagli? Quale futuro per le risorse in sanità?* Rome: Censis–Forum per la Ricerca Biomedica, 2012.

Chao, Nadia Jandali and Stanley Martin. 'Recent Developments in the Debate over Private Health Care in Canada'. *Health Law Matters* 241 (2012): 1–3.

Charlesworth, Kate, Michael J. Galsworthy, Kelly Ernst, et al. 'Health Research in the European Union: Over-controlled but Under-measured?' *European Journal of Public Health* 21, no. 4 (2011): 404–6.

Chaudhuri, Shubaum and Patrick Heller. *The Plasticity of Participation: Evidence from a Participatory Governance Experiment.* New York: Institute for Social and Economic Research and Policy, 2003.

Chen, Xiangming, ed. *Shanghai Rising: State Power and Local Transformations in a Global Megacity.* Minneapolis, MN: University of Minnesota Press, 2009.

Chirikova, A. 'Federal Centre and Russian Regions: Search for Optimal Relationship Models'. In *Federalism and Russian Regions*, edited by N. Lapina and V. Mokhov. Institute of Scientific Information for Social Sciences, Russian Academy of Sciences (INION RAN). Moscow, 2006.

Chubarova, T.V. and Schestakova, E.E. *Health Care Reforms.* Moscow: Epikon, 1999.

Cisneros Örnberg, Jenny. 'Alcohol Policy in the European Union'. In *European Union Public Health Policies: Regional and Global Perspectives*, edited by Scott L. Greer and Paulette Kurzer. Abingdon: Routledge, 2012: 168–80.

Collicelli, Carla, Vittoria Coletta, and Maria Antonietta Di Candia. 'Qualità e Impatto Sociale dei Servizi Sanitari in Italia'. In *Rapporto Sanità 2012*, edited by Gian Franco Gensini, Anna Lisa Nicelli, Marco Trabucchi, et al. Bologna: Il Mulino, 2012: 43–94.

Collier, Roger. 'In the Record'. *Canadian Medical Association Journal* 180, no. 10 (2009): 1109.

Collier, Ruth Berins and David Collier. *Shaping the Political Arena.* Princeton: Princeton University Press, 1991.

Commission on Devolution in Wales (Chairman Mr Paul Silk). 'Empowerment and Responsibility: Financial Powers to Strengthen Wales', 2012. http://commissionondevolutioninwales.independent.gov.uk/files/2013/01/English-WEB-main-report1.pdf.

Commission on Scottish Devolution (Chairman Sir Kenneth Calman). 'Serving Scotland Better: Scotland and the United Kingdom in the 21st Century'. Edinburgh, 2009. www.commissiononscottishdevolution.org.uk/.

Confindustria. *Struttura e Performance della Filiera della Salute (anni 2007–2010)*. Rome: Confindustria, 2012.

Conlan, Timothy. *New Federalism: Intergovernmental Reform from Nixon to Reagan*. Washington, DC: Brookings Institution Press, 1988.

Connolly, Sheelah, Gwyn Bevan, and Nicholas Mays. *Funding and Performance of Healthcare Systems in the Four Countries of the UK Before and After Devolution*. London: The Nuffield Trust, 2011.

Costa-Font, Joan and Scott L. Greer. *Federalism and Decentralization in European Health and Social Care*. Basingstoke, Hampshire: Palgrave Macmillan, 2012.

—— 'Territory and Health: Perspectives from Economics and Political Science'. In *Federalism and Decentralization in European Health and Social Care*, edited by Joan Costa-Font and Scott L. Greer. Basingstoke, Hampshire: Palgrave Macmillan, 2012: 13–43.

Cotta, Maurizio and Luca Verzichelli. *Political Institutions in Italy*. Oxford, UK: Oxford University Press, 2007.

Council of Australian Governments. 'National Health Reform Agreement', 2011.

Creswell, Julie and Reed Abelson. 'A Giant Hospital Chain is Blazing a Profit Trail'. *The New York Times*, 12 August 2012.

Daley, John, Cassie McGannon, and Jim Savage. *Budget Pressures on Australian Governments* [in English]. Carlton, Vic.: Grattan Institute, 2013.

Deber, Raisa B. 'Health Care Services: Public, Not–for–profit or Private?' Discussion Paper Number 17. Saskatoon, SK: Commission on the Future of Health Care in Canada, August 2002.

Dehousse, Renaud. 'Comparing National and EC Law: The Problem of the Level of Analysis'. *The American Journal of Comparative Law* 42, no. 4 (1994): 761–81.

Deorukhkar, Sumedh and Alicia Garcia Herrero. *Five Challenges for India in 2013*. New York: World Policy Institute, 2013.

Department of the Parliamentary Library. *Federal–State Financial Relations: The Deakin Prophecy*, by Denis James. Research Paper no. 17 (1999–2001). Canberra, 2000.

Deutsche Krankenhausgesellschaft. *Bestandsaufnahme zur Krankenhausplanung und Investitionsfinanzierung in den Bundesländern*. Berlin: Deutsche Krankenhausgesellschaft, 2012.

DiMaggio, Paul J. and Walter W. Powell. 'The Iron Cage Revisited: Institutional Isomorphism and Collective Rationality in Organizational Fields'. In *The New Institutionalism in Organizational Analysis*, edited by Walter W. Powell and Paul J. DiMaggio. Chicago: The University of Chicago Press, 1991: 63–82.

Dolls, Mathias, Clemens Fuest, and Andreas Peichl. 'Automatic Stabilizers and Economic Crisis: US vs. Europe'. *Journal of Public Economics* 96, no. 3 (2012): 279–94.

Donahue, John D. and Richard J. Zeckhauser. 'Public–Private Collaboration'. In *The Oxford Handbook of Public Policy*, edited by Michael Moran, Martin Rein, and Robert E. Goodin. Oxford: Oxford University Press, 2008: 496–525.

Duckett, Stephen. 'The Continuing Contest of Values in the Australian Health Care System'. In *Access to Health Care: Solidarity and Justice*, edited by A. den Exter. Erasmus University Press, 2008.

Duckett, Stephen and Annalise Kempton. 'Canadians' Views about Health System Performance'. *Healthcare Policy* 7, no. 3 (2012): 88–104.

Dyson, Kenneth. *The Politics of the Euro-zone: Stability or Breakdown?* Oxford: Oxford University Press, 2001.

Dyson, Kenneth and Kevin Featherstone. *The Road to Maastricht: Negotiating Economic and Monetary Union.* Oxford: Oxford University Press, 1999.

Echo of Moscow, Skvortsova V.I. (8 December 2013: Moscow) radio interview.

Eckholm, Erik. 'The SARS Epidemic: China Admits Underreporting Its SARS Cases'. *The New York Times*, 21 April 2003.

Elamon, Joy, Richard W. Franke and Bappukunju Ekbal. 'Decentralization of Health Services: The Kerala People's Campaign'. *International Journal of Health Services* 34, no. 4 (2004): 681–708.

Elazar, Daniel J. *Exploring Federalism.* Tuscaloosa, AL: University of Alabama Press, 1987.

—— *How the Prismatic Form of Canadian Federalism Both Unites and Divides Canada.* Jerusalem, Israel: Jerusalem Center for Public Affairs, 1999.

—— 'Comparative Federalism'. *Polis* 5 (1995): 106–15.

Elhauge, E. *The Fragmentation of US Health Care.* Oxford, UK: Oxford University Press, 2010.

Elias, Norbert. 'Technization and Civilization'. *Theory, Culture & Society* 12, no. 3 (1995): 7–42.

Encarnación, Omar G. 'Federalism and the Paradox of Corporatism'. *West European Politics* 22, no. 2 (1999): 90–115.

Engelmann, Frederick C. and Mildred A. Schwartz. 'Perceptions of Austrian Federalism'. *Publius* 11, no. 11 (1981): 81–93.

Erk, Jan. 'A Federation without Federalism'. *Publius* 34, no. 1 (2004): 1–20.

Ernst, Christian and Andrea Szczesny. 'Spezialisierungs- und Selektionsanreize fester Krankenhausbudgets 1993–2002: Eine empirische Analyse'. *Betriebswirtschaftliche Forschung und Praxis* 58, no. 6 (2006): 566–84.

Ernst, Kelly, Rachel Irwin, Michael Galsworthy, et al. 'Difficulties of Tracing Health Research Funded by the European Union'. *Journal of Health Services Research and Policy* 15, no. 3 (2010): 133–6.

Essue, Beverley, Patrick Kelly, Mary Roberts, et al. 'We Can't Afford My Chronic Illness! The Out–of–pocket Burden Associated with Managing Chronic Obstructive Pulmonary Disease in Western Sydney, Australia'. *Journal of Health Services Research & Policy* 16, no. 4 (October 1, 2011): 226–31.

Eurostat. 'Eurostatistics. Data for Short-term Economic Analysis'. Luxembourg: Publications Office of the European Union, 2014.

Fahy, Nick. 'Who is Shaping the Future of European Health Systems?' *BMJ* 344 (2012): e1712.

Falkner, Gerda. *The European Union's Decision Traps: Comparing Policies.* Oxford University Press, 2011.

Fallend, Franz. 'Austria: A Federal, a Decentralized Unitary, or "Hybrid State"? Relations between the Welfare State and the Federal State'. In *Routledge Handbook of Regionalism and Federalism*, edited by John Loughlin, John Kincaid, and Wilfried Swenden. Abingdon: Routledge, 2013: 235–47.

Farrar, Shelley, Fiona Harris, Tony Scott, et al. 'The Performance Assessment Framework: Experiences and Perceptions of NHS Scotland', 2004. www.scotland.gov.uk/library5/health/pafr.pdf.

Farrell, Anne-Maree. 'The Emergence of EU Governance in Public Health: The Case of Blood Policy and Regulation'. In *Health Governance in Europe: Issues, Challenges and Theories*, edited by Monika Steffen. Abingdon: Routledge, 2005: 134–51.

Feng, Xingyuan, Christer Ljungwall, Sujian Guo, et al. 'Fiscal Federalism: A Refined Theory and its Application in the Chinese Context'. *Journal of Contemporary China* 22, no. 82 (2013): 573–93.

Ferrario, Caterina and Alberto Zanardi. 'Fiscal Decentralization in the Italian NHS: What Happens to Interregional Redistribution?' *Health Policy* 100, no. 1 (2011): 71–80.

Ferrera, Maurizio. 'The Rise and Fall of Democratic Universalism: Health Care Reform in Italy, 1978–1994'. *Journal of Health Politics, Policy and Law* 20, no. 2 (1995): 275–302.

Fierlbeck, Katherine. 'Three Approaches to Cost Containment in Health Care Federalism'. In *Bending the Cost Curve*, edited by Gregory Marchildon and Livio de Matteo, forthcoming publication. Toronto: University of Toronto Press, 2014.

Flood, Colleen M. and Subit Choudhry. 'Strengthening the Foundations: Modernizing the Canada Health Act'. Commission on the Future of Health Care in Canada. Discussion Paper no. 13 (2002). http://www.law.utoronto.ca/documents/chaoulli/romanow_report.pdf.

Fonseca, Cristina Maria Oliveira. *Saúde no Governo Vargas (1930–1945): Dualidade Institucional de um Bem Público.* Rio de Janeiro: Fiocruz, 2007.

France, George and Francesco Taroni. 'The Evolution of Health-policy Making in Italy'. *Journal of Health Politics, Policy and Law* 30, no. 1–2 (2005): 169–88.

France, George, Francesco Taroni, and Andrea Donatini. 'The Italian Health Care System'. *Health Economics* 14, no. S1 (2005): S187–S202.

Gadelha, Carlos Augusto, *José Manuel Santos de Varge Maldonado, and Laís Silveira Costa*. 'O Complexo Produtivo da Saúde e Sua Relação Com o Desenvolvimento: Um olhar sobre a dinâmica da inovação em saúde'. In *Políticas e Sistema de Saúde no Brasil*, 2nd edition, edited by Ligia Giovanella, Sarah Escorel, Lenaura de Vasconcelos Costa Lobato, et al. Rio de Janeiro: Fiocruz/Cebes, 2012: 247–81.

Gagnon, Alain-G. and Raffaele Iacovino. *Federalism, Citizenship and Quebec: Debating Multinationalism*. Toronto: University of Toronto Press, 2001 and 2007.

Gallego, Raquel. 'Las políticas sanitarias de las comunidades autónomas'. In *Estado de bienestar y comunidades cutónomas*, edited by Raquel Gallego, Ricard Gomá, and Joan Subirats. Madrid: Tecnos, 2003: 102–22.

Gawande, Atul. 'Big Med'. *New Yorker*, 13 August 2012.

Ge, Yanfeng and Sen Gong. *Chinese Health Care Reform*. Beijing: China Development Publishing, 2007.

Gerlinger, Thomas and Kai Mosebach. 'Die Ökonomisierung des deutschen Gesundheitswesens: Ursachen, Ziele und Wirkungen wettbewerbsbasierter Kostendämpfungpolitik'. In *Privatisierung von Krankenhäusern. Erfahrungen und Perspektiven aus Sicht der Beschäftigten*, edited by Nils Böhlke, Thomas Gerlinger, Kai Mosebach, et al. Hamburg: VSA Verlag, 2009: 10–40.

Gil-Serrate, Ramiro, Julio López-Laborda, and Jesús Mur. 'Revenue Autonomy and Regional Growth: An Analysis of the 25-Year Process of Fiscal Decentralisation in Spain'. *Environment and Planning* 43, no. 11 (2011): 2626–48.

Glauser, Wendy. 'Private Clinics Continue Explosive Growth'. *Canadian Medical Association Journal* 183, no. 8 (2011): E437–8.

Glinos, Irene. 'Worrying about the Wrong Thing: Patient Mobility Versus Mobility of Health Care Professionals'. *Journal of Health Services Research and Policy* 17, no. 4 (2012): 254–6.

Glinos, Irene, Rita Baeten, Matthias Helble, et al. 'A Typology of Cross-border Patient Mobility'. *Health & Place* 16, no. 6 (2010): 1145–55.

Gnatyk, O.P., K.A. Tkhapa, V.A. Scherbakov, et al. 'Program of Health Care System Modernization and its Influence on Quality of Health Care in Regions of the Russian Federation'. In *Smolensk and Novosibirsk areas and Khabarovsk Territory. Final Projects*. Moscow, 2013.

Gonçalves, Reinaldo. 'Governo Lula e o Nacional-desenvolvimentismo às Avessas'. *Revista da Soc. Bras. Economia Política* no. 31 (2012): 5–30. http://www.sep.org.br/revista/download?id=219.

Gong, Peng, Song Liang, Elizabeth J. Carlton, et al. 'Urbanisation and Health in China'. *The Lancet* 379, no. 9818 (2012): 843–52.

Gottweis, Herbert and Elisabeth Baumandl. 'Gesundheitspolitik'. In *Politik in Österreich. Das Handbuch*, edited by Herbert Dachs, Peter Gerlich, Herbert Gottweis, et al. Vienna: Manz, 2006: 753–67.

Goulart, Flávio. *Municipalização: Veredas. Caminhos do Movimento Municipalista de Saúde no Brasil*. Rio de Janeiro-Brasília: Abrasco–Conasems, 1996.

Grant, Hugh M. and Jeremiah Hurley. 'Unhealthy Pressure: How Physician Pay Demands Put the Squeeze on Provincial Health-care Budgets'. *School of Public Policy Research Papers*. University of Calgary: 6/22 July 2013.

Greenwood, Justin. *Interest Representation in the European Union*. Basingstoke: Palgrave Macmillan, 2003.

Greer, Scott L. *Territorial Politics and Health Policy: UK Health Policy in Comparative Perspective*. Manchester: Manchester University Press, 2004.

—— 'Uninvited Europeanization: Neofunctionalism and the EU in Health Policy'. *Journal of European Public Policy* 13, no. 1 (2006): 134–52.

—— 'Devolution and Divergence in UK Health Policies'. *BMJ* 338, no. 7686 (2008): 78–80.

—— 'The Changing World of European Health Lobbies'. In *Lobbying in the European Union*, edited by David Coen and J.J. Richardson. Oxford: Oxford University Press, 2009a.

—— 'How Does Decentralization Affect the Welfare State?' *Journal of Social Policy* 39, no. 2 (2009b): 1–21.

—— *The Politics of European Union Health Policies*. Buckingham: Open University Press, 2009c.

—— 'How Does Decentralisation Affect the Welfare State? Territorial Politics and the Welfare State in the UK and US'. *Journal of Social Policy* 39, no. 2 (2010): 181–201.

—— 'The Weakness of Strong Policies and the Strength of Weak Policies: Law, Experimentalist Governance, and Supporting Coalitions in European Union Health Policy'. *Regulation & Governance* 5 (2011): 187–203.

—— 'The European Centre for Disease Prevention and Control: Hub or Hollow Core?' *Journal of Health Politics, Policy, and Law* 37, no. 6 (2012a): 1001–30.

—— 'Polity-making without Policy-making: European Union Health Care Services Policy'. In *Policy Dynamics in the European Union*, edited by Jeremy J. Richardson. Oxford: Oxford University Press, 2012b.

—— 'Avoiding Another Directive: The Unstable Politics of European Union Cross-border Health Care Law'. *Health Economics, Policy and Law* 1–7 (2013a).

—— 'Glass Half Empty: The Eurozone and Internal Market Overshadow the Health Effects of Maastricht'. *European Journal of Public Health* 23, no. 6 (2013b): 907–8.

—— 'Structural Adjustment Comes to Europe: Lessons for the Eurozone from the Conditionality Debates'. *Global Social Policy*, 2013c.

—— 'Power Struggle: The European Union and Health Care Services'. Brussels: Observatoire Social Européenne. www.ose.be.

Greer, Scott L. and Alan Trench. *Health and Intergovernmental Relations in the Devolved United Kingdom*. London: The Nuffield Trust, 2008.

Greer, Scott L. and Paulette Kurzer, eds. *European Union Public Health Policies: Regional and Global Perspectives*. Abingdon: Routledge, 2013.

Greer, Scott L. and Simone Rauscher. 'When Does Market-marking Make Markets? EU Health Services Policy at Work in the UK and Germany'. *Journal of Common Market Studies* 49, no. 4 (2011).

Griffith, Gareth. 'Commonwealth–State Responsibilities for Health – "Big Bang" or Incremental Reform?' edited by New South Wales Parliament. Sydney: New South Wales Parliamentary Library Research Service, 2006.

Grigorieva, N.S. and T.V. Chubarova. 'Modern Health Care: Policy, Economics, Management'. Author's academy. Moscow, 2013.

Guilhem, Fabre. *The Lion's Share: What's Behind China's Economic Slowdown.* FMSH-WP-2013-53, 7 October 2013.

Gunlicks, Arthur. *The Länder and German Federalism.* Manchester: Manchester University Press, 2003.

Gupta, Amit Sen. 'National Health Policy 2002: A Brief Critique'. *The National Medical Journal of India* 15, no. 5 (2002): 215–16.

Gupta, Devendra B. and Anil Gumber. 'Decentralisation: Some Initiatives in the Health Sector'. *Economic and Political Weekly* 34, no. 6 (1999): 356–64.

Gusmano, Michael K., Li Luo, Daniel Weisz, et al. 'Health Improvements in Shanghai Since 2000: A Look at the Evidence'. Unpublished manuscript. Garrison, NY: The Hastings Centre, 2014.

Haas, Ernst B. *The Uniting of Europe: Political, Social and Economical Forces 1950–1957.* London: Stevens & Sons, 1958.

Hacker, Jacob and Theodore Marmor. 'How Not to Think About "Managed Care"'. *University of Michigan Journal of Law Reform* 32, no. 4 (1999): 661–84.

Hadley, Charles D., Michael Morass, and Rainer Nick. 'Federalism and Party Interaction in West Germany, Switzerland, and Austria'. *Publius* 19, no. 4 (1989): 81–97.

Hall, Peter A. 'The Role of Interests, Institutions, and Ideas in the Comparative Political Economy of the Developed Nations'. In *Comparative Politics: Rationality, Culture, and Structure*, edited by Mark Irving Lichbach and Alan S. Zuckerman. Cambridge: Cambridge University Press, 1997.

—— 'The Economics and Politics of the Euro Crisis'. *German Politics* 21, no. 4 (2012): 355–71.

Hall, Peter and Rosemary Taylor, 'Political Science and the Three New Institutionalisms'. *Political Studies* XLIV (2001): 936–57.

Ham, Chris. 'Reforming the NHS From Within'. London: King's Fund, 2014. http://www.kingsfund.org.uk/time-to-think-differently/publications/reforming-nhs-within.

Hancher, Leigh and Wolf Sauter. *EU Competition and Internal Market Law in the Health Care Sector.* Oxford: Oxford University Press, 2012.

Hardin, Garrett. 'The Tragedy of the Commons'. *Science* 162, no. 3859 (1968): 1243–8.

—— 'Extensions of "The Tragedy of the Commons"'. *Science* 280, no. 5364 (1998): 682.

Harper, Stephen. 'Letter to Premier Ralph Klein'. Ottawa, ON: Office of the Prime Minister, 31 March 2006.

Hashemian, M., W. Qian, K.G. Stanley, et al. 'Temporal Aggregation Impacts on Epidemiological Simulations Employing Microcontact Data'. *BMC Medical Informatics and Decision Making* 12, no. 132 (2012).

Hatzopoulos, Vassilis and Tamara Hervey. 'Coming into Line: The EU's Court Softens on Cross-border Health Care'. *Health, Economics, Policy and Law* 8, no. 1 (2013): 1–5.

Hauray, Boris. *L'Europe Du Médicament: Politique – Expertise – Intérêts Privés.* Paris: Presses de Sciences Po, 2006.

—— 'The European Regulation of Medicines'. In *European Union Public Health Policy: Regional and Global Trends*, edited by Scott L. Greer and Paulette Kurzer. Abingdon: Routledge, 2013.

Hayek, Friedrich. 'Economics and Knowledge'. *Economica* 4 (1937): 33–54.

—— *Individualism and the Economic Order.* Chicago, IL: University of Chicago Press, 1939.

Hazell, Robert. 'Three Policies in Search of a Strategy'. In *The English Question*, edited by Chen Selina and Tony Wright. London: Fabian Society, 2000: 29–44.

Heard-Laureate, Karen. 'Europeanization of Health Policy: The Role of EU Institutions'. In *The Europeanization of European Politics*, edited by Charlotte Bretherton and Michael L. Mannin. Palgrave Macmillan, 2013.

Heitzmann, Karin and August Österle. 'Lange Traditionen und neue Herausforderungen: Das österreichische Wohlfahrtssystem'. In *Europäische Wohlfahrtssysteme*, edited by Klaus Schubert, Simon Hegelich, and Ursula Bazant. Wiesbaden: VS Verlag, 2008: 47–69.

Helderman, Jan-Kees, Gwyn Bevan, and George France. 'The Rise of the Regulatory State in Health Care: A Comparative Analysis of the Netherlands, England and Italy'. *Health Economics, Policy and Law* 7, no. 1 (2012): 103–24.

Heritier, Adrienne and Martin Rhodes. *New Modes of Governance in Europe: Governing in the Shadow of Hierarchy.* Basingstoke: Palgrave Macmillan, 2011.

Hervey, Tamara K. 'If Only it Were So Simple: Public Health Services and EU Law'. In *Market Integration and Public Services in the European Union*, edited by Marise Cremona. Oxford: Oxford University Press, 2011.

Hervey, Tamara K. and Jean V. McHale. *Health Law and the European Union.* Cambridge: Cambridge University Press, 2004.

Hesketh, Therese and Xi Z. Wei. 'Health in China: From Mao to Market Reform'. *British Medical Journal* 314 (1997): 1543–5.

Heß, Werner. *Krankenhäuser im Spannungsfeld zwischen Reformdruck und Finanznot.* München: Economic Research, Allianz Group, Dresdner Bank, 2005.

Hibbard, Judith H., Jean Stockard, and Martin Tusler. 'Does Publicizing Hospital Performance Stimulate Quality Improvement Efforts?' *Health Affairs* 22, no. 2 (2003): 84–94.

Hipgravel, David, Sufang Guao, Yan Mu, et al. 'Chinese-style Decentralisation and Health System Reform'. *PLOS Medicine* 9, no. 11 (2012): 1–4.

Hirschman, Albert O. *Exit, Voice, and Loyalty: Responses to Decline in Firms, Organizations, and States.* London: Harvard University Press, 1970.

Hix, Simon. *The Political System of the European Union.* New York: Palgrave Macmillan, 2005.

HM Treasury. *House of Lords Select Committee on the Barnett Formula: The Government's Response.* London: TSO, 2009. http://www.official-documents. gov.uk/document/cm77/7772/7772.pdf.

Hochman, Gilberto. *A Era do Saneamento: As Bases da Política de Saúde Pública no Brasil*. São Paulo: HUCITEC-ANPOCS, 1998.

Hofmarcher, Maria M., Herta M. Rack, and Annette Riesberg. 'Health Systems in Transition: Austria', edited by WHO Regionalbüro für Europa im Auftrag des Europäischen Observatoriums für Gesundheitssysteme und Gesundheitspolitik. Kopenhagen: European Observatory on Health Systems and Policies, 2006.

Hofmarcher, Maria M. and Wilm Quentin. 'Austria. Health System Review'. In *Health Systems in Transitions*, edited by European Observatory on Health Systems and Policies. Brussels, 2013: 1–292.

Hood, Christopher. 'Public Service Management by Numbers: Why Does it Vary? Where Has it Come From? What are the Gaps and the Puzzles?' *Public Money and Management* 27, no. 2 (2007): 95–102.

Hood, Christopher and Ruth Dixon. 'The Political Payoff from Performance Target Systems: No-brainer or No-gainer?' *Journal of Public Administration Research and Theory* 20, no. s2 (2010): i281–98.

Hooghe Liesbet, Gary Marks, and Arjan H. Schakel. *The Rise of Regional Authority: A Comparative Study of 42 Democracies*. London: Routledge, 2010.

House of Representatives. *The Blame Game: Report on the Inquiry into Health Funding*. Canberra: Standing Committee on Health and Ageing, 2006.

Hu, Zuliu and Mohsin S. Khan. 'Why is China Growing So Fast?' International Monetary Fund, *Economic Issues* no. 8 (1997). www.imf.org/EXTERNAL/PUBS/FT/ISSUES8/INDEX.HTM.

IBGE (Instituto Brasileiro de Geografia e Estatística). 'Indicadores IBGE. Principais destaques da evolução do mercado de trabalho nas regiões metropolitanas abrangidas pela pesquisa, 2003–2013'. Rio de Janeiro: IBGE, 2014. http://www.ibge.gov.br/home/estatistica/indicadores/trabalhoerendimento/pme_nova/retrospectiva2003_2013.pdf.

Imbeau, Louis M., Réjean Landry, Henry Milner, et al. 'Comparative Provincial Policy Analysis: A Research Agenda'. *Canadian Journal of Political Science* 4 (2001): 779–804.

Immergut, Ellen. *Health Politics: Interests and Institutions in Western Europe*. Cambridge: Cambridge University Press, 1992.

Independent Commission on Funding and Finance for Wales (Chairman G. Holtham). *Funding Devolved Government in Wales: Barnett and Beyond*. Cardiff, 2009. http://wales.gov.uk/funding/financereform/report/firstreport/?lang=en.

Ingram, Helen. 'Policy Implementation through Bargaining: The Case of Federal Grants-in-aid'. In *American Intergovernmental Relations*, 2nd ed., edited by Laurence J. O'Toole, Jr. Washington, DC: CQ Press, 1993: 281–9.

Institute of Medicine. *Best Care at Lower Cost: The Path of continuously Learning Health Care in America*. Washington, DC: National Academies Press, September 2012.

International Innovation. 'A Glimpse into the Future of Medicine', 12 (2013).

IPEA (Instituto de Pesquisa Econômica Aplicada). 'Duas décadas de desigualdade e pobreza no Brasil medidas pela PNAD/IBGE'. Comunicados do IPEA, no. 159. Brasília: IPEA, 2013. http://www.ipea.gov.br/portal/images/stories/PDFs/comunicado/131001_comunicadoipea159.pdf.

Ivins, Courtney. 'Inequality Matters: BRICS Inequality Fact Sheet'. Brasilia, Brazil: OXFAM, 2013.

Jacobs, Lawrence R. 'The Medicare Approach: Political Choice and American Institutions'. *Journal of Health Politics, Policy and Law* 32, no. 2 (2007): 159–86.

Jarman, Holly and Scott L. Greer. *Just Add Hierarchy: The Hardening of European Fiscal Governance*. Ann Arbor, 2013.

JHPPL. 'Managed Care Backlash'. *Journal of Health Policy, Politics and Law* 24 (Special Issue, 5 October 1999).

Jian, Weiyan, Kit Yee Chan, Daniel D. Reidpath, et al. 'China's Rural–Urban Care Gap Shrank for Chronic Disease Patients, but Inequities Persist'. *Health Affairs* 29, no. 12 (2010): 2189–96.

John, T. Jacob. 'Is India Ready for an Overhaul in Healthcare?' *Economic and Political Weekly* 45, no. 20 (2010): 14–17.

Johnson, Craig. *Decentralisation in India: Poverty, Politics and Panchayati Raj*. London: Overseas Development Institute, 2003.

Jordan, Andrew and Camilla Adelle. *Environmental Policy in the EU: Actors, Institutions and Processes*. London and New York: Routledge, 2013.

Jordan, Jason. 'Federalism and Health Care Cost Containment in Comparative Perspective'. *Publius: The Journal of Federalism* 39, no. 1 (2008): 164–86.

Jütting, Johannes, Céline Kauffmann, Ida McDonnell, et al. *Decentralisation and Poverty in Developing Countries: Exploring the Impact*. Paris: OECD Development Centre, 2004.

Kaiser Family Foundation. 'Americans Rank Health Care Near the Top of their Economic Woes. New Poll Find' (press release), 29 April 2008. www.kff.org.

Kane, N.M. 'Cost, Productivity and Financial Outcomes of Managed Care'. In *Implementing Planned Markets in Health Care*, edited by R.S. Saltman and C. Von Otter. Buckingham–Philadelphia: Open University Press, 1995: 113–32.

Karanikolos, Marina, Philipa Mladovsky, Jonathan Cylus, et al. 'Financial Crisis, Austerity, and Health in Europe'. *The Lancet* 381, no. 9874 (2013): 1323–31.

Karlhofer, Ferdinand. 'Sozialpartnerschaftliche Interessenvermittlung in föderativen Systemen. Ein Vergleich Deutschland–Österrreich–Schweiz'. In *Föderalismus: Analysen in entwicklungsgeschichtlicher und vergleichender Perspektive*, edited by Arthur Benz. PVS Sonderband 32. Wiesbaden: Westdeutscher Verlag, 2002: 234–50.

Karlhofer, Ferdinand and Günther Pallaver. 'Strength through Weakness: State Executive Power and Federal Reform in Austria'. *Swiss Political Science Review* 19, no. 1 (2013): 41–59.

Katznelson, Ira. 'The Great and Grudging Transformation'. *The New York Review of Books* 61, no. 6 (2014): 58–60.

Kelemen, R. Daniel. *Eurolegalism: The Transformation of Law and Regulation in the European Union*. Cambridge, MA: Harvard University Press, 2011.

—— 'Eurolegalism and Democracy'. *Journal of Common Market Studies* 50 (2012): 55–71.

Kingdon, John. *Agendas, Alternatives, and Public Policies*. Boston: Little, Brown and Company, 1984.

Klenk, Tanja. 'Ownership Change and the Rise of a For-profit Hospital Industry in Germany'. *Policy Studies* 32, no. 3 (2011): 263–75.

—— 'Krise und Krisenmanagement in kommunalen Krankenhäusern'. In *Lokale Politik und Verwaltung im Zeichen der Krise?*, edited by Michael Haus and Sabine Kuhlmann. Wiesbaden: Springer, 2013: 215–33.

Kneebone, Ronald. 'How You Pay Determines What You Get: Alternative Financing Options as a Determinant of Publicly Funded Health Care in Canada'. *School of Public Policy Research Papers* 5, no. 21 (June 2012). http://www.policyschool.ucalgary.ca/sites/default/files/research/r-kneebone-althealthpayfinal.pdf.

Koivusalo, Meri. 'The State of Health in all Policies (HIAP) in the European Union: Potential and Pitfalls'. *Journal of Epidemiology and Community Health* 64, no. 6 (2010): 500–503.

Kurzer, Paulette. 'Non-communicable Diseases: Europe Declares War on "Fat"'. In *European Union Public Health Policies: Regional and Global Perspectives*, edited by Scott L. Greer and Paulette Kurzer. Abingdon: Routledge, 2012: 155–67.

Lamping, Wolfram. 'European Integration and Health Policy: A Peculiar Relationship'. In *The Governance of Health in Europe*, edited by Monika Steffen, 18–49. London: Routledge, 2005.

Lancet, The. 'Editorial: What Can Be Learned From China's Health System?' *The Lancet* 379, no. 9831 (2012): 777.

Lapina, N. Yu. 'Centre-regions in Post-Soviet Russia: History, Relationships and Future'. *Politex: Political Expertise. Scientific Journal* 2, no. 2 (2006).

—— 'State Control Over Regional Development: Spatial Structure of Governance and Regional Economic Policies'. PhD thesis, Novosibirsk, 2006.

Lawson, Rick. 'The Irish Abortion Cases: European Limits to National Sovereignty?' *European Journal of Health Law* 1, no. 2 (1994): 167–86.

Le Grand, Julian. *Motivation, Agency, and Public Policy: Of Knights and Knaves, Pawns and Queens*. Oxford: Oxford University Press, 2003.

—— *The Other Invisible Hand: Delivering Public Services through Choice and Competition*. Woodstock: Princeton University Press, 2007.

Leach, Matthew, Leonie Segal, Adrian Esterman, et al. 'The Diabetes Care Project: An Australian Multicentre, Cluster Randomised Controlled Trial [Study Protocol]'. *BMC Public Health* 13, no. 1212 (2013).

Leal, Victor Nunes. *Coronelismo, Enxada e Voto*. Rio de Janeiro: Forense, 1986.

Lee, Philip R. 'Medicine and Public Health in the People's Republic of China: Observations and Reflections of a Recent Visitor'. *Western Journal of Medicine* 120 (1974): 30–437.

Lehmbruch, Gerhard. *Parteienwettbewerb im Bundesstaat: Regelsysteme und Spannungslagen im politischen System der Bundesrepublik Deutschland*. Wiebaden: VS Verlag, 2000.

Lehner, Karl. *10 Jahre Krankenanstaltenfinanzierung in Österreich. Eine kritische Betrachtung*. Vienna: Facultas WUV, 2008.

LeMay-Boucher, Philippe and Charlotte Rommerskirchen. 'An Empirical Investigation into the Europeanisation of Fiscal Policies'. *Comparative European Politics*, forthcoming. Doi: 10.1057/cep.2014.1.

León, Sandra. 'Who Is Responsible for What? Clarity of Responsibilities in Multilevel States: The Case of Spain'. *European Journal of Political Research* 50, no. 1 (2011): 80–109.

—— 'How Do Citizens Attribute Responsibility in Multilevel States? Learning, Biases and Asymmetric Federalism. Evidence from Spain'. *Electoral Studies* 31, no. 1 (2012): 120–30.

Levi-Faur, David, ed. *The Oxford Handbook of Governance*. Oxford: Oxford University Press, 2012.

Li, Zhijian, Jiale Hou, Lin Lu, et al. 'On Residents' Satisfaction with Community Health Services after Health Care System Reform in Shanghai, China, 2011'. *BMC Public Health* 12, suppl. no. 1 (2012): S9.

Lijphart, Arend. 'Non-majoritarian Democracy: A Comparison of Federal and Consociational Theories'. *Publius* 15, no. 2 (1985): 3–15.

Lima, Luciana. 'O processo de implementação de novas estruturas gestoras do Sistema Único de Saúde: Um estudo das relações intergovernamentais na CIB do Rio de Janeiro'. Master's thesis, Universidade do Estado do Rio de Janeiro, 1999.

—— 'Conexões Entre o Federalismo Fiscal e o Financiamento da Política de Saúde no Brasil'. *Ciênc. saúde coletiva* 12, no.2 (2007): 511–22. http://dx.doi.org/10.1590/S1413-81232007000200027.

—— *Federalismo, Relações Fiscais e Financiamento do Sistema Único de Saúde: A Distribuição de Receitas Vinculadas à Saúde nos Orçamentos Municipais e Estaduais*. Rio de Janeiro: Editora Museu da República, 2007.

Lima, Luciana and Ana Luiza Viana. 'Descentralização, regionalização e instâncias intergovernamentais no Sistema Único de Saúde'. In *Regionalização e Relações Federativas na Política de Saúde do Brasil*, edited by Ana Luiza Viana and Luciana Lima. Rio de Janeiro: Contra Capa, 2011.

Lin, Wanchuan, Gordon G. Liu, and Gang Chen. 'The Urban Resident Basic Medical Insurance: A Landmark Reform Towards Universal Coverage in China'. *Health Economics* 18 (2009): S83–S96.

Lindblom, Charles E. *The Intelligence of Democracy: Decision Making through Mutual Adjustment*. New York: Free Press, 1965.

Liu, Yuanli. 'Reforming China's Health Care: For the People, By the People?' *The Lancet* 373 (2009): 281–3.

Lobato, Lenaura and Luciene Burlandy. 'The Context and Process of Health Care Reform in Brazil'. In *Reshaping Health Care in Latin America – A Comparative Analysis of Health Care Reform in Argentina, Brazil and Mexico*, edited by Sonia Fleury, Enis Baris, and Susana Belmartino. Ottawa: International Development Research Centre, 2000: 79–102.

Long, Qian, Ling Xu, Henk Bekedam, et al. 'Changes in Health Expenditures in China in the 2000s: Has the Health System Reform Improved Affordability?'. *International Journal for Equity in Health* 12 (2013): 40.

Longley, Marcus, Neil Riley, Paul Davies, et al. 'United Kingdom. Wales: Health System Review'. *Health Systems in Transition* 14, no. 11 (2012): 1–84.

Lowi, Theodore J. *The End of Liberalism.* New York: Norton, 1979.

Lukes, Steven. *Power: A Radical View.* Oxford: Macmillan Press, 1974.

Machado, Cristiani and Ana Luiza Viana. 'Descentralização e Coordenação Federativa na Saúde'. In *Saúde, Desenvolvimento e Território*, edited by Ana Luiza Viana, Nelson Ibañez, and Paulo Eduardo Elias. São Paulo: HUCITEC, 2009.

Machado, Cristiani, Luciana Dias de Lima, and Carla Lourenço Tavares de Andrade. 'Federal Funding of Health Policy in Brazil: Trends and Challenges'. *Cad. Saúde Pública, Rio de Janeiro* 30, no. 1 (2014): 187–200. http://dx.doi.org/10.1590/0102-311X00144012.

Madrick, Jeffrey. 'Innovation: The Government was Crucial After All'. *The New York Review of Books* 61, no. 7 (2014): 50–53.

Mahal, Ajay, Vivek Srivastava, and D. Sanan. 'Decentralization and Public Sector Delivery of Health and Education Services: The Indian Experience'. Discussion paper no. 20 (2000). Bonn, Germany: Center for Development Research.

Mahoney, Christine. *Brussels versus the Beltway: Advocacy in the United States and the European Union.* Washington, DC: Georgetown University Press, 2008.

Maier, Charles S. *Recasting Bourgeois Europe: Stabilization in France, Germany and Italy in the Decade after World War I.* Princeton University Press, 1975.

Maiz, Ramon, Francisco Caamaño, and Miguel Azpitarte. 'The Hidden Counterpoint of Spanish Federalism: Recentralization and Resymmetrization in Spain (1978–2008)'. *Regional & Federal Studies* 20, no. 1 (2010): 63–82.

Majone, Giandomenico. *Regulating Europe.* London: Routledge, 1996.

—— *The Transformation of the Regulatory State.* Osservatorio sull'Analisi di Impatto della Regolazione, 2010. www.osservatorioair.it.

Mapelli, Vittorio. *Il sistema sanitario italiano.* Bologna: il Mulino, 2012.

March, James G. and Johan P. Olsen. 'The New Institutionalism: Organizational Factors in Political Life'. *The American Political Science Review* 78 (1984): 734–49.

Marchildon, Greg. 'The Future of the Federal Role in Canadian Health Care Federalism'. In *Health Care Federalism in Canada*, edited by Katherine Fierlbeck and William Lahey. Kingston and Montreal: Queen's University Press, 2013: 177–91.

Marmor, Theodore R. 'Health Care Politics and Policy in the United States'. *One Issue, Two Voices. Health Care in Crisis: The Drive for Health Reform in Canada and the United States.* Washington, DC: The Canada Institute, 2008: 14–28.

—— *Fads, Fallacies and Foolishness in Medical Care Management and Policy.* Singapore: World Scientific Publishers, 2009.

—— 'The Unwritten Rules of Cross-national Policy Analysis'. *Health Economics, Policy, and Law* 7, no. 1 (2012): 19–20.

Marmor, Theodore R. and Jonathan Oberlander. 'Health Reform: The Fateful Moment'. *New York Review of Books* 56, no. 13 (2009): 69–74.

Marmor, Theodore R., Kieke G.H. Okma, and J. Rojas. 'What It Is, What It Does and What It Might Do: A Review of Michael Moore's *Sicko*', 113 minutes, Dog Eat Dog Films, USA. *The American Journal of Bioethics* 7, no. 10: 408–50.

Marmor, Theodore R., Kieke G.H. Okma, and S.R. Latham. 'Values, Institutions and Health Politics. Comparative Perspectives'. In *Soziologie der Gesundheit. Kolner Zeitschrift fur Soziologie und Sozialpsychologie, Sonderheft*, edited by C. Wendt and C. Wolf, 46 (2006): 383–405.

Marmor, Theodore, Richard Freeman, and Kieke Okma. 'Comparative Perspectives and Policy Learning in the World of Health Care'. *Journal of Comparative Policy Analysis* 7, no. 4 (2005): 331–48.

—— eds. *Comparative Studies and the Politics of Modern Medical Care*. New Haven: Yale, 2009.

Marmor, Theodore and Rudolf Klein. *Politics, Health, and Health Care*. New Haven: Yale University Press, 2012.

Martinsen, Dorte Sindbjerg. 'Towards an Internal Health Market with the European Court'. *West European Politics* 28, no. 5 (2005): 1035–56.

—— 'Conflict and Conflict Management in the Cross-border Provision of Healthcare Services'. *West European Politics* 32, no. 4 (2009): 792–809.

Martinsen, Dorte Sindbjerg and Karsten Vrangbaek. 'The Europeanization of Health Care Governance: Implementing the Market Imperatives of Europe'. *Public Administration* 86, no. 1 (2008): 169–84.

Mathur, Kuldeep and James Warner Björkman. *The Practice of Policy Making in India: Who Listens? Who Speaks?* New Delhi: Har Anand Publications, 2009.

Mattei, Lauro. 'Gênese e agenda do novo desenvolvimentismo brasileiro'. *Revista de Economia Política* 33, no. 1 (130) (2013): 41–59.

Mätzke, Margitta. 'The Organization of Health Policy Functions in the German Federal Government'. *Social Policy & Administration* 44, no. 2 (2010): 120–41.

—— 'Federalism and Decentralization in German Health and Social Care Policy'. In *Federalism and Decentralization in Health and Social Care*, edited by Joan Costa-Font and Scott L. Greer. Basingstoke: Palgrave MacMillan, 2012: 190–207.

Mayntz, Renate. 'Politische Steuerbarkeit und Reformblockaden: Überlegungen am Beispiel des Gesundheitswesens'. In *Die Zukunft der sozialen Sicherung in Deutschland*, edited by Klaus-Dirk Henke, Joachim Jens Hesse, and Gunnar Volke Schuppert. Sonderheft zur Zeitschrift Staatswissenschaften und Staatspraxis, Sonderheft 1. Baden-Baden: Nomos Verlagsgesellschaft, 1991: 21–45.

Mazzucato, Mariana. *The Entrepreneurial State: Debunking Public vs. Private Sector Myths*. London: Anthem Press, 2014.

McClelland, Siobhan. 'Health Policy in Wales Distinctive or Derivative?' *Social Policy and Society* 1, no. 4 (2002): 325–33.

McKee, Martin, Elias Mossialos, and Rita Baeten. *EU Law and the Social Character of Health Care*. Brussels: Peter Lang, 2002a.

—— *The Impact of EU Law on Health Care Systems*. Brussels: Peter Lang, 2002b.

McKinnon, Ronald I. 'The Logic of Market-preserving Federalism'. *Virginia Law Review* 83 (1997): 1573–80.

Mendelson, Danuta. 'Devaluation of a Constitutional Guarantee: The History of Section 51(xxiiia) of the Commonwealth Constitution'. *Melbourne University Law Review* 23, no. 2 (1999): 308–44.

Messina, Gabriele, Nicola Vigiani, Lucia Lispi, et al. 'Patient Migration among the Italian Regions in 2003'. *Italian Journal of Public Health* 5, no. 1 (2008): 45–52.

MGEPA. 'Krankenhausplan NRW 2015'. Düsseldorf: Ministerium für Gesundheit, Emanzipation, Pflege und Alter des Landes Nordrhein-Westfalen, 2013.

Ministero del Lavoro e delle Politiche Sociali. 'Rapporto sulla non autosufficienza in Italia 2010'. Rome: Ministero del Lavoro e delle Politiche Sociali, 2011.

Ministero della Salute. 'Rapporto annuale sull'attività di ricovero ospedaliero. Dati SDO 2012'. Rome: Ministero della Salute, 2013.

Ministero dello Sviluppo Economico. 'Filiere produttive e territori. Prime analisi'. Rome: Ministero dello Sviluppo Economico, 2012.

Ministry of Health for Brazil. 'Cadastro Nacional de Estabelecimentos de Saúde'. http://cnes.datasus.gov.br/.

Minow, Martha. 'Private and Public Partnerships: Accounting for the New Religion'. *Harvard Law Review* 116 (2003): 1229–70.

Mladovsky, Philipa, Divya Srivastava, Jonathan Cylus, et al. *Health Policy Responses to the Financial Crisis in Europe*. Copenhagen: World Health Organization, 2012.

Moran, Terry. 'The Future of the Australian Public Service: Challenges and Opportunities'. In *CPA Australia's Neil Walker Memorial Lecture*, 2010.

Moreno, Luis. 'Federalization and Ethnoterritorial Concurrence in Spain'. *Publius* 27, no. 4 (1997): 65–84.

—— *Reformas de las políticas del bienestar en España*. Madrid: Siglo XXI, 2009.

Morgan, Steven, Jamie Daw, and Michael Law. 'Rethinking Pharmacare in Canada'. C.D. Howe Institute, Commentary no. 384, June 2013. http://www.cdhowe.org/pdf/Commentary_384.pdf.

Morris, Alan. 'The Commonwealth Grants Commission and Horizontal Fiscal Equalization'. *The Australian Economic Review* 35, no. 3 (2002): 318–24.

Mosca, Ilaria. 'Is Decentralisation the Real Solution? A Three Country Study'. *Health Policy* 77, no. 1 (2006): 113–20.

Mossialos, Elias, Govin Permanand, Rita Baeten, et al. *Health Systems Governance in Europe: The Role of EU Law and Policy*. Cambridge: Cambridge University Press, 2010.

Narayana, Delampady and K.K. Hari Kurup. *Decentralisation of the Health Care Sector in Kerala: Some Issues*. Thiruvananthapuram: Centre for Development Studies, 2000.

Nathan, Richard P. 'Federalism and Health Policy'. *Health Affairs* 24, no. 6 (2005): 1458–66.

National Academy of Social Insurance. 'Strengthening Social Security: What Do Americans Want?' Washington, DC: National Academy of Social Insurance, 2013.

National Assembly for Wales. 'The Review of Health and Social Care in Wales'. Cardiff: National Assembly for Wales, 2003.

National Commission on Macroeconomics and Health (NCMH). 'Report of the National Commission on Macroeconomics and Health'. New Delhi: Ministry of Health and Family Welfare, 2005.

National Health and Hospitals Reform Commission. 'Beyond the Blame Game: Accountability and Performance Benchmarks for the Next Australian Health Care Agreements'. Canberra, 2008.

—— 'A Healthier Future for All Australians – Final Report of the National Health and Hospitals Reform Commission'. Canberra, 2009.

Naughton, Barry. 'Deng Xiaoping: The Economist'. *The China Quarterly* 135 (Special Issue: Deng Xiaoping: An Assessment) (1993): 491–514.

Navarro, Vicente. *Social Security and Medicine in the USSR*. Lexington, MA: Lexington Books, 1977.

—— *El Estado de Bienestar en España*. Madrid: Tecnos/ UPF, 2004.

Nuti, Sabina, Chiara Seghieri, and Milena Vainieri. 'Assessing the Effectiveness of a Performance Evaluation System in the Public Health Care Sector: Some Novel Evidence from the Tuscany Region Experience'. *Journal of Management and Governance* 17, no. 1 (2013): 59–69.

O'Neill, Ciaran, Pat McGregor, and Sherry Merkur. 'United Kingdom. Northern Ireland: Health System Review'. *Health Systems in Transition* 14, no. 10 (2012): 1–91.

Oates, Wallace. *Fiscal Federalism*. New York: Harcourt Brace Jovanovich, 1972.

Obinger, Herbert. 'Föderalismus und wohlfahrtsstaatliche Entwicklung. Österreich und die Schweiz im Vergleich'. *Politische Vierteljahresschrift* 43, no. 2 (2002): 235–71.

—— 'Austria: Strong Parties in a Weak Federal Polity'. In *Federalism and the Welfare State. New World and European Experiences*, edited by Herbert Obinger, Stephan Leibfried, and Francis G. Castles. Cambridge: Cambridge University Press, 2005: 181–221.

Office of the Parliamentary Budget Officer. 'Fiscal Sustainability Report 2013'. September 2013. http://www.pbo-dpb.gc.ca/files/files/FSR_2013.pdf.

Oizumi, Keiichiro. 'A Geographical View of China's Economic Development – Observations Focusing on 337 Prefecture-level-cities'. *Pacific Business and Industries* X, no. 35 (2010): 2–32.

Okma, Kieke G.H. 'Health Care and the Welfare State: Two Worlds of Welfare Drifting Apart?' In *Social Security in Transition*, edited by J. Berghman, A. Nagelkerke, K. Boos, et al. Leiden: Kluwer Law International, 2002a: 229–38.

—— *What is the Best Public–Private Mix for Canada's Health Care?* Montreal: Institute for Research on Public Policy, 2002b.

Okma, Kieke G.H. and Luca Crivelli, eds. *Six Countries, Six Reform Models: The Healthcare Reform Experience of Israel, the Netherlands, New Zealand, Singapore, Switzerland and Taiwan. Healthcare Reforms 'Under the Radar Screen'.* Singapore: World Scientific Publishers, 2010.

Okma, Kieke G.H and Theodore R. Marmor. 'Understanding Welfare State and Health Care Reforms in North America and Western Europe'. *American Journal of Public Administration*, forthcoming.

Olson, Mancur. *The Logic of Collective Action.* Cambridge: Harvard University Press, 1965.

Ong, Lynette H. 'Fiscal Federalism and Soft Budget Constraints: The Case of China'. *International Political Science Review* 33, no. 4 (2012): 455–74.

Organisation of Economic Cooperation and Development (OECD). 'Health at a Glance 2013'. http://www.oecd.org/els/health-systems/Health-at-a-Glance-2013. pdf (p. 155).

—— 'OECD Health Data 2014'. Paris, 2014.

Page, Edward C. 'The European Union and the Bureaucratic Mode of Production'. In *From the Nation State to Europe: Essays in Honour of Jack Hayward*, edited by Anand Menon. Oxford: Oxford University Press, 2001: 139–57.

—— 'The European Commission Bureaucracy: Handling Sovereignty through the Back and Front Doors'. In *European Disunion: Between Sovereignty and Solidarity*, edited by Jack Hayward and Ruediger Wurzel. Basingstoke: Palgrave Macmillan, 2012: 82–98.

Pahwa, Divya H. and Daniel Beland. 'Federalism, Decentralisation, and Health Care Policy Reform in India'. *Public Administration Research* 2, no. 1 (2013): 1–10.

Palier, Bruno and Claude Martin. 'From "a Frozen Landscape" to Structural Reforms: The Sequential Transformation of Bismarckian Welfare Systems'. *Social Policy & Administration* 41, no. 6 (2007): 535–54.

Pallarés, Francesc, José-Ramon Montero, and Francisco-José Llera. 'Non State-wide Parties in Spain: An Attitudinal Study of Nationalism and Regionalism'. *Publius* 27 (1997): 135–69.

Pallarés, Francesc and Michael Keating. 'Multilevel Electoral Competition: Regional Elections and Party Systems in Spain'. *European Urban and Regional Studies* 10, no. 3 (2003): 239–56

Palley, Howard A. 'Canadian Abortion Policy: National Policy and the Impact of Federalism and Political Implementation on Access to Services'. *Publius: The Journal of Federalism* 36, no. 1 (2006): 565–86.

Palley, Howard A., Marie-Pascale Pomey, and Owen B. Adams. *The Political and Economic Sustainability of Health Care in Canada: Private-sector Involvement in the Federal Provincial Health Care System.* Amherst, NY: Cambria Press, 2012.

Palley, Howard A., Pierre Gerlier-Forest, and Marie-Pascale Pomey. 'Examining Private and Public Provision in Canada's Provincial Health Care Systems:

Comparing Ontario and Quebec'. *International Political Science Review* 32, no. 1 (2011): 79–94.

Park, Albert and Fang Cai. 'The Informalization of the Chinese Labor Market'. In *From Iron Rice Bowl to Informalization: Markets, State and Workers in a Changing China*, edited by Ching Kwan Lee and Mary Gallagher. Ithaca, NY: Cornell University Press, 2011: 17–35.

Pelinka, Anton. 'The (In)Compatibility of Corporatism and Federalism: Austrian Social Partnership and the EU'. *West European Politics* 22, no. 2 (1999): 116–29.

Peres, Leon M. 'The Politics of Industrial Policy'. In *Industrial Australia, 1975–2000: Preparing for Change*. Proceedings of the 40th Summer School, Australian Institute of Political Science, edited by Australian Institute of Political Scienc. Sydney: Australia and New Zealand Book Co., 1974.

Pérez Durán, Ixchel. 'Assessing Formal Accountability for Public Policies: The Case of Health Policy in Spain'. *International Review of Administrative Sciences*, forthcoming.

Pérez-Giménez, Roser. 'Políticas sanitarias y desigualdades en España'. In *Cambios en el Estado del bienestar. Políticas sociales y desigualdades en España*, edited by José Adelantado. Barcelona: Icaria, 2000: 251–84.

Permanand, Govin. *EU Pharmaceutical Regulation: The Politics of Policy-making*. Manchester: Manchester University Press, 2006.

Peters, David H., K. Sujatha Rao, and Robert Fryatt. 'Lumping and Splitting: The Health Policy Agenda in India'. *Health Policy and Planning* 18, no. 3 (2003): 249–60.

Peters, Guy B. *American Public Policy: Promise and Performance*, 7th ed. Washington, DC: CQ Press, 2007.

Peterson, Paul E. *City Limits*. Chicago: The University of Chicago Press, 1981.

Pierson, Paul. *Dismantling the Welfare State? Reagan, Thatcher and the Politics of Retrenchment*. Cambridge: Press Syndicate of the University of Cambridge, 1994.

Piola, Sérgio, Andrea Barreto de Paiva, Edvaldo Batista de Sá, et al. 'Financiamento público da saúde: uma história à procura de rumo'. Texto para discussão 1846. Instituto de Pesquisa Econômica Aplicada. Brasília, Rio de Janeiro: Instituto de Pesquisa Econômica Aplicada, 2013. http://www.ipea.gov.br/portal/images/stories/PDFs/TDs/td_1846.pdf.

Polanyi, Karl. *The Great Transformation: The Political and Economic Origins of Our Time*, 2nd ed. Boston, MA: Beacon Press, 2001.

Pollit, Christopher. 'Decentralization. A Central Concept in Contemporary Public Management'. In *The Oxford Handbook of Public Management*, edited by Ewan Ferlie, Laurence E. Lynn, Jr., and Christopher Pollitt. Oxford: Oxford University Press, 2005: 371–94.

Pressel, Holger. *Der Gesundheitsfonds*. Wiesbaden: Springer, 2012.

Pressman, Jeffrey and Aaron Wildavsky. *Implementation: How Great Expectations in Washington Are Dashed in Oakland or, Why It's Amazing That Federal Programs*

Work at All, This Being a Saga of the Economic Development Administration as Told by Two Sympathetic Observers Who Seek to Build Morals on a Foundation of Ruined Hopes. Berkeley: California University Press, 1973.

Pritchard, Peter and Jane Hughes. *Shared Care: The Future Imperative?* London: Royal Society of Medicine Press, 1995.

Propper, Carol, Matt Sutton, Carolyn Whitnall, et al. 'Did "Targets and Terror" Reduce Waiting Times in England for Hospital Care?' *Health Care* 8, no. 2 (2008): 5.

—— 'Incentives and Targets in Hospital Care: Evidence from a Natural Experiment'. *Journal of Public Economics* 94, no. 3 (2010): 318–35.

Putnam, Robert. *Making Democracy Work: Civic Traditions in Modern Italy*. Princeton: Princeton University Press, 1993.

Qian, Yingyi and Barry Weingast. 'Federalism as a Commitment to Preserving Market Incentives'. *Journal of Economic Perspectives* 11, no. 4 (1997): 83–92.

Queen's University. 'Creating Strategic Change in Canadian Healthcare: Conference Summary'. Toronto, ON: Queen's University, 15–16 May 2015.

Rainey, Hal G., and Young Han Chun. 'Public and Private Management Compared'. In *The Oxford Handbook of Public Management*, edited by Ewan Ferlie, Laurence E. Lynn, Jr., and Christopher Pollitt. Oxford: Oxford University Press, 2005: 72–102.

Ranade, W., ed. *Markets and Health Care: A Comparative Analysis*. New York: Addison Wesley Longman, 1998.

Rao, Govinda and Nirvakir Singh. *Political Economy of Federalism in India*. New Delhi, ND: Oxford University Press, 2005.

Ray, Amal. 'The Sarkaria Commission's Perspective: An Appraisal'. *Economic and Political Weekly* 23, no. 22 (1988): 1131–3.

Reagan, Michael D. *The New Federalism*. New York: Oxford University Press, 1972.

Reddy, K. Srinath, Vikram Patel, Prabhat Jha, et al. 'Towards Achievement of Universal Health Care in India by 2020: A Call to Action'. *The Lancet* 377 (2011): 760–68.

Regie de l'Assurance Maladie du Québec. 'Liste des professionels de la santé non-participants ou désengagés au régime de l'assurance maladie du Québec avec adresse de Québec'. Québec: Regie de l'Assurance Maladie du Quebec, 18 July 2013.

Reinhardt, Ewe. 'The Swiss Health System: Regulated Competition without Managed Care'. *Journal of the American Medical Association* 292, no. 10 (2004): 1227–31.

Requejo, Ferran. 'Federalism and Democracy: The Case of Minority Nations – A Federalist Deficit'. In *Federal Democracies*, edited by Michael Burgess and Alain Gagnon. Routledge: London and New York, 2010: 275–98.

RIA Rating (Group RIA News). 'Rating of Social-economic Situations in Subjects of the Russian Federation: 2012 Final Results', 2013.

Riedel, Monika and Gerald Röhrling. 'Ursachen für Kostensteigerungen und zukünftige Herausforderungen im österreichischen Gesundheitssystem'. *WISO Wirtschafts – und Sozialpolitische Zeitschrift* 32, no. 1 (2009): 93–112.

Riggs, Frederick W. *Administration in Developing Countries: The Theory of Prismatic Society.* Boston, MA: Houghton Mifflin Company, 1965.

Ritchie, Murray and Robbie Dinwoodie. 'McLeish Caves in on Free Care for Elderly. Threat of Defeat in Parliament Forces Last Minute Labour U-turn'. *Herald Scotland.* http://www.heraldscotland.com/sport/spl/aberdeen/mcleish-caves-in-on-free-care-for-elderly-threat-of-defeat-in-parliament-forces-last-minute-labour-u-turn-1.201003. Last modified 26 January 2001.

Rodden, Jonathan A. *Hamilton's Paradox: The Promise and Peril of Fiscal Federalism.* Cambridge: Cambridge University Press, 2005.

Rose, Richard. *Representing Europeans: A Pragmatic Approach.* Oxford: Oxford University Press, 2013.

Rosenau, Pauline V. *The Competition Paradigm: America's Romance with Conflict, Contest and Commerce.* New York: Russell Sage Foundation, 2007.

Rosenau, Pauline V. and Christiaan J. Lako. 'An Experiment with Regulated Competition and Individual Mandates for Universal Health Care: The New Dutch Health Insurance System'. *Journal of Health Politics, Policy and Law* 33, no.1 (2008): 1031–55.

Rosenbrock, Rolf and Thomas Gerlinger. *Gesundheitspolitik. Eine systematische Einführung.* Bern: Huber, 2006.

Rosenthal, Marilyn and Jay Greiner. 'The Carefoot Doctors of China: From Political Creation to Professionalism'. *Human Organisation* 41, no. 4 (1982): 330–41.

Rothermund, Ditmar. *India: The Rise of an Asian Giant.* New Haven, CT: Yale University Press, 2008.

Rothgang, Heinz, Mirella Cacace, Simone Grimmeisen, et al. 'The Changing Role of the State in Healthcare Systems'. *European Review* 13, no. 1 (2005): 187–212.

Royal Commission on the Constitution, 1969–1973 (Chairmen: Lord Crowther (1969 –1972), Lord Kilbrandon (1972–1973)). 'Report' (Command 5460). London: HMSO, 1973.

Royal Commission on Long Term Care (Chairman Professor Sir Stewart Sutherland). *With Respect to Old Age: Long Term Care – Rights and Responsibilities.* London: The Stationery Office Limited, 1999.

Rudolph, Lloyd I. and Susanne Hoeber Rudolph. 'The Old and the New Federalism in Independent India'. In *Routledge Handbook of South Asian Politics: India, Pakistan, Bangladesh, Sri Lanka, and Nepal,* edited by Paul R. Brass. London: Routledge, 2010: 147–61.

Saich, Tony. *Governance and Politics of China,* 3rd edition. New York: Palgrave Macmillan, 2011.

Saltman, Richard B., Vaida Bankauskaite, and Karsten Vrangbaek, eds. *Decentralization in Health Care: Strategies and Outcomes.* London: Open University Press, 2007.

—— 'The Role of Comparative Health Studies for Policy Learning'. *Health Economics, Policy, and Law* 7, Special Issue 1 (January 2012): 11–13.

Scharpf, Fritz W. 'The Joint-decision Trap: Lessons from German Federalism and European Integration'. *Public Administration* 66 (1988): 239–278.

—— 'The European Social Model: Coping with the Challenges of Diversity'. *Journal of Common Market Studies* 40, no. 4 (2002): 645–70.

Schelkle, Waltraud. 'EU Fiscal Governance: Hard Law in the Shadow of Soft Law'. *Columbia Journal of European Law* 13 (2006): 705.

—— 'The Contentious Creation of the Regulatory State in Fiscal Surveillance'. *West European Politics* 32, no. 4 (2009): 829–46.

Schischkin, S.V., ed. *Health Care in Regions of the Russian Federation: Financing and Management Tools.* Moscow: Pomatur Press, 2006.

Schumacher, Ernst F. *Small is Beautiful: Economics as if People Mattered.* London: Harper Perennial, 2010.

Scotton, Richard B. and Christine R. Macdonald. *The Making of Medibank* 76. Sydney: School of Health Services Management, University of NSW, 1993.

Scully, Sharon. 'Does the Commonwealth Have Constitutional Power to Take over the Administration of Public Hospitals?' Research paper 2008–2009, 36. Canberra: Parliamentary Library, 2009.

Secretaries of State for Health, Wales, Northern Ireland and Scotland. 'Working for Patients'. Cm 555. London: HMSO, 1989.

Secretary of State for Health. 'The New NHS: Modern, Dependable'. Cm 3807. London: The Stationery Office, 1997. www.dh.gov.uk/en/Publicationsand statistics/Publications/PublicationsPolicyAndGuidance/DH_4008869.

—— 'The NHS Plan'. CM 4818-I. London: The Stationery Office, 2000. www.dh.gov. uk/en/Publicationsandstatistics/Publications/PublicationsPolicyAndGuidance/ DH_4002960.

—— 'Delivering the NHS Plan'. Cm 5503. London: Stationery Office, 2002. www. dh.gov.uk/prod_consum_dh/groups/dh_digitalassets/@dh/@en/documents/ digitalasset/dh_4059526.pdf.

Select Committee on the Barnett Formula. 'The Barnett Formula'. HL Paper 139. House of Lords, London: The Stationery Office, 2009.

Senate. 'Implementation of the National Health Reform Agreement'. Finance and Public Administration References Committee. Canberra, 2013.

Shangai Municipal Health Bureau. 'On Improving the City's Community Health Services: Research Report', 2010.

Sharman, Campbell. 'Executive Federalism'. In *Intergovernmental Relations and Public Policy*, edited by Brian Galligan, Owen Hughes, and Cliff Walsh. Singapore: Allen & Unwin, 1991: 23–39.

Simon, Michael. 'Die Umsetzung des GSG im Krankenhausbereich: Auswirkungen der Budgetdeckelung auf die Aufnahme- und Verlegungspraxis von Allgemeinkrankenhäusern'. *Zeitschrift für Gesundheitswissenschaften* 4, no. 1 (1996): 20–40.

—— *Krankenhauspolitik in der Bundesrepublik Deutschland: Historische Entwicklung und Probleme der politischen Steuerung stationärer Krankenversorgung.* Wiesbaden: VS Verlag, 2000.

—— *Das Gesundheitssystem in Deutschland.* Bern: Huber, 2005.

—— *Sechzehn Jahre Deckelung der Krankenhausbudgets.* Berlin: ver.di., 2008.

Singh, Nirvikar. 'Decentralization and Public Delivery of Health Care Services in India'. *Health Affairs* 27, no. 4 (2008): 991–1001.

Sinha, Aseema. *The Regional Roots of Developmental Politics in India.* Bloomington: Indiana University Press, 2005.

Smee, Clive. *Speaking Truth to Power: Two Decades of Analysis in the Department of Health.* Oxford: Radcliffe Press, 2005.

Smith, Charles. 'Is Premier Gordon Campbell's Conversation on Health Part of a Hidden Agenda to Introduce Private Health Insurance?' *News Features*, 2007, 1–4. http://www.straight.com/news/premier-campbell-conversation-health-part-agenda-introduce-private-health-insurance.

Smith, R.D. 'Responding to Global Infectious Disease Outbreaks: Lessons from SARS on the Role of Risk Perception, Communication and Management'. *Journal of Social Science and Medicine* 63 (2006): 3113–23.

Sobolev, Boris and L. Kuramoto. 'Cluster-randomized Design for Simulation-based Evaluation of Complex Healthcare Interventions'. *Journal of Simulation* 4 (2010): 24–33.

Souza, Celina. 'Governos e sociedades locais em contextos de desigualdade e de descentralização'. *Ciência & Saúde Coletiva* 7/3 (2002): 431–41.

—— 'Para Entender a Nossa Barafunda Federativa'. Insight Inteligência 2013. http://www.insightinteligencia.com.br/61/PDFs/pdf4.pdf.

Souza, Luiz Eduardo and Pedro Fonseca. *O processo de substituição de importações.* São Paulo: Livraria Ciência e Tecnologia Editora Ltda, 2009.

Stark, Kirk J. 'Rich States, Poor States: Assessing the Design and Effect of a US Fiscal Equalization Regime'. *Tax Law Review* 63 (2009): 957–1008.

Starr, Paul. *Remedy and Reaction: The Peculiar American Struggle over Health Care Reform.* New Haven, CT: Yale University Press, 2011.

Statement of Defense and Counterclaim. 'Canadian Independent Medical Clinics Association v. Medical Services Commission of British Columbia', 2009.

Statistisches Bundesamt. 'Gesundheit. Grunddaten der Krankenhäuser'. Wiesbaden: Statistisches Bundesamt, 2013.

Steele, David and Jonathan Cylus. 'United Kingdom and Scotland: Health System Review'. *Health Systems in Transition* 14, no. 9 (2012): 1–150. http://www.euro.who.int/en/who-we-are/partners/observatory/health-systems-in-transition-hit-series/countries-and-subregions.

Steffen, Monika. *Health Governance in Europe: Issues, Challenges and Theories*, edited by Monika Steffen. Abingdon: Routledge, 2005.

—— 'The Europeanization of Public Health: How Does it Work? The Seminal Role of the AIDS Case'. *Journal of Health Politics, Policy, and Law* 37, no. 6 (2012): 1057–89.

Stepan, A. 'Para uma nova análise comparativa do federalismo e da democracia: federações que restringem ou ampliam o poder do Demos'. *Dados* 42, no. 2 (1999). http://dx.doi.org/10.1590/S0011–52581999000200001.

Stepan, Alfred, Juan Linz, and Yogendra Yadav. *Crafting State-nations: India and Other Multinational Democracies*. Baltimore: The Johns Hopkins University Press, 2011.

Stigletz, Joseph. *The Price of Inequality*. New York: W.W. Norton, 2012.

Stillman, Michael and Monalissa Taylor. 'Dead Men Walking'. *The New England Journal of Medicine* 369, no. 20 (2013): 1880–81.

Stone, Deborah. *Policy Paradox: The Art of Political Decision-Making*, 3rd ed. New York and London: W.W. Norton and Co., 2012.

Stone Sweet, Alec. 'Judicial Authority and Market Integration in Europe'. In *Institutions and Public Law: Comparative Approaches*, edited by Tom Ginsburg and Robert A. Kagan. Frankfurt: Peter Lang, 2005: 99–140.

Streeck, Wolfgang. 'Noch so ein Sieg, und wir sind verloren. Der Nationalstaat nach der Finanzkrise'. *Leviathan* 38, no. 2 (2010): 159–73.

Studlar, Donley. 'Tobacco Control Policy in Europe'. In *European Union Public Health Policies: Regional and Global Perspectives*, edited by Scott L. Greer and Paulette Kurzer. Abingdon: Routledge, 2012: 181–93.

Sudarshan, Hanumappa and Nuggehalli Srinivas Prashant. 'Good Governance in Health Care: The Karnataka Experience'. *The Lancet* 377 (2011): 790–92.

Supreme Court of Canada. 'Chaoulli v. Quebec (Attorney General)', [2005] S.C.R. 35. Sara Thomson, Robin Osborn, David Squires, et al. International Profiles of Health Care Systems, 2013. Commonwealth Fund pub. 1717, November 2013.

Surel, Yves. 'The Role of Cognitive and Normative Frames in Policy-making'. *Journal of European Public Policy* 7, no. 4 (2000): 495–512.

Sutherland, Kim and Nick Coyle. *Quality in Health Care in England, Wales, Scotland, Northern Ireland: An Intra-UK Chart Book*. London: The Health Foundation, 2009.

Swerissen, Hal and Stephen Duckett. 'Federalism and Health: Negotiating the Problems of "Fiscal Squabbles", "Waiting" and "Waste"'. In *Analysing Australian Health Policy: A Problem Orientated Approach*, edited by S. Barraclough and H. Gardner. Marrickville: Elsevier, 2007.

Tálos, Emmerich. 'Sozialpolitik zwischen Expansion und Restriktion'. In *Politik in Österreich. Das Handbuch*, edited by Herbert Dachs, Peter Gerlich, Herbert Gottweis, et al. Vienna: Manz, 2006: 624–36.

Tang, Shengian. 'Public Health Programs in China: Has Reform Improved Equity and Effectiveness?' China Health Policy Report. Duke Global Health Institute, 4 January 2013.

Tediosi, Fabrizio, Stefania Gabriele, and Francesco Longo. 'Governing Decentralization in Health Care Under Tough Budget Constraint: What Can We Learn from the Italian Experience?' *Health Policy* 90, no. 2 (2009): 303–12.

Théret, Bruno. 'Regionalism and Federalism: A Comparative Analysis of the Regulation of Economic Tensions between Regions by Canadian and American Federal Intergovernmental Transfer of Programmes'. *International Journal of Urban and Regional Research* 23, no. 3 (1999): 479–512.

Theurl, Engelbert. 'Some Aspects of the Reform of the Health Care Systems in Austria, Germany and Switzerland'. *Health Care Analysis* 7, no. 4 (1999): 331–54.

—— 'Die österreichische Gesundheitspolitik der letzten Jahre im Lichte der internationalen Entwicklung'. In *Der Sozialstaat auf dem Prüfstand. Analysen und Perspektiven*, edited by Engelbert Theurl. Heidelberg: Physica Verlag, 2001: 135–70.

Thompson, James D. *Organizations in Action Social Science Bases of Administrative Theory.* New York: McGraw Hill, 1967.

Tiebout, Charles M. 'A Pure Theory of Local Expenditure'. *The Journal of Political Economy* 64, no. 5 (1956): 416–24.

Timmins, Nicholas. *Never Again. The Story of the Health and Social Care Act.* London: King's Fund, 2012. http://www.kingsfund.org.uk/publications/never-again.

—— *The Four UK Health Systems. Learning from Each Other.* London: King's Fund, 2013. http://www.kingsfund.org.uk/publications/four-uk-health-systems-june-2013.

Tödter, Karl-Heinz and Michael Scharnagl. 'How Effective are Automatic Stabilisers? Theory and Empirical Results for Germany and other OECD Countries'. Frankfurt: Discussion paper series 1/Volkswirtschaftliches Forschungszentrum der Deutschen Bundesbank, 2004.

Tomblin-Murphy, Gail. 'Governing Challenges in Implementing Needs-based Health Human Resources Planning'. In *Health Care Federalism in Canada*, edited by Katherine Fierlbeck and William Lahey. Kingston and Montreal: Queen's University Press, 2013: 118–38.

Topol, Eric. *The Creative Destruction of Medicine.* New York: Basic Books, 2012.

Torbica, Aleksandra and Giovanni Fattore. 'The Essential Levels of Care in Italy: When Being Explicit Serves the Devolution of Powers'. *European Journal of Health Economics* 6, no. S1 (2005): 46–52.

Trebilcock, Michael J. and Edward M. Iacobucci. 'Privatization and Accountability'. *Harvard Law Review* 116, no. 5 (2003): 1422–53.

Trubek, Louise G., Thomas R. Oliver, Chih-Ming Liang, et al. 'Improving Cancer Outcomes through Strong Networks and Regulatory Frameworks: Lessons from the United States and European Union'. *Journal of Health Care Law and Policy* 14, no. 1 (2011): 119–51.

Trukeschitz, Birgit, Ulrike Schneider, and Thomas Czypionka. 'Federalism in Health and Social Care in Austria'. In *Federalism and Decentralization in European Health and Social Care*, edited by Joan Costa-Font and Scott L. Greer. Houndmills: Palgrave Macmillan, 2012: 154–89.

Tuohy, Carolyn Hughes. *Accidental Logics: The Dynamics of Change in the Health Care Arena in the United States, Britain, and Canada.* Oxford: Oxford University Press, 1999.

—— 'Single Payers, Multiple Systems: The Scope and Limits of Subnational Variation under a Federal Policy Framework'. *Journal of Health Politics, Policy and Law* 34, no. 4 (2009): 453–96.

Tuschen, Karl Heinz and Michael Quaas. *Bundespflegesatzverordnung: Kommentar mit einer umfassenden Einführung in das Recht der Krankenhausfinanzierung.* Stuttgart, Berlin; Köln: Kohlhammer, 2001.

Twomey, Anne and Glenn Withers. 'Federalist Paper 1 Australia's Federal Future: Delivering Growth and Prosperity'. Council for Australian Federation, 2007.

Vaishnav, Milan. 'Is the Regional Wave Over?' *Sunday Times of India*, 17 November: 12 – excerpt from 'The Complicated Rise of India's Regional Parties'. Washington, DC: Carnegie Endowment for Peace, 2013. http://carnegieendowment.org.

Valentine, Vikki. 'Health for the Masses: China's "Barefoot Doctors"'. National Public Radio Online, 4 November 2005. http://www.npr.org/templates/story/story.phpstoryId=4990242.

Van De Gronden, Johan W. 'Cross-border Health Care in the EU and the Organization of the National Health Care Systems of the Member States: The Dynamics Resulting from the European Court of Justice's Decisions on Free Movement and Competition Law'. *Wisconsin International Law Journal* 26, no. 3 (2008): 705–60.

Van De Gronden, Johan W., E. Szyszczak, U. Neergaard, et al. *Health Care and EU Law.* New York: Springer-Verlag, 2011.

Vandamme, Thomas. 'From Federated Federalism to Converging Federalism? The Case of EU Subsidiarity Scrutiny in Spain and Belgium'. *Regional & Federal Studies* 22 no. 5 (2012): 515–31.

Vardomsky, L.B. and E.E. Skaterschikova. *External Economic Activities of Russian Regions.* Moscow: Arkti Press, 2002.

Vauchez, Antoine. *L'Union par le Droit: L'invention d'un Programme Institutionnel pour L'Europe.* Presses de Sciences Po, 2013.

Venkat Raman, Appaswamy and James Warner Björkman. *Public–Private Partnerships in Health Care in India: Lessons for Developing Countries.* London: Routledge, 2009.

Verband der Ersatzkassen (vdek). 'vdek-Basisdaten des Gesundheitswesens 2012/2013'. Berlin: vdek, 2013.

Vereschagina, E.L. *European Territorial Cooperation: Influence on Decision-making in EU (1980–1990s).* Moscow, 2008.

Vining, Aidan and Anthony Boardman. 'Public–Private Partnerships in Canada: Theory and Evidence'. *Canadian Public Administration* 51, no.1 (2008): 9–44.

Vladeck, Bruce C. 'The Market vs. Regulation: The Case for Regulation'. *Health and Society* 59 (1981): 209–23.

Vladeck, Bruce C. and Thomas Rice. 'Market Failure and the Failure of Discourse: Facing Up to the Power of Sellers'. *Health Affairs* 28, no. 5 (2009): 1305–15.

Vogel, Ezra. *Deng Xiaoping and the Transformation of China.* Cambridge, MA: Belknap Press of Harvard University, 2011.

Von Hagen, Jürgen, Ludger Schuknecht, and Guido Wolswijk. 'Government Bond Risk Premiums in the EU Revisited: The Impact of the Financial Crisis'. *European Journal of Political Economy* 27, no. 1 (2011): 36–43.

Wang, Hufeng, Michael K. Gusmano, and Qi Cao. 2010. 'Review and Evaluation of Community Health Organisation Policy in China: Will the Priority of New Healthcare Reform in China Succeed?' *Health Policy.* doi:10.1016/j.healthpol.2010.07.003.

Ward, Ann and Lee Ward, eds. *The Ashgate Research Companion to Federalism.* Farnham, Surrey: Ashgate, 2009.

Ward, Lee. 2007. 'Montesquieu on Federalism and Anglo-gothic Constitutionalism'. *Publius* 37, no. 4 (2007): 551–7.

Watts, Ronald. *Comparing Federal Systems.* Montreal and Kingston: McGill University Press for the Institute of Intergovernmental Relations, 2008.

Webster, Charles. *The Health Services Since the War. Volume I. Problems of the National Health Service Before 1957.* London: HMSO, 1988.

Wei, X., D. Zakus, H. Liang, et al. 'The Shanghai Case: A Qualitative Evaluation of Community Health Reform in Response to the Challenge of Population Ageing'. *International Journal of Health Planning and Management* 20, no. 3 (2005): 269–86.

Weingast, Barry R. 'The Economic Role of Political Institutions: Market-preserving Federalism and Economic Development'. *Journal of Law, Economics, and Organization* 11, no. 1 (1995): 1–31.

Wendt, Claus. 'Mapping European Healthcare Systems: A Comparative Analysis of Financing, Service Provision and Access to Healthcare'. *Journal of European Social Policy* 19 (2009): 434–45.

Wendt, Claus and Jürgen Kohl. 'Translating Monetary Inputs into Health Care Provision: A Comparative Analysis of the Impact of Different Modes of Public Policy'. *Journal of Comparative Policy Analysis: Research and Practice* 12, no. 1–2 (2010): 11–31.

Wendt, Claus, Lorraine Frisina, and Heinz Rothgang. 'Healthcare System Types: A Conceptual Framework for Comparison'. *Social Policy & Administration* 43, no. 1 (2009): 70–90.

West, Loraine A. and Christine P.W. Wong. 'Fiscal Decentralisation and Growing Regional Disparities in Rural China: Some Evidence in the Provision of Social Services'. *Oxford Review of Economic Policy* 11, no. 4 (1995): 70–84.

Wetzel, Deborah. *Decentralization in the Transition Economies: Challenges and the Road Ahead. Decentralization in the Transition Economies: Challenges and the Road Ahead.* Washington, DC: World Bank, 2001.

Wheare, Kenneth C. *Federal Government.* London: Oxford University Press, 1963.

White, Kevin N. 'The State, the Market, and General Practice: The Australian Case'. *International Journal of Health Services* 30, no. 2 (2000): 28–308.

Williams, Ross. 'History of Federal–State Fiscal Relations in Australia: A Review of the Methodologies Used'. *Australian Economic Review* 45, no. 2 (2012): 145–57.

Wilsford, David. 'Path Dependency, or Why History Makes It Difficult but Not Impossible to Reform Health Care Systems in a Big Way'. *Journal of Public Policy* 14, no. 3 (1994): 251–83.

—— 'The Logic of Policy Change: Structure and Agency in Political Life'. *Journal of Health Politics, Policy, and Law* 35, no. 4 (2010): 663–80.

Wiltshire, Kenneth. 'Chariot Wheels Federalism'. In *Upholding the Australian Constitution: Proceedings of the Twentieth Conference of the Samuel Griffith Society*. Sydney: The Samuel Griffith Society, 2008.

Wright, Deil S. 'Models of National, State and Local Relationships'. In *American Intergovernmental Relationships*, 2nd ed., edited by Lawrence J. O'Toole, Jr. Washington, DC: CQ Press, 2000: 74–88.

Wright, Gavin. *Sharing the Prize: The Economics of the Civil Rights Revolution in the American South*. Cambridge, MA: Belknap Press/Harvard University Press, 2014.

Writ of Summons. 'Canadian Independent Medical Clinics Association v. Medical Services Commission of British Columbia', 2009.

Wyke, Alexandra. *Fixing Healthcare: The Professionals' Perspective*. London: Economist Intelligence Unit, 2009.

Yakabuski, Konrad. 'The Common Sense Question that Bouchard Dared to Ask'. *Globe and Mail*, 11 August 2004, B2.

Young, Anne F. and Annette J. Dobson. 'The Decline in Bulk-billing and Increase in Out-of-pocket Costs for General Practice Consultations in Rural Areas of Australia, 1995–2001'. *Medical Journal of Australia* 178, no. 3 February (2003): 122–6.

Yusuf, Farhat and Stephen Leeder. 'Can't Escape It: The Out-of-pocket Cost of Health Care in Australia'. *Medical Journal of Australia* 199, no. 7 (2013): 475–8.

Zhao, Q., Z.J. Huang, S. Yang, et al. 'The Utilization of Antenatal Care Among Rural-to urban Migrant Women in Shanghai: A Hospital-based Cross-sectional Study'. *BMC Public Health* 12 (2012): 1012. http://www.biomedcentral.com/1471–2458/12/1012.

Zubarevich, N.V. *Russian Regions: Non-equality, Crisis, Modernization*. Moscow: Independent Institute of Social Policies, 2010.

Index

abortions 155
Abrucio 180, 187
Abruzzo 63, 71, 73, 75
academic 80–81, 106
accelerate 46, 143, 170, 173
access 3–4, 6, 53, 55, 84, 117, 140–41,
        146, 155, 165, 169–70, 175–7, 185,
        189, 199, 203, 213–14, 216, 220,
        222–4
    to ambulatory specialist services 132
    barriers 145, 176
    to capital markets 9, 39–40, 45
    to drugs 207
    to elective surgery 127
    to health care 50, 95, 97, 139–40, 147,
        172, 211
    to health information 52, 54
    to Medicaid 145
    to running water 155
    to services 128, 158, 160, 203–4
accident 33, 199
accord 109, 112–14
    bilateral 109
Accord on Health Care Renewal 112
accountability 3, 5–7, 9–10, 12, 47, 51–2,
        54, 56, 58–61, 82–4, 88–9, 97,
        100, 110, 133, 135, 163, 182, 215,
        217–19, 221, 223
achievement 118, 162
acquis communitaire 96
action 37, 51–2, 84, 96–8, 101–2, 106–7,
        111, 127, 13–9, 185, 191, 221
active 14–16, 24, 33, 36, 49, 59, 70–72,
        74, 85, 93, 108, 114, 119, 123, 128,
        132, 134–5, 141, 170, 177, 190,
        201, 214–15, 228, 248, 274
acute 81, 126, 128, 131, 165, 203
    see also Severe Acute Respiratory
        Syndrome (SARS)
adjustment 99, 104, 138, 183–4, 188

see also Economic Adjustment
    Programmes (EAPs)
administer 140, 144, 160, 177
administration 6, 17, 73, 77, 90, 109,
        112, 115, 118–20, 123, 125, 137,
        139–40, 143–7, 150, 165–6, 169,
        185, 208, 213
    see also Veterans' Health
        Administration (VHA)
administrative 9, 15, 17, 19–20, 31, 48, 64,
        81, 103, 108–9, 120, 143–4, 162–3,
        166, 168, 182, 185–6, 196–7,
        208–10
admission 74–5, 93
adult 140, 161
adulteration 151
advanced 22, 64, 199
advances 13, 103, 188–90, 192, 220
advantage 43–5, 87–8, 113, 118, 205,
        213–14
adverse 12, 137–8, 207, 220
advertise 12
advertising 125
advocacy 80, 110, 133
affiliation 22, 24, 73, 137, 140, 142
after-reform 147
age 70, 127–8, 149, 160, 202
agency 66, 100–102, 126, 185, 204, 209
agenda 21–2, 28, 82, 106, 135, 144, 147,
        188, 224
agent 2, 41, 132, 152, 157
aggregate 2, 132, 152, 157
agreement 22, 25, 35–6, 41, 69, 72–3, 83,
        100, 108–9, 114–15, 125, 135–6,
        138, 146, 179, 189, 193, 209
agriculture 98, 158, 161, 170
AIDS (Acquired Immune Deficiency
        Syndrome) 162, 199
aims 4, 34, 57, 73, 79, 84, 145
airbus 153

Northrine–Westphalia 35
nosologies 208
not binding 115
not-for-profit
    groups 126
    or public hospitals 39
Nova Scotia 114, 120
Novosibirsk 196, 203
NSWPs *see* non-state-wide parties
numerical targets 100
nurses 52, 110
nursing
    care insurance 33
    charge 35
    and residential care facilities 33
    staff 26, 87, 92
nutrition 175

Oates 4, 128
Obama administration 139, 145–7, 213
objectives 56, 65, 86, 103, 112, 118, 160,
        195, 199, 207, 210
oblasts 196, 206
obligations 6, 31, 36, 54, 66, 73, 116, 154,
        195, 199, 207, 209–10
obligatory 36
occupational
    fragmentation 20
    groups 15, 19
    sickness funds 19
occupations 185
OECD (Organisation for Economic
        Cooperation and Development) 34,
        68, 98, 107, 112, 115, 117, 127,
        141, 146, 165
off-budget government revenue 172
official
    budget statistics 169
    gazettes 53, 58
officials 8, 52–3, 96, 98, 132, 143, 166–8,
        174, 177, 224
offloaded 108
oil
    crisis 36
    and gas production 205
    price shocks 21
old-age pension 33
older people 175
oligarchic system 180

oligarchies 180
Ontario Auditor General's review of a
        Private Financing Initiative 113
open
    economies 99
    federalism 112
operate 14, 43, 66, 83, 153, 158, 164
operating
    asset 71
    costs 18
    deficit 72
    result 70
operational
    expenditures 198
    issues 208
    problems 162
    and technical and managerial capacities
        187
operationalising 189
opportunities 131, 143, 154, 204, 211, 219
ordinary statute regions 64
Organic Law 4/2000 50
organisation(s) 2, 13, 15, 19–22, 26, 28,
        30, 34, 52, 60, 65, 85, 87–91, 96,
        98, 102, 107, 117, 126, 134–5, 142,
        145, 159, 163, 165, 167, 173, 183,
        187, 189, 193, 191, 203, 209, 214,
        216–18, 222, 225
    of health services 187
    of medical care 145
    of services 189
Organisation for Economic Cooperation
        and Development *see* OECD
organisational
    arrangements 127
    autonomy 22
    hub 20
    inertia 84
    structures 184
organised crime 73
organs 96, 150, 207
Orissa 161
Ottawa 108–9, 111–15, 118–20
outbreaks 162
outcome 90, 105
out-distanced 141
outgoing
    mobility 76
    patients 74

change 10, 88–9, 95, 144, 147, 166
conceptions 137
conditionalities 104
coordination across jurisdictions 118
debate 106, 144
decisions 3, 6, 100, 139, 218, 222
design 129
development 4, 11, 81, 128, 132, 149,
    214, 223–4
direction 10, 96, 120
divergence 83, 86
elites 146
experimentation 18, 27, 123
fields 10, 15, 17–18, 21, 27
formation 129, 215
formulation 13–14, 96, 214, 224
frame 23
initiatives 128, 151, 181
innovation 24, 28, 118, 174
instruments 138
interventions 132
issues 3, 102
levers 135
-makers 22–3, 29, 97, 161, 163, 176
-making 2, 7–12, 15–16, 19, 21–3, 31,
    81, 100, 104, 106, 115, 139, 144,
    147–8, 199, 219, 221
objectives 86, 210
options 132
paralysis 137
processes 156
recommendations 104, 156
responses 11, 23, 80, 86, 220
responsibilities 129
review process 100
sectors 76
tools 98
political
    accountability 9, 82–3, 97
    actors 10, 149, 186, 225
    affiliations 137
    agenda 21–2, 28, 82, 147
    arena 19
    arrangement 83
    autonomy 47–8, 166
    centralisation 153, 215
    centre 16–18
    change 95
    clout 151

commitment 151
compromise 196
conflict 81, 163
consensus 73
constellations 16
corruption 73
costs 89
culture 11, 204
deadlock 32
devolution 79, 82–3
dynamics 3, 18, 26, 214, 222
entrepreneurs 20
factors 45, 203, 220
feasibility 15, 28
and fiscal federalism 152
force 96, 215
form 137
history 153, 179
influence 17–18
institutions 18, 27, 147, 167
issues 22
legitimacy 182
loyalty 196
mechanisms 181
opposition 134
parties 6, 17, 24, 32, 40, 44, 46, 83,
    123, 153–4, 160, 167
persuasion 133
polarisation 162
powers 196
prejudgment 99
pressure 24
process 115, 137, 222
project 184
relationship 189
representatives 7
responsibility 29, 34, 124
space 120
status 163
strategy 114, 192
strength 181
strife 16
structures 10, 15, 101
system 2, 15–17, 27, 146, 149, 166, 176
unity 47
unrest 170
will 106
window-dressing 119
politically accountable 82

deficits 70
differences 167, 192, 202
disparities 165, 169, 172, 174, 190,
    210, 218
disparity 195, 216, 222
elites 196–7
finances 76
funds 24
government(s) 1–2, 5, 7, 12, 15–17,
    47, 49, 52, 54, 59, 61, 63–6, 70,
    72–3, 77, 82–3, 143, 148, 165, 180,
    195–7, 208–10, 216, 219
governors 24
health care
    systems 71–2, 74–5, 77
    deficit 71–2
hospital expenses 24
hospitals 74, 171
identities 15
imbalances 160
inequalities 10, 167, 177, 185, 191,
    193, 215, 221
interests 27
intervention 67
jurisdictions 6, 149, 196, 210, 217,
    219, 221–3
level 19–20, 24, 66, 77, 118, 144, 189,
    200, 205, 210–11, 220, 222
offices of central departments 144
parties 153–4
pilot projects 211
planning 20
political influence 17
presence 189
presidents 69
programmes 205–6
responsibility 208–9
systems 63–4, 72, 75, 216
tax 181
territory 70
variation in health care 166
veto 27
Regional Associations of Statutory Health
    Insurance Funds 345
Regional Association of Statutory Health
    Insurance Physicians 35
Regional Hospital Association 35
Regional Management Committees 189
regionalisation of health care 69

regionalised decentralisation 143
regionalist parties 59
register of patients 200
registration 52
regressive 155, 172, 174
regulate 9, 20, 45, 52, 54, 57, 124, 144,
    156, 180, 187, 198, 225
regulated competition 146
regulating 19, 105, 118, 191
regulation(s) 5–6, 8–9, 15, 17, 21, 29,
    33–4, 48, 50, 52–6, 85, 98, 101–2,
    104, 108–9, 117, 145, 168, 172,
    182, 188, 199, 201, 204–5, 219–20,
    223
regulatory
    capacity 24
    circuit 20
    EU policies 98
    framework for accountability 51
    and policy coordination 118
    and redistribution policies 168
rehabilitation 25, 63, 131, 188
reimbursable 15
reimbursed 34
reimbursement 29, 32, 34–6, 38, 43,
    141–2, 208
reining in expenditure 145
relations between the federal and substate
    governments 112
relationship(s) 3, 4, 7, 10, 12, 14, 26, 61,
    65, 69, 74, 99, 102–3, 105, 112,
    119, 133, 149, 152, 180, 184–5,
    189, 191, 195, 213, 218, 221–2
religious 30, 126, 179
remittances 155
remodelling 36
remunerating 66
remuneration 19, 53, 126, 142
renal failure 140
renegotiation 133
renovations 198
reorganisation
    of health services 186
    of services 72
repeal 147
repercussions 119, 185
replace 137, 141, 154, 208
representation 48, 82, 193
representative 2, 41, 96, 196

representatives 7, 19, 23, 29, 31–2, 35,
124, 152, 188
reproductive and child health services 159
Republic of
Altay 201
Chechenskaya 201
Dagestan 201, 206
Ingushetia 201–2
Kabardino-Balkariya 201
Karachay-Cherkessiya 201
Mari-El 206
Mordovia 205
North Ossetia–Alania 201
Tyva 201–2, 206
Republican
Governor Mitt Romney 145
majority in the House 146
value preferences 145
republics 195–6
reputation 84, 90, 171
reregulation 95, 98
research 17, 43, 51, 60, 96, 98, 101–2, 118,
145, 175–6, 198, 224
researchers 13, 196, 22
Reserve Bank of India 158
residence 19, 50, 54, 74
residential aged care
facilities 131–2
payments 132
residents 19, 26, 65, 69–70, 74–7, 126,
137, 171, 173–5, 203–4
residual powers 17, 108, 150
resilience 26
resolution 96, 151, 209
resource(s) 3, 6–9, 18, 23–4, 28–9,
40, 45, 47–51, 54–6, 58, 64–5,
67–70, 72–3, 83–4, 87, 113–14,
118, 120, 128, 143, 151–2,
156–9, 162, 165–6, 170, 172,
174, 177, 179–81, 186–93,
196–7, 200, 204–5, 209–10, 219,
221, 223
allocation 174, 188, 191, 193
capacity 160
endowments 158
potential 205
respond 21, 46, 120, 124, 127, 166, 174,
179, 187, 216, 222
response time 85

responsibilities
for enacting legislation 167
for health care 151
in health care 133, 205
realignment 134
of a state 124
responsible
for financing a large portion of public
services 168
for the operation of government 167
responsive 135, 167–8, 215, 217
responsiveness 45, 120, 163, 168, 217
restraining medical expenditure 141
restricted coverage 141
restrictions regarding fees 116
results 6, 13, 24, 43, 47, 51, 54–5, 58–9,
61, 102, 118, 120, 142, 156, 160,
166, 174, 180, 199, 211, 216
retaining 81, 183
retirements 185
retraining 200
retrenchment 22, 174, 176
revenue 5, 8–9, 18, 20, 24–5, 28, 48–9,
107, 125, 129, 134, 157, 163, 168,
216
authority 158
and expenses 173
-generating activities 172
growth 141
from patients 171
raising capacity 126
shock 99
review of legislation 17
reward(s) 64, 77, 84
Rheinland–Pfalz 42
rich 73, 156, 216, 223
right(s) 31, 50, 54–6, 59, 76, 80, 96, 104,
115, 125, 137, 151, 160–62, 176,
180, 182–3, 192, 196, 201, 208–10
-based 162
of co-decision 31–2
to equality 116
to food 154
to free movement 103
of government 150
and responsibilities 208
to work 161
Right to Education Act 161
Rio de Janeiro 189, 191